# The Best of the Independent Rhetoric and Composition Journals

## The Best of the Independent Rhetoric and Composition Journals
SERIES EDITOR: STEVE PARKS

Each year, a team of editors selects the best work published in the independent journals in the field of Rhetoric and Composition, following a competitive review process involving journal editors and publishers. For additional information about the series, see http://www.parlorpress.com/bestofrhetcomp.

# THE BEST OF THE INDEPENDENT RHETORIC AND COMPOSITION JOURNALS

## 2013

Edited by Steve Parks, Brian Bailie, Heather Christiansen, Elisabeth Miller, and Morris Young

Parlor Press
*Anderson, South Carolina*
www.parlorpress.com

Parlor Press LLC, Anderson, South Carolina, USA

S A N: 2 5 4 - 8 8 7 9

ISSN 2327-4778 (print)

ISSN 2327-4786 (online)

1 2 3 4 5

Cover design by David Blakesley.
Printed on acid-free paper.

Parlor Press, LLC is an independent publisher of scholarly and trade titles in print and multimedia formats. This book is available in paper and digital formats from Parlor Press on the World Wide Web at http://www.parlorpress. com or through online and brick-and-mortar bookstores. For submission information or to find out about Parlor Press publications, write to Parlor Press, 3015 Brackenberry Drive, Anderson, South Carolina, 29621, or email editor@parlorpress.com.

# Contents

# Introduction

*Elisabeth Miller and Morris Young*

The articles in this collection feature the rich complexity of rhetoric and composition—of writing, language-use, and communication.
Incisive analyses of topics as diverse as the argument that fetal imaging
technology makes; the role of race in writing across the curriculum; and
how the connection between computer coding and writing showcase
the situated, material, and political nature of our field. Classrooms,
institutions, cultures, and communities are the sites of our research.
Jazz, computer code, humor, immigration papers, and the speech patterns of conservative pundits are the materials of our inquiry. Surveys,
fieldwork, rhetorical and textual analysis, lived experience, teaching
practice, and collaborative writing are the methods and forms of our
investigation.

Such diversity certainly captures the spirit of the 15 independent
journals represented in this collection. These journals thrive under the
substantial pressures and demanding workloads that come with compiling, editing, and distributing academic publications—without support from professional organizations and often limited support from
their institutions. All the while, these independent journals feature
scholarship that challenges the field, push for innovation, and provide
forums for new work that might be seen as "on the margins."

In this introduction, we point to four common threads and complexities that this year's set of articles address: 1) dealing with identity
issues at the institutional level, 2) accounting for material dimensions
of writing and rhetoric, 3) theorizing teaching, and 4) innovating the
methods and form of our scholarship to best address these myriad
complexities. We note, too, that any collection necessarily includes
and excludes, leaves in and leaves out. We draw on some frameworks
from disability studies and universal design to offer one more impor-

tant lens for this collection—and to broaden our thinking as a field. Finally, we close with a few words about the selection process for this collection and an acknowledgment of the many contributors to this anthology's own complex process of development.

## DEALING WITH IDENTITY ISSUES ON THE INSTITUTIONAL LEVEL

Questions of identity, representation, access, inclusion, and exclusion in our classrooms, writing programs, and larger university contexts form the bedrock of Rhetoric and Composition. Language, we know, is inextricable from race, class, gender, (dis)ability, sexuality, and the myriad intersections of these identities. Several articles in this collection grapple with identity on an institutional level. Mya Poe, for one, in "Re-Framing Race in Teaching Writing Across the Curriculum" notes the rich array of scholarship in compositions studies addressing race and pedagogy and a relative dearth of race-conscious work in writing across the curriculum (WAC). Offering examples from her own writing across the curriculum (WAC) teaching and consulting, she seeks to integrate race into classroom and programmatic discussions. The place of race in the university is similarly central to Steve Lamos's "Minority-Serving Institutions, Race Conscious 'Dwelling,' and Possible Futures for Basic Writing at Predominantly White Institutions." Lamos directs attention to both the shrinking of basic writing programs and the lack of race consciousness at predominantly white institutions. Spatial theories of "dwelling" and influencing larger spaces from the inside and the periphery lead Lamos to a number of strategies for ways basic writing programs may thrive in the increasingly neoliberal university.

While Lamos urges basic writing programs to carve out and define their own spaces, Eliot Rendleman, in "Lexicography: Self-Analysis and Defining the Keywords of Our Missions" encourages writing centers to interrogate what they mean by the key terms they use to define their programming. Performing extensive survey research, Rendleman offers a "lexicographical," or definition-based, method for programs to examine their institutional identities.

Looking beyond the university, Michelle Hall Kells's "What's Writing Got to Do with It?: Citizen Wisdom, Civil Rights Activism, and 21st Century Community Literacy" explores the persistent question of the university's relationship with, and obligation to, citizens in the broader community. Kells deftly draws on the "legacy" of Mexican-American civil rights activists to call for action from writing programs and publicly engaged rhetoric beyond "a once-done-always done exercise" (101). She offers her Writing Across Communities program and community writing center as a place where taking agency of writing enables activism and connection.

## ACCOUNTING FOR THE MATERIAL DIMENSIONS OF WRITING AND RHETORIC

Bound as they are to identity, writing and rhetoric's material dimensions push persistently on their social consequences. Kate Vieira's "On the Social Consequences of Literacy" speaks compellingly to this point, drawing on fieldwork to demonstrate writing and documents as "navigational technologies" that alternately limit, enable, constrain, and mobilize access to education and other resources for migrants.

Writing and literacy are further complicated and intertwined with material technologies in Annette Vee and Mark Sample's "The Role of Computational Literacy in Computers and Writing." This piece features short talks from multiple writing and coding scholars at the 2012 Computers and Writing conference's Town Hall "Program or be Programmed: Do We Need Computational Literacy in Computers and Writing?" The article's online publication in *Enculturation* foregrounds the material, including tweets from audience members throughout the text. The text of the provocative talk challenges the very notion of what writing is, proposing computer coding as a kind of writing and asking what role coding should play in composition studies.

The boundaries of writing and rhetoric expand in related ways in two other pieces featured in this anthology: the multimodal webtext "Crossing Battle Lines: Teaching Multimodal Literacies Through Alternative Reality Games" by Scott Nelson, Chris Ortiz y Printice, M. Catherine Coleman, Eric Detweiler, Marjorie Foley, Kendall Gerdes, Cleve Wiese, R. Scott Garbacz and Matt King, featured in *Kairos* and the webtext "Recitative: The Persuasive Tenor of Jazz Culture in Langston Hughes, Billy Strayhorn, and John Coltrane" by Andrew Vogel in *Harlot*. Both pieces engage with the ways materiality makes meaning through gaming and music, respectively, and both articles reach readers through multiple modes, including sound and images. Imagery, the body, and the non-linguistic make their own arguments in Rochelle Gregory's "A Womb with a View: Identifying the Culturally Iconic Fetal Image in Prenatal Ultrasound Provisions." Analyzing public discourse around developing fetal imaging technology, Gregory finds that increasingly vivid images of fetuses are frequently drawn on to make pro-life arguments.

## THEORIZING TEACHING

Classroom practice remains a central concern for teacher-scholars in Rhetoric and Composition and, thus, makes a central appearance in this collection. Writing instruction gets a boost from classical rhetorical theory and the power of humor in Steve Sherwood's "Humor and the Rhetorical Properties in the Writing Classroom." Including wit, levity, and even self-deprecation in the kairotic space of the writing classroom is a move consistent with Aristotle, Quintilian, and Cicero's conception of a rhetorically adept orator—and offer a teaching tool for writing instructors.

Problem-based learning strategies offer another answer for improving student learning, say Paula Rosinski and Tim Peeples in their article, "Forging Rhetorical Subjects: Problem-Based Learning in the Writing Classroom." Problem-based learning puts students in the middle of "ill-structured," open-ended scenarios that demand collaborative thinking and writing. For example, students work in groups to develop a resource for the university library designed to help students purposefully use online search engines.

What students take or transfer from the writing classroom also remains a perennial question for Rhetoric and Composition. Liane Robertson, Kara Taczak, and Kathleen Blake Yancey take up that question in "Notes Toward A Theory of Prior Knowledge and Its Role in College Composers' Transfer of Knowledge and Practice." After offering an extensive review of previous studies on transfer, the authors put forward a fresh approach, developing various "typologies" for the ways students take up prior knowledge, including "assemblage" and "remix"—concrete ways to understand transfer.

Heidi Estrem and E. Shelley Reid flip the script on research about teaching in "What New Writing Teachers Talk about When They Talk about Teaching," suggesting that much work has been done on teaching practices in composition, but less on how new teachers learn to teach writing. Conducting a multi-site interview study, Estrem and Reid begin to sketch ways of learning about teaching, calling for longer, more sustained teaching training and opportunities for conversation to match the recursive learning process.

## INNOVATING METHODS AND FORM

With so many layers of complexity bound up in the situated practices of writing and rhetoric, scholars featured in this collection strategically and compellingly employ multiple methods for researching and forms for presenting their findings. Ethnographic research by Vieira; long-range, multi-site qualitative research by Estrem and Reid; and extensive survey research by Rendleman all attest to the multiple ways research is conducted and knowledge is made in our field. And the texts by Vogel and Nelson et al. put into practice the theories of multimodality that they extol.

Rebecca Jones and Heather Palmer also work creatively with form, telling an engaging narrative in "Counter-Coulter: A Story of Craft and Ethos." The two authors weave a tale of drafting—and extensively revising—a speech responding to conservative pundit Ann Coulter, who visited their university to give a talk. Their narration smartly demonstrates and comments on rhetorical choices and the complexities of developing ethos with an audience. Their article's method, content, and form nicely complement one another.

Form, method, and content also converge compellingly in "Prison Collaborative Writing: Building Strong Mutuality in Community-Based Learning," by Grace Wetzel with a response by "Wes," a prisoner who participated in the community-based learning project featured in the article. In addition to its smart reflection on peer-reviewing and collaboration in a university-community project at a prison, the form of the article truly embodies the community literacy value of writing *with* and actively collaborating with the communities we study. Collaboration, indeed, makes a strong showing through this collection. Six of the fifteen articles are co-written by two or more authors, embodying our field's value of writing as a social act.

## ANOTHER LENS: DISABILITY AND UNIVERSAL DESIGN

As a way of contributing to this already innovative collection and pushing for new work in the field of rhetoric and composition more broadly, we want to turn briefly to disability and universal design as important, under-examined, under-represented concepts that point to rich directions for our scholarship. As we well know as a field, there is always danger of invisibly assuming and catering to a normative—white, male, heterosexual, middle or upper-middle class, able-bodied—notion of students, administrators, teachers, and researchers. Countering that danger, we pause to emphasize the importance of valuing the diversity of ability generated by a range of bodies and minds. As Jay Dolmage argues in his recent *Disability Rhetoric*, disability should not be ignored or considered a problem to accommodate, but valued for its inventive and subversive potential to generate new meaning and new ways of making meaning.

To read this collection—and our field—through the critical lens of disability would push us not just to include mention of disabled people or to critique ableist spaces, but to read differently, as Dolmage says, crookedly, for the varied ways bodies and minds are productively imperfect. Taking the trends we identified in this collection, how, then, are the bodies of students, writing program administrators, and teachers, normed by the institutions in which we study, work, and teach? Where is the body in the material—as individuals engage with computers and code, with games, with documents? And how do different kinds of bodies and minds both run into normative barriers and create new ways of engaging with the material we explore?

How, further, may universal design—the idea that building or creating environments that provide the greatest level of access to persons with all kinds of abilities and disabilities—challenge our understanding of our classrooms? Of humor as a connecting or disconnecting force, of teacher training and the best ways to meet new teachers' needs as learners with all kinds of abilities? How might universal design change our research methods—and the forms in which we present research? Could, and should, interviews move further away from strictly in-the-moment, verbal responses? Could research influenced by disability and universal design be conducted in increasingly collaborative ways to include ever more perspectives and ways of making meaning? How could our findings be presented in accessible online spaces and in increasingly multimodal forms like so much of the work in *Kairos, Enculturation*, and *Harlot*? By posing disability and universal design as important lenses, we identify not so much a gap in the current collection, but an opportunity for a different—perhaps a crooked—kind of reading and researching.

## THE PROCESS OF THIS COLLECTION

Finally, we want to briefly discuss the process behind the volume you have in front of you, *The Independent Rhetoric and Composition Journals*. Each journal featured in this collection submitted options for review. To recognize the exciting work happening in this diverse set of journals, we called upon an equally varied set of Associate Editor reviewers. We sought these individuals from a range of institutions, from research universities to teaching colleges and at a number of different points in their careers, including graduate students, full- and part-time instructors, and tenure-track faculty. Each of these individuals read the articles using the following criteria and rankings:

- Article demonstrates a broad sense of the discipline, demonstrating the ability to explain how its specific focus in a subdisciplinary area addresses broader concerns in the field.
- Article makes original contributions to the field, expanding or rearticulating central premises.
- Article is written in a style which, while based in the discipline, attempts to engage with a wider audience or concerns a wider audience.

Based upon their recommendations, the Editors of this collection selected the final list of essays included in this volume.

Before moving onto the essays featured in this book, then, we hope you will take a moment to read this partial list of Associate Editors who have helped organize or participate in our reading groups. Their willingness to volunteer time, actively discuss, and help assess the work speaks to the spirit of collaboration and conversation which marks the "best" of our field: Amanda Adams-Handy; Geghard Arakelian; Brian Ashland; Tamara Bassam Issak; Anthony Black; Phil Bratta; Ronisha W. Browdy; Tessa Brown; Rubén Casas; Libby Catchings; Shannon Dale; Lisa Chow; Kathleen Daly; Riley Dawson; Daphne Desser;

Sue Doe; Candace Epps-Robertson; Miriam Fernandez; Jennifer Fisch-Ferguson; Maureen Fitzsimmons; Matt Frye; John T. Gagnon; Dax Garcia; Romeo Garcia; Julia Garrett; Laura Gonzales; Monika Grzesiak; Margaret Bertucci Hamper; Rebecca Hayes; Sterling Higa; Tobi Jacobi; Erica Kalnay; Vani Kannan; Theresa Keicher; Kate Kiefer; Akbar Khan; Carrie Lamanna; Lance Langdon; Lisa Langstraat; Emily LaPadura; Stephanie Larson; Johnna Lash; Jasmine Lee; Megan Lemming; Jens Lloyd; Emily Loney; Kristina Lum; Skyler McAlister; Ti Macklin; Rajiv Mohabir; Georganne Nordstrom; Whitney Orth; Lydia Page; Mike Pak; Jess Pauszek; Anna Plemons; Shelly Reid; Jenna Saito; Caitlyn Schuchhardt; Chad Seader; Lisa Shea; Neil Simpkins; Paige Takeya; Ken Tokuno; Aaron Vieth; Sharon Yam.

For this help and support, we want to express our sincerest gratitude: Finally, we want to express our gratitude to Dave Blakesley, Parlor Press, for supporting this project's aims of having funds generated by sales go to support independent journals.

## WORKS CITED

Dolmage, Jay Timothy. *Disability Rhetoric*. Syracuse, NY: Syracuse University Press. 2014. Print.

# THE BEST OF THE INDEPENDENT
# RHETORIC AND COMPOSITION JOURNALS

# ACROSS THE DISCIPLINES

*Across the Disciplines* is on the Web at http://wac.colostate.edu/atd//?utm_source=The_Journal_Database

*Across the Disciplines*, a refereed journal devoted to language, learning, and academic writing, publishes articles relevant to writing and writing pedagogy in all their intellectual, political, social, and technological complexity. *Across the Disciplines* shares the mission of the WAC Clearinghouse in making information about writing and writing instruction freely available to members of the CAC, WAC, and ECAC communities.

### Re-Framing Race in Teaching Writing Across the Curriculum

In this article, Poe notes the dearth of scholarship on race and racial identities in both WAC research and presentations of WAC practice, an absence that is all the more puzzling because of the comparative wealth of such scholarship in rhetoric/composition more generally. To ameliorate this insufficiency, Poe offers several distinct "frames" for introducing race into WAC classrooms, such as situating it in local contexts, understanding our own expectations as they relate to assessment in particular, and understanding the connections (and differences) between multilingualism and race. This is an important piece that fills a notable gap in the WAC literature, not only grounding its argument in theory and research but also providing a number of practical teaching strategies that can be put to immediate use in WAC workshops and classrooms.

# 1 Re-Framing Race in Teaching Writing Across the Curriculum

*Mya Poe*

*Abstract: Although faculty across the curriculum are often faced with issues of racial identity in the teaching of writing, WAC has offered little support for addressing race in assignment design, classroom interactions, and assessment. Through examples from teaching workshops, I offer specific ways that we can engage discussions about teaching writing and race productively.*

A graduate Health Policy class is discussing The Immortal Life of Henrietta Lacks by Rebecca Skloot. The book traces the life of Henrietta Lacks, a cancer patient, a poor African American woman, a mother, a wife, and likely the world's most important cell donor. Lacks' cells were taken without her consent and were used to create an "immortal" cell line, which has led to major advances in biomedical research and huge profits. Lacks died shortly after her cells were taken in 1951, although her cells are still used today in labs around the world.

In discussing the ethics of using a patient's cells, a white student argues that taking the cells of an African American cancer patient and using the cells without her consent was acceptable "because it was legal at that time." An African American student bristles and questions, "just like slavery?" Two Indian students in the class are puzzled at this exchange. The remainder of the class is silent.

Last spring, John, a faculty member in Health Policy and Administration, shared this story with me during one of our discussions about teaching writing. John was disturbed by the interaction among the students in his class; not only had the white student missed an important point about bioethics but she had also missed seeing how bioethical issues could be related to race and socioeconomic status. The retort from the African American student did not further the conversation, and John could not get any of the students to meaningfully discuss issues related to patient consent, ownership of genetic material, and the implications of these issues for different groups after this class exchange. Although John was frustrated by this event, he also saw it as an important window into student learning and thought this incident would make an ideal writing opportunity. So, he contacted me to help him design a meaningful writing assignment around this class exchange in hopes that it might help students understand the ways that a professional in the discipline might think through these issues. The bioethical issues presented in The Immortal Life of Henrietta Lacks are complex, and John wanted his students to think more critically about those issues, especially as they relate to poverty and race, before writing their final papers for the semester. The goal for John was not for students to write about their personal feelings on the topic but to use writing to think through the ethical issues in the Lacks case from a professional point of view.

In my time as a writing across the curriculum (WAC) director, I have worked with many faculty like John who have an interest in using writing to help students think through technical issues of identity, ethics, and policy. In John's case, the topic of race could have served as a roadblock to writing instruction; he could have dropped the class discussion and moved on. Instead, he saw the exchange as an opportunity for writing and reflection.

Stories like John's have led me to believe that we need to anticipate these moments where race and writing come together across the curriculum and share ways of working through these moments as we work with faculty and teaching assistants in helping them design, deliver, and assess writing. The WAC literature, however, offers little help in understanding these intersections. While the WAC literature provides a stunning number of resources on developing faculty workshops, tracking changes in student writing over time, and managing successful programs (Young & Fulwiler, 1986; McLeod, Miraglia, Soven, & Thaiss, 2001; Soliday 2011), it is decidedly less helpful in attending to issues of students' racial identities. In "Black holes: Writing across the curriculum, assessment, and the gravitational invisibility of race," Chris Anson (2012) explains that the dearth of information on racial identity is "puzzling," given WAC's openness to diverse forms of discourse and the populations who produce those forms (p. 16). Anson provides an extensive search of the WAC literature, including the WAC Clearinghouse, CompPile, collections, and annotated WAC bibliographies, to find information related to WAC and race. His search yields only a handful of references. For example, the WAC Clearinghouse does include a bibliography related to "diversity," but most of the entries are related to gender, not racial identity. Anson notes that WAC leaders are not disinterested in issues related to race but that "the subject of race is perceived to generate layers of additional complexity over principles, theories, and pedagogies already challenging to faculty in various disciplines to interpret and apply to their teaching" (2012, p. 19). Likewise, WAC scholars may worry about being perceived as foregrounding the values of composition studies over those of other disciplines. Besides, when WAC principles are distilled to brief faculty workshops with a focus on best practices in generic assignment design and assessment, issues of diversity seem "beside the point" (Anson, 2012, p. 19).

More recently, a number of WAC articles have been devoted to multilingual writers (Johns, 2005; Cox & Zawacki, 2011), but often these articles ignore students' racial identities in favor of their linguistic identities. Our field's interest in literacy practices makes a focus on linguistic identity understandable, but as scholars in English Language Learning have noted, "Through teaching and learning a second language, racialized images of the teacher, students, and people that appear in teaching materials get produced and reproduced" (Kubota & Lin, 2009 p. 1). Indeed, ESL/EFL researchers have begun to acknowledge that a critical perspective on multilingual writers also means paying attention to issues of power and racial identity (For example, see the special issue of TESOL Quarterly, Kubota & Lin, 2006, dedicated to the topic.) Ryuko Kubota and Angel Lin (2009) identify four areas for study, including learner/teacher identities and race; manifestations of race in pedagogy, curriculum, materials, and technology; language policy, language ideology, and race; and critical (classroom) discourse analysis and race (p. 15-16). Each of these reminds us that language teaching is merely not about the dissemination of technical skills but about the interactions that inform those instructional contexts both in the classroom and in the ideologies that pervade those contexts.

To take a racialized perspective on WAC suggests a critical stance toward the field. Scholars such as Donna LeCourt (1996), Victor Villanueva (2001), and Michelle Hall Kells (2007) have called for critical perspectives on WAC practices, especially as related to ethno-linguistic identity. LeCourt, for example, has called for changes that allow students to bring in their alternative literacies. The Writing Across Communities initiative at the University of New Mexico is attempting to do just that by integrating WAC and service-learning through an eco-composition agenda that is meaningful to students from the local community. Kells (2007) writes of the program:

> The challenge for the Writing Across Communities initiative at UNM is enhancing opportunities to build identification with the cultures of the academy as well as to cultivate appreciation across the university for the cultures and epistemologies our students bring with them. (p. 96)

WAC's limited engagement with race stands in contrast to the rich body of literature in composition studies on ethnic rhetorics and literacies. One gesture to bring race to WAC scholarship is to draw on this body of research. However, because WAC operates throughout the university community, it is also important to consider that simply importing theory into our practices will likely fail. We have to engage the other frames about race that circulate in the university community—frames that are often deployed by administrators and other powerful stakeholders in the university community.

My goal in this article is to offer specific ways that we can integrate discussions about race in our interactions with faculty, graduate students, and administrators across the curriculum. First, I explain several other frames about race that operate in the university. I then go on to explain three ways that we can reframe race within WAC to make race a meaningful part of our discussions about teaching writing across the curriculum. In my discussion, I use examples from faculty workshops and writing intensive courses to illustrate these points. By understanding the new diversity, recognizing how stereotypes matter, and drawing on linguistic diversity, I contend that we will better help faculty teach writing and improve their ways of responding to student writing.

## Existing Frames

As Chris Anson (2012) notes, one of the reasons that WAC scholars may be reluctant to engage with the topic of race is that it complicates existing relationships with faculty in other disciplines. This is true, but not because composition scholars are the only ones who bring racialized frames to the table. Quite to the contrary, we can find quite powerful other frames for race in university communities.

In The Activist WPA: Changing Stories About Writing and Writers (2008), Linda Adler-Kassner explains how framing—"the idea that stories are always set within and reinforce particular boundaries" (p. 4)—allows for the creation of larger narratives and help individuals make sense of everyday experiences (p. 11). Quoting Deacon, Adler-Kassner goes on to write that "frames define stories that both reflect and perpetuate dominant cultural values and interest rather than 'stimulating the development of alternative conceptions and values' that are 'critical' to those values and interests" (p. 12).

Drawing on the notion of frames allows us to interrogate the stories we already have available to discuss race and writing as well as related notions about achievement and language use. Ironically, often the most powerful, visible frame for race on university campuses are not those deployed by faculty researchers but frames deployed by university administration. For instance, a common frame for discussing race comes is the multicultural frame. A multicultural frame about race might go as follows:

> The challenges in working with an ever-growing pluralistic school population encompass many areas. The provision of relevant multicultural curriculums, the use of culturally sensitive assessment and intervention strategies, the training of school staff in the provision of these services, the recruitment and retention of multicultural and diverse professionals, and the integration of diverse communities and parents in an authentic and empowering manner are only a few of the critical issues facing those working with today's students. (Sanchez et al., 1995, para. 3)

In the multicultural frame, the term race is often synonymous with diversity or a number of other ways that we might characterize individuals in a pluralistic society (gender, ethnicity, religion, etc.), thus race is just one of many variables through which we may recognize difference. The stories in this frame emphasize "cultural sensitivity" or awareness, suggesting that increased understanding of our differences will lead to a more tolerant society. As a result, multicultural approaches tend to focus on training and community building. Even very good initiatives, such as anti-racism initiatives, however, don't engage with student literacies (St. Cloud State University, 2012; University of Puget Sound, 2012).

Although the multicultural frame has been a powerful way to open up discussions of difference, it not free from problems. The approach conjures notions of attending "diversity workshops" that include "warm and fuzzy conversations about diversity that raise consciousness but rarely upset or threaten" (Denny, 2010, p. 33). As Jennifer Trainor notes (2008), attempts in multicultural education to interrogate white privilege have fallen short with white audiences (p. 7) and can actually have the effect of fortifying existing identities and refocusing only on the struggles of working class whites (p. 19).

Another common frame in discussion about race is the achievement gap frame. An achievement gap frame might sound like the following:

> Black ghetto students will get statistically significant higher scores on measures of abstract thinking when they have mastered the grammar of standard English...the mean IQ scores of black ghetto students will go up when they learn to speak and write standard English. (Farrell, 1983, p. 479, 481)

In the achievement gap frame, race is an identifying marker for grouping individuals who share a set of physical characteristics. For example, in the quote above, black individuals who live in poor, urban areas share a common set of attributes. By changing the linguistic practices of this group, the story goes, there will be a change in their cognitive abilities. Achievement gap frames, such as the example above, employ a comparative approach to race; for example, race is tied to a trait, such as IQ, that can be contrasted to the IQ of another raced group.

The achievement gap frame can be found in high-profile books such as the Bell Curve: Intelligence and Class Structure in American Life (Herrnstein & Murray, 1996) and, more recently, Academically Adrift: Limited Learning on College Campuses (Arum & Roska, 2011). To be fair, arguments such as the one in the Bell Curve suggest a biological rationale for differences in performance while Academically Adrift makes no direct argument. However, Academically Adrift like many such publications works within the achievement gap frame, deploying a language of static racial identity correlated with assessment results without considering whether the decisions being made from those assessment results are valid. In the end, the achievement gap frame can be difficult to challenge because administrative audiences gravitate to stories that rely on statistical evidence that seems irrefutable.

In addition to the multicultural frame and the achievement gap frame, other frames that circulate in academic contexts include the post-racial frame and a post-structural frame. In the post-racial frame—a frame that students often work within—racial identity should no longer be a factor in selection processes because U.S. culture now longer operates through the lens of racial prejudice (Trainor, 2008; For a critique of color blindness, see Bonilla-Silva, 2006). In the humanities and social sciences, it is not uncommon to find researchers working within a post-structural frame in which identity is a fluid, discursive construction that has meaning in cultural contexts only because individuals in those contexts assign value to racial constructions (Hall, 1996). Other faculty may bring an anti-racist frame or a culturally-responsive one (Ladson-Billings, 1997). For social scientists like John in Health Policy, race may be a social construction, but it has very real material consequences as related to access to healthcare, quality of care, health outcomes, and legal and Civil Rights implications. For faculty like John, I do not need to bring him a theory of race from composition studies; he already has an understanding of race that is meaningful in his disciplinary context. He needs help teaching writing.

In the end, all of the above frames have meaning to the audiences who deploy them, and we are unwise not to acknowledge that these frames shape individuals' views of teaching ethno-linguistically diverse populations. Each frame provides the language and logics that make certain conclusions seem commonsensical. What interests me is not locating one "right" frame for race but identifying a frame that allows for meaningful discussions of teaching writing to ethno-linguistically diverse students. For example, none of the above frames tells us how to turn the heated Health Policy discussion in John's class into a meaningful writing assignment. In what follows, I suggest ways that we can reframe race in our work with faculty, administrators, and students across the curriculum so the place of racial identity (and its intersections with gender, language, socioeconomic status, geography, and so on) "make sense" in understanding how to better teach writing.

My suggested reframing of race draws on three inter-related principles: (1) making race local, (2) identifying expectations, and (3) acknowledging the racial aspects of linguistic diversity and its meanings in the disciplines.

## A FRAME FOR RACE AND WRITING ACROSS THE CURRICULUM

Brian Huot (2002) argues that assessment of writing should be site-based, locally-controlled, context-sensitive, rhetorically-based, and accessible. Huot's taxonomy is a good model for thinking about how we might reframe race in WAC scholarship; reframing race means reframing the way we think about teaching and responding to student writing across the disciplines. My proposed frame is about what race means in teaching writing, not a theory of race that sits outside of writing. Such a frame makes research locally meaningful, whether we focus on classroom or program-level concerns. Thus, the stories that we should tell about race and writing are ones based on the specific needs of students and teachers at our specific institutions. The research we propose should be based on sound principles of writing research, namely that writing is a rhetorical act, shaped by our linguistic-cultural backgrounds. The writing instruction we propose—be it assignment design, peer review practices, or assessment—should not be based solely on generic best practices, but on practices attuned to the contexts in which writing is taught at our institutions and the students who are the recipients of that instruction. Finally, the conclusions that we draw about students writing abilities across the curriculum should be validated at our institutions with our own values and not solely through external measures.

### Situating Race Locally

Instead of starting with generalizations about teaching writing to racially diverse student populations, it is better to start with discussions about local students and local needs. By describing specific students—students in our classrooms and programs—we can root our conversations locally, where all teaching and assessment stories should begin. The specificity of these discussions is key because terms like "international" or "minority" do not really give us much useful information in these local situations. Moreover, it's too easy to over-generalize our students' motivations and performances when we use generic labels. Instead, a conversation that begins as follows is more helpful:

> The students in my Health Policy class include two African American women, four Euro-American men and four Euro-American women, two Asian American women, and two men from India. In talking to my students, I've found that at least half them know another language and use it on a regular basis. One of the African American women comes from a privileged background and already has a job with a pharmaceutical company. The other African American woman is a returning student; she's interested in becoming a hospital administrator. Of my Euro-American women, one is a former nurse and a widow whose husband died in Iraq. The other three women are traditional college-age students who are interested in pursuing a Masters degree in Health Administration. One of those students speaks Russian at home and is interested in health policy because her mother was diagnosed with breast cancer.

By talking with greater specificity about the actual students in our classrooms, we can move past generalizations about "international students," "basic writers," or "transfer students." Of course, we often need help in figuring how out to elicit such information from students, especially in large classes. Informal writing prompts can be used to gather some of this information. Rather than using close-ended surveys, I prefer to use open-ended writing prompts so that students can articulate their identities in ways that make sense to them (Although research such as by Araiza, Cárdenas, & Garza, 2007, show that surveys can yield very good context-specific information). In asking students to articulate their identities in ways that make sense to them provides us emic descriptions of identity.

By describing students with greater specificity in our classrooms, we will likely find that initial notions about race become more complicated. Those more complicated notions of race allow us to respond more meaningfully to student writing. For example, a first year writing teacher explained in a WAC workshop how a peer review discussion went awry when a Dutch Indian student who grew up in Tanzania used the term "mulatto" in her essay. What was the student's reasoning in selecting the term "mulatto" and how could the instructor guide a class conversation in such a way that would acknowledge the various ways that different students understood that term and its historical legacy in different national contexts?

Working locally, we will also likely find that within the disciplines, the monolithic constructions of students starts to pull apart. For example, my colleagues in the sciences do not simply work with "Asian" students in their labs. They work with Indian-American, Indian, Chinese, Taiwanese, Asian American, and American-Sri Lankan students who come with various linguistic backgrounds (and possibly cultural expectations about the nature of scientific research). Each of those students brings specific writing needs that cannot be addressed with broad characterizations as English as Second Language (ESL) learners or as "Asian" students.

Finally, by describing the students in our programs with greater specificity, we can design multiple levels of support that are meaningful to those populations. For example, if our students are Hmong, Generation 1.5 learners from the local area, then how does that make us rethink the guidance we are giving new teachers about responding to student writing, training our teachers about peer review, and what kinds of program support we need for these new teachers to help them support the local Hmong students who are in our classrooms? In attempting to describe students in our programs with greater specificity, we often find that existing institutional identifiers are insufficient. Comparing our emic definitions with those etic labels can be enlightening in revealing institutional frames for racial identity.

In the end, asking about context-specific demographics allows us to think about racial identity as more dynamic, especially when we bring together "domestic diversity" and "international diversity." It also allows us to make connections to the multiple, shifting identities that students bring to writing classrooms (Canagarajah, 2004). Most importantly, by reframing race as one situated within the specific contexts in which we teach writing, we can move to specific strategies for teaching writing across the curriculum that is attuned to the identities of the students at our institutions.

## Understanding What Expectations We Bring To Writing Instruction

Once we have greater specificity as to our understanding of students in our classrooms, then we can design writing instruction that is better suited to those students. The next question, then, is how good are those assignments and our assessments. What do we do when we find that some students do not perform as well as other students? What do we do when performance seems to be linked to race? Rather than using an achievement gap frame and explaining differences through static identity groupings, it's more useful to consider what expectations teachers and students bring to rhetorical situations across the curriculum. Turning questions of difference into moments of dialog aligns with WAC's emphasis on "pedagogical reform rather than curricular change" (Townsend, 1994, p. 1301); our goal is to help improve the teaching of writing, not tell departments what their students should be writing.

On one hand, it's simple enough to argue that students come with different motivations to learn and different ability levels. Some students take more easily to the expectations of a writing intensive class, for example, than others. Differences in writing development are normal; learning to write is a complex activity and students' personal and cultural identities sharply affect their relationship to writing (Herrington & Curtis, 2000; Ivanič, 1998; Inoue, 2012). Problems arise, however, when systemic barriers or our own biases lead to erroneous conclusions about race and writing ability. It goes without saying that race does not cause individuals to perform in certain ways because of some innate ability associated to that person's race. But racial stereotypes can lead to performance differences.

What is needed is a better understanding of what expectations faculty and students bring to writing classrooms. For example, at one institution where I gave a workshop, instructors of the first year seminar courses brought up the subject of race; African American, Native American, and Latino/a students in their first year writing classes needed more help but would not approach them, they explained. After some discussion, I found that instructors were making an implicit connection between students' race and a university-sponsored bridge program. They assumed that all Latino/a, Native American, and African American students in first year courses were from the bridge program and came with a common set of writing issues. I questioned if they were making assumptions about students too quickly and ignoring the writing needs of other students—namely, white and Asian students who were also in the bridge program. We also talked about how their expectations for those students—expectations that those students came to recognize very quickly—effectively shut down dialog about teaching writing with those students.

While the notion of stereotypes may seem simplistic when discussed in general terms, stereotype research has actually been quite compelling when done in context. Stereotype research on teaching practices has shown that stereotypes do impact teaching and learning (McKown & Weinstein, 2007; Rose, 1989; Pollock, 2001: Ferguson, 1998). Sandra Kamasukiri (1996), for example, showed that teacher's attitudes towards language use had a direct impact on the way that they taught students. Meredith Bulinski et al. (2009) found that white teachers provided more comments to white students than to students of color but that Latino/a students received more comments on grammar than other students. What was surprising in the Inoue et al. study was that white teachers typically shied away from commenting extensively on the writing from students of color. Arnetha Ball (1997), on the other hand, found that African American teachers were more likely to score the writing of African American students lower than white teachers because of their sense of expectations for writers.

The research on teachers' assessments of second language writing is mixed. Donald Rubin and Melanie Williams-James (1997), for example, found that raters favored Asian writers over other native writers. On the other hand, they also found that teachers' ratings of non-native writers "were best predicted by the number of surface errors they detected" (p. 139). And Deborah Crusan (2011) in a study involving more than 100 faculty across the disciplines found that altering racial/ national identifications on student papers influenced the scores that readers gave to writers; scorers gave writers who they believed were born in the U.S. lower holistic scores on their essays.

In addition to research on teachers' assessment practices, Claude Steele's research on stereotype threat (1997) has been influential in understanding how students bring stereotypes to learning contexts. According to Steele (1999), stereotype threat is "the threat of being viewed through the lens of a negative stereotype, or the fear of doing something that would inadvertently confirm that stereotype" (p. 798). Contrary to the belief that low-achieving students are likely to have difficulty on academically difficult tasks, Steele has shown that students who are aware of stereotypes about their group and who highly identify with a domain—e.g., school ("high achievers") —are the students who are most likely to be effected by "threat." It is not that such students believe the negative stereotype; quite to the contrary, such students understand that the negative stereotype is a social construction of their identity, not an actual representation of their ability. As Claude Steele and Josh Aronson (1995) write, "It is important to understand that the person may experience a threat even if he or she does not believe the stereotype" (p. 798). For these students, the desire to overcome the perception of a negative stereotype leads to depressed performance.

Writing researchers have also sought to understand what expectations students bring to writing classrooms. Jennifer Mott-Smith (2009), for example, looked at the experiences of five Generation 1.5 students on a writing proficiency exam and found that her students were keenly that they were labeled as "high risk." Zandra Jordan's research (2012) on African American language (AAL) at a historically black college showed that negative stereotypes were common in such contexts. When Jordan interviewed students about their use of African American language, she found that students characterized AAL as "not professional" and described it as "ignorance that plagues the African American community and allows other races to believe 'we' are less intelligent" (p. 98). Yet, Jordan also found that students did not passively accept negative stereotypes. They sought to change stereotypes, as one student explained, "I do believe that professors should realize that students come from different walks of life. . . speaking 'African American English' is a cultural thing, not meant to harm anyone" (2012, p. 98).

In my own work (2006) on racial stereotypes and writing assessment, I found that students were aware of stereotypes about race and academic performance. For example, one African American student explained:

> Schools give minority students a benefit over the white students because they feel the minority student can't compete with the white student, for this reason white professors will look at the test of a minority student and if they sound the least bit intelligent, the professors are surprised and hype up their grade a few notches. So I feel that the grading professor will grade me on the fact that I'm a black male. (p. 93)

What is telling about research on ethno-linguistic stereotypes from students' perspectives is the persistence with which students feel stereotypes are perpetuated and their resistance to those stereotypes. The research also suggests that students carry their understanding of stereotyping into subsequent classroom interactions. For example, in a study conducted by Geoffrey Cohen, Claude Steele, and Lee Ross (1999), they found that African American students did not respond to the typical "buffered" feedback offered by white teachers. Students did not believe in feedback that they perceived to be insincere platitudes. Instead, Cohen, Steele, and Ross found:

> When feedback was accompanied both by an invocation of high standards and by an assurance of the student's capacity to reach those standards, Black students responded as positively as White students and both groups reported enhanced identification with relevant skills and careers (p. 13)

In sum, both teachers and students bring raced expectations to educational contexts, and those expectations shape the ways that teachers respond to student writing and the ways that students respond to teacher feedback. Often simple practices in understanding stereotypes can lead to meaningful changes in practice. For example, simply counting the kinds of comments we provide different students provides a self-assessment tool for understanding how we respond to writing. Likewise, marking student papers with the names removed is a useful exercise to see if our judgments are affected by subtle biases. Getting students to articulate their own assumptions about learning and disciplinary content can reveal their raced expectations.

Situating race locally is critical, but only a starting point. Understanding what expectations we bring to writing classrooms—be they first-year writing courses, writing intensive courses, or disciplinary courses in which writing plays a role—is important if we are to think about what kinds of changes we make in teaching practices. Rather than thinking of race as an added complexity to WAC workshops or individual consultations, a focus on the raced expectations that we bring to classrooms can improve teaching and even lead to department-led initiatives to better support student writing in the major.

## Understanding the Connection Between Multilingualism and Race

The third element in reframing race across the curriculum is paying attention to the connection between multilingualism and race. In making the connection between language and racial identity, however, I do not want WAC practitioners to explain linguistic and rhetorical practices through essentialized cultural explanations. Instead, I want us to think about how to make connections between home and professional literacies. In doing so, I want us to pay greater attention to how our characterizations of linguistic diversity are often raced in subtle ways. As Lan Hue Quach, Ji-Yoen O. Jo, and Luis Urietta, Jr. (2009) argue, "U.S. linguicism creates inferior identities for nonnative English speakers and ethnolinguistic minority groups . . . Policing Standard English as the only valid linguistic form subordinates and devalues the identities and experiences of ethnolinguistic-minority students" (p. 121).

In disciplinary writing contexts, there are many instances when paying attention to the racialized assumptions of linguistic diversity is critical. In professions such as Health Policy understanding linguistic diversity is enormously important. As John explained to me, hospital administrators as well as nurses, doctors, and other hospital workers interact with individuals from diverse backgrounds. Too commonly, misconceptions arise based on patients' linguistic practices—misconceptions that are located at the intersection of a patient's linguistic and racial identities. Those misconceptions can lead to disastrous consequences, or at the very least, distrust of the healthcare system. Thus, teaching Health Policy students about that connection between race and language use and its implications for professional practice are an essential part of disciplinary education.

Two bodies of literature are useful in integrating linguistic diversity and its racial implications in WAC practice. First, we can draw on the large body of research in linguistic, education, and writing studies on the rhetorical and language patterns of various groups. Such research, for example, has shown us that language patterns are codified and taught, often implicitly through everyday practice. For example, Shirley Brice Heath's ethnography of families in Roadville and Trackton, Ways With Words (1983), illustrates the ways that children learn to use language through the patterns and practices found in their own families. Some of these practices map onto language and literacy practices found in school while many do not. Thus, for scholars like Heath, writing is a cultural practice and the diversity of language use is a cultural resource, not error-ridden linguistic patterns that need to be swept away (see also Taylor, 1983; Purcell-Gates, 2007; Genishi

& Dyson, 2009). Narratives by Keith Gilyard (1991) and Victor Villanueva (1993) critique the ways that attempts to eliminate linguistic variation reap social and personal tolls and remind us that purely cultural explanations for writing practices do not sufficiently account for the personal and social ways that individuals use language.

Second, contemporary theories of multilingualism are valuable. Such theories posit the "multiple and fluctuating character of English as not a single, unchanging world language, or lingua franca, but a constellation of ever changing Englishes" (Horner, Lu, & Matsuda, 2010, p. 2). Multilingual researchers have turned their attention to global Englishes, investigating the varieties of English spoken and written internationally (Lu & Horner, 2004). Even when the end-goal is still Standard English, multilingual theory asks us to consider, "Whose version of Standard English?" Through such questioning, we can move beyond absolutist positions on grammar and move to practices that recognize language use in context: When and where is linguistic variation a standard part of disciplinary practice? When is it more limited and why? Whose interests are represented in those differences?

Understanding the racialized implications linguistic diversity, thus, can be a valuable resource for teaching writing in many disciplines. If the goal is to help prepare students for real-world rhetorical situations, then teaching writing across the curriculum means preparing students for the multilingual spaces in which they will be writing and working. In classroom interactions, we can ask students to identify their own grammatical and spelling patterns, noting when and where they find certain patterns more effective and where deviations from a particular dialect can be strategically useful (Young, 2007).

In writing classrooms, a place where difficulties over linguistic variation often surfaces is in peer review (Leki, 2001). For example, in a biological engineering course I co-taught, students wrote a grant for their final class project. At the end of the semester, students participated in a "study section" that was modeled on the National Institutes of Health process for peer review of grants. In their reviews, students were asked not to make specific comments about the researcher and only focus on the criteria of significance, innovation, and approach. However, when commenting on the writing of Ye-jun, a Korean student, another graduate student (herself a second language writer) commented:

> Overall, this proposal is well organized and clearly planned. However, there are many missing words and grammatical errors in the background section – PROOFREAD! (e.g., "every year, it cause over five hundred million people", etc). SCORE: 2.5 (without the language errors, I would give this grant a higher score).

While it is certainly plausible to argue that this writer could have gotten additional editorial help with his writing, the student reviewer's belief that the errors were a matter of the writer's lack of effort (PROOFREAD!) shows a misunderstanding of language use. To our and our students' detriment, we did not take this chance to initiate a class discussion about linguistic diversity in professional contexts. For example, it is worth debating why this reviewer felt compelled to comment and score the grant on a feature that was not indicated on the scoring rubric—a choice that meant this grant would not be funded in our class scenario. Finally, it's useful to ask if such reactions are stronger toward students of certain racial identities than others.

Ultimately, simply asserting that linguistic diversity is a good thing does not help us teach writing better. In fact, many faculty may agree with the spirit of linguistic diversity but reject multilingualism in disciplinary contexts because of the belief that Standard English is the only dialect used in professional work. Thus, in reframing race in relation to linguistic diversity in teaching writing across the curriculum, several points are important. First, the linguistic diversity that our students bring to writing classrooms across the curriculum is a reflection of the shifting demographics of higher education. It does us little good to think of linguistic diversity in terms merely of error. To help students learn writing, we need to recognize that language use is tied to identity and that students may conflate our responding to their writing as a statement about their racial identity. It is not unreasonable to ask students to learn the linguistic conventions used in disciplinary writing, but it's also useful to recognize that those patterns may be broken or "meshed" with other linguistic forms in specific contexts. Moreover, we have to consider what we want to teach students about the connection between linguistic diversity and professional practice. The myth of linguistic homogeneity is strong in the disciplines as English language publishing is now common in many disciplines. But just because Standard English is required for publishing doesn't mean that it's used all the time in professional practice, and, in fact, encountering linguistic diversity is a normal part of daily practice for many professionals.

## CONCLUSION

Integrating race in WAC practice has the potential to address very real teaching problems that are experienced by teachers across the curriculum. For this reason, I believe it is essential that we ground discussions of race in local contexts and in ways that have specific meaning for teaching writing. By talking about students in specific contexts, we can help teachers like John develop meaningful writing assignments and assessments of student writing. In John's case, we devised a writing assignment for his Health Policy students in which they were asked to review an informed consent document from a local hospital. Although informed consent is now required for medical procedures, its usefulness remains debated, primarily because many patients do not understand the documentation, and doctors will not treat patients under normal circumstances unless given consent. Students were not asked to speculate how Henrietta Lacks or other patients might read the document. Instead, they were asked to provide their personal interpretation of the document, articulating their analysis through their own identities. Those analyses illustrated the varied expectations that readers bring to rhetorical situations and the subtle ways that race and other identities inform those interpretations. In the end, whether it be researching the expectations that teachers and students bring to writing situations or drawing on linguistic diversity as a resource in contemporary disciplinary practice, re-framing race in writing across the curriculum means being attuned to the contexts in which writing is taught at our institutions and how race is meaningful for us and our students at the institutions at which we teach.

### NOTES

1. I use the terms race and ethno-linguistic diversity throughout this article. Although the term "ethnicity" may sometimes be used to distinguish a cultural identity from a national or racial identity, I avoid such distinctions because such terms are not clearly delineated in U.S. culture. Moreover, any ethnic identification is ultimately subsumed in U.S culture under a racialized interpretation. For my own definition of race, I follow Michael Omi and Howard Winant's (1994) description of racial formations—"a process of

historically situated projects in which human bodies and social structures are represented and organized" (p. 55-56). Racial formations, including whiteness, are linked to hegemony and their representations are always in flux.

2. My characterization here of multicultural frames does not suggest that all multicultural education approaches work in this way. For example, culturally responsive pedagogy approaches, such as advocated by Sonia Nieto (2010) and Gloria Ladson-Billings (1997), take a decidedly more critical perspective.

3. I am not suggesting here that we should not be collecting race-based assessment data. Quite to the contrary, race-based data should be collected if needed to make meaningful conclusions about writing assessment results. It is impossible to make valid conclusions about a portfolio assessment, for example, at an ethno-linguistically diverse institution, if data are not collected on students' racial and linguistic identities.

4. Many fields that have taken up issues related to identity, especially racial identity. For example, the technical fields include publications such as the Journal of Women and Minorities in Science and Engineering that are dedicated to issues related to the teaching of under-represented groups in the sciences and engineering.

5. Institutions like George Mason support students' explorations of their multiple identities through publications like Diversity at Mason: The pursuit of transformative education (Habib & Mallett, 2011), Valuing written accents: Non-native students talk about identity, academic writing, and meeting teachers' expectations (Zawacki et al., 2007).

6. As our conversation continued, I wondered if faculty in the disciplines were also linking race to these same students: Why was race linked to writing instruction in one context and not another?

## References

Adler-Kassner, L. (2008). The activist WPA: Changing stories about writing and writers. Logan, UT: Utah State UP.

Anson, C. (2012). Black holes: Writing across the curriculum, assessment, and the gravitational invisibility of race. In A. Inoue and M. Poe (Eds.), Race and writing assessment (pp. 15 29). New York: Peter Lang.

Araiza, I., Cárdenas, H., & Garza, S. (2007). Literate practices/language practices: What do we really know about our students? In C. Kirklighter, D. Cárdenas, & S. W. Murphy (Eds.), Teaching writing with Latino/a students: Lessons learned at Hispanic-serving institutions (pp. 87-97). Albany, NY: SUNY Press.

Arum, R. & Rosa, J. (2011). Academically adrift: Limited learning on college campuses. Chicago, IL: University of Chicago Press.

Ball, A. F. (1997). Expanding the dialogue on culture as a critical component when assessing writing. Assessing Writing, 4(2), 169-202.

Bonilla-Silva, E. (2006). Racism without racists: Color-Blind racism and the persistence of racial inequality in the United States. (2nd ed). Lanham, Maryland: Rowman & Littlefield P.

Bulinski, M., Dominguez, A., Inoue, A. B., Jamali, M., McKnight, M., Seidel, S., & Stott, J. (2009, March). "Shit-plus," "AWK," "frag," and "huh?": An empirical look at a writing program's commenting practices. Paper presented at the Conference on College Composition and Communication, San Francisco, CA.

Canagarajah, S. (2010). An updated SRTOL? CCCC diversity blog. Retrieved from http://cccc blog.blogspot.com/2010/11/updated-srtol.html

Cohen, G., Steele, C. M., & Ross, L. D. (1999). The mentor's dilemma: Providing critical feedback across the racial divide. Personality and Social Psychology Bulletin, 25(10), 1302-1318.

Cox, M. & Zawacki, T. (2011). WAC and second language writing: Cross-field research, theory, and program development [Special issue]. Across the Disciplines, 8(4). Retrieved from http://wac.colostate.edu/atd/ell/index.cfm

Crusan, D. (2011, October). The problem of bias: Achieving fair and equitable L2 writing assessment. Paper presented at the Conference on Writing Education Across Borders. State College, PA.

Denny, H. (2010). Facing the center: Toward an identity politics of one-to-One mentoring. Logan, UT: Utah State UP.

Farrell, T. (1983). IQ and Standard English. College Composition and Communication, 19(4), 470-484.

Ferguson, R. P. (1998). Teachers' perceptions and expectations and the black-white test score gap. In C. Jencks & M. Phillips (Eds.), The Black-White Test Score Gap (pp. 273-317). Washington DC: Brookings Institution.

Genishi, C. & Dyson, A. (2009). Children, language, and literacy. New York: Teachers College Press.

Gilyard, K. (1991).Voices of the self: A study of language competence. Detroit, MI: Wayne State UP.

Habib, A., & Mallett, K. (2011). Diversity at Mason: The pursuit of transformative education. Fairfax, VA: George mason University.

Hall, S. (1996). Introduction: Who needs identity. In S. Hall & P. Du Gay (Eds.), Questions of cultural identity (pp. 1-17). London: Sage Publications.

Heath, S. (1983) Ways with words: language, life, and work in communities and classrooms. Cambridge, UK: Cambridge UP.

Herrington, A. & Curtis, M. (2000). Persons in process: Four stories of writing and personal development in college. Urbana, IL: National Council of Teachers of English.

Herrnstein, R. & Murray, C. (1996). The bell curve: Intelligence and class structure in American life. New York: The Free Press.

Horner, B., Lu, M., & Matsuda, P. (2010). Cross-language relations in composition. Carbondale, IL: Southern Illinois UP.

Huot, B. (2002). (Re)Articulating writing assessment for teaching and learning. Logan, UT: Utah State University Press.

Inoue, A. (2012). Grading contracts: Assessing their effectiveness on different racial formations. In A. Inoue and M. Poe (Eds.), Race and writing assessment (pp. 78-94). New York: Peter Lang.

Ivanič, R. (1998). Writing and identity: The discoursal construction of identity in academic writing. Amsterdam: John Benjamin Publishing Company.

Johns, A. (2005). The linguistically diverse student: Challenges and possibilities across the curriculum [Special issue]. Across the Disciplines, 2. Retrieved from http://wac.colostate.edu/atd/lds/index.cfm

Jordan, Z. (2012). Students' right, African American English, and classroom writing assessment: Considering the HBCU. In A. Inoue and M. Poe (Eds.), Race and writing assessment (pp. 98-110). New York: Peter Lang.

Kamusikiri, S. (1996). African American English and writing assessment: An Afrocentric approach. In E. M. White, W.D. Lutz, & S. Kamusikiri (Eds.), Assessment of writing: Politics, policies, practices. New York: Modern Language Association of America.

Kells, M. (2007). Writing across communities: Deliberation and the discursive possibilities of WAC. Reflections: A Journal of Writing, Service-Learning, and Community Literacy, (6)1, 87-109.

Kubota, R. & Lin, A. (2006). Race and TESOL [Special issue]. TESOL Quarterly, (40)3.

Kubota, R. & Lin, A. (2010). Race, culture, and identities in second language education: Exploring critically engaged practice. New York: Routledge.

Ladson-Billings, G.J. (1997). The dreamkeepers: Successful teachers of African-American children. San Francisco, CA: Jossey-Bass.

LeCourt, D. (1996). WAC as Critical Pedagogy. JAC, 16(3), 389-405.

Leki, I. (2001). A narrow thinking system: Nonnative-English-speaking students in group projects across the curriculum. TESOL Quarterly, 35, 39-67.

McKown, C. & Weinstein, R. (2008). Teacher expectations, classroom context, and the achievement gap. Journal of School Psychology, 46(3), 235-261.

McLeod, S., Miraglia, E., Soven, M., & Thaiss, C. (2001). WAC for the new millennium: Strategies for continuing writing across the curriculum programs. Urbana, IL: National Council of Teachers of English.

Mott-Smith, J. (2009). Responding to high-stakes writing assessment: A case study of five generation 1.5 students. In M. Roberge, M. Siegal, & L.

Harklau (Eds.), Generation 1.5 in college composition (pp. 120-134). New York, NY: Routledge.

Nieto, S. (2010). The light in their eyes: Creating multicultural learning communities. New York: Teachers College Press.

Omi, M., & Winant, H. (1994). Racial formations in the United States: From the 1960s to the 1990s (2nd ed.). New York: Routledge.

Poe, M. (2006). Race, representation, and writing assessment: Racial stereotypes and the construction of identity in writing assessment. (Doctoral dissertation). University of Massachusetts, Amherst. Retrieved from http://scholarworks.umass.edu/dissertations/AAI3206201

Pollock, M. (2001). How the question we ask most about race in education is the very question we most suppress. Educational Researcher, 30(9), 9-12.

Purcell-Gates, V. (2007). Cultural practices of literacy: Case studies of language, literacy, social practice and power. Mahwah, NJ: Lawrence Erlbaum.

Quach, L. H., Jo, J., & Urrieta, L. (2009). Understanding the racialized identities of Asian students in predominately white schools. In Kubota, R. & Lin, A. (Eds.), Race, culture, and identities in second language education: Exploring critically engaged practice (pp. 118-137). New York: Routledge.

Rose, M. (1989). Lives on the boundary: A moving account of the struggles and achievements of America's educationally underprepared. New York: Penguin.

Rubin, D. & Williams-James, M. (1997). The impact of writer nationality on mainstream teachers' judgments of composition quality. Journal of Second Language Writing, 6(2), 139-153.

Sanchez, W. (1995). Working with diverse learners and school staff in a multicultural society. Washington DC: United States Department of Education. Retrieved from http://www.eric.ed.gov:80/PDFS/ED390018.pdf

Smitherman, G. & Villanueva, V. (2003). Language diversity in the classroom: From intention to practice. Carbondale, IL: Southern Illinois UP.

Soliday, M. (2011). Everyday genres: Writing assignments across the disciplines. Carbondale: Southern Illinois Press.

St. Cloud State University. Community Anti-Racism Education (CARE) strategic plan. Retrieved from http://www.stcloudstate.edu/care/strategic.asp

Steele, C. M. (1997). A threat in the air: How stereotypes shape intellectual identity and performance. American Psychologist, 52(6), 613-629.

Steele, C. M., & Aronson, J. (1995). Stereotype threat and the intellectual test-performance of African-Americans. Journal of personality and Social Psychology, 69(5), 797-811.

Steele, C. M. (1999). Thin ice: 'Stereotype threat' and black college students. The Atlantic Monthly. Retrieved from http://www.theatlantic.com/issues/99aug/9908stereotype.htm

Taylor, D. (1983). *Family literacies*. Portsmouth, NH: Heinemann.

Townsend, M. (1994). Writing across the curriculum. In A. Purves, L. Pap, & S. Jordan (Eds.), *English studies and language arts* (Vol. 2), (pp. 1299-1302). New York: NCTE.

Trainor, J. (2008). *Rethinking racism: Emotion, persuasion, and literacy education in an all white high school*. Carbondale, IL: Southern Illinois UP.

University of Puget Sound. Race and pedagogy initiative. Retrieved from http://www.pugetsound.edu/academics/academic-resources/race--pedagogy-initiative/

Villanueva, V. (1993). *Bootstraps: From an American academic of color*. Urbana, IL: National Council of Teachers of English.

Villanueva, V. (2001). The politics of literacy across the curriculum. In S. McLeod, E. Moraglia, M. Soven, & C. Thaiss (Eds.), *WAC for the new millennium* (pp. 165-178). Urbana, IL: National Council of Teachers of English.

Young, V. (2007). *Your average nigga: Performing race, literacy, and masculinity*. Detroit, MI: Wayne State UP.

Young, A. & Fulwiler, T. (1986). *Writing across the disciplines: research into practice*. Portsmouth, NH: Boynton/Cook Publishers.

Zawacki, T., Hajabbasi, E., Habib, A., Antram, A., Das, A. (2007). *Valuing written accents: Non-native students talk about identity, academic writing, and meeting teachers' expectations*. Fairfax, VA: George Mason University.

# COMMUNITY LITERACY JOURNAL

*Community Literacy Journal* is on the Web at http://www.communityliteracy.org

The *Community Literacy Journal* publishes both scholarly work that contributes to the field's emerging methodologies and research agendas and work by literacy workers, practitioners, and community literacy program staff. We are especially committed to presenting work done in collaboration between academics and community members We understand "community literacy" as the domain for literacy work that exists outside of mainstream educational and work institutions. It can be found in programs devoted to adult education, early childhood education, reading initiatives, lifelong learning, workplace literacy, or work with marginalized populations, but it can also be found in more informal, ad hoc projects. For us, literacy is defined as the realm where attention is paid not just to content or to knowledge but to the symbolic means by which it is represented and used. Thus, literacy makes reference not just to letters and to text but to other multimodal and technological representations as well.

## What's Writing Got to Do with It?: Citizen Wisdom, Civil Rights Activism, and 21st Century Community Literacy

Kells's article, part of a *CLJ* special issue on "Writing Democracy" and guest edited by Shannon Carter and Deborah Mutnick, is timely and notable for its focus on "what a pedagogy of public rhetoric and community literacy might look like based on an understanding of twentieth century Mexican American civil rights rhetoric." Kells's careful and insightful analysis of writing, citizenship, and civic literacy is indicative of the kind of work that we aspire to publish in the *Community Literacy Journal*.

# 2 What's Writing Got to Do with It?: Citizen Wisdom, Civil Rights Activism, and 21st Century Community Literacy

*Michelle Hall Kells*

*Abstract: This article examines what a pedagogy of public rhetoric and community literacy might look like based on an understanding of twentieth century Mexican American civil rights rhetoric. The inductive process of examining archival materials and conducting oral histories informs this discussion on the processes and challenges of gaining civic inclusion. I argue that writing can be both a healing process and an occasion for exercising agency in a world of contingency and uncertainty. To illustrate, I describe several key events shaping the evolution of the post-World War II Mexican American civil rights movement in New Mexico. Taking a case study approach, I begin this chapter by examining the civic discourses of one prominent New Mexico leader in the post-World War II civil rights movement: Vicente Ximenes. As a leader, Ximenes confronted critical civil rights issues about culture and belonging for over fifty years ago beginning in Albuquerque, New Mexico. It is a historical moment worth revisiting. First, I set the stage for this examination about writing, citizenship, and civic literacy by analyzing two critical rhetorical moments in this life of this post World War II civil rights activist. Secondly, I connect the Ximenes legacy to a growing movement at the University of New Mexico and the ways that we are making critical responses to current issues facing our local communities in New Mexico. By triangulating social acts of literacy, currently and historically, this article offers organizing principles for Composition teachers and advocates of community literacy serving vulnerable communities in their various spheres of practice.*

Marking the ten year anniversary of 9/11, the Albuquerque Cultural Conference recently took as its theme: "Cultural Survival in Difficult Times" to signal the stark reality that our vulnerable communities (locally and nationally) are becoming increasingly fragile economically, culturally, and politically. This post 9/11 kairotic moment calls to mind the concept of solastalgia or what Glen Albrecht terms human ecosystem distress. Albrecht defines solastalgia as the embodied effects of isolation and the inability to exercise agency over place. Solastalgia can be mapped to such endemic social conditions as drug abuse, physical illness, mental illness, and suicide. I believe that we as a nation have been trying to resolve a kind of collective solastalgia or post-traumatic stress syndrome for the past decade. Moreover, the kind of border tensions that we are facing today, the current anti-immigration hysteria, and the omnipresent English Only movement are historically connected and politically relevant to the current work in public writing and community literacy education (Kells, Balester, and Villanueva; Kells "Mapping"). Writing can be both a healing process and an occasion for exercising agency in a world of contingency and uncertainty.

Literacy and civic engagement figure prominently in issues of agency as do issues of higher education access and Composition Studies as a gateway to enfranchisement. If the past twenty-five years of scholarship in Rhetoric and Composition has taught us anything, it is that there is no panacea, no single prescription for teaching literacy practice. Composition Studies is not a science. And I don't say that disparagingly. I do not mean to negate the kinds of work that calls for the use of scientific and quantitative methods. It just seems that research on literacy practice and communicative action resists absolute predictability and generalizability. Language leaks. My own earliest language attitude studies adopted empirical research methods and applied a quantitative interpretative frame to issues related to ethnolinguistic identity (Kells, "Leveling;" "Linguistic Contact Zones"). And much to my surprise, I have found those early fragments of discovery circulated and cited in our field. The key word here is surprise. The consequences of writing myself into and out of dissonance never cease to surprise me (Kells and Balester, "Voices of the Wild Horse Desert"). The hermeneutics of research can help to position us as scholars and teachers to attend to phenomena otherwise invisible to us. Moreover, research and writing can take us by surprise. Cultivating literacy prac-

tice is not about prescription-writing but making discoveries, sometimes and often by accident.

It is with that same kind of inquisitive wonder and interrogative
impulse that I have applied another set of questions and interpretive
frames to issues related to ethnolinguistic identity and civic engagement. For the past ten years, I have been asking: what a pedagogy
of public rhetoric and community literacy might look like based on
an understanding of twentieth century Mexican American civil rights
rhetoric. The inductive process of examining archival materials and
conducting oral histories has helped me to pay attention to the processes and challenges of gaining civic inclusion. As a result, I have been
imagining a program, a national consortium that examines different
civic discourses and the premises of rhetorical agency embedded in
them (Kells "Rhetorical Imagination"; Rose and Paine). Why don't
we, why haven't we, why couldn't we cultivate think tanks for civic engagement and help students analyze and generate texts that represent
their spheres of belonging? Language is how we transmit culture—
the implicit codes and expectations that hold us together as families,
as neighborhoods, as institutions. Recently Marilyn A. Martinez, a
self-published writer in Albuquerque, New Mexico reminded me of
the intrinsic, humanizing value of language and the role of literacy
in communities beyond the university. Our meeting was nothing less
than serendipitous; the lessons learned were far deeper than expected.

## DISABLING FICTIONS AND COMMUNITY LITERACY

I have been troubled by disabling fictions within literacy education
for a number of years. I am reminded in the most unlikely places why
this particular intellectual pre-occupation, this predilection for confronting "disabling fictions," has a place in academe. The story begins
on a Southwest Airlines flight from Austin, Texas to Albuquerque,
New Mexico in late August 2010, the tail-end of a year-long sabbatical nibbled away by the demands of my department and university. I
was returning home from a trip to the Lyndon B. Johnson Presidential
Library to complete archival research on my current book project,
*Vicente Ximenes & LBJ's Great Society: The Rhetoric of Mexican
American Civil Rights Reform*. It was the proverbial eleventh hour.
Packing in what I hoped to do at the beginning of my sabbatical at
the very end. It was what I wanted to do before New Mexico's State

Secretary of Higher Education called me at home a year ago as I was just beginning to settle into the lovely calm of my sabbatical. The State Secretary of Higher Education wanted me to help him revamp the state's core curriculum because of the role I had played at the University of New Mexico mobilizing the Writing Across Communities initiative for the previous five years. It was a rare opportunity—a worthy risk.

The first six months of my sabbatical were spent scrambling as chair of the UNM Core Curriculum Task Force. We finally put a bow on the final task force report in May 2010; then I promptly jumped into writing the Ximenes book over the summer. When I left for Texas in August, I had five working chapters under construction and needed just one last sweep through the LBJ Presidential Library archives to wrap up the primary research. I was feeling pretty single-minded when I met the person who would unequivocally re-affirm my commitment to the nebulous notion of "Writing Across Communities."

I sat on the aisle seat on my return flight to Albuquerque, the middle seat between the woman at the window and me was empty. We both sat quietly for the duration of the flight, both of us writing in notebooks with pencils. I was reflecting on my findings at the LBJ Library. We both ordered ginger ales to drink. I passed her the glass from the flight attendant and noticed the fingers of my fellow passenger that made grasping the flimsy plastic cup awkward and difficult. Precarious.

The descent into Albuquerque was bumpy as it always is during the summer monsoon season. The turbulence flying over the Sandia Mountains was especially troubling this day. I closed up my things as the woman's notebook slipped off her table onto the floor between us. I reached down and handed it back to her. She thanked me graciously. It was then that I noticed that her speech was slightly halting which she corrected by repeating her sentences deliberately, slowly for my benefit. As the plane pitched over the mountains, we slipped into a casual conversation. "I like to write," she confided. "I write all the time." And it was at that point that I became very interested and wanted to hear her story. "I wrote a book," she told me. "My name is Marilyn Martinez." I thought I heard her say, "The title of my book is 'Battling Debasement.'"

I have to admit that I had difficulty hearing and understanding the words over the engine noise, and I struggled to string together the details. I did realize, however, that Marilyn was talking about battling the stigma of developmental disabilities. I also realized that Marilyn was managing multiple developmental challenges indexed by her speech as well as large and small motor skills. I wasn't sure which disabilities that Marilyn was living with but within some deep intuitive place of my consciousness, I knew they were serious. With the engine noise and the soft modulation of her voice, I couldn't catch everything. I remember this though. Marilyn invited me to attend her book signing during the following week. "We're going to have cantaloupe, and strawberries, and watermelon," she explained. "I love watermelon, do you like watermelon? The director of the Disabilities Center says we can have watermelon because this will be my special day." I had to make a snap decision at this moment. Accept or politely decline this invitation. I took my UNM business card from my purse and handed it to Marilyn. "Please email me and send me the details for your book signing."

On Monday morning, an email message from Marilyn was waiting for me with the details of her book release celebration. In between meetings and classes of that first week of the semester, I attended the book signing for Marilyn Martinez's, Battling the Basement, a chronicle of her journey with Cerebral Palsy. And I ate watermelon and strawberries with Marilyn and her friends at the UNM Center for Development and Disability. There was joy. And after nearly fifteen years in the field of Rhetoric & Composition, I learned a lot about writing and agency that day. I will let Marilyn speak for herself. In the preface of her book, she explains:

> Basement Mentality is when people don't want you to grow in the world. You want to get out of the Basement by going one step higher, but some people want to keep you there in the comfort zone. They don't want you out of that box. You are only allowed to be on the one level where they can protect you—and no higher. But the Basement isn't for me. I have always wanted to get out and go higher, to live my own independent life.

In a word, this is what education is all about: self-authorization. This is the key idea behind the Writing Across Communities initiative at the University of New Mexico: invigorating the public sphere, cultivating civic literacy on behalf of our most vulnerable communities—creating discursive spaces for historically excluded student populations.

And so it is language, community literacy, civil rights, citizenship, and belonging that will frame this article. Literacy can be a generative act of resistance to the indignities and despair of marginalization. In this post-9/11 America, Marilyn Martinez reminds us that there are many different groups assigned to many different kinds of civic "basements." There are entire communities literally and metaphorically kept underground, under-served, and under-represented. So the thorny questions around which I hang all these ideas are: what role does the rhetoric of disputation play in resolving the persistent question of who belongs in America (Beasley)? How might we engage the dissonances of (intellectual, geographical, linguistic) border-crossing in the hermeneutics of citizenship?

To illustrate, I wish to describe several key events shaping the evolution of the post-World War II Mexican American civil rights movement in New Mexico. Taking a case study approach, I begin this article by examining the civic discourses of one prominent New Mexico leader in the post-war movement: Vicente Ximenes. As a leader, Ximenes confronted critical civil rights issues about culture and belonging over fifty years ago beginning in Albuquerque, New Mexico. It is a historical moment worth revisiting.

First, I begin by setting the stage for this examination about writing, citizenship, and civic literacy by analyzing two critical rhetorical moments in the life of this post- World War II civil rights activist. Secondly, I connect the Ximenes legacy to a growing movement at the University of New Mexico and the ways that we are making critical responses to current issues facing our local communities in New Mexico. By triangulating social acts of literacy, currently and historically, I offer some organizing principles for Composition teachers and advocates of community literacy serving vulnerable communities in their spheres of practice. The liminal spaces and geo-political borders in and beyond the Composition classroom are the literacy sites that most concern me here in New Mexico where I teach.

## IMMIGRATION AND THE NATIONAL IMAGINARY

Border anxieties continue to ignite across the country. Perturbations in the national imaginary were dramatically illustrated in May 2010 when several California high school students wore American flag t-shirts to cinco de mayo celebrations. In a strange post-9/11 American patriotic reversal, the students were expelled from school for promoting incendiary rhetorical statements. Wearing the American flag was grounds for expulsion as their Latino classmates donned the colors of the Mexican flag. The rogue demonstrators violated not only good taste but the boundaries of political tolerance at Live Oak High School. Against the backdrop of the recent immigration law SB 1070 enacted by the state of Arizona, this act of public rhetoric takes on multiple layers of significance.

What is particularly rich about the Live Oak, California incident is that the young men wearing the offending American symbol were both Mexican American and Anglo American students. This is not too surprising, however. Ambivalence toward immigrants has been a litmus test of belonging among many social groups for centuries. But I have to agree with syndicated columnist Leonard Pitts that the decision by the Live Oak High School administration to take a disciplinary response rather than use the moment for collective deliberation was a grave mistake. Certainly, there is a teachable moment here—not only for the students of Live Oak High School but for us as nation as the immigration debate once again unravels us at our seams (Pitts). To help us understand the nuances of these current political statements, we need to revisit the 1950s Cold War Mexican American civil rights movement.

There are a few still with us reading the national sign posts, those who took the long view and offered a hand to draft the larger map of US civil rights reform. There are a few whose voices provide contour and dimension to the flat, linear surface of history-making. Vicente Ximenes is one of those rare historical figures. Ximenes' style of leadership resonated with the post-war Mexican American generation and eventually bridged the World War II generation reformers of the 1950s with the Chicano activists of the 1960s. Ximenes's political impulse and rhetorical imagination rested upon four dimensions of democratic practice. Dissent, deliberation, dissonance, and disputation—these framed the guideposts of Ximenes's earliest activist work as a community organizer.

Vicente Ximenes and I met for the first time in November 2002 in Corpus Christi, Texas at the premiere release of the PBS film "Justice for My People," documenting the life and work of Vicente's friend and partner, Dr. Héctor P. García. Vicente told me his own story:

From the time I was a grade school student in the 1920s until today the subjects of discrimination, race, color, national origin, and human rights have been a part of my life. From the first grade in a Mexican American segregated school in Texas until I received a Master's degree at the University of New Mexico, I had a preponderant majority of teachers that did not value my culture, language, custom, national origin, music, or food. Even my mother's tasty bean burritos and tortillas were ridiculed in school. I never had a Mexican American or Hispanic teacher during my formal education.

After the past eight years examining archival materials, conducting oral histories, and listening to the stories of Vicente Ximenes, I discovered that this generation of civil rights activists acquired citizen wisdom and civic literacy through the everyday experiences of growing up on the borders of American citizenship, in the liminal spaces of literacy practice.

Civic action for Vicente Ximenes and the World War II generation of reformers reflect many of the qualities identified by Hannah Arendt in her work, The Promise of Politics. Political action, as such, represents: "venturing forth in speech and deed in the company of one's peers—beginning something new whose end cannot be known in advance; founding a public realm; promising and forgiving one another. None of these actions can be realized alone, but always and only by people in their plurality." What Hannah Arendt describes in the work of restorative justice in the aftermath of World War II, reflect the same principles advanced by Desmond Tutu in the wake of South Africa apartheid. The gift-giving economy of democracy is, first and foremost, a discursive process. Civic literacy is our capacity to read and respond to the world through language, symbol, and art. It is our ability to construct our experience together and to reinvent the public sphere. Civic literacy is our collective need to fabricate the narratives of history, and to construct imaginative fictions for the future, and to reconcile ourselves with one another.

Twentieth-century Mexican American civil rights history suggests that in order for social movements to affect enduring institutional change, they must get into the sinew of governing organizations. They must shape and exercise the muscle and connective tissue of policy and practice from the inside out. It is not enough to stir a movement for social change. Activists must mentor advocates to implement and administer institutional transformation. The influence of a social activist is enhanced, and is best measured, by the effective and strategic placement of representatives within the dominant social structure.

Ximenes and the post-war Mexican American activists advanced a social movement that did not passively wait for justice and an invitation into the national conversation. Rather, they operated on the assumption that change was possible and stirred their own exigences for rhetorical access. They cultivated the rhetorical resources and literacy practices necessary to engage the inevitable dissonance of resistance and promote the requisite disputation toward social reform. This approach informed Ximenes's leadership style for over seven decades, including his tenure as Commissioner for President Lyndon B. Johnson's Equal Employment Opportunity Commission, Chairman of the Inter Agency of Mexican American Affairs, and coordinator of the landmark 1967 Presidential Cabinet Committee Hearings on Mexican American Affairs in El Paso, Texas.

It is important to note the anti-communist hysteria of the McCarthy age shaped the political situation of this twenty-year period of the postwar civil rights era from 1948-1968. The xenophobia and redbaiting discourses of the McCarthy age shaped the rhetorical situation of the twenty-year period of the postwar civil rights era from 1948-1968. As Ellen Schrecker notes in The Age of McCarthyism, Cold War liberals of all ilk found themselves precariously aligned in the struggle against communism at home and overseas. Bobby Kennedy joined the ranks of anti-communist McCarthy democrats through the 1950s. He was in good company. Many Cold War liberals, like Minnesota Senator and future Vice President Hubert H. Humphrey, wanted to expand the welfare state and eliminate racial segregation to protect the world from the expansion of communism.

Albert O. Hirschman in The Rhetoric of Reaction: Perversity, Futility, Jeopardy calls this tactic the "imminent-danger thesis" (153). Deployed throughout the Cold War era, social progressives argued for transferring resources from wealthier groups to poorer populations as a safeguard against the advances of communism. These advocates asserted that civil rights reform and welfare state programs were "imperatively needed to stave off some threatening disaster." The rhetorical resources available to Ximenes and his cadre of American GI Forum organizers were replete with the inconsistencies and fluencies of the

Cold War rhetorical situation within which he exercised agency as a grassroots leader.

The peculiar problem facing Ximenes as new community orga-nizer in Albuquerque sixty years ago in 1951 was how to structure his arguments for Mexican American civil rights reform out of the hostile strands of rhetoric circulating within the Cold War cultural context. Ximenes responded to the local political climate by helping to orga-nize Mexican American veterans in New Mexico around civil rights issues under the umbrella of the American GI Forum. This veterans' rights organization had been originally established in Corpus Christi, Texas by Dr. Hector P. Garcia just three years earlier (Kells, Héctor P. García). Ximenes adapted the vision and mission of the American GI Forum for the New Mexico situation. While the name "American GI Forum" hardly sounds radical to us today, it was sufficiently sub-versive enough to warrant persistent observation by the FBI. Vicente remembers:

> The organizational meeting of the Albuquerque GI Forum was held in the basement of the Sacred Heart Church. Eight persons came together and I was elected chairman of the GI Forum in 1951. Two months after the first meeting I received a frantic call from Monsignor Garcia. The FBI had been by to ask him questions that the Monsignor could not answer about the GI Forum. If word got out in public that the FBI had questioned the Monsignor, the GI Forum would be doomed. I was scared because I had brought together friends to join the GI Forum and I knew the McCarthy Communist scare tactics had ruined the lives of many people. My professor of government had been literally run out of job by the adherents of Senator McCarthy and for a few hours after the Monsi-gnor's call I was frozen with fear of what might happen. Then I picked up the GI Forum constitution and by-laws and head-ed for the FBI office. I presented myself to FBI officials and told them I could answer any questions they had about the GI Forum. Our membership was open to anyone who would swear allegiance to the U.S. flag. The FBI person listened to all I had to say without any response to my statements. I then satisfied the Monsignor as to the legitimacy of the GI Forum.

This is the backdrop that ultimately informed the choices Ximenes exercised on behalf of his constituencies.

Ximenes conceptualized his leadership style from a practical perspective rather than an abstract, theoretical model. He employed a pragmatic approach to civil rights reform, using grassroots community organizing strategies. Ximenes looked to the social realities of New Mexico and the Southwest to construct his understanding of civil rights reform and human rights activism. He believed that giving voice to the personal realities of citizens was the first step to promoting social change. The impetus for literacy practice for Ximenes and his contemporaries rested in the collective as well as the personal.

## CIVIC LITERACY AND MEXICAN AMERICAN CIVIL RIGHTS RHETORIC

On December 20, 1951 Vicente Ximenes circulated one of his first acts of public rhetoric in the form of a letter to the editor of the Albuquerque Journal. The message embedded within this 300 word statement thoughtfully identifies the major issues and Cold War themes motivating the formation of the American GI Forum in Albuquerque that same year. Ximenes opens his letter with this declaration: "This is a letter about death." He then constructs a contrast between "death in New Mexico" and "death in Korea." The illustrative narrative that follows describes a recent event in Lovington, New Mexico. Ximenes delineates:

> On November 16, the Hobbs Daily News-Sun reported the death of two Mexican children from starvation. I assume that they meant that the children were American citizens of Mexican extraction, since it was reported that their legal residence was Yoakum, Texas. It seems no welfare funds were available for these American citizens because the law prevented disposition of funds to non-state residents. Furthermore, it seems that a nurse could not help the children because the nurse could not speak Spanish. Since when does a nurse have to speak Spanish in order to detect malnutrition. I always thought malnutrition was a health condition, not a language.

Ximenes charges the state welfare system and then Senator Clint Anderson for his neglect of local conditions and for the consequent deaths of these two children. Ximenes contrasts the deaths of the two children in New Mexico with the deaths of one hundred and eight US Hispanic soldiers in Korea who gave their lives as American citizens.

This alignment seeks to establish a moral distinction between the noble and honorable Mexican American soldiers killed fighting in battle overseas and the disgraceful and dishonorable deaths of two innocent Mexican American children starved to death in the US homeland. Ximenes deals with the particular classes, not general categories. Ximenes closes his letter of protest with a critique of New Mexico lawmakers and candidates campaigning for election and promoting various economic programs in the state. Ximenes argues:

> Not one single law-maker or would-be law-maker uttered a word about solving New Mexico's situation with reference to the two children that starved in Lovington, New Mexico. Perhaps silence means consent.

Significantly, Ximenes signs his letter as "chairman" of the newly founded American GI Forum in New Mexico. Representing this new civic advocacy organization, Ximenes declares a new public presence in the region. The claims delineated in his letter are far-reaching. Ximenes tackles Cold War liberal issues alongside Mexican American civil rights questions related to national citizenship, regional identity, economic disparities, heritage language, and political representation. He would take up these very same themes for public action six years later in 1957.

## PHRONESIS, RESISTANCE, AND AMERICAN DEMOCRATIC PRACTICE

Ximenes conceptualized his leadership style from the perspective of particular cases rather than theoretical models. He employed a pragmatic epistemic approach to the construction of knowledge, using inductive and deliberative processes. Phronesis, according to Aristotle's Nichomachean Ethics, inextricably connects the dimensions of ethos, deliberation, and praxis—or purposeful choice. Or as Mary Whitlock Blundell argues, "Phronesis guides the process of deliberation and hence plays an essential role in purposeful choice, which in turn is the moving cause of praxis (action)." Consistent with these characteristics of phronesis, Ximenes looked to the social realities of New Mexico and the Southwest to construct his understanding of civil rights reform and human rights activism.

Dramatically illustrating the contradictions of inclusion for Mexican American citizens, this second civil rights incident involved one of the institutions of Constitutional era US culture: the Daughters of the American Revolution. In February 1957, Art Tafoya, chairman of the Denver American GI Forum, along with Jose Ontiveros and Molly Galvan of the Pueblo chapter, reported a racist incident in Colorado to Ximenes. Their reports indicated that the local chapter of the Daughters of the American Revolution had refused to allow a Mexican-origin boy to carry the American flag at a President Lincoln Day ceremony for the Colorado Industrial School for Boys in Golden, Colorado scheduled for February 12, 1957. The correctional institution was populated largely by Mexican-origin boys, many of whom were born in the United States to parents who were immigrant Mexican nationals. Questions of race, national identity, and cultural belonging were at the center of the controversy.

As national chairman of the American GI Forum, Vicente took the lead on the issue and expressed outrage to the local and national press. He immediately fired off a telegram to DAR National President Frederíc Graves and all chapters of the American GI Forum. Within twenty-four hours, thousands of responses poured out in protest. Senator Dennis Chávez of New Mexico sent a telegram in rebuke, reminding public officials in Colorado that Mexican Americans had carried the US flag at Bataan in World War II. Governor McNichols of Colorado, in response, suspended all pending DAR activities in the state.

The symbolic value of this incident was clear to Ximenes. The American flag was a powerful symbol for his civic group; the colors were woven into the official emblem for the American GI Forum. The denial by the DAR of a Mexican-origin child to carry the US flag was a civil rights violation in Ximenes's mind, potentially as incendiary as the catalyzing event that propelled Dr. Héctor García and the American GI Forum into the national limelight in 1949. The refusal of a funeral director in Three Rivers, Texas to bury Mexican American soldier, Private Félix Longoria, had successfully cemented the reputation of the American GI Forum as a civil rights organization nearly a decade before. Ximenes did not waste any time to act on the infraction. He stirred public debate and demanded immediate redress.

The Denver Star and Amarillo Globe-Times noted that the Lincoln Day flag-carrying pageant had been immediately cancelled following Ximenes's complaint. Charlotte C. Bush, chair of the Denver Chapter of the DAR Patriotic Education Committee, publically defended her position: "I wouldn't want a Mexican to carry 'Old Glory,' would you?" This offensive rhetorical question was advanced by Charlotte Bush in her capacity as a DAR official. Her statement not only revealed the character and attitudes of the speaker but the expressed goals of the organization. The premises of Charlotte Bush's assertion include: first, Mexican-origin people are not American citizens; second, only American citizens are entitled to carry the flag. The assertion was sufficiently damaging to DAR that it called for immediate action from the national headquarters.

DAR National President Frederic Graves responded immediately by pulling the charter from the local Denver DAR chapter. She contacted Ximenes and offered to travel to Albuquerque to exchange flags with the American GI Forum as an act of reconciliation. Ximenes had to decide how much more negative press he wanted to promote, heaping political coals on the head of the DAR. However, Ximenes chose to take a restorative justice approach to the conflict, engaging in negotiations with DAR President Frederic Graves. The flag exchange ceremony was promptly staged in front of the American GI Forum building in Albuquerque. The US flag was carried by Roberto Duran, son of New Mexico American GI Forum organizer, Zeke Duran. President Graves delivered a statement regretting the incident and delineating the action she took to punish the Colorado DAR chapter and person who had refused to allow a Mexican American boy to carry the American flag. Ximenes formally accepted the apology and the National DAR's presentation of the American flag.

Symbolically, the American GI Forum raised the gift of the American flag in front of the newly constructed building that would become the permanent national headquarters of the American GI Forum here in Albuquerque. Equally important, the event signaled the authority of Ximenes as an emerging national leader, demonstrated his prudent exercise of citizen wisdom, and publically resisted the second class status of Mexican Americans in Cold War America. In effect, Ximenes asserted a new trajectory for Mexican American civil rights activism.

Ximenes exploited the flag-raising occasion toward a productive and peaceful outcome. He promoted an act of resolution through which both parties could recover honor and esteem. The flag exchange ceremony in Albuquerque, New Mexico provided a public occasion within which the American GI Forum, representative of Mexican American citizens, and the DAR, representative of Constitutional era America, could regain honor. Reverence and ceremony transformed drama and discord. Most importantly, the public event restored the dignity of the community.

## COMMUNITY LITERACY AND CULTIVATING CITIZEN WISDOM

Why are these stories important today? The current historical moment of healing national division and international polarization calls for models of democratic practice that promote dissent, engage difference, cultivate debate, and negotiate the noise of dissonance. As Hannah Arendt reminds, the promise of human freedom is realized through community—by plural human beings, "when and only when we act politically."

In brief, this is what democratized education is all about: cultivating conditions for self-governance and citizen wisdom (Woodruff). And this is the key idea behind the Writing Across Communities initiative at the University of New Mexico. My students and I have envisioned Writing Across Communities as a platform for invigorating the public sphere and cultivating civic literacy among our most vulnerable communities—creating spaces for historically excluded peoples.

Who constitutes our historically-excluded student populations? At the University of New Mexico, our vulnerable communities include a broad range of student groups: First generation college students, economically-vulnerable citizens, linguistically-diverse students, international students, Native American, Mexican American, African American student groups, non-traditional (re-entry) student populations, the unemployed, economically-disadvantaged students, physically and mentally disabled students, returning veterans and their families, political refugees, former prisoners (most of whom are disproportionately male students of color), LGBT students and survivors of hate crimes, sexual abuse, and domestic violence. In other words, I mean nearly the entire student population of the University of New Mexico constitute the intended beneficiaries of the Writing Across Communities initiative.

The impetus for Writing Across Communities at UNM began with some nagging questions about language and diversity. The most significant outcome of these past seven years is that Writing Across Communities continues to complicate the culture of writing at UNM with questions centering on issues of language, literacy, identity, and social justice. In a nutshell: the vision of the UNM Writing Across Communities initiative is to help students cultivate authority and alacrity across multiple contexts in order to develop the knowledge, understanding, and ethical habits of mind for citizenship in intellectually and culturally diverse academic, professional, and civic communities.

Let me code shift here for a moment. The Spanish term bien estar or wellbeing sums it nicely, I think. There are two different verbs of "being" in the Spanish linguistic system: ser (a stable, intrinsic state of being) and estar (a process of being). Writing Across Communities calls attention to the processes of being, of becoming literate members and citizens of our multiple diverse communities.

What I offer is a set of principles. I need to be honest about the organic and evolutionary nature of Writing Across Communities. There is no "blueprint" for Writing Across Communities. I have invited a number of my colleagues locally and nationally to help create this story. Mi compadre Juan Guerra from the University of Washington likens the UNM Writing Across Communities to "rhizomes:" he says that we are growing a forest of social activists from a single root. In reality, we are a work-in-progress. This provisional nature of Writing Across Communities is not only appropriate; it is intentional (Kells, "Writing Across Communities"). Literacy is a fluid, organic process. In other words, literacy is a human process. The notion that mastering any single literacy practice or writing genre is sufficient to becoming an educated and engaged citizen in the 21st century is a flawed notion.

The intellectual engine and the political operating space of Writing Across Communities begin and end with our students—not faculty, not administrators, not curriculum, per se). Our graduate and undergraduate students are the mobilizing force keeping the conversation going. When folks ask me where I find inspiration for this embattled initiative I respond that without a doubt, the story of the post-war Mexican American civil right movement and Vicente Ximenes provides me with the necessary "invisible means of support."

I would like to report that at the end of these past seven years of persistent mobilization that the UNM administration recognizes, supports, and promotes Writing Across Communities university-wide. This is not the case. Infrastructure support remains limited and largely symbolic with annual small grants. We have no budget, nor director, no staff, no office, no formal infrastructure support whatsoever. We do have a WAC logo though, a website, and letterhead. Nonetheless, Writing Across Communities programs and events have served thousands of undergraduate students, included numerous community groups, supported graduate students from across the disciplines, and engaged hundreds of faculty members across the curriculum.

On the one hand, we have been called "an annoying insurgent movement" by administrators. Some would like the messy work of Writing Across Communities to just go away. A few would like a more traditional WAC program in its place "without all the political stuff." On the other hand, we have generated close to ninety-thousand dollars in cross-departmental grant support over the past seven years of mobilization, keeping our programs and events open and free to the public. We have our allies and beneficiaries.

My role as program chair, has been largely as a behind-the-scenes organizer. In practice, I am more of a network operator than an administrator. This protean role has required finding new ways to mobilize diverse constituencies toward a collective re-evaluation of how we teach writing across the university. In this ever changing game of role-shifting, I have also served as chair for the UNM Civil Rights Symposia series for over five years. We have foregrounded African American, Mexican American, and Native American civil rights issues as well as sexual justice issues. Our 2011 Civil Rights Symposium was focused on Mental Health and Social Justice. My graduate students and I have coordinated these university-wide events to mark landmark events in US civil rights reform as well as to call attention to current social justice issues. The response for 2007, 2008, 2009, and 2011 events exceeded our imagination. Hundreds have filled our sessions. We have practiced the deliberative ethics of peaceful social engagement. I have seen meeting rooms gushing over with students from high school to graduate school. Building on this history, our Spring 2012 Writing the World Symposium featured invited speakers, Paul Matsuda (Arizona State University) on second language writing issues and Michelle Eodice (University of Oklahoma) on writing center pedagogies. One young undergraduate student commented to me at the close of our

2012 Writing the World Symposium, "This is even better than a TED Talk."

## Writing Across Communities: Changing the Culture of Writing

I have faith in deliberative processes and the possibilities of community engagement that promote healing, justice, and social connection. Our experience through Writing Across Communities suggests that it is possible to influence cultures of writing within and beyond the university, if we more fully represent and respond to the range of literacy practices associated with the civic, cultural, professional, and academic experiences of our students. Equally important, I have faith in the legacy of civil rights activists like Vicente Ximenes who resist the notion that civil rights reform is a once-done-always-done exercise. I am inspired by leaders like Marilyn Martinez who continue to call attention to the injustices and inconsistencies in our national terms of belonging. And I am especially concerned about the implicit racism embedded in literacy education programs nation-wide. As Leonard Pitts argues in his editorial essay following the Live Oak High School t-shirt ban, "The challenge for schools is to balance kids' impetuousness against their right of free speech" (A8). Pitts's recommendations for alternative responses to the Live Oak High School controversy that promote deliberative action and democratic practice reflects the kind of discursive public sphere that educational institutions (K-16) need to be cultivating. Pitt suggests:

> Imagine if [the principal of Live Oak High School] had corralled the most articulate of the T-shirt boys and the cinco de mayo celebrators and required them to research and represent their points of view in a formal debate before the entire school. The T-shirt kid could have challenged his classmates to explain why he felt the need, if he is an American, to celebrate a foreign holiday. The classmate could have pressed the T-shirt kid on why he felt threatened by a simple acknowledgment of heritage and cultural origin" (Pitts A8).

Regretfully, punitive action and silencing the ruptures in the democratic public imaginary continue to obscure and truncate these kinds deliberative processes necessary for political inclusion and national

transformation. Civic literacy must be as central to public education (K-16) as alphabetic and numerical literacy are to the national
core curriculum (Guerra, "Nomadic Consciousness;" "Transcultural
Citizenship"). Multiculturalism or "diversity" courses as isolated add-
on requirements rather than embedded across-the-curriculum obfus-
cate the intrinsic value of pluralism woven into the national fabric of
democracy.

Our nation has subscribed to racial and linguistic purity myths
since the Constitutional era when the first naturalization laws were
drafted (Kells, "Questions of Race;" López). The legalistic discourse
of racial difference continues to inform our social institutions, our attitudes, our uneven distribution of resources and justice. In a country
where people of color are disproportionately represented on the front
lines of our military operations and in the jail cells of our prisons, we
need to admit that our nation is seriously out of whack. When one of
the greatest human rights tragedies in our history is being played out
on our southernmost borders we need to acknowledge that racism is
alive and well. When we fail to consider the impact of our economic, political, and immigration policies on the vulnerable communities
whose transnational ties and connective tissue endure beyond the geo-
political divisions that separate them from their families—whose economic conditions leave them subsisting at our nation's edges, I need to
say, in spite of the landmark moment when this nation elected a black
man to the White House, we are not living in a post-racial world.

There is a subtext to my title here: "What's writing got to do with
it?: Citizen Wisdom, Civil Rights Activism and Community Literacy."
I have to admit, I keep hearing Tina Turner belting out the words:
"What's love got to do with it?" Honestly. I think love and writing
have a lot to do with it. Certainly, that is a thematic thread weaving
throughout Battling the Basement: The Trials and Triumphs of Marilyn A. Martinez. Similarly, Juan Guerra in his book, Close to Home:
Oral and Literate Practices in a Transnational Mexicano Community,
examines the connective tissue of literacy (and writing) and its importance in sustaining and supporting families and their communities
on both sides of the US border. What is so profound about Guerra's
work is that his ethnographic study illustrates that writing is not only a
personal skill, it is a social good, a community resource. Both Marilyn
Martinez and Juan Guerra illustrate a common insight: giving voice to

the personal realities of marginalized citizens represents the first step to promoting social change.

## WRITING PROGRAMS AND PEDAGOGIES OF LEADERSHIP

So how can we respond? I believe that we each need to exercise the power of public rhetoric—moving between our spheres of concern and exercising authority (citizen wisdom, if you will) within our spheres of influence. Events like those offered through the Writing Across Communities initiative help us as a community protect the public sphere and promote dissent, deliberation, dissonance, and disputation. We need more opportunities and conduits for the cultural arts of resistance, disputation, difference, and debate. Our educational system (K-16) needs to move beyond passive models of literacy education that fail to critique and engage citizens as active "authors" of democracy. The enduring problem of public education is not rankings and test scores but intellectual and political passivity. Well-intentioned literacy programs stop short of cultivating active citizens when they stop short of promoting the full range of literacy practices—writing as well as reading. Teaching reading without cultivating writing (productive responsiveness) is like inviting guests to a party and not letting them speak. Those of us teaching undergraduate and graduate students in university settings have tremendous access to cultivating new leaders in community literacy.

My Spring 2012 graduate seminar, ENGL 640: Ideologies of Literacy, recently served as a deliberative space to examine the embedded assumptions and beliefs informing writing program administration at the University of New Mexico. The exigence for this course was the growing momentum toward institutionalizing Writing Across Communities at UNM and the establishment of the new ABQ Community Writing Center by our graduate students. Additionally, we needed a reflective space for designing the new proposed ENGL 102 (WAC) Writing Intensive Course and cultivating our cross-institutional partnerships through the ABQ Community Writing Center. The messy work of democratizing literacy education is here to stay at UNM as long as we have engaged graduate students troubling the system. The issues of disparity and inequitable distribution of wealth and resources in New Mexico are historical and are not just going to go away. Literacy and social justice are inextricably connected in our local and national Constitutional-based system of governance.

The problem of the transparency of literacy is illustrated across academic, professional, and civic contexts. The value of literacy is so embedded in our social system we cannot see it even as educators. We simply take it for granted. That transparency is not a problem, so to speak, for educators and strategic planners in elite, exclusive institutions that mystify access and the practices of intellectual authority. In fact, the invisibility of literacy actually serves to maintain limited access and retain authority and exclusivity to an elite group of intellectuals. However, the invisibility of literacy is a real problem for diverse, open access institutions like the University of New Mexico and other two-year and four-year colleges across the nation where we are seeking to distribute knowledge and authority to historically-excluded social groups. Transparency of literacy is a problem for our students who do not have the culturally-prescribed literacies of elite, privileged social groups (see Appendix).

The new ABQ Community Writing Center is the heart and soul of the Writing Across Communities initiative. The pilot project is now located in the Albuquerque Public Main Library downtown as a drop-in center to assist local citizens with whatever writing task they want: a work-in-progress poem, a job application, a letter to the editor, a campaign flyer. Writing is and has always been a community endeavor. Admittedly, Plato was very suspicious about the lethal potential of writing. But the architects of the US Constitution were less reticent to wed writing to self-governance, more optimistic about the potential dimensions of literacy and democracy through the written codification of democratic principles. For the American democratic experiment civic literacy and democracy are inextricably intertwined. As the emerging community literacy scholarship suggests, the scope of writing education cannot be limited to the classroom and cannot be approached in a one-size-fits-all model. In Writing and Community Engagement: A Critical Sourcebook, Thomas Deans, Barbara Roswell, and Adrian J. Wurr observe, "One key insight proffered by nearly every community-engaged scholar is that each university/community partnership is shaped by local opportunities and limitations, local people and priorities" (5). We need to attend to difference.

Thanks to a dedicated team of graduate student social activists what once was a vague vision is now a reality for the citizens of Albuquerque. Expanding on the community writing center model instituted by Tiffany Rousculp with the Salt Lake Community Writing Center in 2001, the ABQ Community Writing Center is extending the vision and principles of Writing Across Communities to the larger New Mexico community (Rousculp). While we commemorate the losses and travesty of 9/11 as a nation, we also need to recognize the generative responses and healing endeavors like the work of Rousculp in Salt Lake City launched a decade ago. We at the University of New Mexico are building this vision on the belief that writing can be a healing balm as well as a catalyst for change. Writing can help us cultivate mindfulness as well as collective deliberation at local, national, and global levels. In closing, writing has everything to do with it. Democracy is a living text that we must re-vision and re-invigorate with each generation of citizens.

The goal at this point in the journey is not constructing a monolithic discourse or grand narrative, but sustaining and extending the conversations seeded by the Writing Across Communities initiative over the past seven years beyond the boundaries of the University of New Mexico. This is the purpose of the newly established National Consortium of Writing Across Communities (NCWAC) which my colleagues and I launched in April 2011 in Atlanta during the 2011 Conference of College Composition and Communication (Kells "National Consortium"). Recognizing the tenth anniversary year of 9/11, our hope was to offer educators across the nation a generative vision for literacy education and civic engagement that transgresses the traditional boundaries of our discipline as well as the limits of institutional constraints. The NCWAC stakeholders affirm educational principles and cultural practices that promote the maintenance and wellbeing of human communities through literacy and writing. Moreover, NCWAC seeks to guide curriculum development, stimulate resource-sharing, cultivate networking, and promote research in language practices and literacy education throughout the nation, and to support local colleges and universities working to serve vulnerable communities within their spheres of influence.

The 2012 NCWAC Summer Summit in Santa Fe included three days of discussions about how we as scholars, teachers, writers, and leaders across institutional and regional sites can more effectively align the multi-faceted dimensions of our field in Rhetoric and Composition(and our multiple subfields such as Writing Program

Administration, WAC, Writing Centers, ESL, Basic Writing, Second Language Writing, and Community Literacy to better support future leaders (graduate students and new faculty) seeking to serve the vulnerable communities via sponsored literacy projects within their spheres of influence. Rather than a single book or a static product, the members of NCWAC plan to establish a dynamic online resource site to serve educators nationwide (especially junior faculty and graduate students) who are sponsoring literacy projects and working in and beyond the college classroom. The list of thirty affiliated institutions reads like a litany of hope. The hermeneutic space of the 2012 NCWAC Santa Fe Summit, marking the one-hundredth anniversary of New Mexico statehoood—the only state in the nation whose Constitution is written in both English and Spanish—offers each participant an imaginative site for considering new approaches to writing program that reaches beyond the borders of their institutions.

Writing can be both a pharmakon: both healing balm and an occasion for exercising agency (stirring aggravation) in a world of contingency and uncertainty. Through rhetorical listening and the act of exegesis of the text, the common thread that weaves the stories of members of vulnerable communities, the current narratives of survivors like Marilyn Martinez and historical narratives of leaders like Vicente Ximenes, is the generative possibilities of exercising authority through diverse literacy practices. Community literacy as an advocacy movement offers an imaginative space that resists the debasement of exclusion and marginalization. In a socio-economic climate of scarcity, in a political environment conditioned by fear and shame, the capacity to read and respond to the world through the act of writing represents not only an occasion of agency but an affirmation of our humanity. Physically and mentally disabled peoples, linguistically-diverse students, transnational refugees, homeless veterans, the unemployed— the many groups we serve in our classrooms and beyond—all share a common condition of isolation and the inability to exercise agency over place. The invitation to write represents an opportunity to realize the rhetorical possibilities of turning transgressive power into transformative potential. Whatever challenge writers find themselves battling, the dignity and efficacy of self-representation through semiotics of the text are gifts we must keep in circulation.

## Notes

1. I wish to extend my debt of appreciation to the insightful reflections on the agency of literacy offered in: Marilyn A. Martinez. Battling the Basement: The Trials and Triumphs of Marilyn A. Martinez. Santa Fe: MG Publishing, 2010: n.p.

2. The role of nomos and the concept of discursive democracy as a gift-giving economy are developed further in my presentation for the 2012 Watson Conference, "The Rhetorical Imagination of Writing Across Communities: Nomos and Literacy Education as a Gift-Giving Economy."

3. Segments of this article have been presented at the Writing Democracy Conference (March 2011), the Albuquerque Cultural Conference (September 2011), and the Watson Conference (October 2012).

4. Ellen Schrecker, The Age of McCarthyism: A Brief History with Documents. 2nd ed (New York: Bedford/St. Martins, 2002), 99.

5. Vicente Ximenes interview by author, October 9, 2006.

6. Vicente Ximenes letter to editor, December 20, 1951, Box 141, Folder 2, Héctor P. García (HPG) Papers. Mary and Jeff Bell Library. Texas A&M University-Corpus Christi.

7. Vicente Ximenes letter to editor, December 20, 1951, Box 141, Folder 2. HPG Papers.

8. For further discussion on phronesis, see: Mary Whitlock Blundell "Ethos and Dianoia Reconsidered" in Amélie Oksenberg Rorty, ed. Essays on Aristotle's Poetics (Princeton: Princeton University Press, 1992), 156.

9. Vicente Ximenes interview by author, March 4, 2008.

10. "Racial Issue Halts Lincoln Day Affair" Amarillo Globe Times n.d.; n.p. Box 146, Folder 20. HPG Papers.

11. Vicente Ximenes interview by author, March 9, 2008.

12. I remain indebted to the support and leadership of our Graduate Assistant Writing Across Communities Alliance leaders who have worked so diligently and generously over the past seven years organizing Writing Across Communities events and programs: Beverly Army Gillen, Leah Sneider, Bernadine Hernandez, Dan Cryer, Greg Evans Haley, Erin Penner Gallegos, Brian Hendrickson, and Genevieve García de Mueller.

13. I wish to acknowledge the graduate student Writing Fellows in my ENGL 640 Ideologies of Literacy Seminar who helped to envision the ENGL 102 Writing Intensive Learning Communities Pilot Project during the Spring 2012: Dan Cryer, Christine Beagle García, Genevieve García de Mueller, Brian Hendrickson, Mellisa Huffman, and Lindsey Ives.

14. A special word of acknowledgment is due to the co-founders and leaders of the ABQ Community Writing Center: Brian Hendrickson, Erin Penner Gallegos, Genevieve García de Mueller, Anna Knutson, and Deb Paczynski.

## Works Cited

Aristotle. Nicomachean Ethics. 2nd ed. Trans. Terence Irwin. Indianapolis: Hackett, 1999.

Albrecht, Glenn. Solastalgia: A New Concept in Human Health and Identity. Philosophy Activism Nature (2005) 3:41-44.

Allsup, Carl. The American GI Forum: Origins and Evolution. Austin: Center for Mexican American Studies, 1982, 99.

Arendt, Hannah. The Promise of Politics. New York: Schocken Books, 2005: xx.

Beasley, Vanessa. Who Belongs in America: Presidents, Rhetoric, and Immigration. College Station: Texas A&M University P, 2006.

Blundell, Mary Whitlock. "Ethos and Dianoia Reconsidered" in Amélie Oksenberg Rorty, ed. Essays on Aristotle's Poetics. Princeton: Princeton UP 1992: 156.

Carson, Rachel. Silent Spring. Cambridge: Riverside P, 1962.

Guerra, Juan C. "Writing for Transcultural Citizenship: A Cultural Ecology Model." Language Arts. 85.4 (March 2008): 296-304.

_____. "Putting Literacy in Its Place: Nomadic Consciousness and the Practice of Transcultural Repositioning." Rebellious Reading: The Dynamics of Chicano/a Literacy. Ed. Carl Gutierrez-Jones. Center for Chicana/o Studies: University of California Santa Barbara, 2004: 19-37.

_____. Close to Home: Oral and Literate Practices in a Transnational Community. New York: Teachers College Press, 1998.

Hirschman, Albert O. The Rhetoric of Reaction: Perversity, Futility, Jeopardy. Cambridge: Harvard UP, 1991.

Jarrett, Susan C. Rereading the Sophists: Classical Rhetoric Refigured. Carbondale: Southern Illinois UP, 1991.

Kells, Michelle Hall. Héctor P. García: Everyday Rhetoric and Mexican American Civil Rights. Carbondale: Southern Illinois UP, 2006.

_____. "Leveling the Linguistic Playing Field in the Composition Classroom." Attending to the Margins: Writing, Researching, and Teaching on the Front Lines. Eds. Michelle Hall Kells and Valerie Balester. Portsmouth: Heinemann-Boynton/Cook, 1999:131-49.

_____. "Linguistic Contact Zones: An Examination of Ethnolinguistic Identity and Language Attitudes" Written Communication 19.1 (January 2002): 5-43.

_____. "The Rhetorical Imagination of Writing Across Communities: Nomos and Literacy Education as a Gift-Giving Economy." JAC (Forthcoming 2014).

Kells, Michelle Hall. "National Consortium of Writing Across Communities." http://www.unm.edu/~wac/NCWAC.html

Kells, Michelle Hall. "Writing Across Communities: Deliberation and the Discursive Possibilities of WAC." Journal of Reflections 6.1 (Spring 2007): 87-108.

Kells, Michelle Hall and Valerie Balester. "Voices from the Wild Horse Desert." Attending to the Margins: Writing, Researching, and Teaching on the Front Lines. Eds. Michelle Hall Kells and Valerie Balester. Portsmouth: Heinemann-Boynton/Cook, 1999: xiii-xxiii.

Kells, Michelle Hall, Valerie Balester, and Victor Villanueva, eds. Latino/a Discourses: Language, Identity, and Literacy Education. Portsmouth: Heinemann-Boynton/Cook, 2004.

_____. "Lessons Learned in Hispanic Serving Institutions." Eds. Cristina Kirklighter, Diana Cárdenas, and Susan Wolff Murphy. Teaching Writing With Latino/a Students. Albany: State University of New York P, 2007: vii-xiv.

Kells, Michelle Hall "Mapping the Cultural Ecologies of Language and Literacy" eds. Bruce Horner, Min-Zhan Lu, and Paul Kei Matsuda. Cross-Language Relations in Composition. Carbondale: Southern Illinois UP, 2010: 2004-11.

Kells, Michelle Hall "Writing Across Communities: The Diversity, Deliberation, and the Discursive Possibilities of WAC." Reflections 11.1 (2007): 87-108.

López, Ian F. Haney. White By Law: The Legal Construction of Race. New York: New York UP, 1996.

Martinez, Marilyn A. Battling the Basement: The Trials and Triumphs of Marilyn A. Martinez. Santa Fe: MG Publishing, 2010: n.p.

Pitts, Leonard. "T Shirt Ban Free Speech Issue." Albuquerque Journal May 20, 2010: A8.

Rose, Shirley and Chuck Paine. "On the Crossroads and at the Heart: A Conversation." WPA: The Journal of the Council of Writing Program Administration 35.2 (2012): 160-78.

Rousculp, Tiffany. "When the Community Writes: Re-envisioning the SLCC DiverseCity Writing Series." Reflections 5.1 (2006): 67-88.

Schrecker, Ellen. The Age of McCarthyism: A Brief History with Documents. 2nd ed (New York: Bedford/St. Martins, 2002), 99.

Woodruff, Paul. First Democracy: The Challenge of an Ancient Idea. New York: Oxford UP, 2005.

APPENDIX

## ENGL 640: IDEOLOGIES OF LITERACY

### DR. MICHELLE HALL KELLS

This seminar will examine the historical, cultural, economic, political, and educational dimensions of "literacy." The conceptualization, mythology, and practice of "literacy" (reading and writing) has become integral to social access in our 21st century cosmopolitan universe (full civic, economic, and cultural participation—locally, nationally, and globally). As teachers (of English Studies and Education), we need to apply a critical lens to the metaphors and models of literacy we adopt and promote.

We will examine the question of literacy as a key social value in the national imaginary. Literacy is not only a practice (and outcome of public K-16 education) but a core value of both American Constitutional culture and the Western tradition of higher learning.

Literacy is: how we reason from the data; how we gain authority and authorship in and across diverse intellectual spheres; how we engage (and organize) our social worlds.

We can define literacy as the processes and products related to generating, interpreting, and circulating symbolic systems of meaning (e.g. alphabetic, mathematical, digital, visual, scientific symbol systems). These are all culturally conditioned processes and products for which we need to become socialized (educated) to interpret (read) and write (produce).

The problem of the transparency of literacy is illustrated across academic, professional, and civic contexts. The value of literacy is so embedded in our social system we can't see it (even as educators). We simply take it for granted. That transparency is not a problem, so to speak, for educators and strategic planners in elite, exclusive institutions (e.g. Harvard, Stanford, etc.) that mystify access and the practices of intellectual authority. In fact, the invisibility of literacy actually serves to maintain limited access and retain authority and exclusivity to an elite group of intellectuals. However, the invisibility of literacy is a real problem for diverse, open access institutions like the University of New Mexico (and other two-year and four-year colleges across the nation) where we are seeking to distribute knowledge and authority to historically-excluded social groups. Transparency of literacy is a problem for our students who do not have the culturally-prescribed literacies of elite, privileged social groups.

The literacy skills (informational, digital, numerical, alphabetic, environmental, scientific, etc) of our professoriate and our student body affect every facet of our enterprise as an institution of higher education:

- Recruitment
- Retention
- Graduation Rates
- National Ranking & Distinction
- Placement (job and graduate school)
- Classroom success

Literacy is not only the principal practice of what we do every day in our work and personal lives; it is a deeply held core value of American citizenship and belonging, so integral to who we are—our national identity—it is the concept around which we fashion our system of self-governance through the drafting and continuous revision (and reinterpretation) of the U.S. Constitution. Deliberative literacy (as exemplified in U.S. constitutional rhetoric) is the only core value around which we in our explosive and exponential national diversity can concur. Perhaps we could call literacy one of those "venerable" American ideals.

**NOTE:** This course has been designed for graduate students of Rhetoric & Writing as well as in Education. We will focus on a broad range of arguments (across genres and discourse communities in public/popular cultures). Final course projects will be adapted to the specific needs, interests, and genre-practices of the graduate students in my course with respect to their different sub-areas of Rhetorical Studies and Education.

**Learning Outcomes:**
Course readings, assignments, and class discussions are designed to promote the following learning outcomes:

- Apply and integrate concepts of literacy studies;
- Guide and participate in class discussions of course readings;
- Historicize the intellectual traditions of Western literacy education;
- Critically analyze notions of literacy across academic and public cultures;
- Use the writing process as recursive stages (from invention to editing) for writing tasks;
- Engage in purposeful and productive peer review;
- Connect classroom learning to teaching writing;
- Generate intellectual project (seminar paper) productive to future professional development (conference paper, MA portfolio or dissertation chapter, journal article, etc.);
- Cultivate alliances with peers and work collaboratively toward common goals.

**Required Texts:**
Ellen Cushman, Eugene R. Kintgen, Barry M. Kroll, and Mike Rose eds. Literacy: A Critical Sourcebook

Paolo Freire Pedagogy of the Oppressed.

James Paul Gee Social Linguistics and Literacies: Ideology in Discourses.

Keith Gilyard. Composition and Cornel West: Notes Toward a Deep Democracy.

Antonio Gramsci. Selections from the Prison Notebooks.

Jacqueline Jones Royster. Traces of a Stream: Literacy and Social Change Among African American Women.

Raymond Williams Key Words: A Vocabulary of Culture and Society

Victor Villanueva. Bootstraps: From an American Academic of Color.

# COMPOSITION FORUM

*Composition Forum* is on the Web at http://compositionforum.com/

*Composition Forum* is a peer-reviewed journal for scholars and teachers interested in the investigation of composition theory and its relation to the teaching of writing at the post-secondary level. The journal features articles that explore the intersections of composition theory and pedagogy, including essays that examine specific pedagogical theories or that examine how theory could or should inform classroom practices, methodology, and research into multiple literacies. *Composition Forum* also publishes articles that describe specific and innovative writing program practices and writing courses, reviews of relevant books in composition studies, and interviews with notable scholars and teachers who can address issues germane to our theoretical approach.

### Notes Toward A Theory of Prior Knowledge and Its Role In College Composers' Transfer of Knowledge and Practice

This article exemplifies *Composition Forum*'s commitment to publishing research addressing the intersections of composition theory and pedagogy. The article's focus on transfer demonstrates current and topical conversations in writing studies, and it draws upon important scholarly work on the subject.

# 3 Notes Toward A Theory of Prior Knowledge and Its Role In College Composers' Transfer of Knowledge and Practice

*Liane Robertson, Kara Taczak and Kathleen Blake Yancey*

*Abstract: In this article we consider the ways in which college writers make use of prior knowledge as they take up new writing tasks. Drawing on two studies of transfer, both connected to a Teaching for Transfer composition curriculum for first-year students, we articulate a theory of prior knowledge and document how the use of prior knowledge can detract from or contribute to efficacy in student writing.*

During the last decade, especially, scholars in composition studies have investigated how students "transfer" what they learn in college composition into other academic writing sites. Researchers have focused, for example, on exploring with students how they take up new writing tasks (e.g., McCarthy, Wardle); on theorizing transfer with specific applicability to writing tasks across a college career (e.g., Beaufort); and on developing new curricula to foster such transfer of knowledge and practice (e.g., Dew, Robertson, Taczak). Likewise, scholars have sought to learn what prior knowledge from high school first-year students might draw on, and how, as they begin college composition (e.g. Reiff and Bawarshi). To date, however, no study has actively documented or theorized precisely how students make use of such prior knowledge as they find themselves in new rhetorical situations, that is, on how students draw on and employ what they already know and can do, and whether such knowledge and practice is efficacious in the new situation or not. In this article, we take up this task, within a specific view of transfer as a dynamic activity through which students, like all composers, actively make use of prior knowledge as they respond to new writing tasks. More specifically, we theorize that students actively make use of prior knowledge and practice in three ways: by drawing on both knowledge and practice and employing it in ways almost identical to the ways they have used it in the past; by reworking such knowledge and practice as they address new tasks; and by creating new knowledge and practices for themselves when students encounter what we call a setback or critical incident, which is a failed effort to address a new task that prompts new ways of thinking about how to write and about what writing is.

In this article, then, we begin by locating our definition of transfer in the general literature of cognition; we then consider how students' use of prior knowledge has been represented in the writing studies literature. Given this context and drawing on two studies, we then articulate our theory of students' use of prior knowledge, in the process focusing on student accounts to illustrate how they make use of such knowledge as they take up new writing tasks.[1] We then close by raising questions that can inform research on this topic in the future.[2]

## MODELS OF TRANSFER

Early transfer research in the fields of psychology and education (Thorndike, Prather, Detterman) focused on specific situations in which instances of transfer occurred. Conducted in research environments and measuring subjects' ability to replicate specific behavior from one context to another, results of this research suggested that transfer was merely accidental, but it did not explore transfer in contexts more authentic and complex than those simulated in a laboratory.

In 1992, Perkins and Salomon suggested that researchers should consider the conditions and contexts under which transfer might occur, redefining transfer according to three subsets: near versus far transfer, or how closely related a new situation is to the original; high-road (or mindful) transfer involving knowledge abstracted and applied to another context, versus low-road (or reflexive) transfer involving knowledge triggered by something similar in another context; and positive transfer (performance improvement) versus negative transfer (performance interference) in another context. With consideration of the complexity of transfer and the conditions under which it may or may not occur, Perkins and Salomon suggest deliberately teaching for transfer through hugging (using approximations) and bridging (using abstraction to make connections) as strategies to maximize transfer (7).

In composition studies, several scholars have pursued "the transfer question." Michael Carter, Nancy Sommers and Laura Saltz, and Linda Bergmann and Janet Zepernick, for example, have theorized that students develop toward expertise, or "write into expertise" (Sommers and Saltz 134), when they understand the context in which the writing is situated and can make the abstractions that connect contexts, as Perkins and Salomon suggest (6). David Russell likewise claims that writing happens within a context, specifically the "activity system" in which the writing is situated, and that when students learn to make connections between contexts, they begin to develop toward expertise in understanding writing within any context, suggesting that transfer requires contextual knowledge (Russell 536). In a later article, Russell joins with Arturo Yañez to study the relationship of genre understanding to transfer, finding, in the case of one student, that students' prior genre knowledge can be limited to a single instance of the genre rather than situated in a larger activity system; such limited understanding can lead to confusion and subsequent difficulty in writing (n.p.).

Other research has contributed to our understanding of the complexity of transfer as well, notably of the role that motivation and metacognition play in transfer. For instance, Tracy Robinson and Tolar Burton found that students are motivated to improve their writing when they understand that the goal is to transfer what they learn between contexts, an understanding also explored by Susan Jarratt et al. in a study involving interview research with students in upper-division writing courses to determine what might have transferred to those contexts from the first-year composition experience. Results of the research offer three categories from which students accounted for transfer: (1) active transfer, which requires the mindfulness that Perkins and Salomon define as high-road transfer, (2) unreflective practice, in which students cannot articulate why they do what they do, and (3) transfer denial, in which students resist the idea of transfer from first-year composition or don't see the connection between it and upper-division writing (Jarratt et al. 3). The Jarratt et al. study, perhaps most importantly, suggests that metacognition students develop before transfer occurs can be prompted; students may not necessarily realize that learning has occurred until they are prompted, but this is the point at which transfer can occur (6).

Metacognition as a key to transfer is identified by Anne Beaufort as well: in College Writing and Beyond, Beaufort suggests conceptualizing writing according to five knowledge domains, which together provide a frame within which writers can organize the context-specific knowledge they need to write successfully in new situations. These domains—writing process knowledge, rhetorical knowledge, genre knowledge, discourse community knowledge, and content knowledge—provide an analytical framework authors can draw on as they move from one context to another. Using this conceptual model, students can learn to write in new contexts more effectively because they understand the inquiry necessary for entering the new context. Beaufort suggests that the expertise students need to write successfully involves "mental schema" they use to organize and apply knowledge about writing in new contexts (17).

More recent scholarship about transfer, including the "writing about writing" approach advocated by Douglas Downs and Elizabeth Wardle, suggests that teaching students about concepts of writing will help foster transfer through a curricular design based on reading and writing as scholarly inquiry such that students develop a rhetorical awareness (553). This writing-as-writing-course-content approach dismisses the long-held misconception that content doesn't matter, and others are pursuing this same end although with different curricular models (e.g., Sargent and Slomp; Bird; Dew; Robertson; and Taczak).

A little-referenced source of research on transfer that is particularly relevant to this study on how students use prior knowledge in new situations, however, is the National Research Council volume How People Learn: Mind, Brain, Experience, and School. Here transfer "is best viewed as an active, dynamic process rather than a passive end-product of a particular set of learning experiences" (53). As important, according to this generalized theory of transfer, all "new learning involves transfer based on previous learning" (53). All such prior learning is not efficacious, however; according to this theory, prior knowledge can function in one of three ways. First, an individual's prior knowledge can match the demands of a new task, in which case a composer can draw from and build on that prior knowledge; we might see this use of prior knowledge when a first-year composition student thinks in terms of audience, purpose, and genre when entering a writing situation in another discipline. Second, an individual's prior knowledge might be a bad match, or at odds with, a new writing situation; in FYC, we might see this when a student defines success in writing as creating a text that is grammatically correct without reference to its rhetorical effectiveness. And third, an individual's prior knowledge—located in a community context—might be at odds with the requirements of a given writing situation; this writing classroom situation, in part, seems to have motivated the Vander Lei-Kyburz edited collection documenting the difficulty some FYC students experience as a function of their religious beliefs coming into conflict with the goals of higher education. As this brief review suggests, we know that college students call on prior knowledge as they encounter new writing demands; the significant points here are that students actively use their prior knowledge and that some prior knowledge provides help for new writing situations, while other prior knowledge does not.

This interest in how first-year students use prior knowledge in composing, however, has not been taken up by composition scholars until very recently. During the last four years, Mary Jo Reiff and Anis Bawarshi have undertaken this task. Their 2011 article, Tracing Discursive Resources: How Students Use Prior Genre Knowledge to Negotiate New Writing Contexts in First-Year Composition, provides a compilation of this research, which centers on if and how students' understanding and use of genre facilitates their transition from high school to college writing situations. Conducted at the University of Washington and the University of Tennessee, Reiff and Bawarshi's study identified two kinds of students entering first year comp: first, what they call boundary crossers, "those students who were more likely to question their genre knowledge and to break this knowledge down into useful strategies and repurpose it"; and second, boundary guarders, "those students who were more likely to draw on whole genres with certainty, regardless of task" (314). In creating these student prototypes, the researchers drew on document-based interviews focused on students' use of genre knowledge early in the term, first as they composed a "preliminary" essay and second, as they completed the first assignment of the term:

> Specifically, we asked students to report on what they thought each writing task was asking them to do and then to report on what prior genres they were reminded of and drew on for each task. As students had their papers in front of them, we were

able to point to various rhetorical conventions and ask about
how they learned to use those conventions or why they made
the choices that they made, enabling connections between
discursive patterns and prior knowledge of genres. (319)

Based on this study, Reiff and Bawarshi identify two kinds of boundary-guarding students, and key to their definition is the use of what
they call "not talk":

The first, what might be called "strict" boundary guarding,
includes students who report no "not" talk (in terms of genres
or strategies) and who seem to maintain known genres regardless of task. The second kind of boundary guarding is less
strict in that students report some strategy-related "not" talk
and some modification of known genres by way of adding
strategies to known genres. (329)

These students, in other words, work to maintain the boundary marking their prior knowledge, and at the most add only strategies to the
schema they seek to preserve. By way of contrast, the boundary crossing student accepts noviceship, often as a consequence of struggling
to meet the demands of a new writing task. Therefore, this writer
seems to experience multiple kinds of flux—such as uncertainty about
task, descriptions of writing according to what genre it is not, and the
breakdown and repurposing of whole genres that may be useful to
students entering new contexts in FYC (329).

What's interesting here, of course, isn't only the prototypes, but
how those prototypes might change given other contexts. For example, what happens to students as they continue learning in the first
term of FYC? What happens when students move on to a second term
and take up writing tasks outside of first-year composition? Likewise, what difference might both curriculum and pedagogy make? In
other words, what might we do to motivate those students exhibiting
a boundary-guarding approach to take up a boundary-crossing one?
And once students have boundary-crossed, what happens then? How
can we support boundary-crossers and help them become more confident and competent composers?[3]

## WHERE MANY STUDENTS BEGIN:
## ABSENT PRIOR KNOWLEDGE

As documented above, it's a truism that students draw on prior knowledge when facing new tasks, and when that acquired knowledge doesn't fit the new situation, successful transfer is less likely to occur; this is so in writing generally, but it's especially so as students enter first-year composition classrooms in college. At the same time, whether students are guarding or crossing, they share a common high school background. Moreover, what this seems to mean for virtually all first-year college composition students, as the research literature documents but as we also learned from our students, is that as students enter college writing classes, there's not only prior knowledge, but also an absence of prior knowledge, and in two important areas: (1) key writing concepts and (2) non-fiction texts that serve as models. In part, that's because the "writing" curricula at the two sites—high school and college––don't align well. As Arthur Applebee and Judith Langer's continuing research on the high school English/Language Arts curriculum shows, the high school classroom is a literature classroom, whereas the first-year writing classroom—which despite the diverse forms it takes, from first-year seminars to WAC-based approaches to cultural studies and critical pedagogy approaches (see Fulkerson; Delivering College Composition)—is a writing classroom. The result for our students—and, we think, others like them––is that they enter college with very limited experience with the conceptions and kinds of writing and reading they will engage with during the first year of postsecondary education.

In terms of how such an absence might occur, the Applebee and Langer research is instructive, especially in its highlighting of two dimensions of writing in high school that are particularly relevant in terms of absent prior knowledge. First is the emphasis that writing receives, or not, in high school classrooms; their studies demonstrate an emphasis placed on literature with deleterious effects for writing instruction:

> In the English classes observed, 6.3% of time was focused on the teaching of explicit writing strategies, 5.5% on the study of models, and 4.2% on evaluating writing, including discussion of rubrics or standards. (Since multiple things were often going on at once, summing these percentages would

> overestimate the time devoted to writing instruction.) To put
> the numbers in perspective, in a 50-minute period, students
> would have on average just over three minutes of instruction
> related to explicit writing strategies, or a total of 2 hours and
> 22 minutes in a nine-week grading period. ("A Snapshot" 21)

Second, and as important, is the way that writing is positioned in the
high school classes Applebee and Langer have studied: chiefly as preparation for test-taking, with the single purpose of passing a test, and
the single audience of Britton's "teacher-as-examiner." Moreover, this
conclusion echoes the results of the University of Washington Study
of Undergraduate Learning (SOUL) on entering college writers, which
was designed to identify the gaps between high school and college that
presented obstacles to students. Their findings suggest that the major
gaps are in math and writing, and that in the latter area, writing tests
themselves limit students' understanding of and practice in writing.
As a result, writing's purposes are truncated and its potential to serve
learning is undeveloped. As Applebee and Langer remark, "Given the
constraints imposed by high-stakes tests, writing as a way to study,
learn, and go beyond—as a way to construct knowledge or generate
new networks of understandings . . . is rare" (26). One absence of pri-
or knowledge demonstrated in the scholarship on the transition from
high school to college is thus a conception and practice of writing for
authentic purposes and genuine audiences.

Writers are readers as well, of course. In high school, the reading
is largely (if not exclusively) of imaginative literature, whereas in college, it's largely (though not exclusively) non-fiction, and for evidence
of impact of such a curriculum, we turn to our students. What we
learned from them, through questionnaires and interviews, is that
their prior knowledge about texts, at least in terms of what they choose
to read and in terms of how such texts represent good writing, is located in the context of imaginative literature, which makes sense given
the school curriculum. When asked "What type of authors represent
your definition of good writing?" these students replied with a list of
imaginative writers. Some cited writers known for publishing popular
page-turners—Michael Crichton, James Patterson, and Dan Brown,
for instance; others pointed to writers of the moment—Jodi Picoult
and Stephenie Meyer; and still others called on books that are likely to
be children's classics for some time to come: Harry Potter, said one student, "is all right." Two other authors were mentioned—Frey, whose A

Million Little Pieces, famously, was either fiction or non-fiction given its claim to truth (or not); and textbook author Ann Raimes. In sum, we have a set of novels, one "memoir," and one writing textbook— none of which resembles the non-fiction reading characteristic of first-year composition and college more generally. Given the students' reading selections, what we seem to be mapping here, based on their interviews, is a second absence of prior knowledge.

Of course, the number of students is small, their selections limited. These data don't prove that even these students, much less others, have no prior knowledge about non-fiction. But the facts (1) that the curricula of high schools are focused on imaginative literature and (2) that none of the students pointed to even a single non-fiction book—other than the single textbook, which identification may itself be part of the problem––suggest that these may not have models of non-fiction to draw on when writing their own non-fiction. Put another way, when these students write the non-fiction texts characteristic of the first-year composition classroom, they have neither pre-college experience with the reading of non-fiction texts nor mental models of non-fiction texts, which together constitute a second absence of prior knowledge.

Perhaps not surprisingly, what at least some students do in this situation is draw on and generalize their experience with imaginative texts in ways that are at odds with what college composition instructors expect, particularly when it comes to concepts of writing.[4] When we asked students how they wrote and how they defined writing, for example, we saw a set of contradictions. On the one hand, students reported writing in various genres, especially outside of school. More-over, unlike the teenagers in the well-known Pew study investigating teenagers' writing habits and understandings––for whom writing inside school is writing and writing outside school is not writing but communication––the students we interviewed do understand writing both inside and outside school as writing. More specifically, all but one of the students identified writing outside school as a place where they "use writing most," for example, with all but one identifying three specific practices––taking notes, texting, and emailing––as frequent (i.e., daily) writing practices. In addition, two writers spoke to particularly robust writing lives; one of them noted, for instance, writing

> [i]nside school. Taking notes. Inside the classroom doing notes. If not its writing assignments. Had blog for a while; blog about everyday life [she and three friends]; high school

sophomore through senior year; fizzled out b/c of life; emails; hand written letters to family members.

A second one described a similar kind of writing life, his located particularly in the arts: "Probably [it would] be texting . . . the most that I write. I also write a little poetry; I'm in a band so I like to write it so that it fits to music; a pop alternative; I play the piano, synth and sing."

On the other hand, given that many of these texts—emails and texts, for example—are composed to specific audiences and thus seem in that sense to be highly rhetorical, it was likewise surprising that every one of the students, when asked to define writing, used a single word: expression. One student thus defined writing as a "way to express ideas and feelings and to organize my thoughts," while another summarized the common student response: "I believe writing is, um, a way of expressing your thoughts, uh, through, uh, text." In spite of their own experience as writers to others, these students see writing principally as a vehicle for authorial expression, not as a vehicle for dialogue with a reader or an opportunity to make knowledge, both of which are common conceptions in college writing environments. We speculate that this way of seeing writing—universally as a means of expression in different historical and intellectual contexts—may be influenced by the emphasis on imaginative authorship in the high school literature curriculum, in which students read poets', novelists', and dramatists' writing as forms of expression. Likewise, the emphasis on reading in high school, at the expense of writing, means that it's likely that reading exerts a disproportionate influence on how these students understand writing itself, especially since the writing tasks, often a form of literary analysis, are also oriented to literature and literary authorship. And more generally, what we see here—through these students' high school curricula, their own reading practices, and their writing practices both in but mostly out of school—is reading culture-as-prior-experience, an experience located in pre-college reading and some writing practices, but one missing the conceptions, models, and practices of writing as well as practices of reading that could be helpful in a new postsecondary environment emphasizing a rhetorical view of both reading and writing. Or: absent prior knowledge.

## A Typology of Prior Knowledge, Type One: Assemblage

While we speculate that college students, like our students, enter college with an absence of prior knowledge relevant to the new situation, how students take up the new knowledge relative to the old varies; and here, based on interview data, writing assignments, and responses to the assignments, we describe three models of uptake. Some students, like Eugene, seem to take up new knowledge in a way we call assemblage: by grafting isolated bits of new knowledge onto a continuing schema of old knowledge. Some, like Alice, take up new knowledge in ways we call remix: by integrating the new knowledge into the schema of the old. And some, like Rick, encounter what we call a critical incident—a failure to meet a new task successfully—and use that occasion as a prompt to re-think writing altogether.

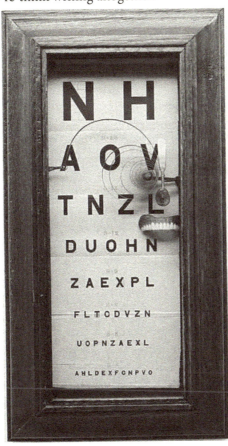

Eugene, who seems to be an example of Reiff and Bawarshi's border guarders, believes that what he is learning in FYC is very similar to what he learned in high school. How he makes use of prior knowledge and practice about writing is what we call assemblage: such students maintain the concept of writing they brought into college with them, breaking the new learning into bits, atomistically, and grafting those isolated "bits" of learning onto the prior structure without either recognition of differences between prior and current writing conceptions and tasks, or synthesis of them. Such bits may take one or both of two forms: key terms and strategies. Taken together, the conception of writing that students develop through an assemblage model of prior knowledge is very like the assemblage "Vorwarts!" in its remaking of the earlier structure of the eye chart: the new bits are added to it, but are not integrated into it but rather on top of it, such that the basic chart isn't significantly changed at all.

When Eugene, a successful AP student in high school whose score enabled him to exempt the first of the two first-year composition courses at Florida State, entered English 1102, the second-term, research and argument course, he articulated a dualistic view of writing—for writing to be successful, "you have the right rhetoric and the right person in the right manner," he observed—and believed that writing operates inside a transmission model through which his writing would allow him "to get his message across." Interestingly, he believed that he was "really prepared for college": "[in high school] we were doing a lot of papers that talked about literary devices so I basically knew a lot of literacy devices so there wasn't a lot more to learn necessarily, I guess more fine-tuning of what I had already learned." And what there was to learn, Eugene didn't find worthwhile, in part because it fell outside what he did know: "I don't like research papers because I don't know how they work very well and collecting sources and analyzing." He noted that he was better at "evaluating an article and finding a deeper meaning," which is the purpose, of course, of the literary analysis texts he wrote in high school.

As he begins his college writing career, then, Eugene establishes a three-part pattern that continues throughout English 1102 and the next term: (1) he confuses and conflates the literary terms of high school and the literacy and rhetorical terms and practices of college; (2) he continues to believe that "there wasn't a lot more to learn"; and (3) he relies on his prior knowledge of writing, one located chiefly in the role of the unconscious in writing process. As he analyzes his progress in terms of writing, for example, he notes the central role of the unconscious:

> my main point is that writing is unconsciously understanding that certain genres that have certain formalities where I have progressed and so where I have progressed is I can put names and places to genres; writing is pretty much unconscious how you are adjusting the person you are talking to and how you are writing.

In this case, the unconscious element of writing provides the central element of Eugene's concept of writing, and as English 1102 continues and in the semester that follows, Eugene struggles to find terms that he can comfortably graft onto that central understanding.

During the course of two semesters, Eugene was interviewed four times, each time nominating his key terms for composing, and in this data set, we can also see Eugene struggling to make his prior conception of writing work with the new conception of writing to which he is being introduced. In all, he nominated 18 terms: audience and genre were both mentioned three times (once each in three of the four interviews), with other terms each suggested once: reflection, tone, purpose, theme, exigence, diction, theory of writing, imagination, creativity, and rhetorical situation. Some of the terms—rhetorical situation and exigence, for instance—came from his first-year composition class, while others—diction and imagination—were terms located in his high school curriculum. As he continued into the semester following English 1102, Eugene held on to genre, saying in one interview immediately following English 1102 that "I still have to go with genre [as] important and everything else is subcategories," in the next that genre was still important but not something he needed to think about, as he worked "unconsciously":

> A lot of my writing is like unconsciously done because it's been ingrained in me to how writing is done. Even though I probably think of genre I don't really think of it. Writing just kind of happens for me.

And in the final interview, Eugene retrospectively notes that what he gained was a "greater appreciation" of genre, "for the role genre plays in writing. [I]t went from being another aspect of writing to the most important part of writing as a result of ENC 1102." Genre for Eugene, then, seems to be mapped assemblage-like onto a fundamental and unchanging concept of writing located in expression and the unconscious.

In the midst of trying to respond to new tasks like the research project and unable to frame them anew, Eugene defaults to two strategies that he found particularly helpful. One of these was multiple drafting, not to create a stronger draft so much, however, as to have the work scaffolded according to goals: "Most useful was the multiple drafts, being able to have smaller goals to work up to the bigger goal made it easier to manage." The second strategy Eugene adopted both for English 1102 and for writing tasks the next semester was "reverse outlining," a practice in which (as its name suggests) students outline a text once it's in draft form to see if and how the focus is carried through the text. This Eugene found particularly helpful: "something new I hadn't experienced before was the reverse outline because it helped me to realize that my paragraphs do have main points and it helps me realize where I need main points." Interestingly, the parts-is-parts approach to writing Eugene values in the smaller goals leading to larger ones in the multiple drafting process is echoed in his appreciation of reverse outlining, where he can track the intent of each paragraph rather than how the paragraphs relate to each other, a point he makes explicitly as English 1102 closes:

> Um, my theory of writing when I first started the class was very immature I remember describing it as just putting your emotions and thoughts on the paper I think was my first theory of writing and I think from the beginning of fall it's gotten to where I understand the little parts of writing make up the important part of writing, so I think in that way it's changed.

As the study concludes and Eugene is asked to comment retrospectively on what he learned in English 1102, he re-states not what he learned, but rather the prior knowledge on writing that he brought with him to college. He observes that, "For me, there wasn't much of a difference between high school and college writing" and

> Like I came from a really intensive writing program in high school, so coming into [the first-year comp] class wasn't that different, so, um, I mean obviously any writing that I do will help me become better and hopefully I will progress and be-

come better with each piece that I write, so in that regard I think it was helpful.

What thus seems to help, according to Eugene, is simply the opportunity to write, which will enable him to progress naturally through "any writing that I do."

And not least, as the study closes, Eugene, in describing a conception of writing developed through an assemblage created by grafting the new key term "genre" onto an unconscious process resulting in writing that is dichotomously "good" or "bad," repeats the definition he provided as English 1102 commenced:

> I mean writing is, like, when you break it down it's a lot more complex than what you describe it to me. I mean you can sit all day and talk about literary devices but it comes down to writing. Writing is, um, it's more complex, so, it's like anything, if you are going to break down, it's going to be more complex than it seems. Writing is emotionally based. Good writing is good and bad writing is bad.

Writing here is complex, something to be analyzed, much like literature, "when you break it down." But it's also a practice: "you can sit all day and talk about literacy devices but it comes down to writing." Likewise, the strategies Eugene appreciated—revising toward larger goals and reverse outlining to verify the points of individual paragraphs—fit with the assemblage model as well: they do not call into question an "unconscious" approach, but can be used to verify that this approach is producing texts whose component parts are satisfactory. Of course, this wasn't the intent of the teacher introducing either the multiple drafting process or the reverse outlining strategy. But as Eugene makes use of prior knowledge, in an assemblage fashion, the conceptual model of unconscious writing he brought to college with him shapes his uptake of the curriculum more broadly, from key terms to process strategies.

## TYPE TWO: REMIX

Students who believe that what they are learning differs from their prior knowledge in some substantive way(s) and value that difference behave differently. They begin to create a revised model of writing we characterize as a remix: prior knowledge revised synthetically to incorporate new concepts and practices into the prior model of writing. Remix, in this definition, isn't a characteristic of hip-hop only or of modernism more generally, but a feature of invention with a long history:

> Seen through a wider lens . . .remix—the combining of ideas, narratives, sources—is a classical means of invention, even (or perhaps especially) for canonical writers. For example, . . . as noted in Wikipedia, Shakespeare arguably "remixed" classical sources and Italian contemporary works to produce his plays, which were often modified for different audiences. Nineteenth century poets also utilized the technique. Examples include Samuel Taylor Coleridge's "Rime of the Ancient Mariner," which was produced in multiple, highly divergent versions, and John Keats' La Belle Dame sans Merci, which underwent significant revision between its original composition in 1819 and its republication in 1820 (Remix). In sum, remixing, both a practice and a set of material practices, is connected to the creation of new texts (Yancey, Re-designing 6).

Here, we use remix with specific application to writing: a set of practices that links past writing knowledge and practice to new writing knowledge and practice, as we see in the experience of Alice.

Alice entered English 1102 with a conception of writing influenced by three sets of experience: preparing for and taking the Florida K-12 writing exams, known as the FCAT; completing her senior AP English class; and taking her English 1101 class, which she had completed in the summer before matriculating at Florida State. Alice had literally grown up as an "FCAT writer," given that the writing curriculum in the state is keyed to these essay exams and for many if not most students, the writing exam is the curriculum (e.g., Scherff and Piazza). In her senior year, however, Alice enrolled in an AP English class, where she learned a different model of text that both built on and contrasted with her experience as an FCAT writer: "[my senior English teacher] explained his concept as instead of writing an intro, listing your three points, then the conclusion, to write like layers of a cake. Instead of spreading out each separate point . . . layer them." The shift here, then, is one of remix: the arrangement of texts was to remain the same, while what happened inside the texts was to be changed, with Alice's explanation suggesting that the shift was from a listing of points to an analysis of them. During the third experience, in the summer before her first year in college, Alice learned a new method of composing: she was introduced to "process writing," including drafts, workshops and peer reviews.

When Alice entered English 1102, she defined writing as a Murray-esque exercise: "Writing," Alice said, "is a form of expression that needs to have feeling and be articulate in order to get the writer's ideas across. The writing also needs to have the author's own unique voice," an idea that provided something of a passport for her as she encountered new conceptions of writing located in key terms like rhetorical situation, context, and audience. In Alice's retrospective account of English 1102, in fact, she focuses particularly on the conception of rhetorical situation as one both new to her and difficult to understand, in part because it functioned as something of a meta-concept: "Rhetorical situation had a lot of things involved in that. It was a hard concept for me to get at first but it was good." By the end of the course, however, Alice was working hard to create an integrated model of writing that included three components: her own values, what she had learned during the summer prior to English 1102, and what she had learned in English 1102:

> I still find writing to be a form of expression, it should have the author's own voice and there should be multiple drafts and peer reviews in order to have the end result of a good and original paper. Along with that this year I learned about concepts such as rhetorical situation. . . . This opened me up to consider audience, purpose, and context for my writing. I need to know why I am writing and who I am writing to before I start. The context I am writing in also brings me to what genre I'm writing in.

Alice's conception of writing here seems to rely on the layering strategy recommended by her AP teacher: voice, mixed with process, and framed rhetorically, defined here layer by layer.

As Alice continues into the term after she completes English 1102, two writing-related themes emerge for her. One: a key part of the process for Alice that begins to have new salience for her is reflecting on her writing, both as she drafts and after she completes a text. Two: she finds that the study itself has helped her develop as a writer but that she needs more time and more writing activity to make sense of all that she's been offered in English 1102.

In English 1102, Alice had been asked to reflect frequently: in the midst of drafting; at the end of assignments; and at the end of the course itself in a reflection-in-presentation where she summarized what she had learned and also theorized about writing. These reflective practices she found particularly helpful and, in the next term, when she wrote assignments for her humanities and meteorology classes, she continued to practice a self-sponsored reflection: it had become part of her composing process. As she explains, her own sense is that through reflection, she is able to bring together the multiple factors that contribute to writing:

> I do know that I really liked reflection, like having that because I haven't done that before. And whatever term was writing with a purpose and I like that so I guess writing with some purpose. Like when you are done writing you do reflection because before I would be done with a writing and go to the next one and so then in between we go over each step or throughout.

As the study concluded, Alice linked reflection and rhetorical situation as the two most important concepts for writing that she learned in English 1102, but as she did earlier, she also includes a value of her own, in this case "being direct," into a remixed model of writing:[5]

> Two of the words I would use to describe my theory of writing would be the key terms, rhetorical situation, reflection and the last that isn't would just be being direct. Rhetorical situation encompasses a lot about anybody's theory of writing. It deals with knowing the purpose of my writing, understanding the context of my writing, and thinking about my audience. I chose being direct for lack of a better term. I don't think my writing should beat around the bush. It should just say what needs to be said and have a purpose. As for reflection that's something we do in life and not just writing. In the context of writing it really helps not just as a review of grammar or spelling errors but as a thought back on what I was thinking about when I wrote what I wrote, and that could change as I look back on my writing.

Being direct, of course, was Alice's contribution to a curricular-based model of writing informed by reflective practice and rhetorical situation. Reflection she defines as a "thought back," a variation of the "talk backs" that students were assigned in English 1102, here a generalized articulation of a meta-cognitive practice helping her "change as I look back on my writing." In addition, Alice works toward making reflection her own as she theorizes about it—"that's something we do in life and not just writing"—in the process seeing it as a life-practice as well as a writing practice. More generally, what we see here is that Alice is developing her own "remixed" model of composing, combining her values with curricular concepts and practices. Not least, reflection was thus more than an after-the-fact activity for Alice; rather, it provided a mechanism for her to understand herself as a learner and prepare for the future whether it was writing or another activity.

Alice, however, is also aware of the impact of the study and of the need for more time to integrate what she has learned in English 1102 into her model and practice of writing. On the one hand, she seems to appreciate the study since, in her view, it functions as a follow-up activity extending the class itself, which is particularly valuable as she takes up new writing tasks the next semester:

> I feel as though I forget a lot about a class after I take it. I defi-
> nitely don't remember everything about my English class, but
> I feel I remember what will help me the most in my writing
> and I think that information will stay with me. This study has
> helped me get more from the class than just taking it and after
> not thinking about it anymore. The study helped me in a way
> to remind me to think about what we went over in English as
> I wrote for my other classes.

On the other hand, Alice understands that she has been unable to use all that was offered in English 1102:

> I feel like I haven't used everything; there were a lot of terms
> that we went over I don't use and there are some that I do and
> those are the ones that [the teacher] used the most anyways. I
> feel like this has helped me remember those that I will use and
> I feel like this has helped me retain a lot of information and
> now I have had to write a lot more besides our class and the
> stuff I gave to you. I was still thinking about what we did in

that comp class, so it has really helped me. But I still think I
could use a lot more experiences with writing papers and getting more from a college class, I mean like getting away from
the FCAT sound. I wrote like that until 10th grade.

Alice hopes that she has identified the best terms from the class and
thinks that she has, given that "those are the ones that the teacher
used the most," which repetition was, as she observes, one reason she
probably remembers them. But because of the interviews, she "was still
thinking about what we did in the comp class": she is continuing to
think about the terms more intentionally than she might have had no
interviews taken place. But as important, Alice believes that she "could
use a lot more experiences with writing papers and getting more from a
college class," here pointing to the need to get "away from the FCAT."
Given that Alice "wrote like that until 10th grade," "getting away from
the FCAT sound" is more difficult than it might first appear.

In sum, there is much to learn from Alice's experience. Through
her integration of her own values, prior knowledge, and new knowledge and practice, we see how students develop a remix model of composing, one that may change over time but that remains a remix. We
see as well how a composing practice like reflection can be generalized
into a larger philosophy of reflection, one more characteristic of expertise. And, not least, we see, through a student's observations, how a
term that we see as a single concept functions more largely, as a meta-
concept, and we see as well how hard it can be to remix prior knowledge, especially when that prior knowledge is nearly deterministic in
its application and impact.[6]

## CRITICAL INCIDENTS: MOTIVATING NEW
## CONCEPTIONS AND PRACTICES OF COMPOSING

Often students, both in first-year composition and in other writing situations, encounter a version of what's called, in fields ranging from air
traffic control and surgery to teaching, a "critical incident": a situation
where efforts either do not succeed at all or succeed only minimally.
What we have found is that writing students also encounter critical
incidents, and some students can be willing or able to let go of prior
knowledge as they re-think what they have learned, revise their model
and/or conception of writing, and write anew. In other words, the set-

backs motivated by critical incidents can provide the opportunity for conceptual breakthroughs, as we shall see in the case of Rick.

The surgeon Atul Gawande describes critical incidents as they occur in surgery and how they are later understood in his account of medical practice titled Complications. Surgical practice, like air traffic control, routinely and intentionally engages practitioners in a collective reviewing of what went wrong—in surgery, operations where the patient died or whose outcome was negative in other ways; in air traffic control, missteps large (e.g., a crash) and small (e.g., a near miss)—in the belief that such a review can reduce error and thus enhance practice. Accordingly, hospital-based surgeons meet weekly for the Morbidity and Mortality Conference, the M&M for short, its purpose both to reduce the incidence of mistakes and to make knowledge. As Gawande explains,

> There is one place, however, where doctors can talk candidly about their mistakes, if not with the patients, then at least with one another. It is called the Morbidity and Mortality Conference—or, more simply, M & M—and it takes place, usually once a week, at nearly every academic hospital in the country. . . . Surgeons, in particular, take the M & M seriously. Here they can gather behind closed doors to review the mistakes, untoward events, and deaths that occurred on their watch, determine responsibility, and figure out what to do differently next time. (57-58)

The protocol for the M&M never varies. The physician in charge speaks for the entire team, even if she or he wasn't present at the event under inquiry. In other words, a resident might have handled the case, but the person responsible—called, often ironically, the attending physician—speaks. First presented is information about the case: age of patient, reason for surgery, progress of surgery. Next the surgeon outlines what happened, focusing on the error in question; that there was an error is not in question, so the point is to see if that error might have been discerned more readily and thus to have produced a positive outcome. The surgeon provides an analysis and responds to questions, continuing to act as a spokesperson for the entire medical team. The doctor members of the team, regardless of rank, are all included but do not speak; the other members of the medical team, including nurses and technicians, are excluded, as are patients. The presentation concludes with a directive about how such prototypic cases should be handled in the future, and it's worth noting that, collectively, the results of the M&Ms have reduced error.

Several assumptions undergird this community of practice, in particular assumptions at odds with those of compositionists. We long ago gave up a focus on error, for example, in favor of the construction of a social text. Likewise, we might find it surprising that the M&M is so focused on what went wrong when just as much might be learned by what went right, especially in spite of the odds, for instance, on the young child with a heart defect who surprises by making it through surgery. Still, the practice of review in light of a critical incident suggests that even experts can revise their models when prompted to do so.

This is exactly what happened to Rick, a first-year student with an affection for all things scientific, who experienced a misfit between his prior knowledge and new writing tasks as he entered English 1102. Rick identified as a novice writer in this class, in part because he was not invested in writing apart from its role in science. A physics and astrophysics major, he was already working on a faculty research project in the physics laboratory and was planning a research career in his major area. He professed:

> I am a physics major so I really like writing about things I think people should know about that is going on in the world of science. Sometimes it's a challenge to get my ideas across to somebody that is not a science or math type, but I enjoy teaching people about physics and the world around them.

Rick credited multiple previous experiences for his understanding of writing, including his other high school and college courses; in addition, he mentioned watching YouTube videos of famous physicists lecturing and reading Einstein's work. He also believed that reading scientific materials had contributed to his success in writing scientific texts: "I think I write well in my science lab reports because I have read so many lectures and reports that I can just kind of copy their style into my writing."[7]

Rick's combination of prior knowledge and motivation, however, didn't prove sufficient when he began the research project in English 1102. He chose a topic with which he was not only familiar but also passionate, quantum mechanics, his aim to communicate the ways in which quantum mechanics benefits society. He therefore approached the research as an opportunity to share what he knew with others, rather than as inquiry into a topic and discovery of what might be significant. He also had difficulty making the information clear in his essay, which he understood as a rhetorical task: "The biggest challenge was making sure the language and content was easy enough for someone who is not a physics major to understand. It took a long time to explain it in simple terms, and I didn't want to talk down to the audience." In this context, Rick understood the challenge of expressing the significance of his findings to his audience, which he determined was fellow college students. But the draft he shared with his peers was confusing to them, not because of the language or information, as Rick had anticipated, but instead because of uncertainty about key points of the essay and about what they as readers were being asked to do with this information.

As a self-indentified novice, however, Rick reported that this experience taught him a valuable lesson about audience. "I tried to make it simple so . . . my classmates would understand it, but that just ended up messing up my paper, focusing more on the topic than on the research, which is what mattered. I explained too much instead of making it matter to them." Still, when the projects were returned, he admitted his surprise at the evaluation of the essay but was not willing to entertain the idea that his bias or insider knowledge about quantum mechanics had prevented his inquiry-based research:

> After everyone got their papers back, I noticed that our grades were based more on following the traditional conventions of a research paper, and I didn't follow those as well as I could have. I don't really see the importance of following specific genre conventions perfectly.

In the next semester, however, these issues of genre and audience came together in a critical incident for Rick as he wrote his first lab report for chemistry. Ironically, Rick was particularly excited about this writing because, unlike the writing he had composed in English 1102, this was science writing: a lab report. But as it turned out, it was a lab report with a twist: the instructor specified that the report have a conclusion to it that would link it to "everyday life":

> We had to explain something interesting about the lab and how that relates to everyday life. I would say it is almost iden-

tical to the normal introduction one would write for a paper, trying to grab the reader's attention, while at the same time exploring what you will be talking about.

Aware of genre conventions and yet in spite of these directions for modification, Rick wrote a standard lab report. In fact, in his high-lighting of the data, he made it more lab-report-like rather than less: "I tried to have my lab report stick out from the others with better explanations of the data and the experiment." The chemistry instruc-tor noticed, and not favorably: Rick's score was low, and he was more than disappointed. Eager to write science, he got a lower grade than he did on his work in English 1102, and it wasn't because he didn't know the content; it was because he hadn't followed directions for writing.

This episode constituted a critical incident for Rick. Dismayed, he went to talk to the teacher about the score; she explained that he indeed needed to write the lab report not as the genre might strictly require, but as she had adapted it. Chastened, he did so in all the next assigned lab reports, and to good effect: "My lab reports were getting all the available points and they were solid too, very concise and fac-tual but the conclusions used a lot of good reflection in them to show that the experiments have implications on our lives." The ability to adapt to teacher directions in order to get a higher grade, as is com-mon for savvy students, doesn't in and of itself constitute a critical incident; what makes it so here is Rick's response and the re-seeing that Rick engages in afterwards. Put differently, he begins to see writ-ing as synthetic and genres as flexible, and in the process, he begins to develop a more capacious conception of writing, based in part on his tracing similarities and differences across his own writing tasks past and present.

This re-seeing operates at several units of analysis. On the first level, Rick articulates a new appreciation for the value of the assign-ment, especially the new conclusion, and the ways he is able to theorize it: "I did better on the conclusions when I started to think about the discourse community and what is expected in it. I remembered that from English 1102, that discourse community dictates how you write, so I thought about it." On another level, while Rick maintains that the genres were different in the lab courses than in 1102, as in fact they are, he is able to map similarities across them:

> One similarity would be after reading an article in 1102 and writing a critique where we had to think about the article and what it meant. This is very similar to what we do in science: we read data and then try to explain what it means and how it came about. This seems to be fundamental to the understanding of anything really, and is done in almost every class.

This theorizing, of course, came after the fact of the critical incident, and one might make the argument that such theorizing is just a way of coming to terms with meeting the teacher's directions. But as the term progressed, Rick was able to use his new understanding of writing—located in discourse communities and genres and keyed to reading data and explaining them—as a way to frame one of his new assignments, a poster assignment. His analysis of how to approach it involved his taking the terms from English 1102 and using them to frame the new task:

> I have this poster I had to create for my chemistry class, which tells me what genre I have to use, and so I know how to write it, because a poster should be organized a certain way and look a certain way and it is written to a specific audience in a scientific way. I wouldn't write it the same way I would write a research essay – I'm presenting the key points about this chemistry project, not writing a lot of paragraphs that include what other people say about it or whatever. The poster is just the highlights with illustrations, but it is right for its audience. It wasn't until I was making the poster that I realized I was thinking about the context I would present it in, which is like rhetorical situation, and that it was a genre. So I thought about those things and I think it helped. My poster was awesome.

Here we see Rick's thinking across tasks, genres, and discourse communities as he maps both similarities and differences across them. Moreover, as he creates the chemistry poster, he draws on new prior knowledge, that prior knowledge he developed in his English 1102 class, this a rhetorical knowledge keyed to three features of rhetorical situations generally: (1) an understanding of the genre in which he was composing and presenting, (2) the audience to whom he was presenting, and (3) the context in which they would receive his work. Despite the fact that this chemistry poster assignment was the first time he had composed in this genre, he was successful at creating it, at least in part because he drew on his prior knowledge in a useful way, one that allowed him to see where similarities provided a bridge and differences a point of articulation.[8]

All this, of course, is not to say that Rick is an expert, but as many scholars in composition, including Sommers and Saltz, and Beaufort, as well as psychologists like Marcia Baxter-Magolda argue, students need the opportunity to be novices in order to develop toward expertise. This is exactly what works for Rick when the challenges in college writing, in both English 1102 and more particularly in chemistry, encourage him to think of himself as a novice and to take up new concepts of writing and new practices. Moreover, the critical incident prompts Rick to develop a more capacious understanding of writing, one in which genre is flexible and the making of knowledge includes application. Likewise, this new understanding of writing provides him with a framework that he can use as he navigates new contexts and writing tasks, as he does with the chemistry poster.

If indeed some college students are, at least at the beginning of their postsecondary career, boundary guarders, and others boundary crossers, and if we want to continue using metaphors of travel to describe the experience of college writers, then we might say that Rick has moved beyond boundary crossing: as a college writer, he has taken up residence.

## CONCLUDING THOUGHTS

Our purpose in this article is both to elaborate more fully students' uses of prior knowledge and to document how such uses can detract from or contribute to efficacy in student writing. As important, this analysis puts a face on what transfer in composition as "an active, dynamic process" looks like: it shows students working with such prior knowledge in order to respond to new situations and to create their own new models of writing. As documented here, both in the research literature and in the students' own words, students are likely to begin college with absent prior knowledge, particularly in terms of conceptions of writing and models of non-fiction texts. Once in college, students tap their prior knowledge in one of three ways. In cases like Eugene's, students work within an assemblage model, grafting pieces of new information—often key terms or process strategies—onto prior understandings of writing that serve as a foundation to which they frequently return. Other students, like Alice, work within a remix model, blending elements of both prior knowledge and new knowledge with personal values into a revised model of writing. And still other students, like Rick, use a writing setback, what we call a critical incident, >as a prompt to re-theorize writing and to practice composing in new ways.

The prototype presented here is a basic outline that we hope to continue developing; we also think it will be helpful for both teaching and research. Teachers, for example, may want to ask students about their absent prior knowledge and invite them to participate in creating a knowledge filling that absence. Put differently, if students understand that there is an absence of knowledge that they will need—a perception which many of them don't seem to share—they may be more motivated to take up a challenge that heretofore they have not understood. Likewise, explaining remix as a way of integrating old and new, personal and academic knowledge and experience into a revised conception and practice of composing for college may provide a mechanism to help students understand how writing development, from novice to expertise, works and, again, how they participate in such development. Last but not least, students might be alerted to writing situations that qualify as critical incidents; working with experiences like Rick's, they may begin to understand their own setbacks as opportunities. Indeed, we think that collecting experiences like Rick's (of course, with student permissions) to share and consider with students may be the most helpful exercise of all.

There is more research on student uptake of prior knowledge to conduct as well, as a quick review of Rick's experience suggests. The critical incident motivates Rick to re-think writing, as we saw, but it's also so that Rick is a science major and, as he told us, science not only thrives on error, but also progresses on the basis of error. Given his intellectual interests, Rick was especially receptive to a setback, especially—and it's worth noting this—when it occurred in his preferred field, science. For one thing, Rick identifies as a scientist, so he is motivated to do well. For another and more generally, failure in the context of science is critical to success. Without such a context, or even an understanding of the context as astute as Rick's, other students may look upon such a setback as a personal failure (and understandably so), which view can prompt not a re-thinking, but rather resistance. In other words, we need to explore what difference a student's major, and the intellectual tradition it represents, makes in a student's use of prior knowledge. Likewise, we need to explore other instantiations of the assemblage model of prior knowledge uptake as well as differentiations in the remix model. And we need to explore the relationship between these differentiations and efficacy: surely some are more efficacious than others. And, not least, we need to explore further what happens to those students, like Rick, who through critical incidents begin to take up residence as college composers.

## NOTES

1. In this article, we draw on two studies of transfer, both connected to a Teaching for Transfer composition curriculum for first-year students: Liane Robertson's The Significance of Course Content in the Transfer of Writing Knowledge from First-Year Composition to other Academic Writing Contexts and Kara Taczak's Connecting the Dots: Does Reflection Foster Transfer?

2. A more robust picture includes an additional dimension of prior knowledge: what we call a point of departure. We theorize that students make progress, or not, in part relative to their past performances as writers— as represented in external benchmarks like grades and test scores. See *Writing Across Contexts: Transfer, Composition, and Cultures of Writing*, forthcoming.

3. The travel metaphor in composition has been variously used and critiqued: for the former, see Gregory Clark; for the latter, see Nedra Reynolds. Regarding the use of such a metaphor in the transfer literature in college composition, it seems first to have been used by McCarthy in her reference to students in strange lands. Based on this usage and on our own studies, we theorize that what students bring with them to college, by way of prior knowledge, is a passport that functions as something of a guide. As important, when students use the guide to reflect back rather than to cast forward, it tends to replicate the past rather than to guide for the future, and in that sense, Reynolds's observations about many students replicating the old in the new are astute. See our *Writing Across Contexts: Transfer, Composition, and Cultures of Writing*, forthcoming.

4. According to *How People Learn*, prior knowledge can function in three ways, as we have seen. But when the prior knowledge is a misfit, it may be because the "correct" prior knowledge, or knowledge that is more related, isn't available, which leads us to conceptualize absent prior knowledge. For a similar argument in a very different context, materials science, see Krause et al.

5. Alice's interest in "being direct," of course, may be a more specific description of her voice, whose value she emphasized upon entering English 1102.

6. Ironically, the function of such tests according to testing advocates, is to help writers develop; here the FCAT seems to have mis-shaped rather than to have helped, as Alice laments.

7. Rick's sense of the influence of his reading on his conception of text, of course, is the point made above about students' reading practices.

8. This ability to read across patterns, discerning similarities and differences, that we see Rick engaging in, is a signature practice defining expertise, according to How People Learn.

## WORKS CITED

Applebee, Arthur, and Judith Langer. What's Happening in the Teaching of Writing? *English Journal* 98.5 (2009): 18-28. Print.

—-. A Snapshot of Writing Instruction in Middle Schools and High Schools. *English Journal* 100.6 (2011): 14–27. Print.

Baxter-Magolda, Marcia B. *Making Their Own Way: Narratives for Transforming Higher Education to Promote Self-Development.* Sterling, VA: Stylus, 2001. Print.

Beaufort, Anne. *College Writing and Beyond: A New Framework for University Writing Instruction.* Logan: Utah State UP, 2007. Print.

Bergmann, Linda S., and Janet S. Zepernick. Disciplinarity and Transference: Students' Perceptions of Learning to Write. *WPA: Writing Program Administration* 31.1/2 (2007): 124-49. Print.

Beyer, Catharine Hoffman, Andrew T. Fisher, and Gerald M. Gillmore. *Inside the Undergraduate Experience, the University of Washington's Study of Undergraduate Learning.* Bolton, MA: Anker Publishing, 2007. Print.

Bird, Barbara. Writing about Writing as the Heart of a Writing Studies Approach to FYC: Response to Douglas Downs and Elizabeth Wardle, 'Teaching about Writing/Righting Misconceptions' and to Libby Miles et al., 'Thinking Vertically'. *College Composition and Communication* 60.1 (2008): 165-71. Print.

Bransford, John D., James W. Pellegrino, and M. Suzanne Donovan, eds. *How People Learn: Brain, Mind, Experience, and School: Expanded Edition.* Washington, DC: National Academies P, 2000. Print.

Britton, James, et al. *The Development of Writing Abilities (11–18)*, London: MacMillan Education, 1975. Print.

Carter, Michael. The Idea of Expertise: An Exploration of Cognitive and Social Dimensions of Writing. *College Composition and Communication* 41.3 (1990): 265-86. Print.

Clark, Gregory. Writing as Travel, or Rhetoric on the Road. *College Composition and Communication* 49.1 (1998): 9-23. Print.

Detterman, Douglas K., and Robert J. Sternberg, eds. *Transfer on Trial: Intelligence, Cognition, and Instruction.* New Jersey: Ablex, 1993. Print.

Dew, Debra. Language Matters: Rhetoric and Writing I as Content Course. *WPA: Writing Program Administration* 26.3 (2003): 87–104. Print.

Downs, Douglas, and Elizabeth Wardle. Teaching about Writing, Righting Misconceptions: (Re)Envisioning 'First-Year Composition' as Introduction to Writing Studies. *College Composition and Communication* 58.4 (2007): 552-84. Print.

Fulkerson, Richard. Summary and Critique: Composition at the Turn of the Twenty-first Century. *College Composition and Communication* 56.4 (2005): 654-87. Print.

Gawande, Atul. *Complications: A Surgeon's Notes on an Imperfect Science.* New York: Holt/Picador, 2002. Print.

Jarratt, Susan, et al. Pedagogical Memory and the Transferability of Writing Knowledge: an Interview-Based Study of Juniors and Seniors at a Research University. *Writing Research Across Borders Conference.* University of California Santa Barbara. 22 Feb 2008. Presentation.

Krause, Steve, et al. The Role of Prior Knowledge on the Origin and Repair of Misconceptions in an Introductory Class on Materials Science and Engineering Materials Science. *Proceedings of the Research in Engineering Education Symposium 2009*, Palm Cove, QLD. Web.

Langer, Judith A., and Arthur N. Applebee. *How Writing Shapes Thinking: A Study of Teaching and Learning.* Urbana, IL: NCTE P, 1987. Print.

Lenhart, Amanda, et al. *Writing, Technology, and Teens.* Washington, D.C.: Pew Internet & American Life Project, April 2008. Web. 12 Jan 2012.

McCarthy, Lucille. A Stranger in Strange Lands: A College Student Writing across the Curriculum. *Research in the Teaching of English* 21.3 (1987): 233-65. Print.

Perkins, David N., and Gavriel Salomon. Transfer of Learning. *International Encyclopedia of Education.* 2nd ed. Oxford: Pergamon P, 1992. 2-13. Print.

Prather, Dirk C. Trial and Error versus Errorless Learning: Training, Transfer, and Stress. *The American Journal of Psychology* 84.3 (1971): 377-86. Print.

Reiff, Mary Jo, and Anis Bawarshi. Tracing Discursive Resources: How Students Use Prior Genre Knowledge to Negotiate New Writing Contexts in First-Year Composition. *Written Communication* 28.3 (2011): 312–37. Print.

Reynolds, Nedra. *Geographies of Writing: Inhabiting Places and Encountering Difference.* Southern Illinois University Press, 2004. Print.

Robertson, Liane. The Significance of Course Content in the Transfer of Writing Knowledge from First-Year Composition to other Academic Writing Contexts. Diss. Florida State University, 2011. Print.

Robinson, Tracy Ann, and Vicki Tolar Burton. The Writer's Personal Profile: Student Self Assessment and Goal Setting at Start of Term. *Across the Disciplines* 6 (Dec 2009). Web. 12 Jan 2012.

Russell, David R. Rethinking Genre and Society: An Activity Theory Analysis. *Written Communication* 14.4 (1997): 504-54. Print.

Russell, David R., and Arturo Yañez. 'Big Picture People Rarely Become Historians': Genre Systems and the Contradictions of General Education. *Writing Selves/Writing Societies: Research From Activity Perspectives.* Ed. Charles Bazerman and David R. Russell. Fort Collins, CO: WAC Clearinghouse and Mind, Culture and Activity, 2002. Web. 12 Jan 2012.

Scherff, Lisa, and Carolyn Piazza. The More Things Change, the More They Stay the Same: A Survey of High School Students' Writing Experiences. *Research in the Teaching of English* 39.3 (2005): 271-304. Print.

Slomp, David H., and M. Elizabeth Sargent. Responses to Responses: Douglas Downs and Elizabeth Wardle's 'Teaching about Writing, Righting Misconceptions.' *College Composition and Communication* 60.3 (2009): 595-96. Print.

Sommers, Nancy, and Laura Saltz. The Novice as Expert: Writing the Freshman Year. *College Composition and Communication* 56.1 (2004): 124-49. Print.

Taczak, Kara. Connecting the Dots: Does Reflection Foster Transfer? Diss. Florida State University, 2011. Print.

Thorndike, E. L., and R. S. Woodworth. The Influence of Improvement in One Mental Function upon the Efficiency of Other Functions. *Psychological Review* 8 (1901): 247–61. Print.

Vander Lei, Elizabeth, and Bonnie LenoreKyburz, eds. *Negotiating Religious Faith in the Composition Classroom.* Portsmouth: Boynton/Cook, 2005. Print.

Wardle, Elizabeth. Understanding 'Transfer' from FYC: Preliminary Results of a Longitudinal Study. *WPA: Writing Program Administration* 31.1–2 (2007), 65–85. Print.

Wikipedia contributors. William Shakespeare. *Wikipedia, The Free Encyclopedia.* 4 Jan. 2012. Web. 12 Jan. 2012.

Yancey, Kathleen Blake, Ed. *Delivering College Composition: The Fifth Canon.* Portsmouth: Boynton/Cook, 2006. Print.

—-. Re-designing Graduate Education in Composition and Rhetoric: The Use of Remix as Concept, Material, and Method. *Computers and Composition* 26.1 (2009): 4-12. Print.

—-, Robertson, Liane, and Taczak, Kara. *Writing Across Contexts: Transfer, Composition, and Cultures of Writing.* Forthcoming.

# COMPOSITION STUDIES

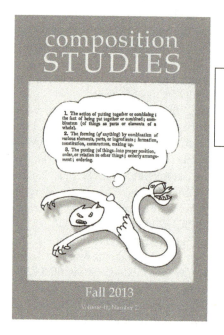

*Composition Studies* is on the Web at http://www.compositionstudies.uwinnipeg.ca

In publication since March 1972, *Composition Studies* holds the distinction of being the oldest independent journal in its field. Consistent with its beginnings as a forum for discussing teaching experiences, *Composition Studies* continues to publish scholarship about teaching writing and has expanded to include a wide range of historical, theoretical, and exploratory studies related to writing, pedagogy, administration, literacy, and emerging areas of interest. The journal's interest in growing with the field is perhaps best illustrated by our call for work that doesn't fit neatly elsewhere.

## Forging Rhetorical Subjects: Problem Based Learning in the Writing Classroom

An excellent representation of the journal's initial pedagogical mission, this piece offers an exploration of the relationship between pedagogy and rhetorical subjecthood. More specifically, the authors detail a reflective approach to problem-based learning intent on exploiting the gap between "abstract theorizing" and "nuts-and-bolts instructional detailing" (11). In this sense, Rosinksi and Peeples's argument embodies the liminal status of the journal itself while also making an important contribution to ongoing conversations about pedagogical effects.

# 4 Forging Rhetorical Subjects: Problem Based Learning in the Writing Classroom

*Paula Rosinski and Tim Peeples*

*Abstract: Following a brief introduction to problem-based learning (PBL) as one type of highly-engaged pedagogy, this article examines how PBL activities in a first-year writing class and an upper-level professional writing and rhetoric class led students to develop rhetorical subjectivities. We conclude that highly engaged pedagogies, like PBL, that purposively situate students/teacher within indetern1inate spaces requiring active reflection and meta-cognition are more likely to forge successful writers, writers who have nlore experience making a wide range of rhetorical choices, have a better sense of writing as contextualized praxis, and know to expect and value the collaborative nature of writing.*

Two students, sitting side-by-side but wearing headphones and probably listening to music, write different sections of the same proposal and drop finished pieces into Google Docs. A third student sits on the ground with his laptop, organizing and reorganizing documents into different piles; he jumps up to retrieve a document from the printer but hesitates when deciding to which pile it belongs. The remaining students work in groups of two, three, or four: they conduct online research, share results and search terms, swap PDF files, rework a Web site's layout and navigation, and design a graph to support an argument. One group of students crowds around the flat screen at their table, pointing and having a slightly contentious debate about which section of video should be edited out and why. With this wide range of writing activities taking place, it is no surprise that the noise level vacillates widely. But stude11ts are engaged enough in their own work that they don't seem bothered by the outbursts of frustration or peals of laughter that erupt from different groups from time to time.

Today, it is commonplace to walk into writing classrooms in colleges and universities across the country and find scenes like the one described above. Students and teachers are regularly found during class time ellgaged with writing, writing technologies, and one another, and within the classroom there is a buzz of activity. If the primary aim of a writing class, at any level, is to develop effective writers, is it the development of successful writers that we are observing when we walk into the buzzing classrooms described above? Hands-on activity by itself certainly does not lead to the development of successful writers. Still, for a variety of reasons, educators in Rhetoric and Composition, as well as a growing number in higher education in general, believe strongly that learning and development are ellhanced significantly through active engagement.

Engaged learning pedagogies, which come into writing classrooms in forms like service learning, project-based learning, and client projects, share features that distinguish them from other pedagogies, like lecture and discussion, and even active pedagogies like workshopping and critique, common in the fine arts. A major distinguishing factor is the way assignments in engaged learning classrooms are designed to situate students within complex, authentic contexts and often require sustained amounts of time. They also commonly require high levels of collaboration, occasionally with others outside of the classroom (see Kuh).

Problem-based learning (PBL) offers another highly engaged pedagogical option for our writing classes. PBL shares with other engaged pedagogies the features listed above, but it distinguishes itself by initiating learning with the introduction of an ill-structured problem around which all learning centers. Service-, project-, and client-based pedagogies can initiate learning and also be designed as ill-structured problems, thus reflecting the distinguishing features of PBL, but PBL always carries these features, making it a distinctly engaged pedagogy.

The ill-structured problem is a hallmark of and key to PBL (see Rhem; Savery). To be ill-structured does not mean poorly, casually, or sloppily designed by an instructor. Ill-structured problems are messy, real-world problems; they are dynamic, without simple, fixed, formulaic, or even "right" solutions; they require a cycle of inquiry, information gathering, and reflection that is likely iterative. PBL revolves around these carefully designed but ill-structured problems. Another hallmark of PBL is the way it initiates learning. One generally thinks of teaching and learning as a process initiated with the introduction of new content, skills, methods, et cetera. After this initial instruction, students are given instruction and time to master the new material that has been introduced. Finally, their mastery is put to the test in one fashion or another before moving on to new sets of content, skills, methods, et cetera. For instance, in most case-based pedagogies, students are introduced to new content, such as the genre of the bad newsletter in business writing, and then they are put to practicing what they have learned by writing a bad newsletter specific to a business world case. In contrast, PBL learning is initiated with the introduction of an ill-structured problem. The new content, skills, methods, et cetera are gathered and gellerated through the process of investigating and addressing the problem, rather than being supplied, studied, and/ or practiced prior to engagement with the problem (see Amador, Miles, and Peters; Duch, Groh, and Allen). In PBL-based medical education, for instance, instruction in new areas might begin with visits to rooms with real patients. The patient in the room, along with all of his or her health details, is the ill-structured problem that initiates learning. What students learn is initiated by and contextualized within this problem.[1]

We chose to examine PBL in the writing classroom for a variety of reasons, but prinlary among them was to improve upon the kinds of engagedleaming already occurring at our institution[2] and in our own classrooms, from first-year composition to advanced courses in Rhetoric and Writing Studies (RWS).[3] While our experiences with PBL do not lead us to herald it as the best or even a better way to teach writing, experimenting with PBL in our actual classrooms helped make obvious, again, the impact pedagogies have on constructing students/ writers- rhetorical subjects- and compelled us to reflect more critically on the student-writer subjectivities being constructed in our classrooms. Our experience leads us to the conclusion that highly engaged pedagogies, like PBL, that purposively situate students/ teachers within open-ended, indeterminate, messy problem spaces requiring active reflection and metacognition are more likely to forge successful writers, or writers who (a) have more experience making a wide range of situated rhetorical choices, (b) have a better sense of writing as contextualized praxis that is mutually constitutive of writers, readers, texts, and contexts, and ( c) know to expect, understand, and value the collaborative, messy nature of non-routine writing.

In what follows, we reflect on our process of developing and teaching PBL assignments for two writing courses: one, a required first-year composition course, and the other, an introductory course in Professional Writing and Rhetoric, required of both majors and minors. Through this assignment-based reflection, we share sample PBL assignments designed specifically for writing instruction, which is in and of itself of some value, for though there is much available in terms of literature and sample assignments for PBL, there is very little focused on writing instruction (see Pennell and Miles). However, our focus, here, is not on applying PBL to writing instruction and sharing PBL writing assignment samples, per se. Our focus is on calling attention to two central questions always involved in the teaching/learning of writing but routinely left in the shadows of either more abstract theorizing or more nuts-and-bolts instructional detailing. Through our reflective process, we call attention to the following two questions:

- "What defines a successful writer?" and
- "How can we best develop/ teach such writers?"

In calling attention to these questions within pedagogy and contextualized in our own pedagogical experiences, we hope to reinvigorate explicit disciplinary, as well as local, conversations about the role our pedagogical practices- PBL in this case-play in forming writers/ people/agents and the significant impact pedagogy has on the formation of rhetorical subjects.

## THE SUBJECT OF WRITING

In *Fragments of Rationality*, Lester Faigley challenges compositionists to consider how sn1dent-writers/ rhetorical subjects are called into being through pedagogy, among other social/ material/cultural practices. The primary focus of argument for Faigley is the distinction and historical transition between the modern construct of the writer/ rhetorical subject as the rational, autonomous individual and the postmodern construction of the fragmented writer/rhetorical subject. One iteration of this difference highlighted by Faigley is the contrast between the pedagogies advocated by Peter Elbow, on the one hand, and Kenneth Bruffee, on the other. Elbow's emphasis on helping students find their authentic voices and helping them learn ways to control language to best express those voices led Bruffee to attack, as Faigley depicts it, Elbow's pedagogy as "encouraging 'rampant individualism'" (226), a hallmark of the modernist construction of the writer/rhetorical subject as a stable, unified self. Bruffee's collaborative pedagogy, Faigley goes on to argue, emphasized "the communal nature of discourse and a view of knowledge as socially negotiated," leading to the construction of writers/rhetorical subjects who understand and practice writing (and themselves, we would add) as part of "ongoing conversations" beyond any stable, unified self (226).

Faigley's challenge to us, though, is more than historical and academic. It leads us to consider the following related questions: Are we aware of the kinds of subjectivities we're inviting students to occupy through our pedagogies? Are they the kinds of subjectivities we want or we should want students to occupy? Are they the kinds of subjectivities that will serve students well in their other college courses, as they engage in casual conversations with peers, as they enter the workplace and become practicing professionals, as they take on adult and domestic responsibilities? Are they the kinds of subjectivities that will help students become responsible, active, ethical citizens? These questions continue to be overlooked in a great deal of pedagogical scholarship, perhaps because teachers and scholars find it unsettling to consider this far-reaching implication of their classroom practice (see Couture; Russell, "Activity Theory"). While Faigley's challenge may have gone largely unheeded on a pedagogical level, other scholarship has e plored, on a theoretical level, how certain pedagogies do indeed invite students to participate in learning and meaning-making in certain ways, and even affect momentarily the way students interact with the world and with others (see Ryan).

## Engaged Pedagogies and (Re)Defining the Successful Writer

If compositionists and academics in the sister fields that make up the broader RWS community are to examine more closely and actively these questions of pedagogical impact on the formation of rhetorical subjects- if we are to reinvigorate explicit disciplinary and local conversations about the significant impact pedagogy has on the formation of rhetorical subjectsengaged learning is one broad pedagogical category RWS should likely investigate. Having grown up in a largely post-Freirian era, Composition Studies has long claimed high ground in discussions about engaged learning. Learning in composition, as well as most technical and profe sional writing classes, is and has been highly engaged. Though this term has shifted in meaning, from simply active learning (e.g., hands on) to something more complex, those of us teaching writing have long been ahead of the curve when it comes to engaged pedagogies. But taking the high ground can also mean assuming a level of invisibility, at least in the explicit conversations about engaged learning. A quick scan of the scholarship being done in this venue highlights disciplines such as psychology and education, particularly for the empirical and theoretical, as well as the sciences, where the focus is more on reports on the implementation and results of engaged pedagogies. Arguably the leader in engaged learning, at least in higher education, is the Indiana University Center for Postsecondary Research (CPR) in the School of Education, out of which come the National Survey of Student Engagement (NSSE), the Faculty Survey of Student Engagement (FSSE), Law School Survey of Student Engagement (LSSSE), and the NSSE Institute for Effective Educational Practice. Only recently (see Consortium for the Study of Writing in College, started 2007-08) have those directly related to RWS entered discussions with comparably strong, expert voices about engaged learning.

When the two of us began incorporating PBL, we began to better understand and articulate more clearly for ourselves reasons we continued to be drawn to other engaged pedagogies, like service-, project-, and client-based assignments. We had each continued to be drawn to these pedagogies in spite of the frustrations they often bring, the additional work they often require of teachers, and the fairly typical resistance teachers receive from students when such pedagogies require them to assume new (highly engaged) ways of being in school: in other words, new subjectivities. PBL was foreign enough to Writing Studies that struggling to think through its value and how to best utilize it helped us begin to rearticulate why we continued to be drawn to the messiness, indeterminacy, dynamism, and sometimes outright frustration of highly engaged pedagogies, in general, such as client-based assignments. The frustrations of project-, problem-, and client-based pedagogies have, in the end, at least, always felt worth it because we saw that our students who were engaged in such learning experiences developed ways of being that seemed a closer fit to our sense of what successful writers are like. These sorts of assignments are so authentic (often almost too real-worldly for classroom comfort) that students daily wrestle with writing as a socially contextualized, dynamic, contested, ideological, meaning-making, iterative, messy process. Within such assignments, *techne*, heuristics, strategies, and procedural knowledge are not simply bits of knowledge learned and applied transactionally. Each of these takes on a life within a specific context, the way experienced writers know they do in actual writing practice. Heuristics, theories, process strategies, et cetera become heuristic themselves, and students find themselves theorizing in context. Students are involved in more sophisticated (and dare we say, authentic) rhetorical praxis. Patricia A. Sullivan and James E. Porter define praxis as "a kind of thinking that does not start with theoretical knowledge or abstract models, which are then applied to situations, but that begins with immersion in local situations, and then uses epistemic theory as heuristic rather than as explanatory or determining" (26). As outlined earlier, all highly engaged writing pedagogies immerse students in complex rhetorical situations that often extend over more than a brief time and often require collaboration, and so they create pedagogical contexts in which students can experience, practice, and learn the *praxical* skills of writers and writing that Sullivan and Porter define. What we experienced and learned through our work with PBL, though, is that PBEs focus on *initiating* instruction and then having all learning arise out of a well crafted, ill-structured problem can heighten the immersive element of engaged pedagogies, which subsequently helps to create learning contexts in which student writers/rhetorical subjects can develop *praxical* subjectivities. *Praxical* writing subjects have developed a sense of themselves as writers who are comfortable with and confident in their ability to immerse themselves in local situations and then use epistemic theory-for example, decontextualized strategies and processes-as a heuristic for determining how to proceed and make wise writerly decisions. This is what we conceive of as a successful writer, it is what we have seen develop through and as a result of highly engaged pedagogies, and it is what we became aware of even more clearly through our implementation of PBL.

But why? What is distinct about what we are referring to as these *highly* engaged pedagogies, including PBL, that more dramatically forges these *praxical* writing subjects? We believe it stems from a change in the meaning and valuing of "engagement."

The meaning of engaged learning shifts when one moves from, say, (a) small group work aimed at ends achieved through discrete processes culminating in well-defined products to (b) immersion in messy writing problems. In the first instance-small group work-engagement is employed as a means for more effectively transferring writerly knowledge. For instance, rather than speak about and then have students individually work on revising, the small peer-group revision workshop functions as a more effective means for transferring that writerly knowledge of revising. The engagement linked to small peer-group interaction is a means to an end: more effective (e.g., experiential) transfer of learning. In the second instance- immersion in messy writing problems-engagement is no longer employed as a means for enhancing the transaction of writerly knowledge. Instead, engagement has become part of *the knowledge* being learned, as well as a context within which writers learn. Being engaged is understood and practiced as an essential part of "being a writer." The student-writer/rhetorical subject shifts from being a receiver of the transfer of knowledge through engaged/ experiential means of teaching-learning (e.g., the small peer-group revision workshop) to being an active agent/writer immersed in/ engaged with messy writing problems. From within this new sense of engagement, what is consiered the successful writer also shifts.

One approach to defining writing success might stem from a general skills model of writing expertise (see Peeples and Hart-Davidson for discussion of the three models of writing expertise referenced here and adopted from Kaufer and Young). In this model, writing expertise is defined by the knowledge and control of general strategies (e.g., inaking diagrams, analogies, and means-ends analyses) that are deemed useful in and transferable to any context; the successful writer is one who can demonstrate having and effectively applying such knowledge. Another approach to defining success might stem from a contextualist model of writing expertise. In this second model, writing expertise is defined by the knowledge and control of context-/ culture-specific norms; the successful writer is one who has accurately read/interpreted local norms and is able to maneuver effectively within those norms through the application of contextual knowledge. In both of these models, successful writing is relatively predictive and dependent on the application of what one has come to know in a transactional way.

Engaged pedagogies qua active learning are valuable in both of these models because they increase motivation and the ability to transfer knowledge learned in one case, for instance, to another. In one of these two models of expertise, the contextualist model, engagement takes on an additional value, beyond enhanced motivation and practice in transfer: the creation of authentic scenarios, situations, and contexts gives students experience reading/interpreting local norms and adapting/adjusting to them. It is presumed that this experience will help students more effectively transfer such knowledge to new contexts.

A third approach to defining success might stem from an interactionist model of writing expertise. In this third model, writing expertise is defined by the sort of *praxical* wisdom and behavior earlier described; the successful writer "relies on a complex ... interaction between context knowledge and general strategies that are in principle articulable and teachable" (Kaufer and Young qtd. in Peeples and Hart-Davidson 101). In this third model, successful writing is messy and less predictive. Like the general skills and contextualist models, the interactionist model values hands-on, active engage1nent as a means for motivation and as a crucial part of learning transfer. In addition, though, the interactionist model values hands-on, active engagement in and of itself, as something that, in and of itself, is instructive. *Through engagement*, students learn *that* writing is messy, open-ended, indeterminate, and iterative; they learn *how* to write within such contexts; and they learn to *value* the process of working through/with this messiness.

When engagement carries these new values, the goals and objectives of engagement change significantly. From the perspective of the first two models, the context for engagement is meant to be a vehicle for learning, and as such, the context should be relatively transparent. When the context itself is problematical, it should be for clearly defined instructive purposes- the problematical should be, in other words, under the control of the teacher. From the perspective of an interactionist model of writerly success, however, the problems posed by contexts- for example, the availability of resources, collaborative differences, shifting and complex matrices of power, shifting timelines, changing goals, et cetera- are themselves uncontrollable, essential, and essentially instructive characteristics of writing. From this perspective, the frustrations teachers and students have with highly engaged pedagogies, such as project- and client-based assignments, mean something very different. Teachers employing and reflecting on these pedagogies from a generalist or contextualist model perceive the problems of context as failures either of themselves, their students, or the contexts. From an interactionist perspective of writing instruction and writerly success, experiences with unpredictable, messy, and dynamic contexts are instructive, not failures.

It may or may not be an accident that many in writing have embraced highly engaged pedagogies. If an accident, we believe it is an accident that might be leading (though accidentally and, thus, not as effectively as might be the case) to the development of a different kind of student-writer/rhetorical subject, one who reflects a more *praxical*, interactionist model, for these student-writers/rhetorical subjects have experienced the messiness that is the nature of most writing. If it is not an accident, then we believe we can more effectively and powerfully develop this *praxical*, interactionist model of expertise by consciously focusing on the development of our highly engaged pedagogical practices, with attention to the changing values of engagement and the writerly experiences and qualities developed as a result.

## THE FORGING OF RHETORICAL SUBJECTS: REFLECTING ON AND THROUGH PBL ASSIGNMENTS

### First-Year Composition, Digital Literacies, and PBL

We designed a set of three digital literacy PBL activities-"Critiquing Search Engines," "Understanding & Using Databases," and "Documenting Digital Sources" (see Appendix for actual assignments)- for College Writing, our university's first-year composition course. Digital literacies were our focus for a variety of reasons, but first and foremost we wanted students to learn that critically engaging online research and documenting online sources is a more sophisticated, rhetorically contextualized, and messy process than a general skills model, or even a contextualist model, of writing sometimes suggests. We assumed that students often put little deliberate thought into selecting search engines and databases, since we repeatedly observed them turning to the same search engines and databases in different research situations, usually because they were the ones students learned about in high school and with which they felt most comfortable, regardless of whether or not they were appropriate or even adequate sources of information for their current research purposes. We also observed that students often failed to appreciate the disciplinary values that are conveyed through documentation standards and, instead, viewed writing citations as a kind of formulaic drudgery. Since this was our first foray into PBL, we chose to design several shorter low-stakes assignments, in the hopes that they would encourage students to embrace the activities without fear of how such an experimental pedagogy might impact their grades or standing in the course (see Anson). The low-stakes nature of these shorter PBL activities also made us, as instructors, more comfortable using this pedagogy for the first time as well.

It is easy enough to provide students with a list of numbered directions for conducting a simple search engine or database search, but in the "Critiquing Search Engines" and "Understanding & Using Databases" digital literacy activities, vve wanted students to experience that how a search engine or database worked- for example, how it was designed and programmed, the search options that were or were not available, the types of sources it catalogued, the kinds of returns that were possible-could affect profoundly the activity of research and the quality of research identified. We also wanted students to learn that the practice of using research technologies is itself part of the meaning-making process, and that search engines and databases are not just mere tools for returning supposedly objective research results. We expected that immersing students in an indeterminate, messy, and openended research context could help them think about research engines and databases as socially and culturally constructed artifacts with biases and limitations, with intended primary and secondary audiences. And since this first-year writing course is charged with preparing students for later writing courses as well as real-world writing situations, we also wanted to disrupt what students thought should happen in writing classrooms and real writing situations by putting them in indeterminate and complex writing and research spaces. These two activities asked students to solve the problem of determilling how exactly different search engines and databases functioned, and to develop strategies for deciding which ones to use for different research situations they were actually facing in their other courses (see Appendix for actual assignments).

We designed the third PBL digital literacy activity, "Documenting Digital Sources," because we wanted students to understand that there is a method behind what often seems like the madness of documentation, that this method reflects academic values and disciplinary

priorities, and that such an understanding can assist one in documenting ever-evolving online sources. Janice R. Walker and Todd Taylor's
*The Columbia Guide to Online Style 2/e* examines what they call "the
logic of citation" and notes five principles of citation style: access, intellectual property, economy, standardization, and transparency (31-36).
While Walker and Taylor's guide goes a long way to demystifying the
process of writing documelltation and understanding its underlying
logic, we sought a more engaged way of teaching students about documentation so that they could approach it as a heuristic, not as a series
of rules to follow. This last digital literacy activity asked students to
solve the problem of identifying the values embodied in the different
documentation features and explaining these values to an audience of
high school students.

What sets each of these three PBL digital literacy activities apart
from other kinds of engaged pedagogies is that they each initiated
instruction with real, and in these cases, deceptively simple, problems-
for example, how do different research engines and databases function? How do you decide which search engine or database to use for
different research situations? What do the different components of an
online citation mean? Then, all learning emerged out of student attempts to answer these questions. Initiating and sustaining all learning through real problems increased student immersion, which in turn
gave students opportunities to experience and practice the praxical
skills of writers and writing. Instead of being given abstract or theoretical knowledge about research engines, databases, and documenting
online sources, students were immersed il1 local, meaningful situations and then had to use epistemic theory- that is, the knowledge they
were creating themselves- as a heuristic for figuring out real answers
to real problems.

Given that a hallmark feature of PBL is the open-endedness of
the learning environment, it was interesting, but not surprising, to
hear our students express disbelief that they could learn anything
from these experiences. They expressed frustration at being given
such open-ended assignments without clearly defined expectations for
how they should respond to them and what exactly they should learn.
With all three activities, students began working silently, either individually or in groups, but as they became more involved with the
problems, the classrooms became animated with collaborative chatter.
Students started to express surprise at the ways they tended to take

certain things for granted or as givens, for example, when they realized that not all search engines returned the same results when using the same search terms, or that using different Boolean functions (or, for that matter, when they learned what a "Boolean" function actually is) returned different results; when they figured out that it was possible to determine what kinds of resources different databases collected and that there were ways to return only certain types of sources (i.e., full-text only, PDF only); or when the previously puzzling way to write a bibliographic citation finally began to make sense when they considered that the various features reflected a discourse community's concerns or values.

In their own ways, each of these digital literacy activities showed students that real engagement- the process of working in indeterminate contexts to solve real problems- is instructive *itself.* We used the "Critiquing Search Engines" and "Understanding Databases" in the middle of the term in our first-year writing classrooms, after the sttldents had completed several shorter writing assignments but before they began longer; research-based projects. These two activities, in particular, highlighted the messy and iterative process of research and writing, because they taught students that neither search engines nor databases are objective tools and that writers need to consider their respective advantages and disadvantages on a technical as well as rhetorical level in each different research situation. What students (and in particular, at our institution, first-year students) often think should happen in a college classroom, and what they often think writers are and do, was also disrupted: instead of sitting quietly in their seats listening to a lecture and then being given explicit instructions about what kind of writing to produce in response to the assignment, students were permitted to, quite simply, decide how they were going to proceed. They were permitted, to their surprise, to physically move about inside or outside of the classroom, to ask each other questions and collaborate, or to e-mail friends or family members they thought could assist them in their inquiry, and to actually begin crafting their responses to the problem in genres of their own choosing (instead of being told, in an assignment handout, in what genre they should respond, usually outside of class time).

Their immersion and engagement in a real writing situation itself helped the students develop sophisticated responses to the problems they were tasked with solving. So, for example, research became for the students not a clearly delineated activity which points to the most obvious research engine or database to use, but rather an imprecise activity which requires writers to develop strategies for selecting the most appropriate research source for any given disciplinary situation, and then to revise iteratively these strategies on the spot as one learns more information either about the database, research engine, or one's research topic. Students first tried to write neat, numbered lists about how to decide which search engine to use or how to conduct effective database research, or they tried to make a list explaining which search engine or database to use in different situations. But as they themselves engaged in the research necessary to construct these lists, the impossibility of composing a series of steps to follow or writing an objective list that would cover all rhetorical situations became apparent. Students then often moved on to create more sophisticated decision-trees, but these also became too complex. Finally, most students decided upon writing responses that were rich in detail about the rhetorical, biased, and complex qualities of search engines and databases, while also emphasizing that their readers would have to make wise decisions based upon their own rhetorical and disciplinary reasons for conducting research. Supported by activity theory's claim that human actions cannot be understood outside of the wider human activity of which it is a part, the very pedagogy underlying these activities required students to take the wider human activity into account (real, student-identified research scenarios, particular research questions grounded in particular disciplines) in order to make informed research and writing decisions (see Dias et al.). So, for example, students composed humorous letters to first-year writing students, warning them not to thoughtlessly rely upon the same search engine for all occasions and encouraging them to research search engines themselves, while considering their own research purposes, before selecting a search engine to use.

We used the "Documenting Digital Sources" activity closer to the end of the term, as students were completing their long-term research project. This activity also immersed students in messy and indeterminate writing spaces and prevented them from simply regurgitating the documentation styles for online sources. Instead of being given abstract knowledge about how to document online sources, they had to use epistemic theory- that is, the knowledge they were creating themselves- as a heuristic for figuring out how to write these entries. So when confronted with the open-ended request to write an explanation

to a less-experienced audience of high school students about the significance of a bibliographic citation's components, our students were
often, at first, at a complete loss about how to proceed. This activity
moved them from this place of certainty (all I have to do is mimic this
set format, or fill in the empty spaces at the Landmark's online citation
generator) to a place of uncertainty (what is the significance of these
various components? why are they in this particular order? what would
high school students already know about online documentation? what
do I take for granted that high school students might not know?). We
viewed their hesitation as a sign of a growing understanding that documenting online sources is not an isolated skill (as the filling-in-the-
blank model implies), but part of a wider human activity (in this case,
the activity of engaging in responsible academic discourse) that is context or disciplinary bound.

Our students first responded to this activity much like they did to
the two earlier digital literacy activities: they tried to compose neat,
orderly lists or explanations that would tell the high school students
exactly how to compose a bibliographic citation for a digital source.
But the students' efforts to write one comprehensive citation description were quickly thwarted as they were confronted with the existence
of such a wide range of digital sources, with the lack of page numbers
or inconsistent numbering practices, with unclear author attributions,
and a plethora of other complications that arise when trying to attri-
bute author, publisher, dates, Web addresses, and even titles to digital
sources. Students ended up responding in ways similar to how they
responded to the previous two activities: by writing letters, or memos,
or a series of short Web pages to their audience of high school students,
imploring them to think about digital citations not as a series of blanks
that can be filled in mindlessly, but as one of the ways we join, participate, and extend academic discussions responsibly. For the remainder
of the term, when students worked on their bibliographies, we often
heard comments about how they were making decisions and choices-
about which information to include, in what order, et cetera- based
upon what the particular disciplinary community expected, cared
about, and which information was necessary so that readers could locate the same exact resource.

This PBL activity also seemed to encourage metacognitive awareness in students because the process of articulating explicitly for a real
audience why various components of an entry are significant to the

academic community highlights that documenting digital sources serves a very specific purpose in academic writing. For instance, documenting digital sources increases the author's ethos and shows that the various entries are not random, but rather indicate what academic communities value in digital sources. Such metacognitive awareness also helps students identify the similarities and differences between academic, real world, and workplace writing as well (see Russell, "Rethinking Genre and Society").

## Entering the Field of Professional Writing through PBL

At the same time we were exploring PBL in the first-year writing classroom, we were exploring how it might fit into and enhance some of our advanced major/minor courses in Professional Writing and Rhetoric. We designed a set of four PBL assignments-" Defining the Field," "Adding to the Conversation about Organizational Context," "Embodying Rhetoric as an Ethical Act," and "Making Space for Good Work"-for our introductory course to the major/minor. Each of the other courses within the major/ minor already included some form of highly engaged pedagogy, such as client- or service-learning-based assignments. The introductory course, unlike most in professional writing, functioned as an introduction to histories, theories, and issues that defined the field, so it did not lend itself as readily to highly engaged pedagogies beyond a case study here and there. Unlike the low-stakes digital literacy activities we designed for our firstyear writing course, we took it as a challenge to meet the majority of our learning objectives for this introductory professional writing and rhetoric course through PBL. Aside from a midterm and final exam, we constructed the entire course around PBL assignments. We focus, here, on the first two assignments, "Defining the Field" and "Adding to the Conversation about Organizational Context."

At the undergraduate level, in general, but particularly within an introductory course, students do not conceive of themselves as participating in defining the field to which they are just then being introduced, nor do they conceive of themselves as being able to contribute in any meaningful way to the conversations that make up the field. Students generally assume, at this level, that they will be fed the content, that all will be defined for them, and that their role is to receive definitive knowledge from another. Two of the objectives of our major/ minor are that students will (a) develop their own clear definition of the field and themselves as writing and rhetoric experts within it and (b) understand their role and the role of writing and rhetoric in the shaping of the worlds in which they participate. "Defining the Field" and "Adding to the Conversation about Organizational Context" embraced those learning objectives, but quite differently through PBL than they had been addressed in prior offerings of the course. Just as it would be easy enough to supply students with clear instructions for conducting a variety of online searches, or generating accurate and appropriate citations, it is relatively easy to present students with a range of information about and within the field of Professional Writing and Rhetoric and then engage them in syntheses of the field and arguments within the field. These PBL professional writing and rhetoric assignments posed deceptively simple problems to students- "How would you define Professional Writing and Rhetoric to a group of novices?" and "What is organizational context and how does it affect the practice of Professional Writing and Rhetoric?" They then engaged students in largely self-directed problem solving that regularly included identifying, reading, and synthesizing disciplinary scholarship and, finally, drawing their own conclusions and crafting their own responses. Student learning was initiated by open-ended questions, and all learning emerged out of the students' own efforts to answer these questions.

As one might imagine, student reaction to the "Defining the Field" assignment after only one week of class was just short of either active rebellion or total paralysis (see Appendix for actual assignment). After initial vocal and kinetic resistance- for example, "You don't really mean you expect us to define the field before you've taught us anything?," "You've got to be kidding?," and looks of disgust exchanged across tables accompanied by much fidgeting- some students started asking productive, problem-solving-oriented questions: "Can we use the class text books?," "Can we ask you questions?," "Can we interview other professors and students?," and "Can we use online sources?" Somewhat surprisingly, the start of such productive questioning and writerly activity actually preceded any individual student's feelings of resolution that "Yes, he really isn't kidding" and certainly preceded any communal sense of positive resolve and proactivity. It was students' *engagement in* problem solving- in writing, in assuming the role of the active rhetorical subject- that led to positive resolve rather than vice versa. By the end of the initial class period in which the assignment was introduced, the majority of students were so engaged, and positively so, they had already surpassed the comfort level with the activity of addressing such a question- "How do you define Professional Writing and Rhetoric?"- that previous students struggled to achieve after two weeks of other teaching-learning activities. We highlight, though, that it was their comfort with *the activity of addressing* such a question that reached higher levels more quickly; they were still very much struggling over the content of their arguments, as should have been the case. On day one, the students addressing this PBL assignment were already deeply iinmersed in the authentic engagement of writing- of being active rhetorical subjects.

Though the students in this course were less surprised to be confronted by another problem-based assignment ilnmediately following the completion of the first, the open-ended, ill-structured problem nature of their second assignment ("Adding to the Conversation about Organizational Context") created similar immediate and ongoing problem-solving challenges for them. In other words, feelings of resistance and disbelief were at the very least less vocal and extreme, but the socio-cognitive challenges- the writing and rhetorical challenges- were equally dramatic. We saw this, in part, as a sign of good learning very early in the course. Writers are constantly faced with new rhetorical challenges, and the expert writer not only expects that but has learned how to work through- that is, problem solve- those challenges effectively. At the very least, our students were already learning how to ad just/manage their affective response to novel rhetorical situations-that is, their PBL assignments. More promisingly, we saw them already developing, or developing-in-action, inventional and collaborative strategies and process knowledge for conducting the work writers routinely face. For example, one group of students developed inventional strategies for how to identify and keep track of resources that should be included in the project; another pair of students began designing a system, involving e-mail, Google Docs, and a free wiki, as a way to share and revise their peers' writing; several other students began generating a list of potential audiences for their organizational context project, taking complex notes on why each potential audience would be interested in such a project and how these different interests meant that the different audiences would expect different kinds of information, different ways of presenting the information, and even different navigational schemes for their project's interface.

The second PBL assignment in this class posed a new challenge: largescale collaboration. In addition to learning about organizational context in order to address the "content problem" of the assignment, the students were experiencing the impact of organizational context building and rebuilding from the start of the project. As Linda Driskill explains, "Context can help explain what a document means, what ideas it contains, why the writer would try to express his or her ideas in a particular way, and why readers who occupy particular roles in different parts of an organization would be likely to respond to a document in particular ways" (108). In other words, writing is not successful simply because it is grammatically or structurally correct, it is successful when its writers have taken into account the organizational context and responded accordingly, for example, by defining the situation, identifying the key individuals and participants and their sometimes conflicting motivations, understanding the external influential parties, and acknowledging that there are multiple direct and indirect audiences for a given text. The students' location within the organizational context of our introductory professional writing and rhetoric classroom became a point of reflective instruction throughout and, particularly, after the completion of the assignment.

In their writing about organizational context and its relationship to Professional Writing and Rhetoric, students often reflected on their own immediate organizational/contextual experience. They would, for instance, comment on the strengths and weaknesses of their own collaborative practices with this particular assignment, as well as other class assignments, and they would begin adopting and adapting language they were learning as they studied organizational context to reflect on their own experiences and to enhance the content they were developing within their assignments. Through that reflective process, they would not only effectively learn about, write about, and revise their own writing about organizational context, but they would at some dramatic, though infrequent, moments revise elements of *their own* organizational contexts. They would, in other words, rewrite a portion of the context of their own immediate writing work and their worlds of action/ subjectivity. To illustrate, one group with high motivation and strong academic skills, but that showed deep frustration early on with learning and employing digital writing technologies within the context of the classroom and the designated time of a class period, reframed their working time and space- their organizational context- to actively integrate outside resources and other spaces. They requested out-of-class time to meet with technology experts on campus, and they devised out-of-class collaborative work times in spaces beyond the classroom to work. These students learned through direct experience and engagement, accompanied by disciplinary study and reflection, about organizational context as an integral, though partially revisable, element of writing and rhetorical action. "Writing" for these students, then, was that fully-engaged, socio-cultural kind that has material consequences and impact, a lesson that is exceptionally difficult to teach in a way beyond the purely abstract. Further, "writing" for these students became a way to reinvent not only the field of Professional Writing and Rhetoric, but their own writerly subjectivities as well (see Slevin). Far from being passive recipients of a lecture from a professor on the field of Professional Writing and Rhetoric and the impact of organizational context on writing situations, and then blandly repeating these descriptions on an exam, the students themselves participated in generatively reconstructing and redefining the field, and recreating their own rhetorical, *praxical* subjectivities, as they engaged in complex and reflective writerly ways of being.

## CONCLUSION

We now return, more directly, to the two central questions we proposed earlier and offer some preliminary responses, in the spirit of igniting further conversations about the role our pedagogical practices play in forming writers and the impact pedagogy can have on the formation of rhetor cal subjects:

- "What defines a successful writer?" and
- "How can we best develop/ teach such writers?"

As we also mentioned earlier, we are not claiming that PBL is the only or even the best pedagogy for creating active learning environments. We are, instead, proposing that by focusing our attention on designing PBL activities and then reflecting on the kinds of writerly behaviors in which they invited students to participate, we became more aware of how the very pedagogies we enacted in class created particular kinds of subjectivities for students to occupy. We found that PBL activities did indeed have the advantage of inviting students to behave more like "real" and what we have come to call "successful" writers, based on an interactionist model of writing. In this model, successful writers understand that writing is messy, iterative, and indeterminate; they know *how* to negotiate writing in such contexts; and they *value* these messy processes as well. Unlike other engaged pedagogies, which rely on a model of presenting information to students first and then asking them to put that information into action second, PBL activities require students to immerse themselves in real-world problems and then generate the knowledge itself, as an act of heuristic invention. This difference seemed to lead to the creation, at least temporarily, of rhetorical, *praxical* student subjects who were confident relying on their own generative knowledge when finding themselves in novel situations that required them to decide how to respond appropriately. With other types of engaged pedagogies, when writerly ways of acting are "pre-packaged" and delivered outside of real writing situations, student writers routinely become flustered when these "pre-packaged" bits of information fail to respond adequately or fail to take into account the complexity of their writing situation. In contrast, students who engaged in generative problem-based learning as they experienced real writing situations and hurdles appear to be more rhetorically flexible and capable of taking responsive action. For example, when the students working on the "Adding to the Conversation about Organizational Context" project realized that one of their secondary, indirect audiences might be future employers, they decided to rethink entirely their project's organizational and navigational schemes. They decided that the academic resources they had been relying upon as examples, and with which they were most comfortable using themselves as students, were inadequate for this newly realized and yet very important audience. Instead of relying upon tried and true, and perhaps even dull, ways of organizing their content, they decided to engage in large-scale audience analysis to support their efforts to create a more audience-responsive organizational scheme.

While we want to be careful and refrain from arguing that PBL is the best pedagogy, we also think it is important to note that PBL does offer something special, and that is its quality of *initiating* instruction with, and then having all learning emerge out of, a well crafted problem. This feature helps to create a learning environment in which student writers/rhetorical subjects develop not only *rhetorical* subjectivities, but *praxical* subjectivities as well. It is worth noting again Sullivan and Porter's definition of praxis as "a kind of thinking that does not start with theoretical knowledge or abstract models, which are then applied to situations, but that begins with immersion in local situations, and then uses epistemic theory as heuristic rather than as explanatory or determining" (26). So in regard to the question of how we can best develop/teach such writers, we argue that one way is by using pedagogies that so intensely immerse students in local and real situations that engagement *itself* becomes part of being a successful writer. This ups the ante, so to speak, on our understanding of engaged learning: it is no longer just the means for transferring effectively writerly knowledge, but rather a way of "being" and acting. In other words, engaged learning becomes, in the interactionist model of writing, rhetorical praxis.

The two courses we use as illustrations here are not even the kind most readily adaptable to PBL, and yet that is in part why we chose to focus on them, both for our own pedagogical exploration and also for scholarly reflection. Courses that most readily spring to mind for adoption of PBL include what we might categorize as advanced practice or performancebased courses. These courses are typically populated by students who bring some advanced-level rhetorical/writing skills and experiences, to which they can turn when addressing complex, ill-structured, novel rhetorical/writing challenges. These practice- or performance-based courses common in RWS curricula (see The Committee on the Major in Writing and Rhetoric's "Writing Majors at a Glance")-"Writing for the Web," "Teaching Writing," "Tutoring Writing," "Environmental Writing," "Report and Grant Writing," "Technical Documentation," "Advanced Editing," "Publications Management," "Document Design," et cetera-also intuitively lend themselves to the creation of writing problems that can initiate and sustain highly engaged learning. For these reasons, advanced practice- and performance-based courses most readily lend themselves to PBL and would be excellent grounds, we say encouragingly, for broader exploration in RWS. However, what we observed happening in our first-year writing and introductory professional writing and rhetoric classes convinced us that even courses less readily adaptable to PBL can use this pedagogy effectively, as a way to immerse students in active learning environments and invite them to engage in rhetorical praxis.

## APPENDIX

### Critiquing Search Engines

Do you use different search engines for different purposes or when looking for different kinds of information? Or do you turn to the same search engine over and over again without really thinking about how the search engine functions or how it might affect the kinds of information you locate? Faculty who teach first-year writing at your university have noticed that a lot of first-year students seem to over rely on just one or two search engines for all of their research needs, which probably isn't the most efficient or productive research strategy. These faculty members have asked that you create some materials or a resource that will help first-year writing students understand how to decide which search engine to use when faced with a new research question or situation, or when looking for a particular kind of source.

Some of the complexities that make this problem unique are that different search engines may have different features (such as options for narrowing or filtering a search, or special Boolean terms), they may identify Web pages or Web sites differently (by their title, by their metadata), they may have user preferences that can be adjusted, or they may focus on particular kinds of sources (i.e., image, video, full-text, PDF file, etc.).

You can decide as a group what you think is the best way to address this problem.

### Understanding & Using Databases

Have you ever felt like you were drowning in information, or conversely, that there was no existing research on the topic you wanted to study? Information that exists "out there" on the Internet or in databases, journals, or books is useless unless you know how to locate it. One way we can locate meaningful and useful information/sources is by using our library's academic databases. Your library has asked your class to create an online resource that will help other student-researchers conduct effective database research and avoid that "drowning in information" or "there's nothing on my topic" experience.

This activity asks you to determine how exactly different databases function and develop some strategies for deciding which ones to use for the different research situations. Some complexities that you might confront when examining databases and developing strategies for selecting among them include determining the sources searched by the databases, figuring out what kinds of advanced searching options or "filtering" options are offered, identifying what kinds of sources the databases return (i.e., journal article citations, and/or abstracts, and/or full-text, PDF, or HTML files), and determining whether certain databases serve particular audiences or disciplines.

How you create this online resource and what it will include is your decision

## Documenting Digital Sources

Your university has close ties with one of the local high schools; professors give guest lectures and the students visit our campus to attend summer classes and special talks. In an effort to help the senior class of high school students be better prepared for college, you've been asked to teach them to use one of the major documentation styles (MLA, APA, or Chicago). So the problem you're tasked with solving is identifying the values embodied in the different documentation features and explaining these values to an audience of high school students. You need to do much more than simply tell the students how to "fill in the blanks" of a Works Cited entry. Instead, you need to figure out a way to explain what the different components of an entry *mean*, and what kinds of *values* these different components convey about what that particular discourse community's values.

It's up to you how you decide to explain these documentation features/ values to the high school students.

## Defining the Field

It's the fall of your junior year, and you have decided that you want to get a summer professional writing internship before you go into your senior year. You figure that in the current slow economy, an internship would give you some much needed experience and possibly even open up a door to a full-time job at your internship site after you graduate.

To prepare, you've talked with your advisor and also a career counselor at the Career Center. Both have given you lots of good advice about narrowing down the kinds of internships you might want and how to go about finding them, but both have also strongly urged you to create a portfolio you can send as a follow-up to your initial application and resume, and then also use in any interviews you might get.

You get good advice about what should be in your portfolio, but one piece that surprised you was a definition of your field of study. When your advisor told you such a piece would be helpful, you only kind of believed her: "I mean she is only a professor. What would she know about job portfolios?" But when the career counselor told you the same thing, you started to think you'd better put some time into this piece.

When talking with the career counselor about this field definition piece, you ask, "Who would want to read that?" The counselor said, "Well, you'll have a person or group of people who may want to know in a quick glance sort of way what your expertise is and what you can bring to them. Then, there may be a second person or group who will want to read that portion of your portfolio to find out more than the quick and dirty. This other group will want to read something that illustrates your depth of knowledge, as well as something that showcases your writing abilities and abilities to reason."

Throughout your discussion with the career counselor, the issue about how professional writing and rhetoric are connected keeps coming up. She is really interested in hearing more about this connection, about how you define rhetoric, and what it means to connect the two. You've gotten the same sort of response from friends and family, most of whom simply leave out the term "rhetoric" when they talk with you about this topic. So far, you aren't able to respond very well to their questions, a situation you figure you shouldn't find yourself in when you're interviewing for internships. Maybe, you think, this is a key topic in your portfolio piece.

## Adding to the Conversation about Organizational Context

*Professional Writing and Rhetoric: Readings from the Field* argues in the "Introduction" that the field of Professional Writing and Rhetoric can be defined as "organizationally situated authorship." But it also says that phrase requires a lot of "unpacking." In other words, you can't just say "organizationally situated authorship" and expect people will understand you, or even that *you* will know what the heck you're talking about.

PWR faculty have talked a long while about creating some sort of source that students in all PWR classes could turn to when trying to get a deeper understanding of professional writing and rhetoric as "organizationally situated authorship/ action."

The following e-mail was sent by a PWR faculty member to all the other PWR faculty after a flurry of e-mail messages related to this issue:

> Hey, y'all -
>
> This "source" we've been talking about sounds like a great research project for a whole class. We've discovered again and again that none of us could handle this project alone, but a whole class could create something very helpful.
>
> In fact, this makes me think of a rhetoric resource site at Georgia Tech that was created by some students there. It's been a helpful and often used resource for people across the country for almost ten years. One of our classes could create something akin to that Tech site.
>
> Since the issue of "organizationally situated authorship" is so closely connected to *Professional Writing and Rhetoric: Readings froni the Field*, which we know is being used in a number of places around the country now, the site would be a great resource for students and faculty outside of our university. That creates an effective and real audience for this work. Plus, our students would be able to point family, friends, internship and job interviewers, grad schools, etc to the site and say, "Hey, I did that!"
>
> What do ya think?

## NOTES

1. Further introductory information about PBL can be found in these valuable sources: James Rhem's "Problem-Based Leaming: An Introduction" (1998); Barbara J . Duch, Susan E. Groh, and Deborah E. Allen's *The Power of ProblemBased Learning* (2001); Jose A. Amador, Libby Miles, and C. B. Peters's *The Practice of Problem-Based Learning: A Guide to Implementing PBL in the College Classroom* (2006); John R. Savery's "Overview of Problem-Based Leaming: Definitions and Distinctions" (2006); and Michael Pennell and Libby Miles's "'It Actually Made Me Think': Problem-Based Learning in the Business Communications Classroom" (2009). Two excellent online sources

for PBL scholarship are *The Interdisciplinary Journal of Problem-based Learning*, hosted by Purdue University, and *The PBL Clearinghouse*, hosted at the University of Delaware.

2. Elon University has n1ade a long-term institutional comn1itment to engaged learning, a commitment which has become a hallmark of the school's reputation. This reputation is recognized externally by the National Survey of Student Engagement (NSSE), in which Elon consistently earns top scores. In 2009, NSSE surveyed 360,000 students from 617 four-year colleges and universities and is considered "one of the most comprehensive assessments of effective practices in higher education" (see http://www.elon.edu/e-web/ news/nsse/). In the 2009 NSSE report, Elon students rated Elon highly on each of the five benchmarks of excellence: Level of Academic Challenge, Active and Collaborative Learning, Student-Faculty Interaction, Enriching Educational Experiences, and Supportive Campus Environn1ent. For example, Elon's scores for a few of the Enriching Educational Experiences benchmark items were as follows:

|  | Elon<br>First Year/ Seniors | NSSE<br>First Year/ Seniors |
|---|---|---|
| Have done/plan to do an internship, field experience, co-op experience or clinical assignment. | 96%/ 92% | 82%/ 76% |
| Have done/plan to do community/volunteer service. | 93%/ 92% | 80%/ 75% |
| Have done/plan to study abroad. | 91%/ 76% | 45%/ 24% |
| Have done/plan to do culminating senior experience (capstone project, thesis). | 76%/ 93% | 50%/ 64% |

The university's internal commitment to engaged learning is evidenced by its focus on study abroad (71°/o of students study abroad at least once before graduating), undergraduate research, service-lean1ing (supported by The Kernodle Center for Service Learning), internships, and civic engagement. The Center for the Advancement of Teaching and Learning (CATL) and the availability of numerous internal grants which aim to enhance pedagogy, active learning, and faculty-student interaction also speak to the university's commitment to engaged learning. Further, student and faculty participation in Student Undergraduate Research Forum (SURF) has steadily increased over the last 15 years. This forum gives students the opportunity to engage in large-scale research projects and present professionally their research at national and regional conferences.

3. Writing curricula objectives we collaboratively established over the years represent significant features of the context within which we studied PBL. Any decisions we would make or evaluations of possible pedagogies would undoubtedly be made with at least indirect reference to our curricula and the goals/objectives we had established for them.

Our first-year writing program goals reflect a significant connection to rhetoric, with special en1phasis on process, strategies, reflection, and social context. In firstyear writing, our goals state, all students will gain:

1. A more sophisticated writing process including invention, peer responding, revising and editing that result in a clear, effective well edited public piece.

2. A more sophisticated understanding of the relationship of purpose, audience, and voice, and an awareness that writing expectations and conventions vary within the academy and in professional and public discourse.

3. An appreciation for the capacity of writing to change oneself and the world.

As part of a mid-sized university with a core of Professional Writing and Rhetoric faculty, some of whom direct first-year composition and the university's writing center, and all of whom teach in the English department's Professional Writing and Rhetoric (PWR) concentration, we conceive of all of our writing classes as being intimately connected, not within a "major" curriculum but by the discipline of Rhetoric and Composition. Therefore, the goals and objectives of the professional writing and rhetoric curriculum reflect, in some significant ways, those of firstyear writing. The assumptions or principles of PWR include the following:

1. We approach professional writing and rhetoric not simply as a functional art limited to means of production, but as a critical social practice that includes engaging in cultural production of social ends.

2. We approach professional writing and rhetoric as a way of acting effectively and wisely within complex situations, corporate, civic, and personal.

3. We understand professional writing and rhetoric to be a situated art.

4. We value the integration of theory and practice.

5. We see professional writing and rhetoric as one, integrated disciplinary field of study and practice.

From these principles, we have established the following set of student-focused objectives:

1. Students will understand that writing participates in socially constructing the worlds within which we Jive, work, play, et cetera.

2. Students will learn, often through working hands on with actual clients, how to analyze, reflect on, assess, and effectively act within complex contexts and rhetorical situations.

3. Students will study a wide variety of rhetorical techne or strategies and, by working within and reflecting on actual rhetorical contexts, learn to adapt and develop rhetorical strategies and heuristics appropriate to specific situations.

4. Students will show an ability to integrate theoretical knowledge and professional practice.

5. Students will adopt a disciplinary identity as a writer and see themselves as experts (i.e., professional writers/rhetors) who bring particular (e.g., rhetorical) ways of seeing and ways of acting in and on the world around them.

As we build curricula, develop new courses, conceive new assignments, assess programmatic effectiveness, et cetera, we actively reflect on and refer to these goals and objectives. Therefore, they have played a significant role in our inquiry about the place and value of PBL in writing instruction.

## WORKS CITED

Amador, Jose A., Libby Miles, and C. B. Peters. *The Practice of Problem-Based Learning: A Guide to Implementing PBL in the College Clas room*. Bolton: Anker, 2006. Print.

Anson, Chris. "Writing in Support of Departmental Writing Goals and Learning Outcomes." Elon University Writing Across the Curriculum Progran1. Elon University. Elon, NC. 11 March 2010. Guest Speaker.

The Committee on the Major in Writing and Rhetoric. "Writing Majors at a Glance." NCTE/Conference on College Composition and Communic tion, 2010. Web. 14 July 2010.

Consortium for the Study of Writing in College. Indiana University, 2009. Web. 10 June 2010.

Couture, Barbara. "Modeling and Emulating: Rethinking Agency in the Writing Process." *Post-Process Theory: Beyond the Writing-Process Par digm*. Ed. Thomas Kent. Carbondale and Edwardsville: Southern Illinois UP, 1999. 30-48. Print.

Dias, Patrick, Aviva Freedman, Peter Medway, and Anthony Pare. "Situating Writing." *Worlds Apart: Acting and Writing in Academic and Workplace Contexts*. Ed. Patrick Dias et al. Mahwah/London: Lawrence Erlbaum, 1999. 17-46. Print.

Driskill, Linda. "Understanding the Writing Context in Organizations." *Professional Writing and Rhetoric: Readings from the Field*. Ed. Tim Peeples. Longman: 2002. 105-21. Print.

Duch, Barbara J., Susan E. Groh, and Deborah E. Allen, eds. *The Power of Problem-Based Learning: A Practical "How To" for Teaching Undergraduate Courses in Any Discipline*. Sterling: Stylus, 2001. Print.

The Faculty Survey of Student Engagement (FSSE). Indiana University, 2010. Web. 12 June 2010.

Faigley, Lester. *Fragments of Rationality: Postmodernity and the Subject of Composition*. Pittsburgh: U of Pittsburgh P, 1992. Print.

Indiana University Center for Postsecondary Research (CPR) . Indiana Un versity, 2010. Web. 12 June 2010.

*The Interdisciplinary Journal of Problem-based Learning*. Purdue University, n.d. Web. 14 Oct. 2009.

Kuh, George D. *High-Impact Educational Practices: What They Are, Who Has Access to Them, and Why They Matter*. Washington: Association of American Colleges and Universities, 2008. Print.

Law School Survey of Student Engagement (LSSSE). Indiana University, 2009. Web. 12 June 2010.

National Survey of Student Engagement (NSSE). Indiana University, 2010. Web. 12 June 2010.

NSSE Institute for Effective Educational Practice. Indiana University, 2010. Web. 10 June 2010.

*The PBL Clearinghouse.* The University of Delaware, n .d. Web. 12 Oct. 2009.

Peeples, Tim, and Bill Hart-Davidson. "Grading the 'Subject': Questions of Expertise and Evaluation." *Grading in the Post-Process Classroom: From Theory to Practice.* Ed. Libby Allison, Lizbeth Bryant, and Maureen Ho rigan. Portsmouth: Boynton/Cook-Heinemann, 1997. 94-113. Print.

Pennell, Michael, and Libby Miles. "'It Actually Made Me Think': Problem-Based Learning in the Business Communications Classroom." *Business Communication Quarterly* 72.4 (2009): 377-94. Print.

Rhem, James. "Problem-Based Learning: An Introduction." *The National Teaching & Learning Forum* 8.1 (1998): 4-7. Print.

Russell, David. "Activity Theory and Process Approaches: Writing (Power) in School and Society." *Post-Process Theory: Beyond the Writing-Process Paradigm.* Ed. Thomas Kent. Carbondale and Edwardsville: Southern Illinois UP, 1999. 80-95. Print.

Russell, David R. "Rethinking Geme and Society: An Activity Theory Ana ysis." *Written Communication* 14.4 (2002): 504-55. Print.

Ryan, Kathleen J. "Subjectivity Matters: Using Gerda Lerner's Writing and Rhetoric to Claim an Alternative Epistemology for the Feminist Wri ing Classroom." *Feminist Teacher: A Journal of the Practices, Theories, and Scholarship of Feminist Teaching* 17.1 (2006): 36-51. Print.

Savery, John R. "Overview of Problem-Based Learning: Definitions and Di tinctions." *The Interdisciplinary Journal of Problem-based Learning* 1.1 (Spring 2006): n. pag. Web. 14 Oct. 2009.

Slevin, James. "Inventing and Reinventing the Discipline of Composition." *Introducing English: Essays in the Intellectual Work of Composition.* Pitt burg: U of Pittsburgh P, 2001. 37-56. Print.

Sullivan, Patricia A., and James E. Poiter. *Opening Spaces: Writing Technol gies and Critical Research Practices.* Greenwich: Ablex, 1997. Print.

Walker, Janice R., and Todd Taylor. *The Columbia Guide to Online Style 2/e.* New York: Columbia UP, 2007. Print.

# ENCULTURATION

*Enculturation* is on the Web at http://enculturation.gmu.edu/

*Enculturation* started in 1996 by two graduate students. In its sixteen years it has never had institutional support beyond web space provided by a university and has never been affiliated with a press or organization. Currently it is hosted on an individual's server and supported with one RA through the University of South Carolina. All of the managerial, editorial, and production work has been done by young faculty and graduate students in the field of rhetoric and composition. The mission of the journal has generally been to publish broader ranging interdisciplinary work related to rhetoric and composition that is more theoretical or media-oriented.

## The Role of Computational Literacy in Computers and Writing"

"The Role of Computational Literacy in Computers and Writing" reworks a town hall meeting from Computers and Writing 2012 on the links between code and writing. This print version presents a multi-authored constellation of texts that track how computation is being taken up in computers and writing and tries to understand this emergence in a broader context. Sample and Vee's introduction offers a wide-ranging set of resources, with links to courses, articles, and news stories and serves as a significant introduction to this burgeoning field. The individual voices represented in the piece—Sample, Vee, David Rieder, Alexandria Lockett, Karl Stolley, and Elizabeth Losh—provide a rich snapshot of how the field is taking up questions of hardware, software, and computation, from Arduino and processing to code switching and the social nature of code, mixed with tweets posted during the original town hall. This collaboration can serve as a model for others in the field looking to present multi-authored work both in digital and print journals.

# 5 The Role of Computational Literacy in Computers and Writing

*Mark Sample and Annette Vee*

If we can measure the significance a new scholarly object by the number of innovative courses, breadth of engaging research, and buzz of online activity, then code has reached a critical moment in writing studies. Scholars such as N. Katherine Hayles and Espen Aarseth have long focused on the function of code in electronic texts, but ever since Mark Marino described the humanistic reading of code as "critical code studies" in 2006, the field has exploded. Often working at the level of code, the computer science scholars Michael Mateas and Noah Wardrip-Fruin are exploring games as narratives. Rhetoricians who program commercially such as Ian Bogost are similarly concerned with procedurality in new media, particularly game code. And works such as Bradley Dilger and Jeff Rice's edited collection From A to <A> foreground code as a mode of writing. Of course, this work builds on early research by Paul Leblanc, Gail Hawisher, Cynthia Selfe, Jim Kalmbach, and Ron Fortune, all of whom endeavored to draw attention to the politics and composition of code in the 1980s and 1990s.

Code has not only made its way into our research, it has also found its way into our classrooms. Kevin Brock's Code, Computation and Rhetoric class at North Carolina State University, Jamie Skye Bianco's Composing Digital Media course at University of Pittsburgh, and James Brown Jr.'s Writing and Coding composition course at University of Wisconsin-Madison are all examples of writing classrooms that now include code. In programs like Communication, Rhetoric and Digital Media at NC State, there is a growing recognition that some expertise in computational thought is a part of future success as a scholar affiliated with the humanities. As David M Rieder has argued, code is blurring into our textual compositions, such that it's no longer possible to bracket it off from writing pedagogy.

It may be that composition and rhetoric teachers are discovering what software developers already know. That is, from the perspective of computer science, programming has long looked like writing. Turing Award-winner Donald Knuth has argued for argued for "literate programming" and Frederick Brooks has drawn a parallel between a parallel between the programmer and the poet. More recent efforts under the name of "computer science for all," "computer programming for everybody," or "computational thinking"—promoted by computer science educators such as Mark Guzdial and Jeannette Wing—have sought to teach computing across the university curriculum, just as writing is now. These educators build on decades-old efforts by Seymour Papert (the designer of Logo) and John Kemeny and Thomas Kurtz (the creators of BASIC), who designed languages that would help a wider spectrum of people learn to code.

Beyond academia, popular initiatives and news stories have made the connection between coding and writing. For example, the Code Year initiative made a big splash in January 2012 with some good PR, as well as a promise by New York Mayor Michael Bloomberg that he would learn code this year; as of this writing, over 450,000 people have signed up to receive weekly code lessons via email. Massively Open Online Courses, or MOOCs, taught by professors at prestigious institutions such as Stanford and MIT have inspired tens of thousands of civilians to enroll in basic computer science courses. Writing for The Guardian in March 2012, John Naughton explains "Why all our kids should be taught to code." Media theorist Douglas Rushkoff caused a stir in 2011, arguing, "In the emerging, highly programmed landscape ahead, you will either create the software or you will be the software. It's really that simple: Program or be programmed."

It is against this backdrop that the Town Hall "Program or be Programmed: Do We Need Computational Literacy in Computers and Writing?" was proposed. The panel organizer, David Rieder, saw the growing interest in software studies and critical code studies, the ever-deepening engagement with computational approaches to the digital humanities, and his own local experiences teaching graduate courses on Arduino and Processing add up to an emerging interest in code and writing studies. Rieder asked Annette Vee to help plan and recruit panelists for the Town Hall, and both were delighted that writing and coding scholars Alexandria Lockett, Elizabeth Losh, Mark Sample, and Karl Stolley agreed to speak.

In this edited iteration of the Town Hall (you can watch the original on Vimeo, courtesy of Dan Anderson), we've provided a more polished version of each panelist's script, along with a few sample tweets from the audience to represent the dialogue with the presenters. This Storify captures a more complete Twitter backchannel during the presentation. Lynn C. Lewis's review review for the University of Michigan's Sweetland Digital Rhetoric Collaborative offers additional context for the original presentations.

As the title of the Town Hall implies, the pieces below are meant to be provocative rather than thorough considerations of the role of code and computational literacy in computers and writing. Rieder begins by arguing against the logocentric bias of writing studies, and asks: why limit texts to their readability? Based on their power and ubiquity, we should understand processes, specifically algorithmic ones, as the new basis of writing. Vee picks up on Rieder's final assertion that those who don't code will be "stuck in the logocentric sands of the past" and breaks down what it means to have "coding" defined by a coterie of specialists. She asks: if coding is central to writing, shouldn't the values associated with good code be as diverse as the values associated with good writing? Yet we cannot ignore the social context already established for code, asserts Sample. Invoking historically saturated statements from the BASIC programming language, Sample outlines concerns about coding style, substance and interpretation to indicate code's social nature. The social nature of code is clear for Lockett, who relates coding culture to code-switching across versions of English and notes the "sponsorship" of a friend with whom she exchanged knowledge about political and rhetorical theory for knowledge about code. The tension between her assertion that she is "not a computer programmer" and her facility with Linux and various coding structures resolves—at least provisionally—in her embrace of the term "hacker," which gives her the latitude to argue for political awareness about the "socio-technical systems" associated with code and software. Finally, Stolley gives us a call to arms: in Computers and Writing, we must become familiar with the tools that define our field. It will not be easy to learn Unix, GitHub, Ruby, and Javascript, but Aristotle argued that "people become builders by building," Stolley reminds us, and ease of acquisition should not dictate what skills we choose to learn.

Responding to these various assertions, Losh reflects on what it might mean to teach and learn code within the context of Computers and Writing. To the anxious instructor struggling to teach students the complexities of writing, much less programming, Losh advises that we think of writing as an "informational art." This perspective can widen the approaches we take as well as the modalities we emphasize in our classes. But to the administrator who must now direct departments to account for programming's role in writing, she offers only tentative models rather than easy answers. Although we ultimately cannot provide an answer to the central question of the panel—"What is the role of computational literacy in computers and writing?"—we hope our provocations contribute to the continuing conversations about coding and composing in writing studies.

## PROGRAMMING IS THE NEW GROUND OF WRITING

*David M Rieder*

Figure 1. Mark Tansey's Picasso and Braque

There are three reasons that I'm beginning this presentation with Mark Tansey's painting, Picasso and Braque (see Figure 1 above).

 David Rieder: #cwcon #townhall Programming is the new ground of writing.

Dennis Jerz

First, the painting is reminiscent of Orville and Wilbur Wright's first successful flight in Kill Devil Hills, North Carolina, which is just a few hours drive from the site of this conference. Second, at a conference on writing, many of Tansey's paintings, including this one, celebrate text in one way or another—especially the printed word. In the painting above, Picasso is flying one of his collages, while Braque surveys his progress from the ground. The point related to Tansey's interest in the printed word is that the flying surfaces of Picasso's collage are made from swaths of newsprint. Arguably, his flying machine is a multimodal writing machine—albeit a curious-looking one because it appears to be more of a combination of kite and plane. It may be more accurate to say it's a machine made from what look like Hargrave cells wrapped in words. Juxtaposed against the photograph below (see Figure 2), Tansey's painting is a bit of a mash-up of histories of flying, Hargrave's kites and the Wrights' plane.

Figure 2. Wikipedia image of Hargrave (left) and Swain

But, getting back on track, in addition to these two points is the third, which includes my main point. In Tansey's painting, the words printed on the swaths of newsprint, the writing, has broken free of its logocentric grounding. It's a relative break (not an absolute deterritorialization) because the writing on those swaths of newsprint is still recognizable as writing—but the words have taken on a value relative to the flying machine that they serve. The words are still readable, but the point here is why bother reading them?

 #cwcon Rieder at Town Hall Why limit the value of text to its readability?

Susan Delagrange

Or, rather (I don't really mean to throw the baby out with the bathwater), why limit their value to their readability? The flying machine, the dynamic medium they now serve, invites us to step away from our conventional stance toward writing, which is writing at a standstill, and unground ourselves.

"In computational media, writing wants to take a walk. It doesn't want to sit on the couch and be analyzed."

#cwcon

Allison Hitt

In computational media, writing wants to take a walk, not sit on a couch to be analyzed.[1] Writing doesn't need to be limited to the faithful representation of the spoken word—it never did, in fact. In computational media, our alphabet is motivated and dynamic. As Richard Lanham explains in The Economics of Attention, it is capable of thinking. In digital media, writing has expanded far beyond the limits of the logocentric tradition, but many of us continue to reinforce it in our teaching. In a comparison of print and digital textuality, Lanham explains that "all of our attention goes to the meaning of the text" in print-based media (81-2). But when text is digitized, meaning is less important than the ways in which it can move and be transformed. When it comes to computational media and the topic of this town hall, if writing can think (i.e., if it is mobile and transformable) then we should turn our focus away from content, which has diminishing value, to algorithmic forms and functions, which are the stasis of meaning in today's attention economy.

So, my third point about Tansey's painting, what I like about it, is that we're all Picasso in flight, whether we know it or not.

"We are all Picasso in flight." #cwcon David Rieder

Anne Frances Wysocki

How many of us were multi-tasking with tablets or laptops during the Computers and Writing conference, partly here, partly somewhere else? We're in flight right now. But here's the problem, or rather the challenge: while we're all comfortable in flight, far fewer of us are willing or able to recognize how writing has taken flight, too.

The new ground, the new basis of writing is algorithmic. Today, the power and profit in writing has less to do with representing speech than serving a computationally-driven, generative process of creation. If you are teaching and practicing writing as a grounded, representational technology, you are missing the proverbial forest for the trees, the machine for the pages of newsprint.

> David Rieder invokes Jill Morris's geek/jerk disctinction to get us thinking about the generative nature of code/algorithm. #cwcon
>
> Scott Reed

I hope you'll forgive the next and final provocation, which I fear smacks of what Jill Morris might characterize as the turn from geek to jerk, but, if you can't write code, if you can't think with code, if you can't write algorithmically, you may eventually find yourself stuck in the logocentric sands of the past.[2]

> Rieder "If you can't write code, if you can't write algorithmically, you might find yourself in the logocentric sands of the past" #cwcon
>
> Noel Radley

## NOTES

1 In the opening pages of Anti-Oedipus, Gilles Deleuze and Felix Guattari write, "A schizophrenic out for a walk is a better model than a neurotic lying on the analyst's couch" (2).

2 In her presentation at Computers and Writing, Jill Morris reprimanded the geeks in the gaming community whose condescensions about insider know-how made them out to be jerks.

## CODING VALUES

*Annette Vee*

Today I want to talk about good code. Experienced programmers often think about what good code is. But they rarely agree.

And here's what I want to say: they don't agree on what good code is because there is no good code. Or, rather, there is no Platonic Ideal of Good Code. Like writing, there is no good code without context.

@anetv "There is no good code without context." //
Yes! #cwcon

Kathie Gossett

Unfortunately, when good code is talked about, it is often talked about as if there's no rhetorical dimension to code. It's talked about as though the context of software engineering were the only context in which anyone could ever write code. As if digital humanists, biologists, web hackers, and sociologists couldn't possibly bring their own values to code.

@anetv Code, too, is rhetorical. Its value and "goodness" depends on context, despite what some programmers say. #cwcon

Amanda Wall

I'll give you just a couple of examples of how this happens, and what this means for us in computers and writing.

One of the earlier articulations of the supposed Platonic Ideal of Good Code was Edsger Dijkstra's infamous "GOTO considered harmful" dictum, from 1968.

This article railed against unstructured programming and the GOTO command for its ability to jump from one place in a program to another without logical program flow. Dijkstra's assertion was so provocative that "considered harmful" soapboxes have proliferated in programming literature and the Web and the "harm" done by goto has been hilariously depicted in an XKCD comic. Many of us first learned the joy of coding through the languages that used the GOTO command such as BASIC. But Dijkstra's statement suggests that the context of the software production workplace should override all other possible values for code. This is fine—as far as it goes, which is software engineering and computer science. But this kind of statement of values is often taken outside of those contexts and applied in other places where code operates. When that happens, the values of hacking for fun or for other fields are devalued in favor of the best practices of software engineering—that is, proper planning, careful modularity, and unit testing. The popular Ruby figure who went by the name "Why the Lucky Stiff" makes this point about conflicting values between software engineering and hacking forcefully and whimsically in "This Hack Was Not Properly Planned."

Here's a more recent invocation of the Platonic Ideal of Good Code. In this comment, we can see that the values of software engineering are more tacit, and more problematic:

> Every piece of academic code I have ever seen has been an un-mitigated nightmare. The sciences are the worst, but even com-puter science produces some pretty mind-crushing codebases. -"Ender7" on HackerNews

"Ender7" is replying here to a thread about a recent Scientific American story that suggested scientists were reluctant to release the code they used to reach their conclusions, in part because they were "embarrassed by the 'ugly' code they write for their own research." According to Ender7, they should be ashamed of their code. Ender7 goes on to say:

> So, I don't blame them for being embarassed to release their code. However, to some degree it's all false modesty since all of their colleagues are just as bad.

Why is academic code an "unmitigated nightmare" to Ender7? Because it's not properly following the rules of software engineering. Again, the rules of software engineering presumably work well for them. I'm not qualified to comment on that. But that doesn't mean that those values work for other contexts as well, such as biology. In this example, software engineering's values of modularity, security, and maintainability might be completely irrelevant to the scientist writing code for an experiment. If scientists take care to accommodate these irrelevant values, they may never finish the experiment, and therefore never contribute to the knowl-edgebase of their own field. The question, then, isn't about having good values in code; it's about which values matter.

Rules and values of software engineering don't necessarily work well in different disciplines #cwcon

Steven J LeMieux

We often hear how important it is to have proper grammar and good writing skills, as if these practices had no rhetorical dimension, as if they existed in a right or wrong space. But we know from writing studies that context matters. Put another way: like grammar, code is also rhetorical. What is good code and what is bad code should be based on the context in which the code operates. Just as rhetorical concepts of grammar and writing help us to think about the different exigencies and contexts of different populations of writers, a rhetorical concept of code can help us think about the different values for code and different kinds of coders.

'Code is rhetorical': thinking of liberatory properties of couching narrative in source code. #cwcon #townhall

V. Manivannan

And this is how coding values are relevant to us in computers and writing. The contingencies and contexts for what constitutes good code isn't always apparent to someone just beginning to learn to code, in part because the voices of people like Ender7 can be so loud and so insistent. We know from studies on teaching grammar and writing that the overcorrective tyranny of the red pen can shut writers down. Empirical studies indicate it's no different with code. Certainly there are ways of writing code that won't properly communicate with the computer. But the circle of valid expressions for the computer is much, much larger than Ender7 or Dijkstra insist upon.

To close, I want to share with you a bit of what might be considered very ugly code, a small Logo program I call, tongue-in-cheek, "codewell":

```
to codewell [
to semicircle repeat 180 [fd .1 rt 1] end
to smallcircle repeat 360 [fd .01 rt 1] end
to smallsemicircle repeat 180 [fd .05 rt 1] end
to smallleftsemicircle repeat 180 [fd .05 lt 1] end
to circle repeat 360 [fd .1 rt 1] end
to randomcolor setcolor pick [ black red orange yellow green blue
violet ] end
penup
lt 90 fd 200
pendown
rt 90 fd 20 lt 90 fd 5 rt 180 fd 10
penup
fd 5
pendown
rt 90 fd 20 rt 180 semicircle lt 90
penup
fd 5
pendown
lt 90 fd 10 penup fd 3 lt 90 pendown smallcircle lt 180
penup
fd 5 rt 90 fd 5 rt 180
Pendown
smallsemicircle rt 180 smallleftsemicircle lt 40 fd 9 rt 40
smallsemicircle
penup
rt 90 fd 20
Pendown
lt 90 fd 10 penup fd 3 lt 90 pendown smallcircle lt 180
penup
fd 5 rt 90 fd 5 rt 180
pendown
smallsemicircle rt 180 smallleftsemicircle lt 40 fd 9 rt 40
smallsemicircle
penup
rt 90 fd 20 lt 90 fd 3

pendown
semicircle semicircle semicircle fd 10 semicircle
penup
fd 10 rt 90 fd 15  lt 90
pendown
semicircle semicircle
penup
rt 90 fd 15 lt 90
pendown
semicircle semicircle
penup
rt 90 fd 15 lt 90
pendown
semicircle semicircle penup  rt 90 fd 11 lt 90 pendown fd 15 bk 21
penup
rt 90 fd 20 lt 90 fd 9 lt 40 pendown repeat 270 [fd .1 lt 1]
penup
rt 50 fd 7 lt 160
pendown
semicircle semicircle
penup
rt 125 fd 13 lt 65 bk 1
pendown
semicircle semicircle penup rt 90 fd 11 lt 90 pendown fd 15 bk 21
penup
rt 90 fd 5 lt 90 fd 7
pendown
semicircle rt 90 fd 11 lt 70 repeat 160 [fd .1 lt 1]
penup
rt 90 fd 6
pendown
smallcircle
penup
fd 60 rt random 360 fd 140 randomcolor
] end
repeat 60 codewell
```

This is bad code because:

- it is uncommented and hard to read
- it is in an old, seldom-used language
- it is baggy and has repeated statements that should be rewritten as functions
- it is not modular or reusable
- it is an "unmitigated nightmare"

If you run the code [on github here] in a LOGO interpreter, it looks like this:

So, in addition to saying my code sucks, you could also say this:

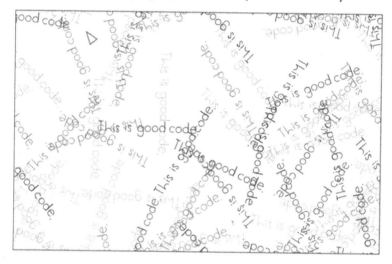

- it could be used to teach people some things about functions and code
- it is a start for a LOGO library of letters that might be kind of cool
- it does what I want it to do, namely, make my argument in code form.

Demonstration of a self-proclaimed sample of an "unmitigated nightmare" code sample by @anetv Allows argument through mess. #cwcon #townhall
Chris Friend

Let's imagine a world where coding is more accessible, where more people are able to use code to contribute to public discourse or solve their own problems, or just say what they want to say. For that to happen, we need to widen the values associated with the practice of coding.

> We need to "widen the values associated with coding," says @anetv Word. #cwcon
>
> Amanda Wall

To Edsger Dijkstra, I'd say: coding values that ignore rhetorical contexts and insist on inflexible best practices or platonic ideals of code should be considered harmful – at least to the field of computers and writing.

## FIVE BASIC STATEMENTS ON COMPUTATIONAL LITERACY

### *Mark Sample*

I want to run through a list of five basic statements about computational literacy. These are literally 5 statements in BASIC, a programming language developed at Dartmouth in the 1960s.

> @samplereality discusses multiple levels of meaning-making in code (beyond executing operations). I love this town hall. #cwcon #critcode
>
> Kevin Brock

BASIC is an acronym for Beginner's All-Purpose Symbolic Instruction Code, and the language was designed in order to help all undergraduate students at Dartmouth—not just science and engineering students—use the college's time-sharing computer system (Kemeny 30).

Each BASIC statement I present here is a fully functioning 1-line program. I want to use each as a kind of thesis—or a provocation of a thesis—about the role of computational literacy in computers and writing, and in the humanities more generally.

### 10 Print 2+3

I'm beginning with this statement because it's a highly legible program that nonetheless highlights the mathematical, procedural nature of code. But this program is also a piece of history: it's the first line of the first program in the user manual of the first commercially available version of BASIC, developed for the first commercially available home computer, the Altair 8800 (Altair BASIC Reference Manual 3). The year was 1975 and this BASIC was developed by a young Bill Gates and Paul Allen. And of course, their BASIC would go on to be the foundation of Microsoft. It's worth noting that although Microsoft BASIC was the official BASIC of the Altair 8800 (and many home computers to follow), an alternative version, called Tiny BASIC, was developed by a group of programmers in San Francisco. The 1976 release of Tiny BASIC included a "copyleft" software license, a kind of predecessor to contemporary open source software licenses (Wang 12). Copyleft emphasized sharing, an idea at the heart of the original Dartmouth BASIC, which, after all, was designed specifically to run on Dartmouth's revolutionary time-sharing computer system (Kemeny 31-32).

## 10 Print "Hello World"

If BASIC itself was a program that invited collaboration, then this—customarily one of the first programs a beginner learns to write—highlights the way software looks outward. Hello, world. Computer code is writing in public, a social text.

 @samplereality 10 PRINT "HELLO WORLD" code, is a social text #townhall #cwcon

 Dennis Jerz

Or, what Jerry McGann calls a "social private text." As McGann explains, "Texts are produced and reproduced under specific social and institutional conditions, and hence…every text, including those that may appear to be purely private, is a social text" (McGann 21). Not co-incidentally, "Hello World" is also the first post the popular blogging platform WordPress creates with every new installation.

## 10 Print "Go To Statement Considered Harmful": Goto 10

My next program is a bit of an insider's joke. It's a reference to a famous 1968 diatribe by Edsger Dijkstra called "Go To Statement Considered Harmful." Dijkstra argues against using the goto command, which leads to what critics call spaghetti code. While Annette Vee addresses that specific debate, I want to call attention to the way this famous injunction implies an evaluative audience, a set of norms, and even an aesthetic priority. Programming is a set of practices, with its own history and tensions. Any serious consideration of code—any serious consideration of computers—in the humanities must reckon with these social elements of code.

## 10 REM Print "Goodbye Cruel World"

The late German media theorist Frederich Kittler has argued that, as Alexander Galloway put it, "code is the only language that does what it says" (Galloway 6). Yes, code does what it says. But it also says things it does not do. Like this one-line program which begins with REM, short for remark, meaning this is a comment left by a programmer, which the computer will not execute. Comments in code exemplify what Mark Marino has called the "extra-functional significance" of code, meaning-making that goes beyond the purely utilitarian commands in the code.

Without a doubt, there is much even non-programmers can learn not by studying what code does, but by studying what it says—and what it evokes.

## 10 Print CHR$(205.5+RND(1));:Goto 10

Finally, here's a program that highlights exactly how illegible code can be. Very few people could look at this program for the Commodore 64 and figure out what it does. This example suggests there's a limit to the usefulness of the concept of literacy when talking about code. And yet, when we run the program, it's revealed to be quite simple, though endlessly changing, as it creates a random maze across the screen.

 Mark Sample's continuously generating maze performs his claim that code can "evoke" things. #cwcon

Amanda Wall

So I'll end with a caution about relying on the word literacy. It's a word I'm deeply troubled by, loaded with historical and social baggage. It's often misused as a gatekeeping concept, an either/or state; one is either literate or illiterate.

> Sample: Hesitant to use the term literacy for its
> misunderstandings & gatekeeping tendencies. Instead,
> use code "competency." #cwcon
>
> Allison Hitt

In my own teaching and research I've replaced my use of literacy with the idea of competency. I'm influenced here by the way teachers of a foreign language want their students to use language when they study abroad. They don't use terms like literacy, fluency, or mastery, they talk about competency. Because the thing with competency is, it's highly contextualized, situated, and fluid. Competency means knowing the things you need to do in order to do the other things you need to do. It's not the same for everyone, and it varies by place, time, and circumstance. Competency also suggests the possibility of doing things, rather than simply reading or writing things.

Translating this experience to computers and writing, competency means reckoning with computation at the level appropriate for what you want to get out of it—or put into it.

## I Am Not a Computer Programmer

*Alexandria Lockett*

I am not a computer programmer. My ability to execute a programming language extends as far as hypertext mark-up language (html), which I learned in the days of crude computing better known as Web 1.0. However, these past couple years, I have been using Ubuntu, the user-friendly Linux desktop environment founded by Mark Shuttleworth. Ubuntu is a Bantu word which means "humanity unto others." This concept not only inspired this piece, but embodies the spirit of generosity embedded in open-source participation.

After a couple of weeks, Ubuntu seemed to completely revitalize my cheap old laptop. The system always booted immediately and it didn't freeze up when I ran multiple programs. Through Ubuntu, I gained access to multiple workspaces, as well as the Ubuntu Software Center, where I could download and try hundreds of free applications. Still perplexed that I didn't have to pay for the operating system, I asked my neighbor (who would soon become one of my best friends),

"Why everyone didn't drop their costly, barely functioning Windows OS's?" Open Source, it seems, thrives on synchronicity. The moment I conspired to murder my machine, a computer programmer appeared at my front door to help me move a heavy piece of furniture. That day my mind was permeated with my technological conflict. I never wanted to use Windows again, and I couldn't afford the expensive membership fees of the iCult. My consumer power seemed muted by my sense that each company was my only option. Of course, my entire technological socialization process in American public schools involved two options: Mac or PC. Both of these companies' global dominance—over market shares, GUI's, and hardware designs—made me feel like I was somehow committing some awful sin when I lusted after the possibility of having additional computing choices. The good neighbor suggested that I stop using proprietary software altogether and consider switching to Linux. I heard the word Linux and I automatically felt crushed. I remembered my high school dork friends with their terminals and their occasional visits with the FBI, on account of their cracking credit cards. How was I to use Linux?

Lockett's first response of Linux (in sum) "how was I to use Linux, that's for the dorks!" ha, yes, a huge gap for many to overcome #cwcon

Kristin Arola

Since I could burn ISO files, I was thrilled I could test out Ubuntu on my sluggish machine. Not only was it super easy to use, but I was pissed that I didn't know this option was available to me. Moreover, I felt dumb not knowing that it wasn't necessary to buy a new computer: Why couldn't I differentiate between a hardware and a software problem? Why had I failed to distinguish a computer from a kitchen appliance such as a blender or toaster—objects you toss in the garbage when they no longer work? The Mac/PC binary logic informing the tiny section of my brain devoted to 'technology and troubleshooting' blurred the communication functions occurring between these two entities entirely.

I asked my neighbor, who would soon become one of my best friends, why everyone didn't drop their costly, barely functioning Windows OS's. After hundreds of thousands of hours, over many long days and long nights, I understood concepts like modularity and proprietary lock-in. In fact, I encouraged him to use the latter concept as a framework for an introduction to computer science course. We discussed some of the ways in which we could resist his pedagogical training. He was frustrated with the textbook and lesson plans because these materials took for granted that C++, albeit the industry standard, was the best or only programming language students should learn. Although the roboticist was required to teach over one hundred and fifty students C++, I urged him to compose his own textbook so that everyone could enjoy two major learning opportunities that integrate technical knowledge and civic participation

First, the format and content of the book would both dismantle the idea that computer science courses should be apolitical. Wikis, by nature, indicate that a given project is too vast for one author due to its need for ongoing, frequent revision. They are never 'done,' so to speak. Furthermore, students' participation on the wiki placed the burden of 'textbook' authorship on the entire class, which would de-centralize my friend's role as the sole source of knowledge. He knew that the wiki-format would require students to demonstrate their in-quisitiveness. Additionally, he could track and evaluate user participa-tion, which helped him customize lesson plans and additional wiki content with their concerns and abilities in mind. As a result, stu-dents practiced three core values of critical pedagogy and hacking: collaboration, active participation, and a curiosity about how things work. Next, he could include supplementary material on social issues in computer programming and computer science, as well as career ad-vice for interested students. Using the hacker name 'Anova8,' I col-laborated with him throughout the summer on some of this Media Wiki-powered book. Indeed, I received a most interesting peer-to-peer education regarding the fundamentals of computer science while he learned about composition and rhetoric pedagogy. In exchange for his knowledge about types, variables, operators, loops, arrays, and struc-tures, he acquired key lessons in Jane Addams' radical pragmatism, Jacqueline Jones Royster's definition of literacy for socio-political ac-tion, Critical Pedagogy, and Resistance Theory. We established that programming instruction was inextricably related to and dependant on writing expertise and opportunities for persuasion. Both writing and programming receive widespread attention as subjects in which few can do well, but nearly everyone needs to learn. Since these prac-tices are so deeply embedded in many people's daily lives, such subjects have a strong influence on how we perceive and measure social progress. However, the dynamic, social, experiential instruction that help us learn these techne is often overlooked.

All codes are languages, all languages are codes.
#cwcon

terfle

Through my neighbor's literacy sponsorship, I came into contact with sites like Slashdot, ReadWriteWeb, and Reddit. I wasn't interested in "becoming" a member of this community, but I did want to know more about the people who wrote the code—their personal experiences, how they interacted. I wanted to visualize their values, beliefs, and ways of seeing the world. I eagerly read Richard Stallman's Manifesto, learned more about Linus Torvalds, Eric Raymond, Alan Turing, Steven Wozniak, Larry Page, Sergey Brin, and Ward Cunningham. When my printer and scanner hard drives weren't compatible with Ubuntu, I perused many discussion threads and figured out how to identify credible advice on how to install them (this was before the HPLIP was accessible in the Ubuntu software center). Successful installation was proof that I could trust the counsel of others. However, I will admit that I did not bother to try out any instructions written by any poster whose post didn't consist of well-sequenced, highly detailed complete sentences. Soon, I began to recognize the characteristics of the Free and Open Source Software Community and its massive impact on other communities. It had a complex history, social languages, intertextuality (i.e. GNU's not Unix), discourses, conversations. All the 'stuff' of a discourse community. Software developments that facilitate(d) web 2.0, our dependence on 'free' applications, and Linux servers running major businesses and the interwebs is striking evidence of its power.

Weirdly excited by Alexandra Lockett's totally unselfconscious/unironic use of the word "interwebs."
#cwcon

Scott Reed

Indeed, I am not a computer programmer, but I began to recognize several commonalities between my perspective as a writing teacher and my friend's perspective as a programmer. The objectives of having access to code, tinkering with the code, running programs for any purpose, and sharing improvements with the community so everyone benefits were tantamount to my pedagogical approaches to rhetoric and composition. Shortly after I changed my operating system to Ubuntu, I renewed connections with those "dork" friends from high school, who were excited to talk about Linux--and hacking, friendship, consciousness, trance music, and the earth's future. Our long conversations helped me recognize what we had in common all along: a love of wit and play, an insatiable curiosity for learning about how things (and people) work, and a knack for solving problems.

I do not feel as if I need to be a programmer to faithfully represent and perform values held by practitioners of Computers and Writing. I have repeatedly stated that I am not a computer programmer, but I am a hacker. I am able to recognize how bureaucratic linguistic practices inhibit me from "tinkering" with language. I see how the humanities' obsession with authors and owners inhibits many people from collaborating, dialoguing about, and innovating scholarly research. In fact, I've been on the border my whole life—switching back and forth from Standard White English and African American Vernacular English, Midwest Plain Style and Decorous Southern Speech. I've used the invisibility and visibility of my identity to push the limits of argumentation beyond the confines of 'normality.' I've been translating language as long as I can remember, trying to understand these rules, poking fun at them, playing with them, succeeding or failing at remixing and subverting them to open up new paths for language use.

Alexandria Lockett--"I've been translating languages as long as I can remember." #cwcon smart thinking on code switching.

Anita DeRouen

Lockett says we can be hackers, subverting institutional restraints on both technology and language. LOVE this metaphor. #cwcon

Amanda Wall

Computational literacy should include a wider range of competencies besides just 'technical' literacy. Coding is a dynamic performance, a demonstration of various levels of competency including: how and why I do code or whether or not I can recognize the ways in which the code influences specific programs I choose to run--in both human and machine interactions. In particular, working with multilingual writers in the writing center for the past year has enabled me to recognize the benefits of using computing as a metaphor for helping them understand grammar. For instance, their understanding of the article as an operation for quantity, or a marker with the capacity to establish degrees of specificity, enables them to go beyond a mechanical tendency to always put 'the' in front of a noun. Rather, these writers can now decide whether or not they should:

1. transform girl to a proper noun and eliminate the need for an article altogether
2. indicate how many 'girls' exist within that context
3. specify what 'the girl' is doing, or where she may be located

By understanding what an article does, multilingual writers can practice grammar with their communication aims, instead of a textbook's static examples, at the forefront of their decision-making. Through my pedagogical and personal experiences with language, I've learned to understand the operational limits and potentials of grammar as code, and recognize its inseparable relationship to technical, cultural, and political ecologies. This talk, for instance, is a program I'm running to facilitate trust between us so that we can acknowledge the value of anyone who wants to tinker with these discourses for the benefit of helping others quench their thirst for knowledge or find out which beverage motivates them to pursue their drink.

 Alexandria Lockett #cwcon operational limits of grammar and coding (politics) flow across and open into each other: possibilities.power

Anne Frances Wysocki

I am not a computer programmer, but should I desire to close the wide gap that exists between what I need to know and what I can possibly learn to become one, I have access to every resource available to me to do so vis-a-vis open educational resources. I don't know C++, Ruby,

Python, or Perl, but I was able to get a sense of the politics surrounding their developments and implementations by visiting their websites, reading discussion forums, current events, trade and scholarly journal articles, and talking to individuals teaching and learning these languages. I highly benefit from experiencing intertwingularity, or the principle that governs the architecture of these collaborative feedback systems whose countless distributed autonomous communities defies unproductive arbitrary hierarchies. I do not teach with technology without discussing the power distributions of socio-technical systems, the ethical responsibilities they inflict upon human users, and the ways in which our grammatical code and linguistic arrangements make it difficult for us to talk about emergence. We need hackers of all gradients—from the computer programmer to the radical pragmatist instructor to the DJ to the comic—to resolve the broader issues of helping students develop enough confidence and generosity to hack language, improve their writing, and self-consciously participate in a much broader effort to do humanity unto others.

## Source Literacy: A Vision of Craft

*Karl Stolley*

### Introduction

> For the things we have to learn before we can do them, we
> learn by doing them. E.g., [people] become builders by building. - Aristotle, Nicomachean Ethics, Book II, Chapter 1

"Program, or be Programmed." That's a dire warning. And being a firm believer in the importance of computational literacy, or source literacy as I prefer to call it, I've issued more than my fair share of dire warnings: What happens if we only write in other people's apps, other people's text boxes. What happens if we think ourselves so privileged as a field that we can pick and choose from the digital buffet of what will and will not be our concerns.

But for the sake of this short polemic, I won't issue any dire warnings. I won't make any direct appeals as to why every member of the Computers and Writing community should immediately learn to program. I won't even want to argue with anyone about whether we should pursue source literacy. For me, the answer is an obvious and unqualified Yes. But debate or even sharing abstract ideas alone is not persuasive. When it comes to programming, like swimming or any other activity whose lived experience differs greatly from its perception or description, only hands-on, long-term experiences will persuade.

What I can offer here is my vision for the field of Computers and Writing. I want to share what it is that we could do and be if we all make learning to program a routine component of our writing and teaching. I will conclude with four things that each member of the field can do immediately to make this vision a reality.

## My Vision

> Do not automate the work you are engaged in, only the materials. - Alan Kay, "Microelectronics and the Personal Computer" (244)

Because this is a vision, I'm going to use the present tense. Not the future tense.

My vision for Computers and Writing places craft at the center of what we do. And what we do is digital production. We make things from raw digital materials: open-source computer languages and open formats. Which is to say, we write digital things. To write digital things, we rely on a strong command of source literacy.

And @karlstolley comes out firing, as expected. Learn to program right after lunch! #cwcon

Michael R. Trice

There are no language tricks with the verb write in this source-literate field I envision. Writing is not a metaphor to explain how writing is accomplished by clicking through a WYSIWYG that generates and automates our work for us. The verb write is literal.

Everyone, of course, writes with web standards: HTML, CSS, and JavaScript. Above all else, the field values digital projects that are accessible from any browser, on any device. In my vision, that value has become pervasive; it's rare anymore to hear of a writing assignment that doesn't require students to adhere closely to web standards.

And while debates rage over different markup and design patterns, the level of discourse and collaboration regarding digital craft has never been more sophisticated. In fact, in the field as I envision it, several members of the Computers and Writing community are now active participants in the working groups that oversee the development of web standards specifications.

But the really remarkable change has been the number and diversity of open-source software projects initiated and maintained by members of the field I envision. It's unusual to find someone in Computers and Writing who doesn't have a GitHub account and a favorite language, or who doesn't attend the special interest group devoted to that language at the 4Cs each year.

From all of this digital production activity, there has been a renaissance in publishing on digital craft in our field. Numerous digital book titles by researchers in Computers and Writing routinely appear on must-read lists outside the field, especially for programmers and developers whose own professional practice has been greatly augmented by a rhetorical approach to thinking about and doing the work of digital craft.

@afwysocki @karlstolley Heck yes, it's all about craft! #cwcon

Kristi Prins

How did this sense of craft emerge? By rejecting a model of computing that is suited to office cubicles and deskilled writers. By embracing, instead, a deep appreciation for the raw materials, the languages, of the digital medium, and seeing digital writing as more than the on-screen result of the machinations of commercial software.

"Craft," in the words of Malcolm McCullough, "is commitment to the worth of personal knowledge" (246). It is commitment to research and learning over technical support and intuitive interfaces. Craft is ultimately the sense of taking responsibility for the digital writing that we unleash on the world. It is the thrill and wonder of watching our collective work emerge from the thousands of lines of hand-written source code that make up the eBooks and web applications that members of the field write every single year.

.@karistolley to #cwcon: 10 EAT LUNCH: LEARN
CODE: PRINT "World, I'm changing you."

Chris Friend

## How to Make this Vision a Reality

Here are four means to making this vision a reality. But do not think
of them as steps. Rather, think of them as representing a radical shift
in digital production that centralizes craft: a shift that you either
adopt, or reject.

    1.   Learn a Unix-like operating system at its command line.

Whether you have a shiny new Mac with the latest version of OS X or
run Ubuntu Linux on an old computer you have laying around, the
first step to source literacy is to get comfortable with relying on the
keyboard to interact with the computer.

    2.   Commit to writing in a text editor with good syntax highlight-
ing, and start writing HTML and CSS.

For everything. Old habits hold people back more than the challenges of learning something new. Even if ultimately you have to submit
something, like a journal article, in Microsoft Word, do your composing in HTML.

    3.   Learn the distributed version control system Git, and establish
a GitHub account.

Experimentation, expansive learning, and even simple revision are all
impossible if we're shackled to the regular file system of a computer,
where versioning happens by renaming files. If the computer is, as
Steve Jobs said, a bicycle for the mind, then Git is a time machine and
guardian angel for the mind's productive digital work.

Share your Github accounts. I want to follow what
you're doing there. ('brocktopus') bit.ly/JG6spo
#cwcon @karlstolley

Kevin Brock

4.  Learn a couple of web-oriented, open-source programming languages.

JavaScript and Ruby are the two languages I wish everyone knew, on top of HTML and CSS. Despite its reputation, JavaScript has matured into an important language, as evidenced by server-side applications such as Node.js. Ruby, courtesy of development frameworks such as Rails and Sinatra, is quickly becoming the language of choice to power web applications. But Ruby has utility in many other domains, such as programming command-line applications that can extend and deepen command-line literacy beyond basic shell scripting.

@karlstolley has a vision for the future in which I fear i may have to live in the woods and go Luddite. Quit scaring me Karl! #cwcon

Kristin Arola

I don't expect any of this will be easy. I engage regularly in all four of the practices above, and have for many years. Yet I still consider myself a learner. And being a learner and valuing learning as itself both craft and challenge, I cannot help but summarily reject 'ease' as a measure of any craft that is valuable or worthwhile.

Just joined GitHub, if only to follow the accounts of other digi-compists. Thx for the push @karlstolley #cwcon

Jen Michaels

## THE ANXIETY OF PROGRAMMING: WHY TEACHERS SHOULD RELAX AND ADMINISTRATORS SHOULD WORRY

*Elizabeth Losh*

The central concept of this panel "Program or Be Programmed" might immediately bring up performance anxiety issues for many composition professionals in the audience. As Stephen Ramsay put it recently, the very notion of the tech-savvy digital humanities as the newest "hot thing" tends to bring up "terrible, soul-crushing anxiety about peoples' place in the world." For those in composition, the anxiety might be even more acutely soul-crushing in light of existing labor politics. Every time the subject of learning code comes up, one can almost see the thought balloons appearing: "How can I learn Python in my spare time when I can't even see over the top of the stack of first-year papers that I have to grade?"

Glad that @lizlosh is addressing the issues of anxiety, code and @sramsay 's "the hot thing" in this town hall. #cwcon

Annette Vee

And for those who care about inclusion, what does it mean to choose the paradigm of computer programming culture, where women and people of color so frequently feel marginalized?

Furthermore, if all these powerful feelings are being stirred up, what questions should we be asking about ideology as an object of study. For example, at the 2010 Critical Code Studies conference, Wendy Chun argued that a desire for mastery over blackboxed systems or access to originary source code shows how a particular dialectic of freedom and control makes it difficult for us to have meaningful discussions about technology and to acknowledge our own limited access to totalizing understanding, even if one might be a software engineer.

Fortunately, after reading the arguments above, our audience should feel a little less anxious as they think about teaching writing as an information art. They should know that doing-it-yourself means doing-it-with-others, whether it is imagining Picasso and Braque building a flying machine, as David Rieder suggests, or installing Ubuntu with the help of a neighbor, as Alexandria Lockett describes. The message to instructors is ultimately comforting: relax, be confident in your own abilities to learn new things, ask questions, facilitate the questions of others, and network in ways that help you make new friends.

However, if you are an administrator as well as an instructor, don't get too relaxed just yet. These talks also bring up some very thorny questions about disciplinary turf. After all, who defines how digital literacy should be taught and who will teach it? Computer scientists? Media artists? Librarians? Writing studies people?

@lizlosh 's response to #cwcon townhall DIY hackers....
good for teachers, but WPAs, admins, beware
promotion discipline boundaries blur blur

Carl Whithaus

Although he uses the word "craft," Karl Stolley asserts that "source literacy" doesn't require an elaborate apprenticeship. All it takes is moving toward a set of everyday common-sense practices involving taking control of command lines and file structures. Mark Sample suggests the term "code competency" as an alternative to "code literacy," because of all the cultural baggage associated with the word "literacy" itself. Trebor Scholz has suggested "fluency" as a better characterization of what we are trying to teach, but Sample notes the limitations of that term.

In a 2010 essay called "Whose Literacy Is It Anyway?" Jonathan Alexander and I pointed to Michael Mateas's work on "procedural literacy" as a way for compositionists to begin to engage with these issues. Mateas worries that universities are often too eager to adopt the training regimes of computer science departments, which is great for graduating computer science majors but not so great for teaching students in other majors or with other passions to use code. Mateas also argues that programming languages like Processing are needed in these curricula, because they can be customized by advanced users outside of technical fields while provide scaffolding for beginners to learn languages like Java and C++. (For more on Processing, see my my "DIY Coding" interview with the language's co-creator Casey Reas.)

So what should be the relationship between writing studies and computer science in the academy? The collegiality common between computer science and computers and writing only gets us so far in our responsibility to teach computational literacy.

i think the ? about programming is at heart a struggle
with collaboration. Academics not so comfortable at
necessary collaboration #cwcon

David Parry

@academicdave IMO, computers and writing has a rich history of collaborative work. Other fields, perhaps not as much. #cwcon

Tim Lockridge

Both Sample and Vee mention Edsger Dijkstra, who was also the author of "On the Cruelty of Really Teaching Computer Science," a decidedly anti-humanistic diatribe on the superiority of formal logic and mathematics as the keys to supposedly real knowledge. Dijkstra's legacy still lives on in many computer science departments, and it is often difficult to have rhetoric taken seriously by stakeholders in many other STEM disciplines. The core curriculum in the Culture, Art, and Technology program that I direct has a digital literacy requirement that generally involves taking a programming course in the computer science department, but not every student feels comfortable crossing those bridges between disciplinary norms.

If there are answers to the questions of who should teach computational literacy, then we have not yet found them. But I'll put in my own GOTO command for writing studies to keep this spaghetti-like discussion going.

## Conclusion

*Annette Vee*

Programming has undeniably made its way into Computers and Writing through our research and teaching, but the role of computational literacy in the field is still in flux. Although we have offered arguments for the importance of computational literacy or competency, we have not offered solutions for how and where to teach this critical skill. We offer only suggestions: the digital literacy requirement that Losh mentions is just one administrative attempt to give students outside of computer science access to programming. Many of us in the field have found space in our syllabi for basic web design or graphical programming in Processing, even if we do not all teach Ruby like Stolley. Yet these practices cannot scale up to 50 sections of first year composition, or across to our colleagues who are expert teachers of writing but not as skilled in digital forms of composition.

What, then, should we teach about programming in our writing classes? As Lockett argues, the politics of software shape our compositions and communications, and we cannot fail to grasp the basic sociotechnical mechanisms behind that. If we consider critical thinking part of our composition teaching mission, critical thinking about our software now seems tantamount to critical thinking about other forms of media that we currently teach in our classes.

But teaching programming per se? Given the diversity of approaches to composition across our field—from rhetorical argument to multimodality to critical engagement—it would be folly to propose a one-size-fits-all solution for how we might fit computational literacy into composition. Each university and each instructor must consider the concerns, futures, and backgrounds of their students along with their local resources before coming to conclusions about the role of computational literacy in their courses.

For now, we hope this collection of provocations has helped put computational literacy on the map of the field of Computers and Writing, but also of writing studies more generally. The algorithmic processes of programming now form a new ground for writing—one that might make us anxious, but one that should invigorate us as well. We teach and compose in writing, and as we expand the modes by which we define writing, we expand its potential as an informational art.

## Works Cited

Altair BASIC Reference Manual. Albuquerque: MITS, 1975. Print.

Aristotle, Nichomachean Ethics. Trans. W.D. Ross. The Internet Classics Archive. Web. 29 Aug. 2012.

Deleuze, Gilles and Felix Guattari. Anti-Oedipus: Capitalism and Schizophrenia. Trans. Robert Hurley, Mark Seem, and Helen R. Lane. Minneapolis: University of Minnesota, 1983. Print.

Dijkstra, Edsger. "Letters to the Editor: Go To Statement Considered Harmful." Communications of the ACM 11.3 (1968): 147–148. ACM Digital Library. Web. 14 Jan 2011.

Galloway, Alexander R. Gaming: Essays on Algorithmic Culture. Minneapolis: University of Minnesota Press, 2006.

Kay, Alan. "Microelectronics and the Personal Computer." Scientific American September 1977: 230-244.

Kemeny, John G. Man and the Computer. New York: Scribner, 1972. Print.

Lanham, Richard. The Economics of Attention: Style and Substance in the Age of Information. Chicago: The University of Chicago Press, 2006. Print.

McCullough, Malcolm. Abstracting Craft: The Practiced Digital Hand. The MIT Press, 1998. Print.

McGann, Jerome. The Textual Condition. Princeton, NJ: Princeton University Press, 1991. Print.

Tansey, Mark. Picasso and Braque. Los Angeles County Museum of Art, Los Angeles, CA. Painting.

Wang, Li-Chen. "Palo Alto Tiny BASIC." Dr. Dobb's Journal of Computer Calisthenics & Orthodontia, Running Light without Overbite May 1976: 12–25. Print.

# HARLOT

*Harlot* is a peer-reviewed digital journal dedicated to exploring rhetoric in everyday life. The journal's title gestures toward historical references to rhetoric as "the harlot of the arts," a pejorative definition that seems widely accepted in contemporary public discourse; *Harlot* seeks to challenge these assumptions by revealing the way that communication of all kinds subtly influences and powerfully shapes the world. The mission of the journal is to create a space for critical—but inclusive and informal—conversations about rhetoric amongst diverse publics, with the aim of bridging rhetorical scholarship and popular discourse.

## Recitative: The Persuasive Tenor of Jazz Culture in Langston Hughes, Billy Strayhorn, and John Coltrane

"Recitative" explores jazz culture as a progressive social force and invites contemporary audiences to enter that "great conversation about the meaning of the modern world." The sleek design complements a nuanced but novice-friendly analysis of aural performances by Hughes, Strayhorn, and Coltrane. Throughout, audio clips slow the audience's reading, shaping an experience that supports Vogel's claim: "By hearing the jazz that permeates our culture, we are all more likely to listen to each other, to compose our thoughts to be spoken deliberately, and thus to invigorate progressive relationships in America today." This article reflects *Harlot*'s drive to connect scholarship and social action; it offers fresh insights on familiar issues while exploiting the affordances of digital publication to deepen audience participation..

# 6 Recitative: The Persuasive Tenor of Jazz Culture in Langston Hughes, Billy Strayhorn, and John Coltrane

*Andrew Vogel*

## CREATOR'S STATEMENT

Jazz is more than music. Jazz is a culture defined by a progressive ethos encoded in sound. By putting the poetry and music of Langston Hughes, Billy Strayhorn, and John Coltrane into conversation, this essay demonstrates the versatility and vitality of jazz culture. However, jazz culture has come to be drowned out in America today, and so I argue for a return to the voices of jazz's past so that we can give a new ear to jazz artists working today. Such listening should be seen as a means to reinvigorate progressive values today and in the future

## HEAD: JAZZ CULTURE

This past summer a dear friend posted one of those provocative questions on a social networking site. She solicited ideas for good music to play while working, something up-tempo to get her motivated. Among the many suggestions submitted was a short list of jazz artists, which she lovingly dismissed as old-fashioned. This is not uncommon. Many find jazz old-fashioned. It's their parents' or their grandparents' music, an endearing but not very compelling reminder of the bygone century.

As Benjamin Schwarz has recently put it in *The Atlantic Monthly*, jazz music is a "relic."

Likewise, when I assign even modern poetry in the American literature classes I teach, the students scarcely even try to conceal their displeasure. "I just don't understand poetry," the bold will announce with defensive pride. This parallels that awkward moment when the subject of my profession comes up among polite acquaintances. People recall fondly a high school or college literature course, list some familiar favorites—Whitman, Dickinson, Frost—and then pine, "I wish I understood poetry," to cover their confession of embarrassing reading habits. This all-too-common embarrassment is confirmed by two recent National Endowment for the Arts studies ("Reading at Risk" and "To Read or Not to Read") that document declining rates of engagement with poetry. Somehow poetry, like jazz, has become a presumptively dead language in the popular imagination.

At one time though, poetry and jazz were highly-respected art forms in America. As industrialization transformed daily life, poets and musicians developed startlingly innovative approaches to their art forms and commanded popular admiration because they spoke to the mixture of wariness and inspiration that people were feeling. By composing sophisticated responses to the troubling realities of modern life out of vernacular materials, America's modernists ignited a new culture, a culture that, following Alfred Appel, I like to think of as jazz culture.

The Original Dixieland Jazz Band, The Great Gatsby, The Waste Land, The Harlem Renaissance, The Jazz Singer, The Modern Jazz Quartet—jazz modernists experimented with an array of compositional techniques to formulate illuminating responses to the startling conditions of life in the modern world. They developed styles of fragmentation, free verse, syncopation, cubism, collage, and stream-of-consciousness to announce their sense that they were living in a new, disorienting world, but the one fundamental feature that pervades jazz culture is the emphasis on sound. Jazz modernists crafted modes of expression to represent the sounds of the new dispensation—the factory's mechanical thunder, the 20th Century Limited tearing across the plains, the subway tunneling under Manhattan, the electric turbine, the noon-time and the midnight street corner, the internal combustion engine, the airplane propeller, the silent film piano, the talkie, and the phonograph. Poetry and music were uniquely well suited to distill and represent the sound of modern life, and the people listened. Yet, although precious little has changed with regard to the fundamental features of modern existence, jazz poetry and music have been crowded out of the marketplace of vital ideas and relegated to the dustbin of university campuses, public radio, and used record stores where they cling to an intensely loyal but arguably diminishing audience.

With this in mind, I would like to reconsider jazz music and poetry together. I want to question why they are generally presumed to be passé when there are so many innovators in these forms working in relative obscurity today. I'd like to think about the aural relationships between jazz poetry and music, and I'd like to think about their sound as fundamentally rhetorical, a persuasive ethos. Considering jazz poetry and music as rhetorical, I want to evoke Gertrude Buck, who argued that persuasion should put the public good before personal interest and that honesty is essential to social progress. In this essay, I focus on Langston Hughes, Billy Strayhorn, and John Coltrane, who embody Buck's imperative in jazz culture. By studying Hughes, Strayhorn, and Coltrane as poet/musicians, I'd like to define the discourse of jazz culture and suggest that by hearing the jazz that permeates our culture we are all more likely to listen to each other, to compose our thoughts to be spoken deliberately, and thus to invigorate progressive relationships in America today.

## SOLO: LANGSTON HUGHES

### "The Weary Blues"

In the essay "Jazz as Communication," Langston Hughes explains that jazz is "a circle, and you yourself are a dot in the middle" (492). He means that jazz is expansive. He argues that jazz is vastly more than merely music; rather, for Hughes jazz is a feeling about modern life that is sometimes expressed musically but that as often "seeps into words" (493). Implicitly jazz is also expressed in relationships, in work, in dance, in sex, and in politics. He suggests that people are drawn to jazz arts because they recognize in it articulations of their own ideas on life in the modern world. Hughes claims that he has been only one of many writers through whom jazz has been "putting itself into words" (494).

In 1923 Hughes wrote probably his most famous jazz poem, "The Weary Blues":

> Droning a drowsy syncopated tune,
> Rocking back and forth to a mellow croon,
>     I heard a Negro play.
> Down on Lenox Avenue the other night
> By the pale dull pallor of an old gas light
>     He did a lazy sway . . .
>     He did a lazy sway . . .
> To the tune o' those Weary Blues.
> With his ebony hands on each ivory key
> He made that poor piano moan with melody.
>     O Blues!
> Swaying to and fro on his rickety stool
> He played that sad raggy tune like a musical fool.
>     Sweet Blues!
> Coming from a black man's soul.
>     O Blues!
> In a deep song voice with a melancholy tone
> I heard that Negro sing, that old piano moan—
>     "Ain't got nobody in all this world,
>     Ain't got nobody but ma self.
>     I's gwine to quit ma frownin'
>     And put ma troubles on the shelf."
>
> Thump, thump, thump, went his foot on the floor.
> He played a few chords then he sang some more—
>     "I got the Weary Blues
>     And I can't be satisfied.
>     Got the Weary Blues
>     And can't be satisfied—
>     I ain't happy no mo'
>     And I wish that I had died."
> And far into the night he crooned that tune.
> The stars went out and so did the moon.
> The singer stopped playing and went to bed
> While the Weary Blues echoed through his head.
> He slept like a rock or a man that's dead.

The poem is a classic of the Harlem Renaissance because in the spirit of jazz it is composed to speak to (and for) a generation of the free children of former slaves who had migrated from the South to the North and stood up to Jim Crow segregation and terrorism. The poem gives voice to the uncertainty, the frustration, and the defiance of the New Negro Movement.

The speaker ostensibly listens while a musician plays and sings, but the speaker really performs both his voice and the musician's. The speaker's voice favors standard American English, but the quoted lyrics of the musician's song are annunciated in African American dialect: "ma self," "gwine," "ma frownin'." Nevertheless, the standard American English of the speaker takes up the characteristics of the music being played. Hughes essentially sings both voices. In Hughes' understated delivery, his voice accentuates the sonorous o and u sounds of "droning," "drowsy," "syncopated tune," for example; he lingers on the word "moan" and quavers on "tone," conveying the emotion of both listening and performing.

The use of occasional end rhyme complements this aural pattern. The poem is built around a series of linked couplets; however, the couplets are irregularly spaced around interjections of various lengths. The first and second couplet, "tune/croon" and "night/light," are interrupted by one line, yet later couplets are interrupted by two lines here, three lines there, and even whole verses of the musician's songs. These rhymes distribute the poem's aural effects throughout the poem, lending a sense of overall cogency to the interplay of the poem's two distinct voices.

Finally, whereas poetry of previous generations followed rigorous prescriptive patterns of stressed and unstressed syllables, Hughes' lines are deliberately uneven and loosely syncopated. The stressed sounds come not from preset, classical patterns. They are improvisational, keyed to the expression of feeling. For instance, the lines "Swaying to and fro on his rickety stool / He played that sad raggy tune like a musical fool" have 11 and 13 syllables respectively, and they each follow an organic voicing rooted in the poem's articulation of emotions. Taking all these features of the poem together, there's little doubt that Hughes is translating the styles of jazz—multiple voices, harmonic interruption, improvisational performance, and syncopation—into his lyrics as he explicitly represents both the voices and the tribulations of black people in a racist world.

## SOLO 2: LANGSTON HUGHES

**"Trumpet Player: 52nd Street"**

Throughout his career, Hughes crafted jazz poems. His 1947 "Trumpet Player: 52nd Street" is another example:

> The Negro
> With the trumpet at his lips
> Has dark moons of weariness
> Beneath his eyes,
> Where the smoldering memory
> Of slave ships
> Blazed to the crack of whips
> about thighs.
>
> The negro
> with the trumpet at his lips
> has a head of vibrant hair
> tamed down,
> patent-leathered now
> until it gleams
> like jet—
> were jet a crown.
>
> The music
> from the trumpet at his lips
> is honey
> mixed with liquid fire.
> The rhythm
> from the trumpet at his lips
> is ecstasy
> distilled from old desire—
>
> Desire
> that is longing for the moon
> where the moonlight's but a spotlight
> in his eyes,
> desire
> that is longing for the sea

where the sea's a bar-glass
sucker size

The Negro
with the trumpet at his lips,
whose jacket
Has a fine one-button roll,
does not know
upon what riff the music slips

It's hypodermic needle
to his soul
but softly
as the tune comes from his throat
trouble mellows to a golden note

Like "The Weary Blues," this poem evokes the legacies of slavery by suggesting that the collective memory of slave ships inspires the musician's playing, and it extends the defiance of the New Negro into the Civil Rights era by evoking cocky urbane fashions and the fraught doctoring of kinky hair. Likewise, "The Trumpet Player" is as ambivalent as "The Weary Blues," both admiring and pitying the black artist's complicated social position. In the cabaret, under the spotlight, the trumpet player is simultaneously the representative of black culture as well as an individual seeking happiness and comfort, for which fame, fashion, alcohol, opiates, and even music are but meager substitutes.

Hughes' arrangement of the poem imitates a jazz solo in which an instrumentalist will improvise on a standard melody through a series of measures. The "melody" of the poem follows on the repeated line, "The Negro / With the Trumpet at his lips." Each verse varies on the theme, describing both the trumpet player and the sources of his musical ideas. The pattern of rhyme and assonance is irregular, evoking improvisation by taking on new variations in each verse. Hughes sings the lines organically, speeding up his tempo in staccato bursts of thought or slowing down to linger in febrile drawls over key words. His voice is both syncopated and melodic, following the sound as much as the sense of the words. Calling attention to the unifying idea of the poem, he growls then glides through the lines, "as the tune comes from his throat / trouble mellows to a golden note." Even his slight unintentional lisp individuates his performance, lending it inimitable personality.

## Chorus: Persuasive Sound

Langston Hughes was a master of jazz poetry because the sound and the power of his lyrics are keyed to progressivism. As a black man, as a gay man, and as an advocate for the disenfranchised, Hughes translates jazz into words as he persistently explores the theme of "trouble" mellowed to that "golden note." His poetry is a model of the style upon which so many poets would innovate and improve—Sterling Brown, Gwendolyn Brooks, Allen Ginsberg, Lawrence Ferlinghetti, Frank O'Hara, Michael Harper, Jayne Cortez, Yusef Komunyakaa, William Matthews, Rita Dove, Robert Pinsky, Nikky Finney, and Terrance Hayes, to name only a few. And certainly Hughes' influence resonates beyond his own medium—in the art of Romare Bearden, for instance, the plays of August Wilson, the novels of Toni Morrison, the films of John Cassavetes and Spike Lee, and the albums of A Tribe Called Quest, Public Enemy, and The Roots. Certainly, Martin Luther King, Jr.'s "I Have a Dream" speech echoes Hughes' Montage of a Dream Deferred. Crucially, Hughes' sound encouraged and inspired jazz musicians.

Hughes' poetry was potent then and it remains popular now because it reminds us, when we really listen, that jazz can be thought of as a distinctive culture with its own attitudes, customs, aesthetics, commitments, and concerns. By seeing jazz as culture we begin to see it as a great conversation about the meaning of the modern world that includes (and evokes) voices working in a variety of modes and mediums from fashion to film to funk. Much of the appeal of jazz culture is rooted in its resistance to a discriminatory status quo. That resistance is encoded in sound, and that sound is conversational, inviting participation. In jazz culture, therefore, women, African-Americans, homosexuals, the poor, and all the marginalized and excluded can listen to, dance to, and reflect upon a sound that defies tradition and thus seeks to establish new social arrangements based on the justice of personal exploration and shared interests.

Such conversation is precisely what Gertrude Buck defined as Platonic speech. Rather than an approach to discourse that advances the interests of the individual by any available and necessary means, Buck sought persuasion based on the common interests of all participants in the public forum. Establishing common interests, Buck explains, demands pursuit of truth. Yet, because truth is relative, those involved in the conversation must be willing to both share personal observations and listen to those of others. Thus, she calls for a conversation based on attention, reflection, sharing, and honesty, all of which are rooted in the careful composition of ideas. That's jazz culture. It's what we hear in the leading practitioners of jazz arts, like Hughes, but also Billy Strayhorn and John Coltrane.

## BRIDGE: BILLY STRAYHORN

### "Lush Life"

Billy Strayhorn's "Lush Life" is notoriously difficult to play as music, but when treated as modernist poetry rather than just song, it makes a lot more sense for musicians. Like Hughes' poetry, the song's peculiar cadences emerge from the organic improvisational play of stressed and unstressed words:

> I used to visit all the very gay places
> those come what may places
> where one relaxes on the axis of the wheel of life
> to get the feel of life
> from jazz and cocktails.
> The girls i knew had sad and sullen gray faces
> with distant gay traces
> that used to be there you could see where
> they'd been washed away
> by too many through the day
> twelve o'clocktails.
> [ Lyrics from: http://www.lyricsty.com/billy-strayhorn-lush-life-lyrics.html ]
> Then you came along with your siren's song
> to tempt me to madness.
> I thought for a while that your pointed smile
> was tinged with the sadness
> of a great love for me.
> Ah yes, I was wrong.
> Again, I was wrong.

Life is lonely again,
and only last year
everything seemed so assured.
Now life is awful again.
and the thoughtful of heart
could only be a bore.

A week in Paris will ease the bite of it;
all I care is to smile in spite of it.
I'll forget you I will,
and yet you are still
burning inside my brain.

Romance is mush,
stifling those who strive.
I'll live a lush life in some small dive,
and there I'll be while I rot
with the rest of those
whose lives are lonely too.

Likewise the shifts of tempo come from the words rather than a time signature. Repetition in the first chorus—"places," "life," "cocktails"—underscores the interchangeability of locations and libations as time drags slowly along. Certain lines rhyme, "faces/traces," "away/day," "madness/sadness," but these are irregular, emerging opportunistically through the narrative, reinforcing the sorrowful rituals of a life without love. The opportunistic rhyming climaxes with the couplet: "A week in Paris will ease the bite of it / All I care is to smile in spite of it." The double rhyme highlights the speaker's fruitless quest for solace in romantic love. Similarly, Strayhorn's performance introduces an unexpected pause in the penultimate line, "while I rot with the rest," and the piano fill in that moment highlights the speaker's understanding of his fate in the modern world of circumstantial love affairs.

Tonally, Strayhorn's performance calls attention to the painful passage of time as he quavers on "day" in the first chorus and enjambs "madness—I" in the second. The piano's blues-minor chord progression harmonically anticipates the mood change between the second and the third chorus, and Strayhorn's voice assumes the feeling, changing the mood of the performance from ironic disregard to pained resignation.

As a student of both Ira Gershwin and modernist poets like e. e. cummings (Hadju 135, 195), Strayhorn uses irregular cadences and opportunistic rhymes to translate certain ambivalent feelings about life and love in the modern world into jazz expression. The poem cynically discounts notions of sentimental love without denying the potency of desire and loneliness. As with Hughes, the poignancy of Strayhorn's performance is tied to the fact that as a gay man his love would be unsanctioned and the worry that he would, therefore, always remain lonely, living the lush life. Yet, such agonies are not exclusively homosexual, because so many people seem to be wearing a mask of gayety to cover their "sad and sullen gray faces," an observation that speaks to the dehumanizing customs that seem to be inherent in the modern condition.

Although Billy Strayhorn's name may be unfamiliar to some, he was jazz royalty. Strayhorn was Duke Ellington's musical collaborator, composing his most famous song, "Take the 'A' Train," a song that also uses experimental modernist lyric as a foundation for music. Strayhorn and Ellington shared a fruitful relationship because Strayhorn understood and contributed to Ellington's sense that music should tell true stories about modern life, and his innovative lyrical arrangements fostered improvisation and individuated performance over prescriptive rote. For Ellington and Strayhorn, music was a vehicle to pose social questions and bring attention to civil rights causes. Strayhorn even cultivated a friendship with Martin Luther King, Jr., the two men drifting into intense personal conversation whenever they encountered one another (Hadju 265). Perhaps these elements of Strayhorn's music— the poetry, the activism, and the sound—are what attracted one of jazz's most innovative visionaries, John Coltrane.

## Rhapsody: John Coltrane

### "Lush Life" and "A Love Supreme"

Coltrane studied both Langston Hughes and Billy Strayhorn, and their styles are audible in Coltrane's cadences (Porter 15). In 1957 John Coltrane recorded "Lush Life" as the title track of an album in which he confirmed that he was moving in new musical directions, taking themes from standards and pop tunes and working them through a complicated series of variations and inversions that anticipated the radical directions his music would explore in the coming years.

The choice of Strayhorn's classic affirms the composer's stature, yet it also indicates the importance of lyric in the forms of experimental jazz that Coltrane would pioneer. Coltrane clearly takes up Strayhorn's lyrics in his solo. He is voicing the words themselves as notes, mimicking through his saxophone Strayhorn's verbal performance. Red Garland's piano accompaniment reinforces this sense as Coltrane soulfully declaims the first two stanzas of the poem. Then as the rhythm section joins in, the final three stanzas of the poem are voiced with Strayhorn's ironic disregard of romance. Donald Byrd on trumpet then follows Coltrane's lead through the choruses, replaying Strayhorn's words and likewise evoking his themes.

Using poetry as a basis for musical composition appealed to Coltrane. As he explained to Michel Delorme in 1965, he liked to use poetry in his compositions because for him this was a way to "capture the essence of a precise moment in a given place [and] compose the work and perform it immediately in a natural way" (DeVito 244). Later, in 1967, Coltrane explained to Frank Kofsky that his music amounted to "a conscious attempt to change what I've found." That is, Coltrane saw music as an instrument to make the world a better place because, as he put it, "it can create the initial thought patterns that can change the thinking of the people" (Porter 261). Like Strayhorn and Hughes, Coltrane conjured the jazz feeling into art, composing a vehicle to pursue social progress.

*A Love Supreme* is perhaps Coltrane's most famous and most personal album. It is a four-part suite that is explicitly a prayer and a meditation on the love of God. It is a work of musical genius; however, the work's power is augmented by the use of poetry. Most famously and obviously the simple four-note theme that is the basis of the entire record is tied to the words "a love supreme," which are annunciated iambically, duh-Da duh-Da.

To highlight these four note/syllables, after the opening fanfare Coltrane plays these notes in sequence, running them through various scales until a chorus of voices take up the simple phrase, chanting "a love su-preme." The rhythm of the chant supplies an elemental rhythmic platform upon which the curtains of Coltrane's musical explorations gambol.

More importantly, however, in the liner notes of *A Love Supreme* Coltrane explains that the poem printed therein is given "musical narration" in the fourth movement, "Psalm." As Lewis Porter has demonstrated, Coltrane was being literal (246). He actually plays the words, which MarleelMystic's youtube video powerfully illustrates.

> I will do all I can to be worthy of Thee, O Lord.
> It all has to do with it.
> Thank You God.
>
> Peace. There is none other.
> God is. It is so beautiful.
> Thank You God.
>
> God is all.
> Help us to resolve our fears and weaknesses.
> In you all things are possible.
> Thank you God.
>
> We know. God made us so.
> Keep your eye on God.
> God is. He always was. He always will be.
>
> No matter what... it is God.
> He is gracious and merciful.
> It is most important that I know Thee.
>
> Words, sounds, speech, men, memory, thoughts,
> fears and emotions--time--all related...
> all made from one... all made in one.
>
> Blessed be his name.
> Thought waves--heat waves--all vibrations--
> all paths lead to God. Thank you God.
>
> His way... it is so lovely... it is gracious.
> It is merciful--Thank you God.
> One thought can produce millions of vibrations
> and they all go back to God... everything does.

Thank you God.
Have no fear... believe... Thank you God.
The universe has many wonders. God is all.

His way... it is so wonderful.
Thoughts--deeds--vibrations,
all go back to God and He cleanses all.

He is gracious and merciful... Thank you God.
Glory to God... God is so alive.
God is.
God loves.

May I be acceptable in Thy sight.

We are all one in His grace.
The fact that we do exist is acknowledgement
of Thee, O Lord.
Thank you God.

God will wash away all our tears...
He always has...
He always will.

Seek him everyday. In all ways seek God everyday.
Let us sing all songs to God.
To whom all praise is due... praise God.

No road is an easy one, but they all
go back to God.

With all we share God.
It is all with God.
It is all with Thee.

Obey the Lord.
Blessed is He.

We are all from one thing... the will of God...

Thank you God.

--I have seen ungodly--
none can be greater--none can compare
Thank you God.

He will remake... He always has and He
always will.
It's true--blessed be His name--Thank you God.

God breathes through us so completely...
so gently we hardly feel it... yet,
it is our everything.
Thank you God.
ELATION--ELEGANCE--EXALTATION--
All from God.
Thank you God. Amen.

The words and the music celebrate a simple idea, a love supreme, as Coltrane explores the manifold implications and applications of the idea of a universal, omnipotent, and loving God. Coltrane's bluesy voicing is suggestive of the difficult "paths," as the poem explains, to knowledge of God. The key image of the poem is tied to Coltrane's sense of himself as a musician. The line, "One thought can produce millions of vibrations," evokes the relationship between Coltrane's musical ideas and his articulations of them. Alluding to the very reed on his lip, the words draw the listener to focus on Coltrane's singularly rich timbre, and the line resolves in the idea that all vibrations "go back to God." Extending this metaphor, Coltrane elaborates, "God breathes through us so completely... so gently we hardly feel it... yet, it is our everything." God's breath passes through each of us just as Coltrane's breath passes through his horn, giving meaning to the instrument and the musician's life. The life of the world is the music of God in word, in music, and in deed. The metaphor illustrates Coltrane's adjuration to "In all ways seek God every day," which lends depth and power to his music and definitively formulates the approach to life that he believes will make the world a better place.

## Coda: Body and Soul

In "Jazz as Communication" Hughes further defines his sense of jazz. He succinctly states, "jazz is a dream deferred" (494). He is observing, in case anybody missed it, that his poetry is jazz and, therefore, a question regarding the progressive promise of the modern world. Certainly the deferred dream Hughes cites is the dream of liberty and equality for African Americans in a segregated country. Less obvious, but no less real and relevant, are the dream's implicit extensions to include gender, sexuality, ability, age, economic class, and so forth. Put simply, the sound of jazz announces the will to pursue and enact a better life for all. Jazz, for Hughes, is "A great big dream—yet to come—and always *yet*—to be-come ultimately and finally true" (494). Listening to Hughes, Strayhorn, and Coltrane, we recognize jazz as a culture of voices discussing the dream and its deferral.

The deferral continues in part because too many well-intentioned individuals claim appreciation for Hughes and the jazz ethos he represents but stop there. Instead of exploring the flourishing voices of jazz culture that resonate throughout American culture through the twentieth century and into the twenty-first, we categorize and separate poetry from jazz, jazz from the blues, the blues from rock & roll, and rock & roll from funk and punk. We divide folk voices from urban voices, straight from gay, black from white, male from female, rich from poor, left from right, old school and old fashioned from contemporary. Hughes becomes categorized as a voice of the Harlem Renaissance, some old-timey movement, rather than a vital voice clamoring with others in the name of more perfect union. By respectfully appreciating Hughes as a great American voice in our classrooms and stopping there, we fail to hear the myriad voices speaking to, with, for, and against him then and now, and that is how we have muted the progressive conversation of jazz culture.

Nevertheless, the improvisational and performative basis of the culture rewards close listening. As we listen, we begin to feel a deeper impulse. We become inspired to use human thought and energy to build a world that is peaceful and just, a world where all people can be free, where the troubled can find support, where the diligent can prosper, where the devout can find spiritual ascension. We hear in jazz an invitation to participate in the discussion of a dream. When the time comes we each compose and play our own version of the tune. As Hughes puts it, "Jazz is a heartbeat—its heartbeat is yours. You will tell me about its perspectives when you get ready" (494). As we speak we hear our voice collaborate and compromise with the voices around us. Imani Perry, for example, listens to a cycle of 31 versions of the jazz standard, "Body and Soul," recorded between 1939 and 2009. In this cycle she hears the "care" of what I am calling jazz culture. The return to "Body and Soul" resonates with the idea of an unruly, obstreperous, disputatious, but welcoming and engaging forum, which is what I picture when I imagine Buck's paradigm for discussion applied to the pursuit of the social good. As a standard returned to again and again, "Body and Soul" illustrates the fundamental spirit of jazz culture—the changes serve as a repository of questions about life in the modern world while simultaneously inviting new arrangements, enunciations, and compositions.

Whether we listen to "Body and Soul," Langston Hughes, Billy Strayhorn, John Coltrane, A Tribe Called Quest, Kevin Young, Fred Moten, Esperanza Spalding, Yoko Miwa, Gerald Clayton, Maria Schneider, the writers in Sascha Feinstein's *Brilliant Corners*, or even the speech of our president, we must recognize that the aesthetic and political dimensions of our world today are rooted in the ethos of jazz culture. As we listen, and then as we start to speak, we must surely hear ourselves questioning and, thus, advancing an aural and rhetorical aesthetics of progress in modernity. Perhaps the ironic cynicism of this postmodern world has made all such sound and fury irrelevant and, indeed, an out-moded relic, but I don't think so. I'd like my students, my acquaintances, and my friends to recognize with me that we know more about ourselves, about our daily work, about our play, and about what we can say when we hear the legacies of jazz culture that remain inflected in voices throughout America today.

## NOTE

The music that is "cited" as background to the three vocal tracks of this essay are taken from performances of the jazz standard "Body and Soul," composed by Johnny Green. The performances are by, in order, Coleman Hawkins, Errol Garner, Benny Goodman, Dave Brubeck, Thelonius Monk, John Coltrane, and Django Reinhardt & Stephane Grappelli. The citation of these performances is meant to evoke the persuasive sound of discursive care that Perry defines.

## ACKNOWLEDGMENTS

I am indebted to the editors of *Harlot*, especially Kate Comer, for their spirited suggestions that strengthened this essay. Many of the ideas for this essay emerged during conversations with Kevin Kjos, so much so that, in the true spirit of jazz, one couldn't clearly discern to whom any of the ideas in this essay truly belong. Additionally, credit for the web design and recording/mixing belongs to Nellie Ortiz and Christopher Burkholder, respectively.

## FAIR USE STATEMENT

1.  The purpose and character of your use: The copyrighted work quoted and referenced in this scholarly project is used to illustrate analysis and provide substantiation for analytical claims. The use is transformative in that all cited work is used as basis for original analysis and commentary that expands upon the ideas developed in the original works.

2.  The nature of the copyrighted work: The copyrighted work utilized is textual and musical. Proper citations can be found within the work and its accompanying bibliography. Readers are strenuously urged to seek out, purchase, and enjoy the original works. They are well worth it.

3.  The amount and substantiality of the work: Most of the copyrighted work cited here is sampled. However, a few works are reproduced in their entirety because complete reproduction is essential to illustrating the thesis of the argument. Sound bites cannot capture and represent the sound that is the basis of jazz culture.

4.  The effect of the use upon the potential market: This scholarly analysis and commentary should only have a positive effect on the markets for jazz and poetry, and these works in particular. No profit will be derived from the publication of this essay. This essay is offered in good spirit and with the sincere hope that individuals persuaded by the thesis will seek out opportunities to support the work of poets and musicians, including those cited and referenced herein.

# Works Cited

Appel, Alfred Jr. Jazz Modernism: From Ellington and Armstrong to Matisse and Joyce. New Haven Yale UP, 2004. Print.

Brubeck, Dave. "Body and Soul." 24 Classic Original Recordings. Fantasy. 1990. CD.

Buck, Gertrude. "The Present Status of Rhetorical Theory." Toward a Feminist Rhetoric: The Writing of Gertrude Buck. Ed. Joann Campbell. Pittsburgh: U Pittsburgh, 1996. 45-51. Print.

Coltrane, John. A Love Supreme. New York: Impulse/Verve, 1965. CD.

—. Lush Life. Prestige. 1958. CD.

—. Interview with Michel Delorme. "Coltrane Star of Antibes: 'I Can't Go Farther,'" Coltrane on Coltrane. Ed. Chris DeVito. Chicago: Chicago Review Press, 2010. 241-246 Print.

Garner, Errol. "Body & Soul." Body & Soul. Sbme Special Markets. 2008. CD.

Goodman, Benny. "Body and Soul." Greatest Hits. RCA. 1998. CD.

Hajdu, David. Lush Life: A Biography of Billy Strayhorn. New York: Farrar Strauss, Giroux, 1996. Print.

Hawkins, Coleman. "Body and Soul." Body and Soul. RCA. 1958. CD.

Hughes, Langston. "Jazz as Communication." The Langston Hughes Reader. New York: George Braziller, 1958. 492-494. Print.

—. Montage of a Dream Deferred. New York: Henry Holt, 1951. Print.

—. "The Weary Blues." The Voice of Langston Hughes. Washington: Smithsonian Folkways, 1995. CD.

—. "Trumpet Player: 52nd Street." Langston Hughes at 100. Beinecke Rare Book & Manuscript Library. 14 Jan. 2013. Web.

Monk, Thelonius. "Body and Soul." Live in Italy. Original Jazz Classics. 1991. CD.

Perry, Imani. "Of Degraded Talk, Digital Tongues, and a Commitment to Care." Profession, 2012. 17-24. Print.

Porter, Lewis. John Coltrane: His Life and Music. Ann Arbor. U Michigan, 1998. Print.

Reinhardt, Django. "Body and Soul." Djangology. Documents Classics. 2005. CD.

Schwarz, Benjamin. "The End of Jazz." The Atlantic, November 2012. Web. 14 Jan. 2013.

United States. National Endowment for the Arts. "Reading at Risk: A Survey of Literary Reading in America." Washington: GPO, 2004. Web.

United States. National Endowment for the Arts. "To Read or Not to Read: A Question of National Consequence." Washington: GPO, 2002. Web.

# THE JOURNAL OF BASIC WRITING

*The Journal of Basic Writing* is on the Web at http://wac.colostate.edu/jbw/index.cfm

*The Journal of Basic Writing* is a refereed print journal founded in 1975 by Mina Shaughnessy and is published twice a year with support from the Office of Academic Affairs of the City University of New York. Basic writing, a contested term, refers to the field concerned with teaching writing to students not yet deemed ready for first-year composition. Originally, these students were part of the wave of open admissions students who poured into universities as a result of the social unrest of the 1960s and the resulting reforms. Though social and political realities have changed dramatically since then, the presence of "basic writers" in colleges and universities, and the debates over how best to serve them, persist. *JBW* publishes articles related to basic and second-language writing as well as freshman writing transitions. Articles that explore the social, political, and pedagogical questions related to educational access and equity are at the core of *JBW*'s history and mission.

## Minority-Serving Institutions, Race-Conscious "Dwelling," and Possible Futures for Basic Writing at Predominantly White Institutions

Basic writing is not alone in its struggle to offer ensured access to the academy for marginalized students. Minority-serving institutions (MSIs) provide longstanding traditions of accessibility and outreach. Expanding on Nedra Reynold's notion of "dwelling" as an inspired form of engagement with and within spaces that challenge educational fairness and justice, Lamos looks to MSIs as models of educational leadership that spark race-conscious ideologies, practices, pedagogies, and service-learning activities. In this way, MSIs are poised to counteract the "contemporary neoliberal higher education climate" that has widely restricted options for basic writers. By tracing the correspondences between MSIs and basic writing, Lamos helps our field envision new spatial and discursive embodiments of educational equity and social justice.

# 7 Minority-Serving Institutions, Race-Conscious "Dwelling," and Possible Futures for Basic Writing at Predominantly White Institutions

*Steve Lamos*

ABSTRACT: *This essay looks to Minority-Serving Institutions (MSIs) for strategies that can be implemented in order to combat contemporary neoliberal attacks against the programmatic and institutional spaces of basic writing within Predominantly White Institutions (PWIs). Working from Nedra Reynolds' notion of thirdspace-oriented "dwelling" and Derrick Bell's notion of "interest convergence," it identifies four race-conscious "dwelling strategies" currently employed by MSIs to promote student success. It then offers four complementary suggestions regarding specific ways in which we in BW might adapt similar race-conscious dwelling strategies in the effort not only to defend our programs against contemporary attacks, but also to grow and cultivate new BW spaces within PWIs.*

## RACE AND THE INSTITUTIONAL SPACES OF BASIC WRITING

Many of us who work in basic writing (BW), and especially those of us who work in BW programs within the context of predominantly white institutions (or PWIs for short), consider our programs to be "race-conscious" spaces—that is, spaces where relationships between and among issues of race, racism, language, and literacy can be openly interrogated, challenged, and reformed when students learn how to write. In this sense, many of us are inspired by assertions like those of Deborah Mutnick that "basic writing[,] for all its internal contradictions, has played a vital role in increasing access to higher education, in particular for working-class people of color" (71–72). Unfortunately, many of us working in BW also know only too well that race-conscious BW spaces have been disappearing with increasing frequency during the last fifteen years or so. BW has been eliminated across the four-year CUNY campuses as part of the termination of its Open Admissions program, fundamentally redefined at the University of Minnesota as part of the dismantling of the General College program, undermined at the University of South Carolina (along with Rhonda Grego and Nancy Thompson's important "Studio" model for BW), and lost within a number of other institutions described within Nicole Greene and Patricia McAlexander's book *Basic Writing in America*. Additional losses within the context of two-year institutions also seem imminent: Pima Community College, one of the largest community colleges in Arizona, is currently attempting to establish baseline placement scores for all of its programs, thereby limiting its longstanding open admissions mission (see Pallack); meanwhile, legislation in Connecticut is currently being debated that would eliminate all remediation from two-year and four-year schools alike (see Fain).

Certainly, this widespread loss of BW space has a great deal to do with the increasing influence of neoliberal impulses that are reshaping higher education, especially PWIs. BW spaces are being or already have been eliminated from four-year and two-year PWIs as these institutions increasingly compete, both nationally and internationally, for ranking and prestige as a function of variables such as faculty research productivity, grant money, student ACT scores, and the like (see Hazelkorn; Ward). The logic driving BW elimination seems to be that institutions cannot compete for prestige if they support supposedly "illiterate" students who do not belong within their walls in the first place.

BW spaces are also being eliminated from PWIs in keeping with the sense that these "remedial" programs can be repackaged and resold as part of larger for-profit educational entities.

For instance, one of the individuals responsible for making the decision to end Open Admissions within CUNY four-year schools in 1999 was Benno Schmidt, a former president of Yale and then-chairperson of the Edison Group, a for-profit K-12 charter school manager. Higher education critics Patricia Gumport and Michael Bastedo point out that Schmidt, along with many other members of the Task Force that decided to terminate Open Admissions on CUNY's four-year campuses, stood to generate a good deal of profit once responsibility for remediation could be shifted away from CUNY and toward the companies that they were associated with (343). And, certainly, Schmidt and his Task Force colleagues were enacting a kind of logic in 1999 that has become increasingly prevalent since. Andrew Rosen, CEO of Kaplan University, has recently argued that for-profit higher educational institutions can and should target underprepared and underrepresented students as an increasingly important "down-market" group that is largely uninterested in traditional educational institutions. For-profit institutions should target this down-market, Rosen says, in much the way that "Wal-Mart and Target [aim] at mass-market consumers who'd prefer to save money rather than shop in a pricey department store" (34-35). In this sense, transforming "remedial" programs such as BW into down-market profit generators seems to be increasingly attractive, especially in a world where higher education increasingly resembles a big-box superstore.

It is certainly worth recognizing, however, that there are other types of higher education spaces outside of the PWI that seem able to maintain a focus on providing effective race-conscious instruction—including race-conscious literacy and writing instruction—even amid contemporary neoliberal pressures. One such space is that of the Minority-Serving Institution (MSI), which is composed of the Historically Black College and University (HBCU), the Hispanic-Serving Institution (HSI), the Tribal College and University (TCU), and the Asian-American-Native-American-Pacific-Islander-Serving Institution (AANAPISI). More than 430 MSIs are presently operating throughout the U.S. to educate roughly 2.3 million students (Harmon 4), including 16% of all African Americans, 42% of all Hispanics, and 19% of all Native Americans enrolled in U.S. higher education (Harmon 4). Furthermore, more than half of these MSIs possess an open admissions mission (Cunningham and Leegwater 178) while most serve "a large number of economically and academically 'at risk' students" (Gasman, Baez, and Turner 6). But especially important to my point here is the fact that most MSIs perceive issues of social and racial justice as central to their missions, even as they serve students from all racial and cultural backgrounds (Gasman, Baez, and Turner 3),

and even as they receive significant amounts of federal funding, total-
ing hundreds of millions of dollars annually, to perform their work.[1]
In a crucially important sense, then, MSIs operate as explicitly race-
conscious (as well as class-conscious) higher education spaces that are
managing to thrive, despite the many pressures that they face within
our contemporary higher education climate.[2]

In the hope of addressing and ultimately reversing the troubling
loss of race-conscious BW space within the PWI, I analyze here some
of the specific strategies and techniques through which contemporary
MSIs successfully cultivate and promote race-conscious education for
their students. I then discuss some of ways in which we in BW can
begin to adopt these MSI strategies and techniques in order to preserve—and perhaps even to expand and grow—the operation of our
own race-conscious spaces within PWI contexts. To help me do so, I
draw directly on two theoretical concepts: Nedra Reynolds' notion of
"dwelling" and Derrick Bell's notion of "interest convergence."

## THEORETICAL FRAMEWORKS: REYNOLDS' "DWELLING" AND BELL'S "INTEREST CONVERGENCE"

Composition theorist Nedra Reynolds defines "dwelling" as the process whereby embodied human beings—that is, human beings whose
bodies are marked by differences such as race, gender, sexuality, and
so on—interact with both the natural and built environments that
they inhabit in ways that actively create and re-create new spaces. For
Reynolds, dwelling constitutes the process whereby racialized individuals make choices about where, how, why, and how long to remain in,
engage with, and / or reflect on particular spaces in ways that directly
impact how these spaces are constructed. She writes:

> People's responses to place—which are shaped in large part
> by their bodies, by the physical characteristics they carry with
> them through the spatial world—determine whether they
> will 'enter' at all, or rush through, or linger—and those deci-
> sions contribute to how a space is 'used' or reproduced. (143)

Reynolds further stresses that dwelling is intimately tied to the construction of discursive space, arguing that

> Discourses don't have roofs or walls or provide shelter, but as many of us recognize from favorite books or stories, discourses can hold memories or represent a meaningful time and place; if familiar, they invite us to dwell within them. If unfamiliar or strange, it takes much longer, and dwelling doesn't happen when people feel excluded or that they don't belong. (163)

Finally, Reynolds stresses that dwelling serves as a mechanism by which to analyze how individuals can create both physical and discursive spaces of "resistance to the dominant culture" (141)—or what she later terms "thirdspaces" in ways resonant with the work of critical geographers such as Henri LeFebvre, Edward Soja, Doreen Massey, and others. Reynolds thereby argues that, during the course of actively dwelling within various physical and discursive spaces, racialized individuals can also dwell upon unfair and unjust practices and relationships within those spaces in ways that can foster thirdspace-oriented change—including change aimed at remedying the troubling effects of racism.

Reynolds' notion of dwelling sheds important light onto some of the key practices—what, for the purposes of this essay, I will call "dwelling strategies"—through which Minority-Serving Institutions are ultimately able to create and maintain race-conscious institutional spaces in the ways that they do. By employing various dwelling strategies, MSIs create thirdspaces in which students are invited to consider how issues of race and racism profoundly shape their educational and literate lives. Furthermore, by employing these dwelling strategies, MSIs challenge the loss of race-conscious space within our contemporary neoliberal higher education climate: these strategies help MSIs to insist that issues of race and space matter fundamentally to educational success in ways that cannot easily be dismissed amid the neoliberal rush for prestige and profit. Or, to put things more simply, MSIs use dwelling strategies to assert that race-conscious educational spaces must be preserved, not eliminated, within contemporary higher education.

In turn, critical race theorist Derrick Bell's notion of "interest convergence" is important for understanding how and why MSI-sponsored dwelling strategies can serve as models to those of us seeking to preserve BW in the context of the PWI. Bell argues that mainstream race-based educational reform efforts (and we can certainly include BW programs among such efforts) need to be perceived as benefitting mainstream white institutions in order to have long-lasting effects within the larger U.S. educational system. Specifically, Bell contends that these efforts need to be perceived as operating within a system where race-based reform "where granted, will secure, advance, or at least not harm societal interests deemed important by middle- and upper-class whites" ("Brown" 22). Bell does acknowledge the glaring irony in this situation: if racial justice efforts ultimately depend on and require the approval of the white mainstream in order to be deemed worthwhile, then such efforts may end up being "of more help to the system we despise than to the victims of that system we are trying to help" ("Racial Realism" 308). Nonetheless, he ultimately concludes that, if we can attend to interest convergence dynamics carefully and critically, we can foster successful institutional change in the form of "policy positions and campaigns that are less likely to worsen conditions for those we are trying to help and more likely to remind those in power that there are imaginative, unabashed risk-takers who refuse to be trammeled upon" (308).

Interest convergence offers us a particularly important tool with which to understand how and why MSI-style race-conscious dwelling can ultimately prove appealing within the context of the contemporary neoliberal PWI. Its principles suggest that race-conscious dwelling will be perceived as important and worthwhile within the PWI to the degree that it forwards PWI goals and interests—goals and interests which do still include the cultivation of at least some level of diversity within the PWI student body. As a quick illustration of this, consider the rhetoric currently being employed by Michael Crow, the well-known current President of Arizona State University and self-described "academic entrepreneur." In the midst of describing his institution as a model for the entrepreneurial (read: neoliberal) PWI of the future, Crow insists that Arizona State must seek to "champion diversity and. . . accommodate the many gifted and creative students who do not conform to a standard academic profile, as well as those who demonstrate the potential to succeed but lack the financial means to pursue a quality four-year undergraduate education" (5). He further insists that Arizona State must "advance global engagement" (3) by serving the needs of international students as well as students from "immigrant households where the primary language is not English" (8). Through such rhetoric, Crow espouses a kind "neoliberalism for PWI diversity" stance, one asserting that prestige, profit, and diversity all fit neatly together. To be sure, we in BW ought to approach such neoliberal rhetoric with great caution, especially given the ways in which it threatens to conceptualize racial, ethnic, linguistic, and cultural diversity as nothing more than assets to be traded by powerful PWIs in the pursuit of their own interests. But we can nonetheless view this sort of rhetoric as offering an important opportunity to assert that our BW programs and the race-conscious dwelling that they promote are fundamental to PWIs' collective ability to achieve their goals of diversity and globalism. In other words, we can assert that the proclaimed diversity interests of PWIs converge directly with our own BW interests in race-conscious dwelling in ways that ought to be recognized and embraced.

## MSIs, Dwelling Strategies, and the Creation of Race-Conscious Institutional Thirdspaces

With this combined framework of Reynolds' dwelling and Bell's interest convergence in mind, I turn now to four specific types of race-conscious dwelling strategies that MSIs routinely use to help interrogate and reform racist social and educational spaces both within and beyond the academy. These include cultivating and supporting explicit race-conscious educational ideologies and practices, offering race-conscious and spatially-oriented writing pedagogies, emphasizing race-conscious service-learning and community service activities, and documenting race-conscious institutional success. Each of these dwelling strategies helps to transform the MSI into a thirdspace of critical reform and change that opposes the neoliberal elimination of race-conscious space within higher education.

### MSI Dwelling Strategy #1: Cultivating and Supporting Explicit Race-Conscious Educational Ideologies and Practices

One of the first important ways in which MSIs promote dwelling is by proclaiming both explicitly and publicly the relationship that they imagine between their work and issues of social and racial justice—by proclaiming, that is, a kind of overt race-consciousness in terms of their institutional missions, goals, and values. MSI researchers Terrell Strayhorn and Joan Hirt describe such race-consciousness as a "defining characteristic" of MSIs (210). Meanwhile, other MSI scholars suggest that this defining characteristic is expressed in somewhat unique ways across different MSI contexts. Within HBCUs, for instance, Elaine Copeland finds a particularly close relationship between race-consciousness and community engagement, arguing that the "Emphasis [at HBCUs] has been and continues to be on cultural values, ethics, character development, civic responsibility, leadership, and service to the [African American] community" (53).[3] In the context of HSIs, Christina Kirklighter, Diana Cardenas, and Susan Wolff Murphy suggest that there is often an explicit emphasis on race-consciousness within the space of the campus: they describe this as the HSI desire to "educate all students, particularly Latino/a students" (3) as part of a larger effort to develop spaces of "difference and educational activism" (1).[4] With respect to the TCU context, Justin Guillory and Kelly Ward argue that there is often a particular stress on Native American languages and cultures which is designed to promote "cultural pride and hope" (91). Finally, with regard to AANAPISIs, Julie Park and Robert Teranishi contend that there is a conscious effort to subvert the stereotype of the Asian American as "model minority," especially given the tendency of this stereotype to "overshadow the unique needs of the broader [Asian American] community and underserved groups" (122). MSI operation and race-consciousness thus go hand-in-hand, even if the expression of this race-consciousness may vary slightly from institutional type to institutional type.

Accompanying this ideological emphasis on race-consciousness within the MSI is an explicit emphasis on student success—that is, on a "belief that all students can learn, regardless of their entering level [of] preparation, and that the role of the institution is to do everything possible to ensure [this]" (Bridges, Kinzie, Laird, and Kuh 228). Such a success orientation is evident in the fact that so many MSIs have open admissions policies predicated on the idea that all students can succeed, regardless of past educational experiences or backgrounds. This orientation is further evident in the fact that many MSIs offer explicit student support mechanisms, especially during the first two years of the undergraduate experience. These mechanisms include first-year support and community-building programs (e.g., "First Year Experience" courses and sequences, bridge programs, and intensive mentoring programs) as well as other advising and feedback programs providing support from faculty and staff. HBCU researcher and administrator Henry Ponder suggests that, on the whole, these kinds of support programs attempt to ensure that "first-year [MSI] students…[possess] the necessary motivation to maximize their efforts and take responsibility for their own learning" (127). MSI researchers Terrell Strayhorn and Melvin Terrell echo this point, suggesting that these mechanisms, especially when staffed by faculty members who work closely with undergraduate students, aim to establish "a close-knit community where students [feel] part of the institutional fabric of the campus" (147).

By espousing an explicitly race-conscious mission, and by coupling this mission with specific race-conscious student support mechanisms, MSIs directly encourage students' successful dwelling. MSIs serve, in other words, as race-conscious "safe spaces" from which students can spend significant time reflecting on the important relationships between a larger racist U.S. culture and their own education as college students. At the same time, MSIs routinely offer race-conscious institutional and material support to students as they dwell, especially in the form of small courses where students are likely to feel a sense of community and belonging, mechanisms that monitor students' academic process and offer extra assistance as needed, and a climate that values frequent and meaningful contact between students and faculty. Furthermore, in stark contrast to many mainstream PWIs, which tend to marginalize student support mechanisms into "remedial" programs or other ghettoized activities in ways that are frustratingly familiar to those of us in BW, race-conscious support mechanisms are viewed as absolutely central to the MSI experience. By stressing race-conscious dwelling in these ways, MSIs ultimately challenge the neoliberal contention that contemporary race-conscious spaces ought to be eliminated from the academy. Instead, MSIs insist, race-conscious spaces need to be preserved and expanded because they are absolutely essential to students' success within higher education.

## MSI Dwelling Strategy #2: Offering Race-Conscious and Spatially-Oriented Writing Pedagogies

A second means by which MSIs promote dwelling is by providing race-conscious and spatially oriented writing pedagogies and curricula. Carmen Kynard and Robert Eddy argue, for instance, that MSIs in general and HBCUs in particular foster at least three important race-conscious writing pedagogies, each premised on identifying and integrating of various types of institutional and discursive spaces. The first of these involves cultivating "Trans-school literacies" (W38), which arise when students integrate and transform home literacies and school literacies into new hybrid thirdspace literacies. The second involves "Collaborative-community teaching and learning" (W38) practices, which require students to bridge classroom and community spaces through various types of race-conscious service-learning and community engagement activities. The third involves fostering "Critical local-national understandings" (W38), which arise from "interrogat[ing] the politics of [students'] institutions, the social crises of their neighboring communities, and their own experiential knowledge as co-terminous realities" (W38). In these ways, Kynard and Eddy argue that HBCUs encourage a focus on the racialized nature of literacy "standards" as they are manifest within and across different spaces, from local to global, in ways that promote thirdspace interrogation and transformation.

A similar relationship between and among issues of race, space, and literacy is posited by Christopher Schroeder within the context of HSI writing pedagogy. HSIs promote, he says, "an alternative model of literacy that can authorize the locations that [their] students and others must negotiate as they write and read" (280). Furthermore, by focusing this issue of "location"—the issue of where students write, for what purposes, and to what audiences—HSIs ultimately concentrate

> less upon approximating a target discourse or upon producing a product and more on the act or performance of negotiating…differences….[HSI writing pedagogy moves] beyond the rejecting of deficiency and embracing difference to seeing difference, particularly the negotiation of differences—linguistic, cultural, epistemological, institutional—as a basic practice of intellectual work. (280)

For Schroeder, then, HSI writing pedagogies demand that students engage carefully and critically with what it means to write and read across spaces in ways that enable them to recognize, negotiate, and transform the problematic power differentials that they encounter.

Still further, Beatrice Mendez-Newman describes some of the key race-conscious pedagogical attitudes and practices that she believes are frequently fostered within the space of HSI writing courses. In particular, she argues that these courses emphasize the need for Freireian critical awareness on the part of teachers: "It is difficult not to rely on Freireian constructs in attempting to understand the HSI environment. There is, when the instructor is white, a profound difference between the teacher / authority figure and the learners" (19). As well, she says that HSI courses demand a race-conscious and supportive teacher attitude toward student literacy learning, asserting that "pedagogical content is far less important than pedagogical attitude. If an environment of trust and respect is not established in the classroom, little if any learning will occur" (19). Finally, she describes a number of specific pedagogical orientations that she sees as crucial to the HSI writing classroom, including 1) critical engagement with the label of "ESL" student as it often fails to apply to many students at HSIs, 2) careful engagement with patterns of error in the context of students' writing, 3) envisioning classrooms as promoting race-conscious "communities of learners," and 4) ensuring that teachers are as accessible to HSI students as possible (23).[5] Thus, for Mendez-Newman, the HSI writing classroom effectively requires race-conscious teaching of many varieties.

Through these types of race-conscious pedagogies and teacher orientations, MSIs posit that dwelling is a decidedly literate practice that spans the spaces of home and school simultaneously. At the same time, MSIs characterize literacy as one of the most important products of successful MSI-centered dwelling—that is, as a set of skills, practices, beliefs, and habits of mind that can be used within, across, and beyond university spaces to do substantive race-conscious work in the world. MSIs thereby challenge neoliberal logic once again: rather than conceding that "remedial" writing instruction does not belong in the contemporary college or university, MSIs insist that spaces for race-conscious literate dwelling are indispensable to any college or university setting that purports to educate students for a diverse and global world.

## MSI Dwelling Strategy #3: Emphasizing Race-Conscious Service-Learning and Community Service Activities

MSIs also promote dwelling through race-conscious service-learning and community engagement programs, especially those focused on writing and literacy instruction. The value of these programs is evident within a recent special issue of the journal *Reflections: A Journal of Writing, Community Literacy, and Service-Learning*, which focuses on a range of programs currently being offered by faculty at HBCUs. This issue highlights, for instance, service-learning activities and curricular options currently being enacted at Spelman College in Atlanta, including a linked "First-Year Experience Seminar" and "Sophomore Experience Seminar" requiring participation in and writing about a sustained local volunteer commitment of students' choice (Jordan 47-8), student volunteer work with and research at a local library dedicated to African American history and culture (49-52), tutoring work with a local middle school (52-55), and work with local teen drinking and drug prevention programs (56-7). It highlights similar initiatives at Jackson State University in Mississippi: as part of the first-year writing curriculum, students are required to participate in a local grade-school tutoring program during one semester (McDaniels Harrion, Glenn, and Gentry 115-19) and to work with a number of local women's groups during the next semester (120-22). Still further, it describes efforts at North Carolina Central University requiring first-year writing students to engage in a letter writing partnership with a local high school designed to "unite and empower [these] two academic communities" (Faulkner-Springfield 66).

Central across these types of HBCU service-learning and community engagement efforts is the way in which they view literacy as bridging the spaces of classroom and community: as Riva Sias and Beverly Moss summarize, these efforts "reveal the close, even 'seamless,' historical, political, and cultural relationship of African American literacy practices and African American community partnerships" (2-3). Also notable is the fact that these HBCU efforts are being mirrored in other MSI contexts, including HSIs and Tribal Colleges,[6] in ways suggesting that the integration of school and community spaces is central to much MSI writing and literacy instruction. And, finally, these MSI service-learning and community engagement efforts offer an important contrast to the more superficial versions of such programs that sometimes arise at other types of institutions, including many mainstream PWIs. Angelique Davi characterizes such uncritical programs as "often populated by white students who are asked to go into poor urban areas to work with diverse communities, and there is a tendency for these students to view community service as [solely] an opportunity for self-fulfillment" (74). Davi's point here is not, of course, that middle-class white students cannot engage in successful or worthwhile service-learning or community engagement activity in the context of a writing course. Rather, her claim is that, when mainstream whites and others engage in this type of activity in uncritical fashion, they run a serious risk of letting the desire to feel good trump the actual doing of good for communities of color, a problem that threatens to reify the very social and racial order that these programs claim to be reforming. MSIs, in contrast, seem well prepared to avoid these problems: because they possess race-conscious missions, support mechanisms, and pedagogies, these institutions are explicitly committed to creating authentic race-conscious thirdspaces that seek to challenge the extant social order directly through writing and literacy work.[7]

In these ways, MSI-sponsored service-learning and community engagement programs do a great deal to promote race-conscious student dwelling. They focus not only on students' dwelling activities within the context of MSI writing classroom but also at the intersection of MSI writing classrooms and community spaces. Or, to phrase things differently, MSIs try to replace divisions between "town" and "gown" with a kind of town-and-gown thirdspace that is explicitly dedicated to reforming the social order through literacy instruction. MSIs thereby insist that contemporary colleges and universities have a responsibility to preserve and expand spaces for such race-conscious literate dwelling, both within their walls and within the larger community, rather than simply allowing these spaces to be eliminated in the pursuit of neoliberal goals.

## MSI Dwelling Strategy #4: Documenting Race-Conscious Institutional Success

Many MSIs are, lastly, attempting to document the positive effects of race-conscious dwelling on factors such as student graduation and retention. This documentation helps to offer "proof" that MSIs provide a worthwhile and effective education, especially for students of color.

Numerous scholars note, for example, that MSIs graduate students of color at considerably higher rates than their peer predominantly white institutions. Noel Harmon points out that MSIs award a far greater percentage of BA degrees in education than their predominantly white counterparts do, including 46% of such degrees nationally for African-American students, 49% for Hispanic students, and 12% for Native American students (6). He notes, too, that MSIs have especially strong track records in Science, Technology, Engineering, and Math (STEM) fields at the BA level, awarding approximately 41% of all STEM degrees for African American students and 54% for Hispanic students (6). Meanwhile, Jaime Merisotis and Kirstin McCarthy mention that 38% of TCU students initially obtaining an AA degree ultimately managed to obtain a BA, while less than 1% from mainstream schools did (53). These statistics suggest that MSI contexts are especially conducive to improving minority students' overall graduation chances.

Another important issue that MSIs routinely highlight is that of undergraduate retention and transfer from two-year AA programs to four-year BA programs. This issue is stressed by Merisotis and McCarthy with respect to both TCUs and HBCUs. Regarding the former, they mention that TCUs had early 1990s retention rates of about 57%, contrasting starkly in with PWI retention rates hovering at around 1% (50). Regarding the latter, they mention that HBCUs increase the likelihood that students of color will initially enroll in and graduate from four-year BA programs rather than two-year AA programs by nearly 20%, an especially important statistic given that that "students who enroll in four-year schools are more likely to complete a bachelor's degree than those who begin at a two-year school" (53). These figures further indicate that MSIs are having documented positive effects on students' chances of remaining in school long enough to graduate with a BA.

Finally, a large number of MSIs are currently participating in research programs and activities designed to publicize their positive effects more widely. One such contemporary effort titled the "Lumina MSI Models of Success Program"[8] is helping MSIs to demonstrate their efficacy with regard to graduation, retention, and satisfaction rates for students of color. This program presently involves more than twenty institutions and institutional consortia spanning HBCUs, HSIs, TCUs, and AANIPISIs, and it aims to describe the specific ways in which MSIs (which Lumina describes as "recognized leaders in educating and graduating students of color" [Harmon 15]), engage in practices that are relevant to all higher education institutions. Another effort titled the "Building Engagement and Attainment for Minority Students" (BEAMS) project seeks to demonstrate the value of MSIs in terms of educating students in the hard sciences, and it is currently operating at 102 MSIs nationwide (DelRios and Leegwater 3). Its goal is to ensure that MSIs can measure and broadcast their benefits despite the fact that many such institutions have traditionally had limited budgets and infrastructures for doing so.

By documenting their work in these various ways, MSIs are actively attempting to prove that their race-conscious dwelling activities produce measurable results, especially in terms of minority student graduation and retention rates. These documentation efforts further attempt to show that MSIs deserve continued funding and support for future student dwelling: indeed, as Pegeen Riechert-Powell argues, data on topics such as graduation and retention rates are foundational to virtually all institutions' "efforts [to] realize financial gains, in the form of tuition dollars, state funding, or future graduates' support as alumni" (667). But it is also important to point out that these MSI documentation efforts, while certainly participating in neoliberal discourses of assessment and accountability as promoted by sponsors such as the Lumina Foundation, ultimately perform a kind of critically minded thirdspace work. MSIs are, in effect, using neoliberal measurement techniques and discourses to prove that their race-conscious dwelling activities are demonstrably beneficial. By doing so, they seem to be trying to "flip the script" of typical neoliberal assessment, using this assessment to prove quantitatively that race-conscious spaces need to be preserved rather than eliminated within the contemporary academy.

## Dwelling Stragegies and Race-Conscious Thirdspaces for Basic Writing

Having discussed these race-conscious MSI dwelling strategies, I now turn to the questions of what might it mean for BW programs to invite students to dwell successfully within the larger context of the PWI and how such dwelling might help to preserve BW spaces in the present and future. In the hope of answering these questions, I discuss four MSI-inspired dwelling strategies that I believe we can adapt for use in PWI-sponsored BW programs. These strategies include telling explicitly race-conscious stories regarding BW, developing and publicizing new race-conscious writing pedagogies within BW, developing new race-conscious BW program and support structures, and documenting the success of race-consciousness within BW. Each of these strategies posits that BW can and should operate as a type of race-conscious thirdspace within the context of the PWI. Each further posits that often-proclaimed PWI interests in student diversity and globalism converge directly with BW interests in promoting race-conscious dwelling—all in ways that render BW spaces indispensable to the future of the PWI.

## BW Dwelling Strategy #1: Telling Explicitly Race-Conscious Stories

As a first MSI-inspired dwelling strategy, we should imagine ways to engage in race-conscious BW "story-changing" work of the sort advocated by Linda Adler-Kassner: this work is designed to afford us a clearer "voice in the frames that surround our work and the tropes that emanate from those frames regarding our classes and students" (37). Specifically, we should imagine new ways to identify and publicize BW as an institutional space explicitly dedicated to success for the increasingly diverse populations that are entering PWIs in greater numbers. These populations include not only U.S.-born students of color but also speakers of English as a global language and "Generation 1.5" students. Speakers of English as a global language consist of individuals who learned English alongside their other native language(s), often in contexts shaped by colonialism: these students are "native speakers" of English in their homelands even though their native varieties and dialects of English may be different from "standard" versions spoken in places such as the U.S., Britain, or elsewhere (see Canagarajah, "Codemeshing"; "The Place"). "Generation 1.5" students, meanwhile, consist of those who may have been born abroad but have had some amount of formal schooling in the U.S. (See Matsuda; diGennaro; Ortmeier-Hooper). They may well need some second-language writing assistance; however, they are also likely, "as a result of their experience in U.S. schools, [to be] familiar with U.S. education, teenage popular culture, and current slang" in ways that differentiate them from international ESL students (diGennaro 65-66). As Paul Kei Matsuda asserts, BW programs must try to serve these types of students in ways that overcome a "distinction between basic writers and second language writers [that] is becoming increasingly untenable" (83). Furthermore, because both of these populations are increasingly prominent within PWIs, we in BW need to stress our ability to serve them effectively: Ryuko Kubota and Kimberly Abels point out that these populations are often highlighted as central to PWI efforts to "internationalize," and so PWIs are facing increasing pressure to provide them with new "educational opportunities and resources" (83).

What would such story-changing concerning race-conscious BW dwelling within the PWI actually require? Taking a direct cue from the work of MSIs, it would require our telling new BW stories that highlight our desire to serve all PWI students, but especially to serve diverse students. We could insist, in other words, that one of the primary missions of BW within the PWI is to offer race-conscious writing and literacy instruction for students of color, speakers of global Englishes, Generation 1.5 students, and others, to support these students with small classes that promote race-conscious dwelling explicitly, and otherwise to ensure students' successful retention and graduation. By telling such stories, we would thus be working against the neoliberal claim that the sole contemporary function of BW is to provide costly "remediation" for "unprepared" students who have no place in higher education. Instead, we would be insisting that BW provides critical assistance that helps diverse students to dwell successfully within the PWI context until they graduate. Such new stories would thereby assert that PWI interests and BW interests in diversity converge directly, and that they do so to the clear benefit of students.

Such race-conscious BW story-changing would also offer a useful rejoinder to the arguments of a number of scholars who seem to perceive the telling of race-conscious stories regarding BW as outdated, or even somewhat regressive, within the contemporary academy.[9] Greene and McAlexander take such a stance, for instance, when they assert that it is an "oversimplification" to continue viewing BW through explicitly race-conscious analytical lenses (8): they argue that, "although the basis for hostility to basic writing programs in the early years might have involved racism, that hostility was later more strongly fueled by intellectual elitism" (8). Greene and McAlexander then conclude that we in BW ought to stop focusing at length on issues of race and racism when we talk about BW, acknowledging instead that our programs "cut across race, ethnicities, and class" (7).[10] I agree that essentialist thinking about issues of race and racism is problematic, especially when it serves to mask classism or intellectual elitism in ways that Greene and Alexander note. I also recognize that contemporary BW programs do serve students from a range of racial, cultural, linguistic, and social class backgrounds, including many mainstream and working-class whites (see Horner and Lu). But I nonetheless contend that it is worthwhile to tell new race-conscious stories regarding contemporary BW spaces and the kinds of dwelling activities that they promote in order to highlight convergence between the interests of PWIs and the interests of race-conscious BW programs.

## BW Dwelling Strategy #2: Developing and Publicizing New Race-Conscious Writing Pedagogies

In order to encourage MSI-inspired BW dwelling further, we can begin to theorize and implement BW pedagogies that are explicitly designed to help diverse populations succeed within PWI contexts. Toward this end, we can examine the potential value of the writing pedagogies currently being employed by MSIs in various writing courses, including some of those described earlier. For instance, both Kynard and Eddy's discussion of trans-school literacies and Schroeder's emphasis on negotiating the "locations" of literacy seem quite helpful for fostering PWI students' critical engagement with the world from the vantage point of BW thirdspace. Mendez-Newman's suggestions regarding teacher attitudes also seem useful for ensuring that PWI students are being given the chance to engage in race-conscious dwelling successfully within BW.

At the same time, we should investigate the value of other contemporary BW pedagogies aimed at encouraging race-conscious dwelling within the PWI. For instance, within "Professing Multiculturalism: The Politics of Style in the Contact Zone," Min-Zhan Lu discusses the various ways in which written "errors" on the part of students from multicultural backgrounds can become the focus of explicitly race-, culture-, and class-conscious BW instruction. Her "can able to" example, which discusses a seemingly simple ESL mistake written by a Chinese-speaking student, illustrates how talk of error, authorial agency, and meaning can become central to any BW space. By exploring ways to adopt this kind of pedagogy more widely within the context of PWI-situated BW courses, we can ensure that all students are encouraged to use our courses as dwelling spaces from which to investigate, understand, and draw on their existing linguistic strengths, cultural backgrounds, and individual agency.[11]

We should pay further attention to "translanguaging" pedagogies as tools for promoting race-conscious dwelling within PWI-situated BW courses.[12] Suresh Canagarajah defines translanguaging as the capacity of the multilingual and multidialectical individual to "shuttle between diverse languages, treating the diverse languages that form their repertoire as an integrated system" ("Codemeshing" 401).[13]

He also implies that pedagogies rooted in translanguaging are likely to promote race-conscious dwelling for at least two reasons. First, these pedagogies are profoundly concerned with spatial dynamics ("The Place" 598) in ways that resonate strongly with the creation of race-conscious BW thirdspaces within the PWI: they are centrally concerned, in other words, with the question of "how we can accommodate more than one code within the boundaries of the same text" (598) in "rhetorically strategic ways" (599). Second, these pedagogies promote important emotional and ethical orientations from both students and teachers that fit squarely with race-conscious dwelling in BW. They assume that

> multilingual people always make adjustments to each other as they modify their accent or syntax to facilitate communication with those who are not proficient in their language. Furthermore, they come with psychological and attitudinal resources, such as patience, tolerance, and humility, to negotiate the differences of interlocutors. ("The Place" 593-594)

Translanguaging pedagogies thus clearly posit that students should attempt to understand and respond to their world using all the racial, cultural, linguistic, and attitudinal resources at their disposal.

By theorizing and implementing these sorts of race-conscious pedagogies, we can insist that diversity interests within the PWI will be promoted directly by the type of race-conscious dwelling that we espouse within BW—especially as we focus on issues of race, space, and literacy simultaneously, as we interrogate notions of student "error" to promote metacognitive and rhetorical awareness of writing and language skills, and as we promote the kind of patience, tolerance, and humility that characterizes positive learning for all manner of diverse students. Furthermore, we can insist that, because we in BW have been engaged in this kind of race-conscious pedagogy as a field for more than forty years, we possess a uniquely successful track-record and knowledge base that deserves to be preserved and supported within the PWI.

## BW Dwelling Strategy #3: Developing Race-Conscious Program and Support Structures

As a third possible BW dwelling strategy, we need to continue developing and implementing MSI-inspired program and support structures that translate race-conscious BW ideologies and pedagogies into institutional action within the PWI. Fortunately, it would seem that BW already has a good start toward such development, especially given our long history of offering literacy learning support to students.

As one example of such a structure, consider Rhonda Grego and Nancy Thompson's Studio model for BW, which was originally developed at the predominantly white University of South Carolina but has since been adopted at a number of locations across the U.S.[14] This Studio model provides small group meetings where students from across a number of first-year courses meet to talk about their assignments, to engage in peer review of one another's work, and otherwise to discuss the demands being placed on them by writing courses across the space of the university (12-13). The Studio thereby prioritizes the explicit support of students in their other classes, forming a kind of instructional thirdspace: the "students and their work, not any course instructor's plan, provide the 'curriculum' of the studio sessions" (10). Furthermore, the specific version of the Studio developed by Grego and Thompson ended up supporting a good deal of race-conscious instruction at both the University of South Carolina and Benedict College, a nearby HBCU. In particular, it helped students and teachers to understand and respond to implicitly racialized university expectations about course requirements at USC (104) as well as to examine various racialized disciplinary expectations about writing and knowledge making (134-140); it also prompted instructors at both South Carolina and Benedict to draw critical conclusions regarding issues of race, schooling, and their own teaching practices (188-199).

Even while recognizing these successes of Grego and Thompson's Studio, however, we can imagine ways to expand its race-conscious work even further, perhaps with the aid of something like the aforementioned translanguaging pedagogies. For instance, we might try to modify the Studio model slightly so that it offers some sort of "mini-curriculum" designed to have students rewrite assignments for other courses using various translanguaging techniques. Or, we might have the Studio engage all of its students, whether U.S- born, foreign-born, Generation 1.5, or otherwise, in explicit discussion of the language politics undergirding the writing assignments that they receive across the PWI. Developing explicitly race-conscious versions of Studio programs like these would certainly help to increase BW students' chances for effective race-conscious dwelling.

As another example of a worthwhile BW support structure, consider the race-conscious BW service-learning program currently operating within the predominantly white space of Bentley College under the direction of Angelique Davi. Davi argues that this course, which encourages BW students to tutor nearby elementary school students, offers a unique dwelling space from which students of color can examine racialized educational practices and power relations:

> In a service-learning composition course [like the one at Bentley]. . . . students of color may find themselves with opportunities to think critically about their lived experiences both inside and outside the classroom, [as well as about] systemic oppression...and dominant ideologies. For example, students of color may find themselves recognizing more subtle forms of racism embedded in the educational system that may have contributed to their sense of their academic performance. (76)

Davi's service-learning course clearly encourages students to dwell upon the ways in which their existing racialized literacy practices are identified as "remedial" in one spatial context (i.e., the mainstream PWI) and as "expert" in another spatial context (i.e., that of their mentoring relationship with younger students) in ways that ultimately promote thirdspace awareness of the shifting nature of literate activity. In turn, this type of course might be adopted for use in other PWI contexts, thereby inviting a greater number of BW students to engage in careful analysis of how issues of race and racism directly impact multiple literate and educational contexts simultaneously.[15]

By stressing race-conscious BW structures of various kinds— whether Studio programs, service-learning / community engagement writing programs, or others—we can emphasize yet again the central importance and value of the kind of dwelling that BW promotes. We can stress, that is, that PWIs' interests in promoting a diverse and global campus are clearly furthered through the kinds of support programs that we in BW already offer. We might argue as well that the PWI need not reinvent the wheel by developing new kinds of race-conscious student support mechanisms; instead, it ought simply to support the race-conscious BW spaces that we have already been offering (and can easily offer more widely if provided with the proper support).

## BW Dwelling Strategy #4: Documenting the Success and Value of Race-Consciousness

Mentioned earlier in this essay are some of the specific ways in which MSIs have begun to document their successes with respect to issues of race-conscious dwelling. Drawing inspiration from this MSI activity, we in BW should seek to document the relationship between race-conscious BW spaces, the specific types of dwelling that we promote through them, and factors such as graduation and retention rates. And, certainly, we should use this documentation to make persuasive arguments to our PWI sponsors that BW programs deserve their continued and unequivocal support.

Some in BW have certainly already begun this work. Greg Glau, for instance, has recently examined enrollment, pass rates, and retention rates for various groups involved in the Stretch program at Arizona State (during a time before President Crow's tenure), focusing in particular on students of color (37). He notes that students from these groups who have enrolled in Stretch are more likely to pass freshman composition than those who take regular courses (38), that retention rates have improved since Stretch was implemented (38), and that these findings have proven useful in opposing last-minute administrative proposals to raise class sizes or otherwise compromise the kind of important work that the Stretch program performs (44).

Matthew McCurrie has similarly analyzed the value of the Summer Bridge program at Columbia College in Chicago, a program that primarily serves underrepresented minority students. His preliminary work indicates that students have a freshman fall-to-spring retention rate that has improved from 61% in 2004 to 68% in 2008 (although he also notes that this rate still lags behind the 84% retention rate for regularly admitted students) (44). From this data, McCurrie concludes that "summer bridge programs can play an important role in improving the learning experiences of at-risk students when they give prospective students a challenging college experience that prepares them for real college-level work and thus builds confidence" (44).

Peter Adams, Sarah Gearhart, Robert Miller, and Anne Roberts have also been tracking the course completion, retention, and graduation rates of students involved in the Accelerated Learning Program (ALP) at their home institution of the Community College of Baltimore County. They find that ALP "doubles the success rate [for course completion], halves the attrition rate [from the first year course], does it in half the time [to graduation]...and costs slightly less per student than the traditional model" (64). They are also currently involved in new research being conducted by the Community College Research Center at Columbia University that will track ALP pass rates, rates of overall college persistence, and other similar data for students from across varying racial and economic backgrounds (65). And their ALP program seems to be generating a great deal of enthusiasm: more than 80 schools nationwide are currently using some form of this program (Adams, personal communication), and interest in the program continues to grow on the basis of the kind of data that the ALP movement has generated thus far. Although ALP has not yet generated considerable amounts of race-conscious data per se, its current activities and popularity suggest that it is likely to do so soon.

Each of these current BW documentation efforts use the discourses and tools of neoliberal assessment to demonstrate that race-conscious dwelling has positive effects within the PWI. However, in order to engage in a kind of critical "script flipping" similar to that of our MSI counterparts, we need to provide even more of this type of work. By documenting our successes with race-conscious dwelling more fully, we can effectively stress the convergences between PWI interests and our own. We can also effectively demonstrate that PWIs are already reaping important benefits from BW in terms of minority students' graduation and retention rates—and that they stand to reap even more of these benefits if they expand their support for our work.

## CONCLUSION

I want to end this discussion on a hopeful note. While it is true that many BW spaces have been lost within the context of the PWI over the last 15 years, it is also true that we are well-positioned to rebuild and strengthen these spaces with the help of MSI-inspired dwelling strategies that promote convergence between PWI and BW interests. It also seems clear that we can capitalize on growing disciplinary and national interest in BW spaces and issues of PWI diversity to help us do so.

At the level of the discipline, for instance, both 2012 CCCC Chair Chris Anson and 2013 CCCC Chair Howard Tinberg have recently underscored the value and importance of BW space, in part at the urging of members of the Council on Basic Writing (CBW). Anson helped to facilitate a number of well-publicized 2012 sessions on the future of BW, including a particularly powerful session featuring BW luminaries Mike Rose, Lynn Troyka, and Peter Adams. Meanwhile, Tinberg's 2013 CCCC "Call for Proposals" featured BW goals, missions, and students explicitly within the body of its text by stressing the ways in which "the novice or basic writer has been the subject of foundational work in composition studies" (par. 1). Also notable is the fact that the 2013 Council on Basic Writing (CBW) conference will be hosting an event at CCCC 2013 titled "Basic Writing and Race: A Symposium" featuring scholars and teachers from a number of MSIs and PWIs. These individuals will be discussing BW activity within their respective institutions as well as imagining new hybrids of BW, MSI, and PWI scholarship. Issues of race-consciousness and dwelling, as well as possible convergences between various institutional goals, will certainly be discussed at length during this symposium.

This resurgence of disciplinary interest in BW and its race-conscious spaces can certainly help our efforts to understand, enact, and publicize race-conscious dwelling strategies for use in the PWI. This resurgence might inspire us, for instance, to take a cue from *Reflections* and its special issue on HBCU service-learning and community engagement by producing our own special issues and edited collections (perhaps even within the pages of *JBW*) that are explicitly dedicated to issues of race, thirdspace, and MSI-inspired dwelling within PWI contexts. This resurgence might also inspire us to facilitate more regular networking and interaction between faculty teaching BW in both MSIs and PWIs, whether through organizations such as CCCC or CBW, through new conferences and symposia, or through new kinds of professional and institutional networks spanning MSIs, PWIs, and other spaces.

Meanwhile, at a more national level, neoliberal administrators like Arizona State's Crow have been garnering increasing media attention for their ideas about the role of racial and ethnic diversity within the PWI. In particular, Crow was named by *Time* magazine in 2009 as one of the ten most important administrators currently working in higher education, and he was praised in particular by the magazine for his attempts to serve "students with a wide range of backgrounds and abilities while giving elite public schools a run for their research money" (Fitzpatrick par. 1). While we in BW obviously need to interpret such praise critically, we can nonetheless use it to help us call public attention to how we in BW have played, and must continue to play, a central role in ensuring that "students with a wide range of backgrounds and abilities" are ultimately well-served by the PWI of the future.

Such media attention might encourage us, for instance, to generate and circulate public responses from groups like CCCC and CBW that stress the central role of BW within the diverse PWI of the future. It might also prompt us to partner (albeit in decidedly critical ways) with neoliberal sponsors such as the Lumina Foundation, the Gates Foundation, and others to document further our successes with race-conscious dwelling within the PWI. It might even inspire us to try capitalizing on the very recent mainstream discourse tying President Obama's recent re-election to the increasingly diverse and global nature of the U.S. population. If groups such as CCCC or CBW could discuss the importance of race-conscious BW dwelling with the (admittedly neoliberal) U.S. Department of Education, thereby emulating recent actions of the Council of Writing Program Administrators in its own meeting with Arnie Duncan's staff, then we might make the case that BW supports diversity in ways that will benefit the Obama administration's educational agenda directly. Each of these strategies would stress convergence between national educational interests and the work of BW in ways that we have not yet fully explored or exploited.

We need to take advantage of our current moment, then, by thinking in race-conscious spatial terms about the future of BW space within the PWI. In particular, we need to recognize the important race-conscious dwelling work currently taking place within MSI thirdspaces and examine how this work directly challenges contemporary neoliberal thinking about the future of higher education. We also need to imagine ways to employ MSI-inspired race-conscious dwelling activity within our own BW thirdspaces—ideologically, pedagogically, materially, and rhetorically—in ways that can directly challenge neoliberal pressures to eliminate BW. And, finally, we need to make effective interest convergence arguments that can persuade PWI stakeholders that their interests and our BW interests align in ways that are profoundly important to our collective futures.

## Notes

1. HBCUs are funded by Title III, "Institutional Aid," of the Higher Education Act (Gasman 23), receiving approximately $235 million during FY 2011 (U.S. Department of Education, "Title III Part B" n. pag.). HSIs are funded under Title V, "Developing Institutions," and received approximately $150 million during FY 2011 (U.S. Department of Education, "Developing Hispanic-Serving" n. pag.). TCUs are funded under Title III, receiving just under $27 million in FY 2011 (U.S. Department of Education, "American Indian" n. pag.). Finally, AANIPISIs also receive federal Title III funding, obtaining about $13.5 million in FY 2011 (U.S. Department of Education, "Alaska Native and Native Hawaiian" n. pag.).

2. This is not to say, of course, that MSIs operate outside of the influence of neoliberalism: these institutions certainly face their own pressures to cultivate particular kinds of prestige and profit. (See Gasman, Baez, and Turner; Harmon; Merisotis and McCarthy). But these institutions have nonetheless held fast to their central race-conscious goals and missions, even in response to these pressures, in ways that are worth understanding and emulating.

3. See also Taylor; Taylor and Helfenbein; Sias and Moss.

4. See also Schroeder; Contreras, Malcom, and Bensimon.

5. See also the many informative chapters within Kirklighter, Cardenas, and Wolff Murphy's volume on teaching writing in MSI contexts, especially Millward, Starkey, and Starkey; Ramirez-Dhore and Jones; Baca; Jaffe; Artze-Vega, Doud, and Torres.

6. See Kirklighter, Cardenas, and Wolff Murphy; Gasman, Baez, and Turner.

7. See also Deans.

8. I recognize that Lumina and other higher education foundations have been rightly critiqued for contributing directly to neoliberal pressures toward particular kinds of "accountability" (see Stuart). But, as I will articulate momentarily, MSIs possess the potential to work with Lumina and other similar foundations in decidedly critical ways.

9. I recognize that a number of contemporary BW scholars, including William Jones, Bruce Horner and Min-Zhan Lu (see especially Representing the Other), Victor Villanueva (see especially Bootstraps; "On the Rhetoric"), Keith Gilyard (see especially Voices; "Basic Writing"), Deborah Mutnick, and others, have long been telling crucially important race-conscious stories about BW spaces past and present. I also recognize that other important BW work from the late 1960s and early 1970s from authors including Geneva Smitherman (see especially "God Don't Never" and Talkin'), Harvey Daniels (see especially "What's Wrong"), and Mina Shaughnessy (see especially "The Miserable Truth") has also featured explicitly race-conscious stories of

student access to higher education. However, these particular race-conscious stories have not frequently been referenced within contemporary accounts of how and why BW spaces are disappearing from the PWI.

10. For similar stories advocating BW colorblindness, see also Parks; Soliday.

11. Lu engages in additional analyses of "error" and the ways in which it might offer new insight into the power dynamics of language and literacy learning within some of her other most well-known articles: see especially "Living English Work" and "An Essay on the Work of Composition."

12. See, for instance, Canagarajah, "Codemeshing"; Horner, Lu, Royster, and Trimbur; Kynard, "The Blues"; Young and Martinez.

13. Canagarajah defines "codemeshing," meanwhile, as the "the realization of translanguaging in texts" (403)—that is, the ways in which individuals treat multiple languages and dialects "as part of a single integrated system" that also "accommodates the possibility of mixing communicative modes and diverse symbol systems (other than language)" (403).

14. See Lalicker; Tassoni and Lewiecki-Wilson.

15. See also Gabor; Pine.

## WORKS CITED

Adams, Peter. Message to the author. 15 May 2012. E-mail.

Adams, Peter, Sarah Gearhart, Robert Miller, and Anne Roberts. "The Accelerated Learning Program: Throwing Open the Gates." Journal of Basic Writing 28.2 (2009): 50-69. Print.

Adler-Kassner, Linda. The Activist WPA: Changing Stories about Writing and Writers. Logan, UT: Utah State UP, 2008. Print.

Artze-Vega, Isis, Elizabeth I. Doud, and Belkys Torres. "Mas alla del ingles: A Bilingual Approach to College Composition." In Teaching Writing with Latino/a Students: Lessons Learned at Hispanic-Serving Institutions. Eds. Cristina Kirklighter, Diana Cardenas, and Susan Wolff Murphy. Albany, SUNY UP, 2007. 99-118. Print.

Baca, Isabel. "It Is All in the Attitude—The Language Attitude." In Teaching Writing with Latino/a Students: Lessons Learned at Hispanic-Serving Institutions. Eds. Cristina Kirklighter, Diana Cardenas, and Susan Wolff Murphy. Albany: SUNY UP, 2007. 145-68. Print.

Bartholomae, David. "The Tidy House: Basic Writing in the American Curriculum." Journal of Basic Writing 12.1 (1993): 4-21. Print.

Bell, Derrick. "Brown v. Board of Education and the Interest Convergence Dilemma." Rpt. in Critical Race Theory: The Key Writings that Formed the Movement. Eds. Kimberle Crenshaw, Neil Gotanda, Gary Peller, and Kendall Thomas. New York: The New Press, 1995. 20–29. Print.

—. "Racial Realism." Rpt. in Critical Race Theory: The Key Writings that Formed the Movement. Eds. Kimberle Crenshaw, Neil Gotanda, Gary Peller, and Kendall Thomas. New York: The New Press, 1995. Print.

Bridges, Brian K., Jillian Kinzie, Thomas F. Nelson Laird, and George D. Kuh. "Student Engagement and Student Success at Historically Black and Hispanic-Serving Institutions." In Understanding Minority-Serving Institutions. Eds. Marybeth Gasman, Benjamin Baez, and Caroline Sotello Viernes Turner. Albany: SUNY UP, 2008. 3-17. Print.

Canagarajah, Suresh. "Codemeshing in Academic Writing: Identifying Teachable Strategies of Translanguaging." The Modern Language Journal 95.3 (2011): 401-17. Print.

—. "The Place of World Englishes in Composition: Pluralization Continued." College Composition and Communication 57.4 (2006): 586-619. Print.

Contreras, Frances E., Lindsey E. Malcom, and Estela Mara Bensimon. "Hispanic-Serving Institutions: Closeted Identity and the Production of Equitable Outcomes for Latino / a Students." In Understanding Minority-Serving Institutions. Eds. Marybeth Gasman, Benjamin Baez, and Caroline Sotello Viernes Turner. Albany: SUNY UP, 2008. 71-90. Print.

Copeland , Elaine Johnson. "Creating a Pathway: The Role of Historically Black Institutions in Enhancing Access, Retention, and Graduation." In How Black Colleges Empower Black Students: Lessons for Higher Education. Ed. Frank W. Hale, Jr. Sterling, VA: Stylus, 2006. 51-62. Print.

Crow, Michael. "The Research University as Comprehensive Knowledge Enterprise: The Reconceptualization of Arizona State University as Prototype for a New American University." Seventh Glion Colloquium. June 2009. Web. 8 Oct 2012.

Cunningham, Alisa, and Lacey Leegwater. "Minority Serving Institutions— What Can We Learn?" In Recognizing and Serving Low-Income Students in Higher Education: An Examination of Institutional Policies, Practices, and Culture. Ed. Adrianna Kezar. New York: Routledge, 2010. 176-91. Print.

Daniels, Harvey. "What's New with the SAT?" English Journal 63 (1974): 6, 11–12. Print.

Davi, Angelique. "In the Service of Writing and Race." Journal of Basic Writing 25.1 (2006): 73-95. Print.

Deans, Thomas. Writing Partnerships: Service-Learning in Composition. Urbana, IL: National Council of Teachers of English, 2000. Print.

Del Rios, Melissa, and Lacey Leegwater. Increasing Student Success at Minority-Serving Institutions: Findings from the Beams Project. Institute of Higher Education Policy. March 2008. Web. 16 May 2012.

diGennaro, Kristen. "Assessment of Generation 1.5 Learners for Placement into College Writing Courses." Journal of Basic Writing. 27.1 (2008): 61-79. Print.

Fain, Paul. "How to End Remediation." Inside Higher Ed. 4 April 2012. Web. 16 May 2012.

Faulkner-Springfield, Shirley. "Letters to Young High School Students: Writing and Uniting an Academic Community." Reflections: Writing, Service-Learning, and Community Literacy 10.2 (2011): 63-107. Print.

Fitzpatrick, Laura. "Nine Presidents to Watch: Michael Crow." time.com 11 November 2009. Web. 17 November 2012.

Gabor, Catherine. "Writing Partners: Service-Learning as a Route to Authority for Basic Writers." Journal of Basic Writing 28.1 (2009): 50-70. Print.

Gasman, Marybeth. "Minority-Serving Institutions: A Historical Backdrop." In Understanding Minority-Serving Institutions. Eds. Marybeth Gasman, Benjamin Baez, and Caroline Sotello Viernes Turner. Albany: SUNY UP, 2008. 3-17. Print.

Gasman, Marybeth, Benjamin Baez, and Caroline Sotello Viernes Turner, Eds. Understanding Minority-Serving Institutions. Albany: SUNY UP, 2008. Print.

Gilyard, Keith. Voices of the Self: A Study of Language Competence. Detroit, MI: Wayne State UP, 1991. Print.

—. "Basic Writing, Cost Effectiveness, and Ideology." Journal of Basic Writing 19.1 (2000): 36–37. Print.

Glau, Greg. "Stretch at 10: A Progress Report on Arizona State University's Stretch Program." Journal of Basic Writing 26.2 (2007): 30-48. Print.

Greene, Nicole Pipenster, and Patricia J. McAlexander. Basic Writing in America: The History of Nine College Programs. Cresskill, NJ: Hampton, 2008. Print.

Grego, Rhonda, and Nancy Thompson. Teaching / Writing in Thirdspaces: The Studio Approach. Carbondale, IL: Southern Illinois UP, 2008. Print.

Guillory, Justin P., and Kelly Ward. "Tribal Colleges and Universities: Identity, Invisibility, and Current Issues." In Understanding Minority-Serving Institutions. Eds. Marybeth Gasman, Benjamin Baez, and Caroline Sotello Viernes Turner. Albany: SUNY UP, 2008. 91-110. Print.

Gumport, Patricia J. and Michael N. Bastedo. "Academic Stratification and Endemic Conflict: Remedial Education Policy at CUNY." The Review of Higher Education 24.4 (2001). 333-49. Print.

Harmon, Noel. "The Role of Minority-Serving Institutions in National College Completion Goals." Institute for Higher Education Policy. Jan 2012. Web. 16 May 2012.

Hazelkorn, Ellen. "The Impact of League Tables and Ranking Systems on Higher Education Decision Making." Higher Education Management and Policy 19.2 (2007): 1–24. Print.

Horner, Bruce, and Min-Zhan Lu. Representing the 'Other': Basic Writers and the Teaching of Basic Writing. Urbana, IL: NCTE, 1999. Print.

Horner, Bruce, Min-Zhan Lu, Jacqueline Jones Royster, and John Trimbur. "Language Difference in Writing: Toward a Translingual Approach." College English 73.3 (2011): 303-21. Print.

Jaffe, Barbara. "Changing Perceptions, and Ultimately Practices, of Basic Writing Instructors through the Familia Approach." In Teaching Writing with Latino/a Students: Lessons Learned at Hispanic-Serving Institutions. Eds. Cristina Kirklighter, Diana Cardenas, and Susan Wolff Murphy. Albany: SUNY UP, 2007. 169-92. Print.

Jones, William. "Basic Writing: Pushing Against Racism." Journal of Basic Writing 12.1 (1993): 72-80. Print.

Jordan, Zandra. "'Found' Literacy Partnerships: Service and Activism at Spelman College." Reflections: Writing, Service-Learning, and Community Literacy 10.2 (2011): 38-62. Print.

Kirklighter, Christina, Diana Cardenas, and Susan Wolff Murphy, eds. Teaching Writing with Latino / a Students: Lessons Learned at Hispanic Serving Institutions. Albany, NY: SUNY Press, 2007. Print.

Kubota, Ryuko, and Kimberly Abels. "Improving Institutional ESL/EAP Support for International Students: Seeking the Promised Land." In The Politics of Second Language Writing: In Search of the Promised Land. Eds. Paul Kei Matsuda, Christina Ortmeier-Hooper, and Xiaoye You. West Lafayette, IN: Parlor Press, 2006. 75-93. Print.

Kynard, Carmen. "'I Want To Be African': In Search of a Black Radical Tradition/African-American-Vernacularized Paradigm for 'Students' Rights to Their Own Language,' Critical Literacy, and 'Class Politics.'" College English 69.4 (March 2007): 356-86. Print.

—. "'The Blues Playingest Dog You Ever Heard of': (Re)positioning Literacy Through African American Blues Rhetoric." Reading Research Quarterly 43.4 (2008): 356-73. Print.

Kynard, Carmen, and Robert Eddy. "Toward a New Critical Framework: Color-Conscious Political Morality and Pedagogy at Historically Black and Historically White Colleges and Universities." CCC 61.1 (2009): 171; W24-W44. Print.

Lalicker, William. "A Basic Introduction to Basic Writing Program Structures: A Baseline and Five Alternatives." In Teaching Developmental Writing: Background Readings (3rd Edition). Ed. Susan Naomi Bernstein. Boston: Bedford St. Martins, 2007. 15-25. Print.

Lu, Min-Zhan. "Conflict and Struggle: The Enemies or Preconditions of Basic Writing?" College English 54 (1992): 887-913. Print.

—. "Professing Multiculturalism: The Politics of Style in the Contact Zone." CCC 45.4 (1994): 442-58. Print.

—. "An Essay on the Work of Composition: Composing English against the Order of Fast Capitalism." CCC 56.1 (2004): 16-50. Print.

—. "Living English Work." College English 68.6 (2006): 605-18. Print.

Martinez, Deirdre. "Coalition Formation among Minority-Serving Institutions." In Understanding Minority-Serving Institutions. Eds. Marybeth Gasman, Benjamin Baez, and Caroline Sotello Viernes Turner. Albany: SUNY UP, 2008. 269-91. Print.

Matsuda, Paul Kei. "Basic Writing and Second Language Writers: Toward an Inclusive Definition." Journal of Basic Writing 22.2 (2003): 67-89. Print.

McCurrie, Matthew Killian. "Measuring Success in Summer Bridge Programs: Retention Efforts and Basic Writing." Journal of Basic Writing 28.2 (2009): 28-49. Print.

McDaniels, Preselfannie E. Whitfield, Kashelia J. Harrion, Rochelle Smith Glenn, and Gisele Nicole Gentry. "African American Students Learn by Serving the African American Community: A Jackson State University Example of 'Challenging Minds and Changing Lives.'" Reflections: Writing, Service-Learning, and Community Literacy 10.2 (2011): 108-35. Print.

Mendez-Newman, Beatrice. "Teaching Writing at Hispanic Serving Institutions." In Teaching Writing With Latino/a Students: Lessons Learned at Hispanic-Serving Institutions. Eds. Christina Kirklighter, Diana Cardenas, and Susan Wolff Murphy. Albany, NY: SUNY Press, 2007. 17-36. Print.

Merisotis, Jaime P. and Kirstin McCarthy. "Retention and Student Success at Minority-Serving Institutions." New Directions for Institutional Research 125 (2005): 45-58. Print.

Millward, Jody, Sandra Starkey, and David Starkey. "Teaching English in a California Two-Year Hispanic-Serving Institution: Complexities, Challenges, Programs, and Practices." In Teaching Writing With Latino/a Students: Lessons Learned at Hispanic-Serving Institutions. Eds. Christina Kirklighter, Diana Cardenas, and Susan Wolff Murphy. Albany, NY: SUNY Press, 2007. 37-62. Print.

Mutnick, Deborah. "The Strategic Value of Basic Writing." Journal of Basic Writing 19.1 (2000): 69-83. Print.

Ortmeier-Hooper, Christina. "English May Be My Second Language, But I'm Not 'ESL.'" CCC 59.3 (2008): 389-419. Print.

Pallack, Becky. "Pima College Seeks to End Some Remedial Classes." Arizona Daily Star. 18 July 2011. Web. 16 May 2012.

Park, Julie J., and Robert T. Teranishi. "Asian American and Pacific Islander Serving Institutions: Historical Perspectives and Future Prospects." In Understanding Minority-Serving Institutions. Eds. Marybeth Gasman, Benjamin Baez, and Caroline Sotello Viernes Turner. Albany: SUNY UP, 2008. 111-26. Print.

Powell, Pegeen Reichert. "Retention and Writing Instruction." CCC 60.4 (2009): 664-82. Print.

Pine, Nancy. "Service-Learning in a Basic Writing Class: A Best Case Scenario." Journal of Basic Writing 27.2 (2008): 29-55. Print.

Ponder, Henry. "What Makes African American Students Successful at Historically Black Colleges and Universities: The First-Year Program." In How Black Colleges Empower Black Students: Lessons for Higher Education. Ed. Frank W. Hale, Jr. Sterling, VA: Stylus, 2006. 119-28. Print.

Ramirez-Dhore, Dora, and Rebecca Jones. "Discovering a 'Proper Pedagogy': The Geography of Writing at the University of Texas-Pan American." In Teaching Writing with Latino/a Students: Lessons Learned at Hispanic-Serving Institutions. Eds. Cristina Kirklighter, Diana Cardenas, and Susan Wolff Murphy. Albany: SUNY UP, 2008. 63-86. Print.

Reynolds, Nedra. Geographies of Writing: Inhabiting Places and Encountering Difference. Carbondale: Southern Illinois UP, 2004. Print.

Rosen, Andrew S. Change.edu: Rebooting for the New Talent Economy. New York: Kaplan Publishing, 2011. Print.

Schroeder, Christopher. "Notes Toward a Dynamic Theory of Literacy." In The Locations of Composition. Eds. Christopher J. Keller and Christian R. Weisser. Albany: SUNY UP, 2007. 267-88. Print.

Shaughnessy, Mina. "The Miserable Truth." Journal of Basic Writing 17.2 (1998): 106–12. Print.

Sias, Riva, and Beverly Moss. "Rewriting a Master Narrative: HBCUs and Community Literacy Partnerships." Reflections: Writing, Service-learning, and Community Literacy 10.2 (2011): 1-16. Print.

Smitherman, Geneva. "God Don't Never Change: Black English from a Black Perspective." College English 34.6 (1973): 828–33.Print.

—. Talkin' and Testifyin': The Language of Black America. Boston: Houghton Mifflin, 1977. Print.

Strayhorn, Terrell L., and Joan B. Hirt. "Social Justice at Historically Black and Hispanic-Serving Institutions: Mission Statements and Administrative Voices." In Understanding Minority-Serving Institutions. Eds. Marybeth Gasman, Benjamin Baez, and Caroline Sotello Viernes Turner. Albany: SUNY UP, 2008. 203-16. Print.

Strayhorn, Terrell L., and Melvin C. Terrell. The Evolving Challenges of Black College Students: New Insights for Policy, Practice, and Research. Sterling, VA: Stylus, 2010. Print.

Stuart, Reginald. "Disproportionately Influential?" Diverse: Issues in Higher Education 27.12 (2010): 16-17.

Tassoni, John Paul and Cynthia Lewiecki-Wilson. "Not Just Anywhere, Anywhen: Mapping Change through Studio Work." Journal of Basic Writing 24.1 (2005): 68-92. Print.

Taylor, Hill. "Black Spaces: Examining the Writing Major at an Urban HBCU." Composition Studies 35.1 (2007): 99-112. Print.

Taylor, L. Hill and Robert J. Helfenbein. "Mapping Everyday: Gender, Blackness, and Discourse in Urban Contexts." Educational Studies 45 (2009): 319-29. Print.

Tinberg, Howard. "The Public Work of Composition: March 13-16, 2013." Conference on College Composition and Communication. Web. 9 Aug. 2012.

U.S. Department of Education. "Title III Part B, Strengthening Historically Black Colleges and Universities Program." U.S. Department of Education. 1 Jul. 2011. Web. 16 May 2012.

—. "Developing Hispanic-Serving Institutions Program—Title V" U.S. Department of Education. 5 Oct. 2011. Web. 16 May 2012.

—. "American Indian Tribally Controlled Colleges and Universities—Title III Part A Programs." U.S. Department of Education. 1 July 2011. Web. 16 May 2012.

—. "Asian American and Native American Pacific Islander Serving Institutions (AANAPISIs) Receive $2.6 Million in Federal Grant Funding." U.S. Department of Education 23 Nov. 2010. Web. 16 May 2012.

—. "Alaska Native and Native Hawaiian Serving Institutions—Title III Part A Programs." U.S. Department of Education. 30 Jun. 2011. Web. 16 May 2012.

Villanueva, Victor. Bootstraps: From an American Academic of Color. Urbana, IL: NCTE, 1993. Print.

—. "On the Rhetoric and Precedents of Racism." CCC 50.4 (1999): 645-661. Print.

Ward, Stephen C. Neoliberalism and the Global Restructuring of Knowledge and Education. New York: Routledge, 2012. Print.

Young, Vershawn Ashanti, and Aja Y. Martinez. Code-Meshing as World English: Pedagogy, Policy, Performance. Urbana, NCTE, 2011. Print.

# JOURNAL OF TEACHING WRITING

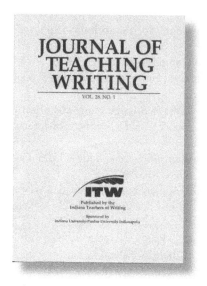

The *Journal of Teaching Writing* is on the web at http://journals.iupui.edu/index.php/teachingwriting/

*The Journal of Teaching Writing*, now in its thirtieth year of publication, is devoted to the teaching of writing at all academic levels, from pre-school to university, and in all subject areas of the curriculum. Our mission is to publish refereed articles that address the practices and theories that bear on our knowledge of how people learn and communicate through writing. Also, an important part of our mission is to demystify the editorial review process for our contributors and to model the teaching of writing as a process of reflection and revision.

### Humor and the Rhetorical Proprieties in the Writing Classroom

An essay about humor in the writing classroom is a rarity in rhetoric and composition journals, and when one crossed my desk with positive reviews, as this one did, I published it as the issue's lead article. Who hasn't thought about using humor in the classroom to connect with students, to build relationships, to foster learning? And who hasn't experienced humor that falls flat—the uncomfortable silence, the smirks and groans? Steve Sherwood offers readers a fresh perspective on humor in the writing classroom, and he brings the classical rhetoricians into his discussion to help us become more thoughtful, more effective users of humor with our students. Drawing on the rhetorical properties of character, circumstance, and audience, Sherwood gives contemporary writing teachers classical lessons on "us[ing] wit to enhance their ethos as good persons speaking well. . . ." In effect, he presents humor as a subject we should know and practice as teachers of rhetoric and composition.

# 8 Humor and the Rhetorical Proprieties in the Writing Classroom

*Steve Sherwood*

A writing emphasis teacher begins class the way he always does, by telling a joke. The joke itself is less important than the students' reaction to it. When the professor delivers the punch line and pauses for laughter, his students look down at their books or stare up at him with stony expressions. The professor turns to a colleague, who is observing the class, and says, "I like to start each day with a joke."

"Do they always go over so well?" the colleague asks. At the que tion, the students erupt in laughter.

This incident illustrates one of the least advantageous ways to use wit in the classroom. A canned joke shows that a teacher may be trying too hard and preparing too much. Such "wit" lacks spontaneity and surprise, especially if the teacher begins every class with a joke. Unless the joke connects to the content of the course, students may see their teacher's attempt at humor as an annoying irrelevance. Also, by telling a daily joke, the teacher obliges his captive audience to laugh, if only out of politeness. The students' silence today suggests they have by this time rejected the burden of this obligation.[1]

Had the great Roman rhetorician and teacher Quintilian witnessed this incident, he might have warned the professor that audiences do not like wit that gives "the appearance of studied premeditation, or smell[s] of the lamp" (*Institutio Oratoria* VI. iii. 33). Other classical rhetoricians, especially Aristotle and Cicero, would offer wisdom of their own. In their discussions of the rhetorical proprieties of cha acter, circumstance, and audience, which governed the use of wit by Arist tle's "truly witty person," by Cicero's *urbanus*, or refined orator, and by

Quintilian's ideal orator, these rhetoricians offer contemporary writing teachers much of what they need to know in order to use humor effe tively in the writing emphasis classroom. These lessons include drawing primarily on self-deprecation and irony, remaining sensitive to circumstance, or *kairos*, and improvising wit to suit a particular group of students (rather than forcing premeditated wit upon an unwilling audience). If contemporary writing teachers can take these lessons to heart, they can learn to use wit to enhance their *ethos* as good persons speaking well, build effective relationships with students, rise above embarrassing moments, soften criticism, stimulate creative thinking, and make their students feel less like prisoners and more like welcome guests in the classroom.

## ARISTOTLE'S WITTY PERSON

When using humor as a rhetorical tool, Aristotle's truly witty person embodies all that is appropriate and tasteful. Such a rhetor uses wit sparingly, makes jokes that "seem to spring from the character" (*Ethics* IV. viii. 3), has the judgment to "regulate [his or her] wit" (IV. viii. 10), and observes the proprieties of character, situation, and audience. At the same time, the truly witty person exercises tact, using humor to amuse, not to hurt. At the extremes of humorous behavior are the buffoon (or βωμολόχος) and the boor (or αγροικος), while the person who engages in true wit (or εὐτρὰπελος) serves as the ideal mean (IV. viii. 3-10). Buffoons violate propriety by making jokes too often or in poor taste–showing themselves as "too fond of fun and raillery" (IV. viii. 3). Buffoons "itch to have their joke at all costs, and are more concerned to raise a laugh than to keep within the bounds of decorum and avoid giving pain to the object of their raillery" (IV. viii. 3). By contrast, the boor "is of no use in playful conversation: he contributes nothing and takes offense at everything" (IV. viii. 11). Throughout the *Ethics*, Aristotle argues for the "middle character" he sees as the representation of refined behavior; in the case of wit, the truly witty person, "will say, and allow to be said to him, only the sort of things that are suitable to a virtuous man and a gentleman" (IV. viii. 3-7). The witty person is versatile or "full of good turns" (IV. viii. 3), responding to a situation as it develops, and uses jokes that "seem to spring from the character" (IV. viii. 3). The witty person also prefers innuendo to the more obvious–and often obscene–humor of the buffoon. As a "cultivated" person, he possesses the judgment to "regulate his wit, and will be as it were a law to himself" (IV. viii. 3-10). In short, the middle character intends his or her humor to amuse, not to hurt, and unlike the buffoon, who often inflicts premeditated humor on an audience, the middle character's wit tends to be subtle and spontaneous, arising out of the opportunities presented by a conversation.

## CICERO'S *URBANUS*

Similar to the truly witty person, Cicero's *urbanus* uses wit sparingly, spontaneously, and "with a delicate charm and urbanity" (*De Oratore* I. v. 17). The *urbanus* remains conscious of his or her dignity, observes the relevant rules of propriety, and uses wit not merely to entertain but to achieve a valid rhetorical purpose (II. lxi. 247). The *urbanus* relies primarily on irony, which combines elegance, wit, and gravity in such a way that the speaker amuses and delights an audience with humorous ambiguities while maintaining a sophisticated and serious demeanor during the presentation of key ideas. Above all, such a rhetor avoids striving overeagerly after wit and can, as circumstances dictate, shift readily from a humorous to a serious demeanor. A keen sensitivity to the proprieties of the rhetorical situation, particularly to *kairos*, makes the truly witty person and the *urbanus* opportunists when it comes to wit–jesting only when circumstances are favorable. Unlike the buffoon, these rhetors tend not to make clumsy, forced, tasteless, offensive, or ill-timed jests.

## QUINTILIAN'S IDEAL ORATOR

In developing the notion of the ideal orator–a good person skilled in speaking (*vir bonus dicendi peritus*)–Quintilian emphasizes many of the same principles governing the wit of the truly witty person and the *urbanus*. Such a person "must above all things devote his attention to the formation of a moral character and must acquire a complete knowledge of all that is just and honorable" (*Institutio Oratoria* XII. ii. 2). On all occasions for speech, Quintilian observes, "Too much insistence cannot be laid upon the point that no one can be said to speak appropriately who has not considered not merely what is expedient, but also what it is becoming to say" (XI. i. 8). This principle applies with particular force to wit since "we pay too dear for the laugh we raise if it is at the cost of our own integrity" (VI. iii. 35). Therefore, the orator who wishes to amuse an audience should do so with care and only when wit is appropriate. When the character of the audience or the seriousness of the situation renders wit inappropriate, the ideal orator should rely on other strategies. And on occasions when wit is appropriate, the orator's "jests should never be designed to wound" (VI. iii. 28) and should avoid arrogance, insolence, sarcasm that targets large groups of people, and remarks that incite revenge or lead to groveling apologies (VI. iii. 33-34). On most occasions, the orator's best approach to wit is to assume a tone of "gentle raillery" (VI. iii. 28). Indeed, Quintilian says, "the most agreeable of all jests are those which are good humoured and easily digested" (VI. iii. 93). Such jests tend, after all, to reveal the intelligence and benevolent intentions of the rhetor and, therefore, win the goodwill of the audience. Of high importance, Quintilian suggests, is an orator's capacity for improvisation—"the crown of all our study and the highest reward of our long labours" (X. vii. 1). Orators cannot prepare for every challenge they may confront in a case, and the intellectual flexibility fostered by the practice of improvisation can help them respond to changing circumstances in the courtroom (or classroom), which often call for the spontaneous exercise of invention and wit (X. vii. 1).

## THE PROPRIETIES AND CONTEMPORARY WRITING TEACHERS

These rules of propriety set forth by Aristotle, Cicero, and Quintilian, aimed at guiding the wit of a refined rhetor, can also guide the wit of college writing teachers. These teachers may find it beneficial, while attempting to deliver instruction, to delight and move their students. After all, teaching writing is often an act of persuasion, with the instructor using all the rhetorical tools in her repertoire—including wit and humor—to convince students of her ability to teach them something valuable. Ideally, of course, all students who take college writing courses should come equipped with high levels of motivation to learn and grow as writers. As Sharon Crowley has observed, however, compulsory composition courses tend to inspire negative attitudes in writing students (242), many of whom resist the efforts of their teachers. Some students, for example, view composition as unnecessary—because they already know how to write—or irrelevant to their chosen field of study; others feel beaten down, having heard during their entire academic careers that they are poor writers. A serious approach to teaching will not necessarily overcome such resistance or guarantee that students take the material or the teacher seriously. Students may rebel when told the importance of a class, of a skill, or of specific information, taking the attitude–perhaps correctly–that they themselves must judge the importance. A good deal of the effectiveness of teaching writing, then, will involve not simply the transmission of facts and knowledge to students through logical means but also the building and maintaining of a teacherstudent relationship conducive to learning. And the viability of such a relationship will often depend upon the teacher's sensitivity to the proprieties of character, circumstance, and audience.

## Proprieties of Character

In a way similar to the truly witty person, the *urbanus*, or the ideal orator, the writing teacher will, when using wit, want to convey the *ethos* of an ethical, intelligent, humble, benevolent person who speaks with sensitivity and good taste–a good person skilled in speaking.[2] Such a person, ever mindful that learning is the primary purpose of the class, seeks a balance between gravity and humor, responding to a given situation with an appropriate demeanor. She must command respect and quiet at times in order to communicate or guide students toward the central ideas of the discipline. At other times, in the service of these ideas, she must draw on her wit in a manner consistent with her own tastes and those of her students. Clumsy, tasteless, or ill-timed attempts at humor will tend to work against the *ethos* of a good person skilled in speaking. So will instances of sarcasm or jests that wound students and reveal, in the teacher, an attitude of arrogance, spite, or intellectual snobbery. We may make someone laugh, but in the process we may sacrifice our dignity or integrity, hurt others, surrender too much authority, and lose track of key classroom goals.

A few years ago, for example, on the first day of a freshman composition course, I failed to maintain the *ethos* of an *urbanus* when a young man glared up at me and said, "I've always hated my English teachers." Instead of ignoring him or responding in a way that spared us both, I took offense at this attack on my profession. With a bit too much asperity, I said, "Well, I'm sure they all *loved* you." This response got a few laughs but started our relationship on the wrong footing. My bitter riposte revealed an inappropriate hostility toward this student, and as a teacher I should have kept a firmer grip on my emotions. It also played into the student's hands, giving him added reason to dislike English teachers. For the rest of the semester, he attempted at every opportunity to erode my authority or question the accuracy of my statements. Targeting him with sarcasm was the act of a boor or a buffoon, not of the gentler, self-deprecatory wit of an *urbanus*, and it did not win me the goodwill of the audience. Perhaps on a better day, I would have nodded and said, "Yeah, no one likes a critic" or "You're right to hate English teachers—we're horrible people."

Such a riposte, witty or not, might have helped me build rather than burn a bridge with this student. After all, modern psychology confirms Quintilian's notion of the power of humor to increase mutual regard between individuals. Psychologist Rod Martin argues that mirth serves important social functions in establishing and maintaining close relationships, enhancing feelings of attraction and commitment, and coordinating mutually beneficial activities" (114), including such mutually beneficial activities as writing workshops. Contemporary Americans, and among them college students, often see humility in authority figures as consistent with a democratic ideal—and therefore the mark of a good and just person. So in spite of Quintilian's caution against the use of self-deprecation as harmful to a rhetor's dignity (*Institutio Oratoria* VI. iii. 82), writing teachers will find that self-deprecatory humor, used judiciously, can enhance rather than detract from their *ethos*. The composition teacher who shows she can laugh with students at her own mistakes or faults reveals that she does not have an inflated, overly serious view of herself or her job. She reveals at once a humble awareness of her fallibility as a human being and an essential confidence in herself and her abilities. And she reveals a willingness to turn her critical judgment—often spent on students' work—on her own flawed speech and actions, poking fun at her factual errors or slips of the tongue. By encouraging students to laugh at and with her, she lets them know such errors are forgivable and invites them to relax and participate in the business of the classroom.

This attitude of self-deprecation becomes especially important when teachers respond to students' insults or criticisms. For example, in one composition classroom, a student told his professor, "I have an uncle who combs his hair like you, to cover up *his* bald spot." The male professor, beginning to lose his hair, could have chosen to take this remark as a personal attack, especially since the student had in earlier meetings issued similar insults. The professor chose instead to smile, run his fingers through the remnants of his hair, and say, "Tell your uncle he has my heartfelt sympathy, as one balding man to another." The professor then continued with the discussion, which the student may have been trying to disrupt, of a new essay assignment. To take the student's remark to heart–registering anger or hurt feelings– might have given the insult far more weight than it deserved. Such a reaction, like the sarcastic remark I made to my student, might also have had several other effects–derailing the legitimate class discussion, eroding the professor's *ethos* and authority, revealing feelings of spite toward the student, and telling other students with questionable motives that they too could "get" to him through mild personal attacks. By accepting the student's observation as a statement of fact, the professor derailed the attempted derailment, demonstrated the quickness of his wit, amused the class, maintained his *ethos* as an intelligent and benevolent person, and kept open the chance of building a better relationship with the offending student, who, as the professor later acknowledged, was a talented writer. In short, selfdeprecation allows writing teachers to rise above such moments.

　　Another beneficial effect of self-deprecatory wit, as it relates to *ethos*, involves the writing teacher's function as a role model, demonstrating appropriate ways of dealing with mistakes, criticisms, or disappointments. Since a great deal of learning to write involves learning to revise, doing so often means coping with setbacks, including the sort of criticism one receives in a workshop session. A teacher who uses wit to deal with criticism and setbacks shows students she has the ability to take what she often dishes out, make corrections, and return to work without undue embarrassment or loss of self-esteem–a useful attitude to take during a writing workshop. As Claudia Cornett says, "Teachers should be models for students. This includes showing how your sense of humor gets you through embarrassing moments and enables you to accept problems that have no solutions. Students learn more from the teachers they laugh with" (32). To the extent that students learn to adopt a self-deprecating attitude toward themselves and their writing, the workshop can become a place where students interact without threatening each other's ego or taking offense at each other's remarks. In such a place, productive collaboration can occur. In the same way, a teacher's demonstration of grace and wit in her communication with students serves as an example of the effective use of rhetorical techniques the students can attempt to put into practice in their own work. Some students may already possess well-developed senses of humor, but they may not know how or when to use this facility with good effect in their speech and writing. Other students may, by observing their teacher's and fellow students' use of wit in the workshop, dare to try their hand at it and learn from the experience. By attending to the proprieties of wit–such as timing, taste, balance, and frequency–the teacher not only builds her *ethos* but also shows student writers how to build their own.

**Proprieties of Circumstance**

The development of a sensitivity to *kairos*, which encompasses both the circumstances out of which a rhetorical need develops and a rhetor's invention of a response to this need, is as important for the contemporary writing teacher as for the sophists of ancient Greece. As John Poulakos has observed, rhetorical situations tend to unfold in unique, unpredictable ways and defy prefabricated responses. A rhetor who understands the contingent nature of discourse "addresses each occasion in its particularity, its singularity, its uniqueness" (Poulakos 61), making her "both a hunter and a maker of unique opportunities, always ready to address improvisationally and confer meaning on new and emerging situations" (61)–some of which may require seriousness and others wit.

In ways strikingly similar to Quintilian's ideal orator, who must improvise arguments in the courtroom, a writing teacher must often improvise responses to the emerging rhetorical situations in the classroom. Just as the orator prepares an argument for a court case, a writing teacher often goes into class each day with a good idea of what she hopes to accomplish, as outlined in her syllabus. And depending on the level of authority she assumes as a teacher, and the extent to which she relies on prepared lectures or lessons, she has a modicum of control over what gets said and done. But interchanges with students often take unexpected turns–sometimes fruitful, sometimes not. Students may interrupt, ask unanticipated questions for which she has no definite answer, and express misunderstandings she needs to address. And one can argue that students have a right to put their teacher on the spot, ask questions, lead the conversation astray, misunderstand points, and resist lessons, especially when such discourse leads them to a deeper understanding of their own or each other's composing processes. Students often ask such challenging questions as "If Cormac McCarthy can use dashes instead of quotation marks, why can't I?" or "How can you be so sure of the difference between an 'A-' and 'B+' paper?" In these cases, learning may hinge on the teacher's ability to improvise situationally appropriate responses—some of which may call for wit. Consider, for example, the question one second-year composition student, a nursing major, asked when given an essay assignment to analyze a piece of children's literature: "We're in the middle of a war and an AIDS epidemic and you want us to write about Dr. Seuss? We should be trying to solve the world's problems, not analyzing fairy tales and children's books."

The professor nodded solemnly and said, "Yes, but you're forgetting Dr. Seuss was a genius. A careful reader can discover answers to some of humankind's great dilemmas in the pages of *Horton Hears a Who*."

A few of the students laughed at the reply, but when the nursing major continued to argue that the assignment was a trivial waste of her time, the professor explained that many children's books have serious themes and suggested she work with one.

"What if I write my own children's book and analyze it?" she asked.

"Even better," the professor said, and though the student's first attempt to write a book explaining AIDS to young children fell short of her own standards, she acknowledged in her analysis how much she learned about the difficulties of writing for children—a lesson not specifically intended by the professor but sparked by their improvised conversation.

Such improvisation is an especially important skill during workshop sessions. After all, as Joseph Petraglia points out, writing is by nature "a variety of what is termed *ill-structured problem solving*" ("Writing" 80, emphasis in original). As Petraglia argues, "In ill-structured problem-solving, contingency permeates the task environment and solutions are always equivocal. The idea of 'getting it right' gives way to 'making it acceptable in the circumstances'" (83). These statements apply both to writing and the teaching of writing. One reason a workshop session helps writers cope with ill-structured problems created by a piece of writing is that the workshop not only tailors learning to fit individual needs but also encourages trial, error, and on-going course corrections. This learning process consists of "on-line anticipation and adjustment," of "continuous detection and correction of error," which Donald A. Schön–who studies the learning processes of architects–calls "reflection-in-action" (26). In the workshop, a writer gains a firsthand knowledge of writing by presenting her work, reflecting on his or her successes and failures, and trying to do better the next time–with feedback, as needed, from others who have negotiated similar intellectual terrain. From the initial plunge (or series of plunges) into writing, during which failure at various levels is likely, the writer learns lessons he or she can apply to subsequent drafts or projects. Meanwhile, the writer also learns to become a better improviser, which Schön believes is an essential aspect of professional artistry. Faced with an unfamiliar situation, in which competing ideas and agendas pose a new and difficult challenge, the writer or artist improvises a solution that draws the diverse parts into a harmonious whole. This act, Schön says, is comparable to the artistry of jazz musicians, who by "listening to one another, listening to themselves, . . . 'feel' where the music is going and adjust their playing accordingly" (30). Ordinary conversation, in which "participants pick up and develop themes of talk . . . is collective verbal improvisation" (30), as is the more purposeful conversation between a teacher and her students.

This type of conversation has several similarities to the Roman *sermo*, the preferred form of discourse for Cicero's *urbanus*. Both the *sermo* and the teacher-student conversation occur in a casual or "plain" style of speech, both consist of exchanges of dialogue, and both have the aim of moving, delighting, or informing an audience. Both also achieve these aims, in part, through the extemporaneous use of wit. In the case of the *sermo*, the *urbanus* uses what Cicero describes as solemn jesting or *severe ludus* (*De Oratore* lixvi. 269), which allows the speaker to use irony or other forms of wit appropriate to the circumstances while keeping the primary focus on the meat of the conversation. Because the conversation is a dialogue, members of the audience also act as speakers, engaging in both serious and witty discourse, which can lead in surprising directions and to unanticipated conclusions. Cicero's solemn jesting, then, could form a natural and appropriate part of the conversations carried on during a writing class. Solemn jesting might involve ironic allusions made by the professor or by the students themselves to points raised as part of a legitimate classroom discussion. In many ways, allusions that play on the ambiguity of a term or concept raised in a lecture heighten students' alertness to what is going on in the class and may even enhance their understanding and memory of an important concept. In creative writing classes, I use the phrase "writing from packages of experience" to describe a technique in which writers examine their life experiences and identify unique experiences that might form the basis of essays, stories, or novels. As I often say, "A large package of experience might lead to a novel, but a smaller package might lead to an essay or short story." One day, a clever student began using "package" as a sexuallycharged double-entendre. With a serious expression, she asked, "Is it okay if the guys show us their packages?" and "But what if someone's package is too small to satisfy the requirements of a good story?" As the teacher, I had to hold to the original, more serious meaning and answer her questions with a straight face even as her fellow students laughed. Otherwise, I risked letting the student twist a useful concept into an obscenity. She continued, during the semester, to put extra emphasis on the term during brainstorming sessions, getting laughs by saying things like, "I'm not so sure I like your *package*," but in some ways, this jest only helped remind her fellow students about both meanings of the term.

As it happens, opportunities for wit and humor occur often, thanks in part to the social tensions inherent in presenting and critiquing student writing, and in part to the ambiguities of intention and meaning that arise. Sometimes, though, the laughter resulting from well-intentioned wit can result in hurt feelings, requiring a spontaneous yet appropriate response from the teacher. One day, for example, a distraught young man stayed after a creative writing class to explain that everyone, including his teacher, had misunderstood his short story, which the class found hilarious. With a wounded expression, he said, "I never meant the piece to be a parody. It's a serious story about a cowboy who can't live with the idea that the evil sheriff stole his ranch, his horse, and his girl." The story contained nearly every dusty cliché ever used in a Western novel, but the author had warped each tired phrase enough to make it, and the story, somewhat fresh and funny. Assuming too much, the teacher had seen these moves as satiric, and so had the student's classmates, but as the student explained, he simply got the clichés wrong. In response, the teacher said he once had the opposite experience when critics took his one-act play–a comedy–more seriously than intended. Produced by a university theater, the play portrayed a scene in which a street artist smeared ketchup on the white wall of a man whose home he had invaded. A bank of critics in the audience later said they saw this mess, intended to satirize graffiti, as a serious artistic statement. One critic even claimed to be so moved by this work of art–created as the audience looked on–that he found it difficult to enjoy the rest of the play.

"At first, I thought he was putting me on," the teacher said. "I never expected anyone to see the ketchup as art."

"What did you say?" the student asked.

The teacher smiled. "What could I say? You can't control how critics will interpret your work."

"So you think I should go with the parody idea?"

"Only if you think the class is right," the teacher said. "If not, maybe you should eliminate the clichés and come up with some fresh metaphors of your own."

In this instance, a misunderstanding led to laughter that hurt the feelings of the student writer who submitted his work. In an effort to salve the student's wounds, the professor improvised a lesson on a number of issues writers often face–cutting clichéd language, coping with unexpected reactions to one's writing, and making decisions about how to proceed. The teacher's selfdeprecatory tale offered these hard lessons together with some consolation and support. Much of a writing teacher's work, whether in the lecture, workshop, or individual conference, will involve a degree of improvisation in order to adjust to changing rhetorical circumstances. And much of this work will involve the impromptu use of wit.

## Proprieties of Audience

While improvising wit appropriate to one's character and circumstances, one must give equal consideration to the character of one's audience–a matter of special importance when the audience consists of student writers. The audience in each writing classroom differs from the audience in every other, due to the specific mixture of students' attitudes, backgrounds, levels of maturity, and personalities. The students in a particular class may feel fatigued, insecure, beaten down by deadlines or poor grades, hostile toward the teacher or toward authority figures in general, or so serious about their studies they have no tolerance for frivolity. In such cases, any attempt at levity on the teacher's part may prove futile–and harmful to her *ethos*. In another class, students who respond positively to wit on one day may on the next reject the teacher's every effort to lighten the mood. Sometimes this rejection occurs for such obvious reasons as the teacher's returning graded quizzes or papers to the students, a proportion of whom will likely receive lower grades than expected. At other times, the rejection may have no apparent cause other than the fickle nature of the audience.

Often, a keen awareness of the classroom *kairos* will alert a teacher to opportunities, or the lack, for wit. So, quite obviously, will the presence or absence of laughter. In any event, a writing teacher should, in the spirit of an *urbanus*, have the sensitivity, taste, and good sense to read and respect each audience's moods and adjust the use of her wit accordingly. She may also wish to avail herself of Plato's version of *kairos*, based on adapting one's speech, whether serious or witty, to fit the souls of one's listeners. This capability, to which Socrates refers in *The Phaedrus*, involves gaining an accurate insight into the sort of people who make up one's audience and choosing the proper words to instruct or persuade them. As Socrates says, one offers to a "complex soul complex speeches containing all the modes, and simple speeches to the simple soul" (277 b-c). A rhetor who addresses a large, diverse crowd may have difficulty judging the nature of the individual souls who make up the crowd and must rely, instead, on his or her best sense of the crowd as an entity. A writing teacher, however, has a far better chance of gaining an accurate insight into the nature of her audience—as a group and as individuals. After all, she not only meets the entire class several times a week, for an entire semester, but also holds individual conferences and reads each student's work, often including essays, stories, and journal entries containing personal information and anecdotes. These encounters—in person and in print—may provide crucial clues to the type of wit that will, and will not, appeal to the students. Something in a student's background may lead him or her to feel offended by a joke that amuses everyone else. For example, a teacher who stumbles over a difficult passage in a reading, and pokes fun at his own stuttering, may unwittingly offend a student whose close relative is a stutterer. If the student has revealed this personal information in conversation or writing, an alert teacher could avoid making such a joke.

By contrast, this knowledge also helps establish the type of wit a teacher can use in appealing to a particular audience. Consider, for example, a conversation that occurred several years ago in an advanced nonfiction writing class composed of fifteen college seniors. In his piece, one of the students used the term "wanker," and the teacher, genuinely puzzled, asked what the word meant. The students laughed and expressed amazement at her ignorance. Finally, the author of the story said, "It's British."

"British for what?"

Another student said, "You know."

"No I don't."

The student rolled his eyes. "Masturbator."

"Seriously?" the teacher asked, and everyone laughed again.

"Why haven't I heard it before?"

The students shrugged. One of them said, "Maybe you don't watch enough TV."

The teacher reflected for a moment. "If you think about it, the term applies to just about everybody, doesn't it?"

Such an exchange would not likely occur in a freshman or sophomore composition class, in part because of the students' ages and in part because "wanker" would not normally appear in an essay composed for such a class. In this writing workshop, though, the students were older and sophisticated enough not only to instruct the teacher on the meaning of a slang term but also to appreciate both the teacher's honest admission of ignorance and her face-saving joke at the end. In any event, they laughed and got back to work. A small, intimate group of writers used to engaging in candid discussions of the actions, scenes, and diction in each other's essays, the students appeared to accept the witticism in the spirit the professor intended, making a conversation that would no doubt be utterly unacceptable in another context, appropriate—or appropriately inappropriate.

Contrast this type of spontaneous wit with the "canned" jokes, props (funny hats, unlit cigars), and skits (which involve adopting personae ranging from Mr. Rogers to Tim "Tool Time" Tailor) Ronald A. Berk urges teachers to use (39-42). Improvisational wit has a bit more risk associated with it, thanks largely to the lack of time to prepare and think through the implications of a joke. The chances of offending someone in the audience therefore increase. And improvised wit can, like prefabricated humor, often bomb. But a writing teacher's willingness to take such risks reveals several important factors relating to audiences. First, by attempting to use wit, she shows she is relaxed and feels sufficiently at ease among the students to let down her guard. Second, by tailoring wit to suit the tastes and needs of a particular group of students, she shows she possesses an intimate knowledge of these students as individuals. Third, by engaging in exchanges of wit, an activity normally reserved for peers, she shows respect for the students as people, treating them as social and intellectual equals. Such treatment is especially important in classrooms rooted in a critical pedagogy, in which a teacher shares a portion of her power of office with students, thus encouraging them to invest and participate in their learning. By improvising wit to suit a particular audience's needs and tastes, a teacher helps her students feel less like unwilling captives and more like welcome guests or even part-owners of a classroom space. In many ways, the students in a writing class truly are members of a captive audience, and, at the least, a teacher shows good manners by making the prisoners' experience more pleasant.

By attending to the proprieties of character, circumstance, and audience, and using wit with the proper mix of gravity and levity, a writing teacher joins a tradition of rhetorical education going back to Aristotle. She acknowledges the reality that one must persuade an audience, including an audience of student writers, to laugh. After all, no teacher can, or should want to, make her students laugh by intimidation or force. The proprieties serve as an overarching heuristic, establishing the parameters within which she can use wit effectively as a teaching tool–in ways that enhance rather than detract from her *ethos* as a good person skilled in speaking and writing, that allow her to adapt to changing conditions in the classroom, and that help her meet the specific needs and tastes of her students. These proprieties, in plainer words, guide the teacher's use of wit to achieve pedagogical goals and construct in the classroom a playful environment in which learning can thrive.

## NOTES

1. Another questionable approach to using humor in the classroom comes from Ronald A. Berk, a professor at Johns Hopkins University School of Nursing and author of two books about using humor as a teaching tool. Sporting an unlit cigar, Berk goes to class dressed as a clown, in comical hats, ties, and a tool belt held up by tape-measure suspenders (Bartlett A8). He makes use of props and stunts in teaching students biostatistics and measurement, arguing that his clowning attracts students' attention and makes lessons memorable (A8-A9). As Berk acknowledges, "'There are people who think that it's frivolous, it's undignified'" (A9). Even so, he cites favorable student evaluations and claims that his playful approach to teaching–which

draws heavily on self-deprecation and avoids sarcasm–cuts tension, makes difficult lessons palatable, improves the student-teacher relationship, and "helps students learn" (A9). In fact, a colleague says he is "'a very effective, engaging teacher'" (A9). One of the chief objections one might raise to a teacher's playing the class clown, complete with funny hat, involves a potential loss of dignity and credibility. To pull off the clown role, a teacher must have a high level of expertise in her field, confidence, good timing and delivery, and the respect and understanding of her students. She must also be funny. If Berk satisfies all these conditions, he may indeed make the clown role work. If not, he risks coming across as a buffoon who, as Cicero tells us, uses humor too often and at the wrong time. Another major disadvantage to going dressed as a clown–or building humor irrevocably into one's syllabus–involves the inability to respond to changing circumstances, or *kairos*. Even if a teacher, such as Berk, could be equally funny every day, the students' needs or responses may often warrant seriousness instead of humor. Dressed for clowning and prepared to deliver stunts or jokes, the teacher may feel so committed to a humorous performance that he or she may be unwilling to change course. Such clowning, then, does not accommodate a flexible approach to teaching.

2. She will also, of course, want to *be* such a person.

## WORKS CITED

Aristotle. *Nicomachean Ethics*. Trans. H. Rackham. Cambridge: Harvard UP, 1934. Print.

Bartlett, Thomas. "Did You Hear the One About the Professor? How One Statistician Learned to Use Humor in the Classroom and Is Now Teaching Others How to Do It." *Chronicle of Higher Education* 49 (25 July 2003): A8-A10. Print.

Berk, Ronald A. Professors Are from Mars®, Students Are from Snickers®: *How to Write and Deliver Humor in the Classroom and in Professional Presentations*. Sterling: Stylus, 2003. Print.

Cicero, Marcus Tullius. *De Oratore*. Books I-II. Trans. E. W. Sutton. Cambridge: Harvard UP, 1942. Print.

Cornett, Claudia E. *Learning through Laughter: Humor in the Classroom*. Bloomington: Phi Delta Kappa, 1986. Print.

Crowley, Sharon. *Composition in the University: Historical and Polemical Essays*. Pittsburgh: U of Pittsburgh P, 1998. Print.

Martin, Rod. *The Psychology of Humor: An Integrative Approach*. Amsterdam: Elsevier, 2007. Print.

Petraglia, Joseph. *Reconceiving Writing, Rethinking Writing Instruction*. Mahwah: L. Erlbaum Associates, 1995. Print.

Plato. *Phaedrus.* Trans. C. J. Rowe. 2nd ed. Warminster: Aris & Phillips, 1988. Print.

Poulakos, John. *Sophistical Rhetoric in Classical Greece.* Columbia: U of South Carolina P, 1995. Print.

Quintilian. *The Institutio Oratoria of Quintilian.* Trans. H. E. Butler. New York: Putnam, 1921. Print.

Schön, Donald A. *Educating the Reflective Practitioner.* San Francisco: Jossey-Bass, 1987. Print.

# KAIROS

Kairos is on the Web at http://www.technorhetoric.net/

*Kairos: A Journal of Rhetoric, Technology, and Pedagogy* is the longest-running online journal in writing studies. The journal was first published in 1996 and maintains its editorial and publishing independence through virtual collaboration by staff members across universities across the world. With no budget, the journal runs exclusively on in-kind donations and volunteer editorial and technical labor. The mission of *Kairos* has always been to publish scholarship that examines digital and multimodal composing practices, promoting work that enacts its scholarly argument through rhetorical and innovative uses of new media. We publish "webtexts," which are texts authored specifically for publication on the World Wide Web. Webtexts are scholarly examinations of topics related to technology in English Studies fields (e.g., rhetoric, composition, technical and professional communication, education, creative writing, language and literature) and related fields such as media studies, informatics, arts technology, and others.

## Crossing Battle Lines: Teaching Multimodal Literacies through Alternate Reality Games

"Battle Lines" offers a compelling game experience that allows student-players to develop rhetorical, community-building, and digital literacies, crossing boundaries between academic and ludic practices. The game was test-run for the first time in a class of undergraduate students at UT Austin over the course of four weeks early in the spring semester of 2012, and the webtext is about that pedagogical practice. In this piece, the inter-relationship between design and the argument is clever, well executed, and is the most accessible (per Web standards) webtext *Kairos* has ever published, which makes it unique and forward-thinking on those grounds alone.

# 9 Crossing Battle Lines: Teaching Multimodal Literacies through Alternate Reality Games

*Scott Nelson, Chris Ortiz y Prentice, M. Catherine Coleman, Eric Detweiler, Marjorie Foley, Kendall Gerdes, Cleve Wiese, R. Scott Garbacz, and Matt King*

*This article was originally published as a webtext at http://www.technorhetoric.net/17.3/praxis/nelson-et-al/index.html and we recommend that you view it there if at all possible.*

In this webtext, we present *Battle Lines*, a pedagogical alternate reality game we developed over the course of two years under the aegis of The University of Texas at Austin's Digital Writing & Research Lab. *Battle Lines* offers a compelling game experience that allows student-players to develop rhetorical, community-building, and digital literacies, crossing boundaries between academic and ludic practices. The game was test-run for the first time in a class of undergraduate students at UT Austin over the course of four weeks early in the spring semester of 2012. Our experiences as game designers and gamemasters, beta testers and data analysts have opened the term *multimodal* for us in theory and practice. Just as important as explanation is demonstration, yet both are still largely reflective practices which emphasize consumption over production. A unique affordance of games is that they involve, at their best, productive activities that include reading, reflection, trial-and-error, revision, and tactics; writing a game is thus no mere transmission of knowledge or instruction, and from this derives all the challenge and advantage of teaching through games.

We have designed this webtext, therefore, not merely to explain nor even to demonstrate but above all to simulate the multimodal experience *Battle Lines* offered both its designers and its players. Crossing Battle Lines, like the game it is named for, is designed to engage readers in multiple sensory dimensions. The goal of this multimodal engagement is to maximize the potential of a digital and online text by presenting evidence and analysis from a combined digital and live-action game (an alternate reality game) in multiple modes: visual, audible, and interactive. Reading our webtext also invites you to watch, listen, interact, and play. We describe this experience across the senses as multimodal following a convention established among composition theorists (Kress, 2001; Lauer, 2009; Selfe, 2007). *Multimodal* is adopted for its emphasis on the semiotic channels of an argument, and on its design and composition, versus *multimedia* or other alternatives with more product-focused shades of meaning. For further perspectives on use of the term *multimodal,* see Claire Lauer's (2012) publication in *Kairos.* We invite you to play, then, engaging in a number of semiotic channels, as you learn what *Battle Lines* was, how it came to be, what questions it raises, and what potentialities it brings into view.

## WHAT ARE ARGS?

Alternate reality games, or ARGs, are part story, part scavenger hunt, part puzzle, part role-playing game, and part community-building exercise. They are set in real and virtual spaces, with players navigating both their environment and the digital media landscape in search of clues and solutions. ARGs have been around since 1996, and some notable ones have been produced by large media companies looking to create buzz about video games or movies (Alternate reality games, n.d.). However, a growing list of educational institutions—including The University of North Texas (Warren, Dondlinger, &McLeod, 2008), Arizona State (Hea, Zimmerman, & Howe, 2010), and Duke (Boluk, Jagoda, & Lemieux, n.d.)—are turning the power of ARGs' collective intelligence skills to educational purposes.

Alternate reality games can run for months (and sometimes years) and thus are usually produced by teams of game masters who create the game's narrative and monitor and adjust the game in real time. This narrative structure is not the usual linear structure, but instead is distributed across various media platforms for players to find and piece together. During gameplay, players' responses to puzzles and characters impact how the game unfolds, with game masters writing players' characters into the storyline and gently guiding teams toward possible puzzle solutions.

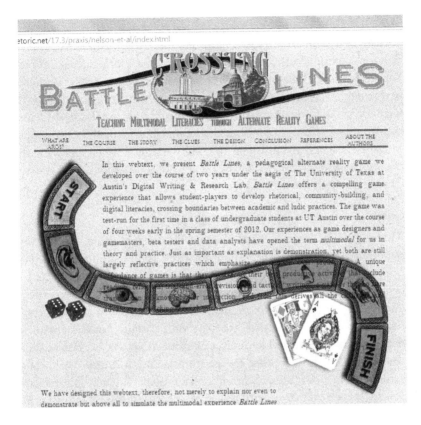

Homepage of *Battle Lines* as originally published in *Kairos*

Caption: Between the main paragraphs on this page lies a stylized board game path, repeating the colors gray, red, brown, and green. Each square in the path has a word or picture inside. They are: Start, an ear, an eye, a brain, an open mouth, a nose, a hand pointing a finger, and Finish. The board game path is wrapped around a pair of black dice showing sixes up and threes on the side, as well as two playing cards, a jack and an ace.

Clues are hidden in websites, on blogs, in emails, in layered pictures, in scrambled YouTube videos, in garbled audio files, and even in the architecture and cityscapes surrounding the players. Each clue is a puzzle, and each puzzle's solution leads the players to another clue. The massive distribution of content and the skills needed to play

ARGs lead to players collaborating and sharing information in organic learning communities.

## Why Use ARGs?

Twenty-first century educators are competing for students' attention—competing with various interactive media, from video games to YouTube to social networking sites to transformative works. Because past pedagogical practices, including lecture, can exclude multimodal learners by reifying dominant power structures—making students consumers of scholarship rather than collaborators in their own education—we feel it is important to combine digital literacy skills with traditional textual research in the composition classroom. One way to do so is through the use of ARGs.

### Games & Social Construction Theory

Although several composition theories inform our game, social construction theory remains at the fore. Even the possibility that contingent subjectivities emerge through social interactions leads us to believe that alternate reality games are ideal spaces for players to experiment with constructing particular identities. While social construction theorists, such as James Berlin (1988), critique power structures that work to naturalize identities, our game supposes a different, but compatible purpose. Taking a page from Kenneth Burke (1969), our game presumes that identification with a range of literacies allows students to experience diversified academic identities by interacting with/in the university environment itself. Though we suspect that academic identifications would occur even without the game, we took that inevitability into account and designed the game to provide students with the agency to construct and negotiate their identities in contexts they may not have experienced otherwise.

### Historical Precedence

Historically speaking, games and rhetoric are so closely intertwined that the rigid distinction between play and rhetorical pedagogy appears new and incongruous—not games in rhetoric, but rhetoric without games. Take any rhetor's education in antiquity: progymnasmata were a series of increasingly difficult modules focused on specific rhetorical challenges that began with fables and simple narrations, leveled up to more developed practices such as the confirmation or refutation of stories or speeches, and eventually culminated in more fully developed role-playing performances such as ethopoiia and, eventually, declamation. This graduated structure epitomizes many of the educationally beneficial qualities contemporary theorists identify in games, such as performance before competence (Gee, 2007, p. 62) and flow (Csikszentmihalyi, 2008, p. 6) or being intensely focused, highly motivated, creatively charged, and working at the very limits of [one's] abilities (McGonigal, 2011, p. 40).

## Role Playing

Classical rhetors also participated in role-playing exercises as part of the progymnasmata: Students tried out different subject positions as part of the process of crafting their own, flexible identities as skilled speakers and writers, often through explicit role-playing in fictional scenarios. The role-playing dimension of declamation tuned out historical or political considerations that distracted from the immediate learning objectives (Winterbottom, 1982, p. 65), making role-playing among the most effective mind-sets for learning. Additionally, literacy scholar James Gee (2008) argued that games teach players necessary skills and knowledge within a Situated Learning Matrix, where content is rooted in experiences a person is having as part and parcel of taking on a specific identity (in terms of the goals and norms stemming from a social group) (p. 26). By teaching through role-playing, games distribute their knowledge and skills as a deep form of value-laden learning (p. 32).

## Games, Pleasure, & Real-World Experience

Fantastical exercises in role-playing or fictional declamation themes, however, are not irrelevant to real-world experience. Rhetorical games are instead lenses through which students can reason about, engage, and assume authority over controversial and complex topics. As Erik Gunderson (2003) put it, ancient declamation reveals a zone of intellectual engagement where the otherwise unapproachable can be handled under the aegis of irrelevance, mere play, and idle fantasy (p. 6). Unlike many of the pedagogical techniques commonly found in the classroom setting, games get players to exercise their learning muscles … without knowing it and without having to pay overt attention to the matter (Gee, 2007, p. 29). Players do not approach games in order to learn a set of skills or a body of knowledge. Rather, skills and knowledge are gained unconsciously as one takes pleasure in mastering the problems and challenges good games offer.

By using both real and fictional controversies, games can sustain students' engagement with real-world issues by providing low-stakes, imaginative, and skills-oriented contexts that also make the learning experience pleasurable. All of these objectives allow for differential rates of learning, keep players invested in the game, and make the often frustrating experience of learning a new skill more pleasant.

## Collaboration & Collective Intelligence

### Harnessing Collective Intelligence

Because the puzzles in ARGs are usually complex enough that one player cannot solve every puzzle alone, players quickly learn to leverage their collective intelligence in their learning communities. The digital media scholar and philosopher Pierre Lévy (1997) defined collective intelligence as a form of universally distributed intelligence, constantly enhanced, coordinated in real-time, and resulting in the effective mobilization of skills (p. 13). Lévy's collective intelligence is the opposite of authoritarian structures that confine individuals to interchangeable parts in service of an overarching purpose. Instead, in a collective intelligence network, each individual possesses skills others do not, and thus is given chances to contribute in an "information on demand" environment. In this environment, individuals find themselves simultaneously mentoring and being mentored by their peers.

### Encouraging Collaboration

In addition, since game content is distributed across many types of digital media applications and real-world locations, ARGs create a necessary condition for productive collaboration: responsibility [rests] on each and every player to come forward with any and all discoveries, so that the entire collective [can] access and process as complete a data set as possible (McGonigal, 2008, p. 11). Because no player is an expert on every facet of a clue, it is more advantageous to share knowledge rather than horde it.

As a result of piecing together the game's structure and mentoring each other, players build communities based on mutually shared knowledge. Jane McGonigal (2008) called this stage in ARGs the collective cognition stage, where players gather and analyze game content, developing a cohesive theory of the game world and a shared language for discussing it. This initial period of intense collaboration provide[s] the players with a sense of community, shared focus, and common knowledge (p. 11).

## Digital Literacy

### Digital Literacies in ARGs

Through the course of an ARG, players must navigate various digital media platforms in search of clues. Additionally, ARGs adapt to player input because players do not merely consume the game, but they produce content as well. Because ARGs require this type of input as well as navigational literacies, players develop a variety of literacies.

Digital literacy can be divided into three types: functional literacy, critical literacy, and rhetorical literacy. Simply stated, when referring to digital literacies, a functionally literate person can use technologies, a critically literate person can question technologies, and a rhetorically literate person can produce technologies (Selber, 2004, p. 25). The structure of ARGs works to develop skills in each of these areas.

Puzzles within ARGs require complex skill sets in a variety of platforms, and getting from clue to clue requires developing these skills. Players, at various moments, may need to comb the source code of a webpage, gradually peel away the layers of a scrambled Photoshop image, or navigate the private databases at one of the campus's libraries. A single player may not possess all of these skills, but, through mentorships formed in her learning communities, she can teach others and in turn be taught by them. In this way, players leave the game familiar with various interface metaphors from a multitude of platforms. The value of this type of literacy comes from knowing how to "work the programs" of our modern digital era. These basic skills, however, are often the limits of traditional methods of instruction. With ARGs, we have a chance to make students questioners and producers of digital media artifacts as well.

### Questioning Digital Media

Because ARGs lay a fictional narrative across real-world technologies, they present prime opportunities to discuss the natures of propaganda and hypermediated societies. Players are constantly questioning the limits of the game, testing the aforementioned hypotheses regarding the storyline, digital media, and reality. When any medium may contain a clue, players become adept at recognizing cues to the veracity of digital media. Traditional instruction in this area may leave students with principles of web credibility, but ARGs force players to put these principles into practice through numerous examples. When players must look beyond the skin of a digital media artifact to find clues, they cultivate critical thinking skills that can translate into a healthy skepticism of the digital media they are exposed to everyday.

### ARGs & Social Action

Finally, in making alternate reality games interactive, we ask players to reflect on these technologies as media of persuasion, deliberation, and social action. More than just following clues from one location to the next, ARGs are participatory media. They ask players to collect, analyze, and critique various sources of information, and the game responds to each of these actions. Seeing a larger system respond to such actions can translate into real-world social action: As Henry Jenkins (2006) found, some alternate reality gaming groups evolve into social action groups, as was the case with the Collective Detective, a think tank whose first task was to try to identify corruption and waste in U.S. federal government spending (p. 244). As one member of the collective noted, the phases of an alternate reality game coincide with real-world practices for analytical thinking as a step toward persuasive discourse (p. 244). Players in ARGs produce media to make a change in the game world, and can in turn use those same practices to change the real one.

## THE COURSE

### Course Context

In the spring of 2012, 21 students signed up for Rhetoric 312, Writing in Digital Environments. While interpretation of just what constitutes "writing" and "digital environments" is up to individual instructors, RHE 312 is a lower-division course taught using networked computers and focused on using, interpreting, and analyzing traditional and emerging technologies (Department of Rhetoric & Writing, 2012–14). All students who enroll in RHE 312 must have at least passed RHE 306, the "Composition 101" of The University of Texas system. For some of these 21 students, RHE 312 was the first exposure they had to college writing with digital technologies.

"Writing," in this sense, referred to a variety of inscription technologies across many modes: verbal, visual, aural, procedural, haptic, and kinesthetic. The course was designed as a type of survey of contemporary expressive technologies, exploring the affordances and constraints of each. Students learned about digital discourse communities and finally presented an argument to an audience of their choice. The hope was that students would leave the course with a greater awareness of not only the communicative power of digital media, but also some of the limitations it imposes upon its users and producers. For this aim, students covered a range of texts that addressed both theory and praxis. All the readings for this course can be found in the left and right columns of this page, and full citations are provided in the References.

The course covered three major units, with each culminating in digital composition and textual reflection. Battle Lines was the first of those units, and thus was designed to introduce students to software and techniques. Using the skills learned in Battle Lines, students later created an infographic for Unit 2 and a researched digital argument for Unit 3. The Digital Writing & Research Lab at UT admittedly provides an environment outside of the norm, as the program has been evolving since 1985 and receives support from the Department of Rhetoric & Writing. However, we believe that most of the principles taught in Battle Lines can be applied using open source software and collaborative exercises.

Given that students were being asked to create multimodal compositions, it made sense that the class materials followed a similar process. Click on the images below for the course's infographic syllabus or the interactive course schedule.

### Reading List

Keith Aoki, James Boyle & Jennifer Jenkins, *Tales from the Public Domain: Bound by Law?*
Roland Barthes, *Rhetoric of the Image*
Stephen A. Bernhardt, *Seeing the Text*
Ian Bogost, *The Rhetoric of Video Games*
Nicholas Carr, *Is Google Making Us Stupid?*
The Computer History Museum, *Remix: Lawrence Lessig on IP in the Digital Economy*

Hanno H.J. Ehses, *Representing Macbeth: A Case Study in Visual Rhetoric*

B.J. Fogg, *The Functional Triad: Computers in Persuasive Roles*

James Paul Gee, *Learning and Games*

Gunther Kress & Theo van Leeuwen, *Colour as a Semiotic Mode: Notes for a Grammar of Colour*

Richard A. Lanham, *The Implications of Electronic Information for the Sociology of Knowledge*

Lev Manovich, *The Language of Cultural Interfaces*

Scott McCloud, *The Vocabulary of Comics & Blood in the Gutter*

Plato, *Phaedrus*

Marshall McLuhan, *The Medium is the Massage*

Martin Solomon, *The Power of Punctuation*

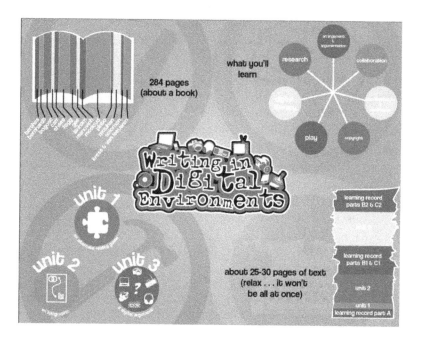

Infographic Syllabus

Caption: The syllabus is divided into four quadrants: Reading, Learning, Writing, and Making. The top left quadrant, Reading, shows an open book divided into sections labelled with author last names. The total reading is 284 pages. The top right quadrant, Learning, lists the Course Strands in a series of connected circles: research, arrangement and argumentation, collaboration, documentation and mechanics, copyright, play, digital literacy. The bottom right quadrant, Writing, says "about 25–30 pages of text (relax ... it won't be all at once). The writing assignments include: learning record part A, unit 1, unit 2, learning record parts B1 & C1, unit 3, and learning record parts B2 & C2. The bottom left quadrant, Making, shows a puzzle piece for unit 1: an alternate reality game. It shows a small stylized infographic for unit 2: an infographic, and it shows several objects clustered around a question mark, including a computer, a camera, a cell phone, and headphones for unit 3: a digital argument. Centered between the quadrants is the title "Writing in Digital Environments" in stylized text with objects clustered around the edges: a CD, a computer, a cell phone, a camera, headphones, a Nintendo controller, an old tv, a camcorder, an iPhone, and a joystick.

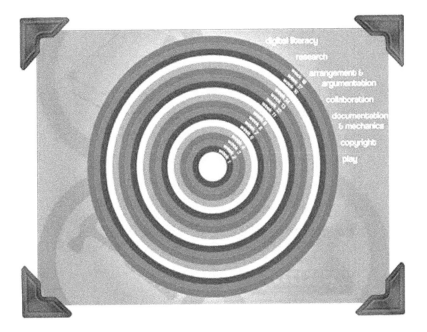

Interactive Course Schedule

Caption: The course syllabus is made up of color-contrasting concentric circles. The colors repeat: navy, blue, olive, green, and dust yellow. Around the top right of the circles, the course strands are listed: digital literacy, research, arrangement and argumentation, collaboration, documentation and mechanics, copyright, and play. Users can roll over each circle to see the assignments for the week.

Each week's assignment is as follows:

| Week | Assignments |
|---|---|
| Week 1 | • Class Introduction/Learning Record Online introduction<br>• Post first observation to your Learning Record<br>• Post questions about LR on main wiki page<br>• Read excerpt from Plato's Phaedrus, Carr's "Is Google Making Us Stupid?" and McLuhan's "The Medium is the Massage" |
| Week 2 | • Questions regarding LRO Part A due<br>• Battle Lines study information<br>• Play Battle Lines<br>• Read Barthes' "Rhetoric of the Image" & Ehses' "Representing Macbeth . . ." |
| Week 3 | • Play Battle Lines<br>• Read Lanham's "The Implication . . ." |
| Week 5 | • Play Battle Lines |
| Week 6 | • Play Battle Lines<br>• Read McCloud's Chs. 2 & 3. |
| Week 7 | • Sketchnotes/Research<br>• Read Kress & Van Leeuwen "Colour . . ."<br>• Copyright discussion<br>• Watch Lessig video, take sketchnotes |
| Week 8 | • Sketchnotes to infographics<br>• Read Bernhardt's "Seeing the Text" & Solomon's "The Power of Punctuation"<br>• Logics of text/Logics of images<br>• Rough sketch of image due |
| Week 9 | • Spring Break<br>• Due Sunday, 3/18: Unit 1 |
| Week 10 | • Discuss Unit 2<br>• Creative Commons resources<br>• Due Sunday, 3/25: Parts B1 & C1 of LR |
| Week 11 | • Audacity discussion<br>• Workshop<br>• Read Bogost, "The Rhetoric of Video Games" & Gee's "Learning & Games" |

| Week 12 | <ul><li>Discussion of video games</li><li>Read Manovich's "The Language of Cultural Interfaces"</li><li>Choosing a venue/interface logics</li><li>Read Fogg's "Persuasive Technology"</li></ul> |
|---------|---|
| Week 13 | <ul><li>Workshop projects</li><li>Project proposals due</li></ul> |
| Week 14 | <ul><li>Workshop projects</li><li>Draft of project due (e.g., storyboard, textual description, mock-up, etc.)</li></ul> |
| Week 15 | Workshop projects |
| Week 16 | <ul><li>Workshop projects</li><li>Unit 2 Due; Final LRO Questions</li></ul> |
| Week 17 | No Class (Finals) |
| Week 18 | Final Learning Record Part B2 & C2 due |

## Assessment

One of the struggles of implementing games in the classroom is working within the more traditional forms of assessment. After all, (most) American universities require that students receive some form of grade for the course, and such a requirement can sap the fun out of any assignment. While there are winners and losers in agonistic games, alternate reality games tend to foster more collaborative efforts among players. We felt to grade students on their performance in each level would unduly emphasize the product rather than the process.

In order to be conducive to gaming structures, the form of assessment used in this course needed to require and allow students to explore their own educational processes. Assessment for the course thus occurred via the Learning Record Online, a portfolio system adapted by Dr. Margaret Syverson of The University of Texas at Austin. The LRO asks that students record and reflect upon their work, with a focus on demonstrable skills and knowledge. While a full discussion of the Learning Record is beyond the scope of this project, we hope the reader will explore this assessment technique further through the Learning Record Online's website.

The Learning Record encourages playful engagement by removing the promise (or threat) of a grade for individual assignments and placing more emphasis on the process of working through the clues. At the midterm and final, students analyzed their own work for evidence across six dimensions of learning (the ways students learn) and seven course strands (what we wanted students to learn). In order for student-players to have evidence to analyze for the Learning Record, it was necessary that they worked through the clues. When the end goal of the course is to present evidence for what you've learned, correct answers count, but much less so than continued engagement and experimentation with the material.

## Course Strands

Digital Literacy

- Through working with various programs in this course, students will gain functional digital literacy through learning how to recognize similar interface logics and manipulate programs for their desired aims.
- Through reading about and studying various programs as well as working with computers, students will learn to think critically about computers' roles in establishing discourse communities and come to see these technologies as value-laden.
- Through creating digital arguments of their own, students will learn to think rhetorically about digital environments.
- By exploring multiple modes of communication, students will learn to think critically about the affordances and constraints of varied media.
- Further, students will learn communication grammars for working with text, sound, static images, video, and interactive technologies.

Research

- Through the process of creating arguments in different media, students will learn to find sound academic research in both digital and analog environments.
- Students will develop a repertoire of research methods to apply in appropriate situations.
- Students will learn what kinds of research are applicable in various venues, and how to build credibility through research avenues.

Arrangement & Argumentation

- Through the projects created in this course and the process of completing a Learning Record, students will learn to plan, draft, and revise their work for maximum effect.
- In creating digital communication, students will learn to apply argumentative and arrangement techniques across a variety of modalities.

Collaboration

- In playing Battle Lines and in creating digital arguments, students will learn the value of voluntary collaboration in digital environments.
- Through the process of creating your own arguments, students will learn to work together toward shared goals and establish themselves within collective intelligence communities.

Documentation & Mechanics

- Students will develop a citation schema to ethically present their sources.
- Further, students will learn to apply accepted mechanical conventions within specific discourse communities.
- Through completing a Learning Record, students will learn to document their learning process for use as evidence in later arguments.

Copyright

- Through the process of remix, students will learn to balance Fair Use and respect for authors' rights.
- Students will learn a variety of resources for ethical use of others' work.

Play

- Through the activities in this course, students will hopefully develop an autotelic personality, one where academic pursuits are internally driven and arise from a sense of curiosity about communication in digital environments.
- Students will learn to balance playful and serious academic inquiry, to push themselves into unfamiliar territory and relish instructive missteps.

## Dimensions of Learning

### Confidence & Independence

- We see growth and development when learners' confidence and independence become congruent with their actual abilities and skills, content knowledge, use of experience, and reflectiveness about their own learning. It is not a simple case of more (confidence and independence) is better. In a science class, for example, an overconfident student who has relied on faulty or underdeveloped skills and strategies learns to seek help when facing an obstacle; or a shy student begins to trust her own abilities, and to insist on presenting her own point of view in discussion. In both cases, students are developing along the dimension of confidence and independence.

### Skills & Strategies

- Skills and strategies represent the "know-how" aspect of learning. When we speak of performance or mastery, we generally mean that learners have developed skills and strategies to function successfully in certain situations. Skills and strategies are not only specific to particular disciplines, but often cross disciplinary boundaries. In a writing class, for example, students develop many specific skills and strategies involved in composing and communicating effectively, from research to concept development to organization to polishing grammar and correctness, and often including technological skills for computer communication.

### Knowledge & Understanding

- Knowledge and understanding refers to the content knowledge gained in particular subject areas. Knowledge and understanding is the most familiar dimension, focusing on the "know-what" aspect of learning. In a psychology class, knowledge and understanding might answer a wide range of questions such as, What is Freud's concept of ego? Who was Carl Jung? What is behaviorism? These are typical content questions. Knowledge and understanding in such classes includes what students are learning about the topics; research methods; the theories, concepts, and practices of a discipline; the methods of organizing and presenting our ideas to others, and so on.

Prior & Emerging Experience

- The use of prior and emerging experience involves learners' abilities to draw on their own experience and connect it to their work. A crucial but often unrecognized dimension of learning is the capacity to make use of prior experience as well as emerging experience in new situations. It is necessary to observe learners over a period of time while they engage in a variety of activities in order to account for the development of this important capability, which is at the heart of creative thinking and its application. With traditional methods of evaluating learning, we cannot discover just how a learner's prior experience might be brought to bear to help scaffold new understandings, or how ongoing experience shapes the content knowledge or skills and strategies the learner is developing. In a math class, students scaffold new knowledge through applying the principles and procedures they've already learned: Algebra depends on the capacity to apply basic arithmetic procedures, for example.

Reflection

- Reflection refers to the developing awareness of the learner's own learning process, as well as more analytical approaches to the subject being studied. When we speak of reflection as a crucial component of learning, we are not using the term in its commonsense meaning of reverie or abstract introspection. We are referring to the development of the learner's ability to step back and consider a situation critically and analytically, with growing insight into his or her own learning processes, a kind of metacognition. It provides the big picture for the specific details. For example, students in a history class examining fragmentary documents and researching an era or event use reflection to discover patterns in the evidence and construct a historical narrative. Learners need to develop this capability in order to use what they are learning in other contexts, to recognize the limitations or obstacles confronting them in a given situation, to take advantage of their prior knowledge and experience, and to strengthen their own performance.

Creativity, Originality, Imagination

- As learners gain confidence and independence, knowledge and understanding, skills and strategies, ability to use prior and emerging experience in new situations, and reflectiveness, they generally become more playful and experimental, more creative in the expression of that learning. This is true not only in creative domains such as the arts, but in nearly all domains: research, argumentation, history, psychology. In all fields the primary contributions to the field are the result of creative or imaginative work. This optional dimension may be adopted by teachers or schools to make explicit the value of creativity, originality, and imagination in students' development and achievement. Among other things, it recognizes the value of creative experimentation even when the final result of the work may not succeed as the student may hope.

**Pedagogical Goals**

In our original proposal for Battle Lines, we ambitiously outlined 28 goals the game would teach. After a year of revision, though, we pared it down to these 18 goals. By playing through the clues we devised, students would learn:

- how to discern the difference between informative and evaluative statements
- how to evaluate websites for veracity
- how to search for Creative Commons digital media artifacts
- how to use image-editing software to crop, resize, and compose images
- how to use popular sound-editing programs
- how to use popular video software
- how to navigate social-networking sites
- how to do reverse image searches
- about the often underused resources at various libraries across campus
- how to navigate the Library of Congress classification system
- how to think critically about their environment and the rhetoric of architecture and design
- to leverage the collective intelligence of groups by collaborating on solving puzzles and clues

- to effectively communicate and organize into learning communities
- about the history of higher education and government in the state of Texas
- about the 128-year history of The University of Texas at Austin
- about the history of Austin, Texas
- about many different artists and public figures from Austin's past and present
- to critically engage controversies by researching and composing arguments in relation to the positions espoused by William Battle and James Ferguson

## THE STORY AND THE CLUES

### The History

In 1916, a dispute broke out between James "Pa" Ferguson, governor of Texas, and William James Battle, president of The University of Texas (Burka, 2011; Gould, 1982; Hogg, 1917). Ferguson, concerned that the university's faculty was misusing taxpayer funds allotted to UT by using those funds to support political campaigns, vetoed the bill responsible for much of the university's funding. Battle, backed by the university's regents, denied any financial misdoings in a commencement speech entitled "Shall Texas Have a University?" (Gould, 1982; Hogg, 1917; "William James Battle"). In addition to the specific issues at hand, the dispute brought up larger issues about the role of universities in the state of Texas and democracies in general (Gould, 1982).

This controversy serves as historical background for *Battle Lines*, with William Battle's name providing a titular pun. The game opens with its protagonist, a present-day UT history student named Amanda, noticing similarities between the educational policies of Ferguson and current Texas governor Rick Perry. She is in the midst of researching those similarities when her email account is hacked. For the student-players in Writing in Digital Environments, the entrance point into *Battle Lines* is a mysterious email containing a link to Amanda's hacked account. From there, Amanda's story unfolds as follows.

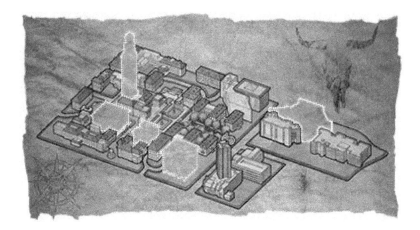

Interactive UT Map

Caption: This image appears on the right side of the screen and is a map of an area of the UT campus with some buildings missing from the map. On the left side of the screen, these missing buildings appear under the various headings describing the game's narrative. When users drag and drop each image on the left to its correct location on the map to the right, the page redirects to a description of the clue that corresponds with that section of the narrative.

## A Hacking in Texas

As she learns more about the controversy between Battle and Ferguson, Amanda gets in two heated exchanges—one with her brother, one with a friend named James—about Texas education policy. Both exchanges are unfolding via email when Amanda realizes her account has been hacked: Seemingly random letters and symbols begin appearing in the subject lines of messages sent between her, James, and her brother. Extracting and rearranging those letters and symbols leads to the website of the apparent hackers: a mysterious organization called the Friends of Texas.

### Level (Clue) 1: Deciphering Correspondence

The game world of *Battle Lines* opened with players receiving an email with an interactive PDF file mimicking the email inbox of Amanda, the protagonist of the game. Players interacted with the inbox image in the same way that they would a real inbox. Scrambled lettering in the subject lines indicated that Amanda's inbox had been hacked and provided players with the first puzzle.

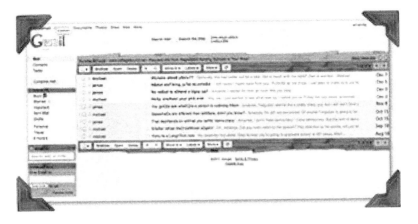

Fake email received by students

Caption: This is relatively simple image of a Gmail inbox. It has some read and some unread emails.

The messages in Amanda's inbox provided backstory and paraphrases of argumentative stances held by James Battle, former president of The University of Texas and a defender of higher education, and former Texas governor James "Pa" Ferguson who objected to universities on account of their tendency to perpetuate intellectual elitism. Players were supposed to identify the best paraphrases and extract strings of inconsistently capitalized letters from subject lines corresponding to web addresses of pages on the Friends of Texas website, which had also been hacked.

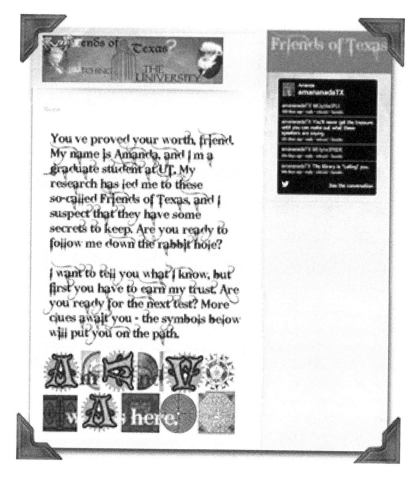

Hacked Friends of Texas Page

Caption: This screenshot of a webpage shows a letter written from a graduate student named Amanda. The webpage's banner indicates that it has some affiliation with the Friends of Texas. Amanda's letter suggests that the readers should somehow make use of the symbols pictured at the bottom of the page to move to the next clue in the *Battle Lines* game.

Players initially attempted to solve these puzzles on their own and with classmates seated nearby. Individual web and social media searches, attempts to analyze images from the Friends of Texas pages in Photoshop, and even pen and paper analysis of data strings quickly gave way to forum collaboration. In the first week of the game, a player requested that the instructor create a page for sharing thoughts and findings on the main course wiki. Players swiftly began sharing information on this page and sifting relevant findings up as static context at the top of the forum page.

The development team expected that at least some players would recognize that the quality of paraphrases in the email corresponded to the correct strings of letters for accessing the pages on the Friends of Texas site, granting access to a Twitter hint system and a portal for requesting access to the designated *Battle Lines* game wiki. Upon accessing the correct pages, players discovered the game's first hint in Amanda's Twitter feed:

Amanda's first tweet

Caption: This image shows a tweet from @amananadaTX, or the graduate student Amanda. The words are a puzzle and include extra letters and numbers in a basic message, which reads "Sort the Sense From the Nonsense" once those letters are removed. Amanda uses a *Battle Lines* hashtag. The tweet has been retweeted three times and marked as a favorite by two people.

Players could view Amanda's tweets on the Friends of Texas pages or on Twitter without signing into the service, but several chose to follow Amanda via existing profiles or by creating new accounts. Hints were posted in real time based on collective progress through game objectives—usually 15 minutes before the end of a 90-minute class session. The development team tweeted additional hints when players still did not recognize paraphrasing as the basis for the puzzle.

Hints given via tweets

Caption: Here, one can see a variety of tweets from Amanda that helped the students move forward in game play. The first tweet reads "Michael sure got mad when I misrepresented Ferguson, huh? I tried a better paraphrase in my response." The second and third tweets have extra numbers and letters added to the words. After removing the extra numbers and letters, the tweets say "Three friends. Three fragments. Three fixes."

Several players discovered the correct pages using these hints and shared the addresses with their classmates on the class wiki. Players solved the first level of the game through experimentation and without demonstrating mastery of the skill of paraphrasing, though they did devote considerable time to perusing online instructional material on paraphrasing tweeted by the development team. Some even attempted to parse this external resource for clues. In response to an inquiry by the instructor regarding the "logic at play" in the level, the first student to solve the puzzle attributed his success to "luck." In the class session following the solution of the puzzle, one player finally identified accurate paraphrasing as the basis for the puzzle.

Due to a fundamental disconnect between the development team's pedagogical intentions and the strategies adopted by players, *Battle Lines* inadvertently began with the most difficult and longest challenge of the game. Level progress was slowed by uncertainty over the digital and real-world boundaries of the game as players intrigued by Amanda's identity searched university directories and social media, discovering numerous false paths. Critical problem solving, logical approaches, and online discussion prevailed over rhetorical analysis or face-to-face collaboration.

## Friends, There Are No Friends

The Friends of Texas's website is awash in various esoteric symbols and slogans, so Amanda counters by hacking into the site's code and making the various symbols function as links to a private wiki she sets up. On that wiki, she posts a brief message to potential collaborators and a mangled audio file pulled from the Friends of Texas's site. On first listen, the file is a cacophonous mix of lines from Battle's Shall Texas Have a University? speech, the Janis Joplin song "Me and Bobby McGee" (Kristofferson & Foster, 1969), and bursts of static. Beneath the static, however, is a series of clues leading Amanda and her collaborators to a Janis Joplin poster in a bar on UT's campus.

### *Level (Clue) 2: Audio Manipulation and Introduction to Photoshop*

In the second week of in-class gameplay, players advanced to the second level of *Battle Lines*. A scrambled Garage Band audio file in the game wiki included several phrases—"a bar," "eating," and "drums"—obscured in multiple tracks. Players had to adjust track volume to decipher these clues which were intended to direct them to the Cactus Café, a historic music venue on The University of Texas campus located near their classroom.

Players readily isolated the clues but hesitated to act on either them or hints tweeted during class. As the first level of the game was entirely digital, players were wary of venturing out during class time. The instructor broadened the game's real-world horizons by encouraging players to pursue their notions regarding the clue. Five players investigated the Cactus Café and swiftly located a poster created for the game. At least one of these players brought a smart phone and scanned in the QR code embedded in the poster, thereby gaining access to the collage challenge.

Janis Joplin–Cass Gilbert Poster

Caption: This poster image shows a photograph of Cass Gilbert and another of Janis Joplin wearing sunglasses. There are QR codes overlain on the sunglasses. The poster headline reads "Janis Joplin with Special Guest Cass Gilbert." There are also a variety of University of Texas buildings pictured, with some of them having been stretched and manipulated to fill the poster space.

Upon returning to class, these players reported their discovery and shared the link from the QR code on the *Battle Lines* wiki forum page. The link in the QR code directed students to the third level of the game—one emphasizing Photoshop. Students also began to note the presence of strings of letters and numbers embedded in the poster, ultimately identifying them as library call numbers for two books located in different libraries on The University of Texas campus.

Two groups of players—one of four and another of three students—visited these libraries and found short phrases attached to the shelves below the books. Players removed these clues and brought them back to share with the class and, according to class observations, initially shared their findings with one another remotely, presumably via text message. These phrases were subsequently posted to the forum page on the game wiki. When combined and added to the Friends of Texas homepage's address, these phrases directed players to a page on the Friends of Texas website with a message from Amanda summoning them to the reference library in the basement of the state capitol, located approximately one mile from the classroom.

A message leading students to the capitol library

Caption: This is another image of the hacked website used by Amanda. The banner indicates that the website is associated with the Friends of Texas. The message appearing on it congratulates students for their hard work and suggests that they visit the library at the Texas Capitol building. There is a Twitter feed appearing in the right sidebar.

The second level of *Battle Lines* laid the groundwork for several subsequent levels, extended the game into real-world space, and challenged conventional classroom practices with an investigative approach to involving students in determining and satisfying the objectives of the game. When the instructor asked the players who visited the Cactus Café and libraries if they would have left the classroom had they not been encouraged to do so, the first student to take the initiative said that they would likely have waited to pursue the clue until after class had concluded.

## University Mysteries

The Joplin poster turns out to contain its own secrets: codes that lead to another page on the Friends of Texas site. Growing increasingly guarded and suspicious of anyone on her trail, Amanda hacks this page as well. Below a message noting that Joplin and famous architect Cass Gilbert both had ties to UT, Amanda adds a series of challenges that will eventually lead anyone serious about aiding her to a pair of books—one on Joplin and one on Gilbert—in UT's libraries.

### Level (Clue) 3: Images

By the third week of the game, most players had progressed to the third level based on the prompt given by Amanda on the page linked to in the QR code. This level required that players create and submit their first digital artifact: a collage assembled in Adobe Photoshop visually expressing their understanding of the relationship between democracy and education and incorporating at least ten layers of visual data. Students in the Writing in Digital Environments course had previously shared their technological proficiencies on the class wiki.

Some students were unfamiliar with Photoshop and uncertain how this software differed from other photo editing or presentation applications. As with the previous level's requirement of a smart phone, camera, or other mobile device and Internet access, the issue of limited or uneven access to technology became significant. Some students inquired whether they could create their collages in other image editing software, but the availability of Photoshop in all Digital Writing & Research Lab facilities allowed use of this particular software to remain a requirement. The development team sought to introduce students to this powerful image editing software by encouraging them to

Student Collage (Cliff)

Caption: This image contrasts an area high up on a cliff and an area at the bottom of the cliff. At the bottom of the cliff are crowds of people who appear similar to paper cutouts. The people are all different colors and are grouped by color. There is a stack of books next to the cliff which people are climbing. At the top of the cliff there are a very few people who appear to have climbed successfully and who are mostly of the same color. At the top of the cliff you can also see a building that looks like the US or Texas Capitol building.

respond to a loosely defined topic with a basic minimum requirement for complexity of composition. Most of the collages submitted grappled with the disjuncture between privilege and merit. Several players created abstract landscapes emphasizing inequality of opportunities for educational advancement. Other players incorporated cartoon and other visual texts, words, and symbols, juxtaposing the meaning of these components with suggestive images and symbolic positionings.

Student Collage (What's Democracy)

Caption: This collage shows an image of a man asking "what's democracy?" with a young woman responding that "democracy is the freedom to elect our own dictators." A variety of other images accentuate the collage: an American flag, a sign saying "VOTE," a picture of Barack Obama with "Progress" written below it, and a road sign that shows the intersection of Church St. and State St.

Student Collage (Cuts and Taxes)

Caption: This image shows crowds of people, some protesting, some in a classroom, some relaxing on a university campus. It also includes a photograph of a ballot with a pen putting an x in one of the squares, as well as the facade of what looks like a university building, a line drawing of a ballot box, and a stack of books.

Student Collage (This is What Democracy Looks Like)

Caption: In this image, the word "Democracy" is repeated four times in the background, from the top of the image to the bottom of the image. Overlain on the words is an image that resembles a flower or a rose window, with each petal a different color. At the bottom of the image, there is a stack of books, a crowd of people, a sign that says "This is What Democracy Looks Like," a line drawing of a monster, and a man using a jeweler's eyepiece.

Some players took a more stylized approach and incorporated allusive images into a unified aesthetic treatment of the controversy.

Players submitted their collages to the game wiki along with a brief written description and commentary on their work. These collages were reviewed and commented on by development team members signed into the wiki under the name 'Amanda.' Players either moved on to the video manipulation level, which commenced with the combined phrases retrieved from the two libraries or revised their submissions. The players also decided among themselves to switch from the main course wiki to the designated game wiki as the primary forum for consolidating their findings.

Significant questions involving the unity or multiplicity of clues and the necessity of individual submissions began to arise at this point in the game. Observers from the development team remarked on most players' willingness to submit individual materials and to progress through game objectives at their own pace. Teams also began to emerge in the class based on classroom seating patterns with enthusiastic players encouraging and guiding others in their immediate vicinity and technically adept players assisting others stuck on previous objectives. An observer on the development team reported that some students appeared to be working with clues that they did not publish on the wiki or share with their classmates, giving rise to a more competitive approach that coincided with other players' willingness to allow clues to be solved for them, but all players ultimately submitted their own collages.

## Capitol Crimes

Amanda plants half a clue under each of the two library books and makes the whole clue lead collaborators back to a new Friends of Texas page she's hacked. In the time the clue buys her, Amanda goes to a reference library in the basement of the Texas Capitol Building—located about a mile from UT—to investigate her situation with one of the Capitol's librarians. She continues to uncover similarities between the Battle/Ferguson controversy and present-day political debates about UT. Unable to put all the pieces together in time, however, she flees the library, leaving behind flash drives with clips of speeches by William Powers, UT's current president, and Rick Perry, Texas's current governor. She is forced to leave unearthing further echoes of Battle and Ferguson to anyone still on her trail.

### Level (Clue) 4: Video Manipulation

The fourth level of *Battle Lines* began when players combined the phrases found in the two libraries and added them to the basic Friends of Texas web address. A message from Amanda summoned them to the reference library in the state capitol. Players hesitated to commence this level at the end of week three on account of the distance between the classroom and capitol, but they collectively discerned that the capitol would be closed on Monday of the following week for a state holiday. Our in-class observer noted that students attempted to arrange group treks to the capitol, but only one student visited the reference library where that student obtained a flash drive from the librarians and then uploaded those findings to the game wiki.

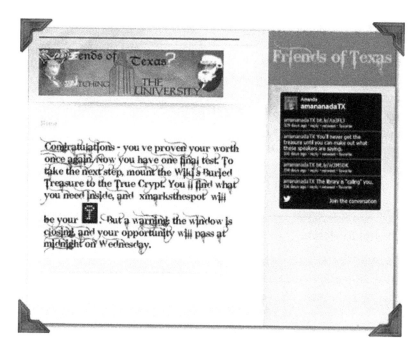

Instructions for the declamation

Caption: This is another image of Amanda's hacked webpage. It is affiliated with the Friends of Texas and has a Twitter feed in the right sidebar. There is a letter that congratulates the viewer on his or her progress and directs the reader to the next level. It also gives a due date for completion of the next level.

The flash drives provided by the development team were loaded with two segments of speeches on education, one by William Powers, the current president of The University of Texas, and one by Governor Rick Perry. Rearranging the segments of these videos in the right order revealed the address of a final page on the Friends of Texas website. On this page, students were prompted to create a final declamation in video or other media format and submit it to the game wiki along with a brief written discussion of their rhetorical stance and the process of creating their artifacts.

## The Vanishing Amanda

Amanda comes across a key to understanding the Friends of Texas and their activities, but refuses to reveal what she's learned to anyone who can't follow the trail she left at the Capitol library. But those who can and do learn the following: The Friends of Texas are a secret society dedicated to debating and guiding Texas education policy. Amanda's interests in Battle and Ferguson led them not to attack her, but to offer a series of disguised challenges aimed at recruiting her for the organization. And now she in turn ventures out to recruit new members she deems worthy.

James, who has been searching for Amanda ever since her email account went silent after the original hacking, finally stumbles across her in Battle Hall, a library on UT's campus named for William Battle. As he calls out to her, however, she disappears around a corner. James pursues to find only an empty hallway, a brief farewell letter Amanda has left behind, and a mysterious figure watching from the shadows behind him. Amanda has yet to be heard from again.

### *Level 5: Declamation*

An encrypted file on the flash drive provided students with raw images and video for use in creating their final declamations. Players expressed frustration with the encryption of the file and when one player succeeded in accessing the data, that player promptly shared the contents of the file on the game wiki. By this stage of the game, players generally realized that they did not necessarily have to participate in solving clues and some began to test the submission and assessment process on the basis of a suspicion that Amanda's feedback to their submissions was automated. Observers from the development team remarked on a loss of some energy among the students when faced with the task of creating a second digital artifact.

Most students devoted class time in the final week of the game to finding additional images and videos for the declamation. These multimodal declamations and written descriptions were accepted or returned with recommendations for revision.

One of the student declamations. https://www.youtube.com/watch?v=eZZt3p0ll-I

Caption: This video begins with electronic music and images of public schools. Then, there is a nuclear explosion on screen and the sounds of an explosion. What follows is a quick montage of sad people. The text on screen indicates that we need to invest in the economy in order to have a better economic future. The rest of the video switches between text on screen that changes colors quickly, and images of students, teachers, and related materials that cycle through quickly. The text argues that we need to give better rewards to good teachers, fire bad teachers, allow teachers more flexibility, and limit the government's role in education.

Successful submissions resulted in players being given a final password which they used to obtain a commemorative game token at Battle Hall. Players were also sent a link to a live-action end-game video. By the end of *Battle Lines*, players had several opportunities to familiarize themselves with the basic use of audio-, image-, and video-editing software by creating digital artifacts responding to the rhetorical situation and main themes of the game. Students submitted a variety of declamations ranging from videos and slideshows to blog entries and collages.

## THE DESIGN

### Podcast

In the following podcast, members of the *Battle Lines* design team discuss the challenges of creating an alternate reality game that is fun and engaging while it teaches rhetoric and digital writing. We discuss the techniques of creating alternate reality by using archival material from this ARG (starting at 1:40); trying to strike a balance between revealing a compelling narrative, requiring digital literacy and skill, and requiring rhetorical engagements with the story (5:19 and 5:57); the problem posed by red herrings and students' inclination to overinterpret false clues that we hadn't intended to leave for them (8:26). As a design team, our on-the-fly course corrections in response to these challenges made significant improvements to our original game design even as the game was unfolding in students' hands. The exigency of keeping students interested, immersed, and on track made designing *Battle Lines* into an exciting recursive composition process in its own right.

Longhorn Gramophone

Caption: This black-and-white line drawing depicts a longhorn bull approaching a phonograph. The bull has long horns and its neck is outstretched toward the phonograph so that its nose is almost touching the phonograph horn. There are small tufts of grass underneath the bull's hooves.

## Podcast Transcript

*[uptempo electronic music theme playing, ends at 0:13]*

[0:13]

NARRATOR: Hi! This is Eric, one of the members of the *Battle Lines* team. Almost any good game needs some sort of conflict to keep it interesting: Mario versus Bowser, red checkers versus black checkers, the blue guy versus the red guy, on and on and on. And as we worked on creating our game, we had our own conflicts to keep things interesting. Not conflicts between the game's creators, fortunately, but conflicts inherent to the process of making an alternate reality game: Choices about which aspects of *Battle Lines* to privilege over others, how to balance our focus and meld the various goals we wanted the game to accomplish. So what follows is our attempt to set up some of those conflicts. Not just as a juicy behind-the-scenes exposé on the creation of *Battle Lines*, but in the hope that documenting our own struggles can help others anticipate and feel up to the challenges that come with building an ARG. We'll try and work through four of these specific conflicts, taking one at a time, though of course they overlapped during our actual process. I'll be talking specifically about some of these challenges in terms of the audio level of *Battle Lines*, a level where students had to use Apple's GarageBand software to find secret code words and messages hidden in an audio file. And I should note that these are just brief introductions to some of these issues; you'll see them pop up many other places in this article.

[1:40]

ERIC: So, first up—

MENACING MALE ANNOUNCER: [interrupting] Round one— fight!

ERIC: No, definitely—definitely not. Nothing that dramatic. First up, the tension between educational gameplay and enjoyable gameplay. Here's Kendall, another member of our Battle Lines team:

KENDALL: *Battle Lines* has a certain educational goal. So it was very difficult in the design of the game to keep in mind the tension between designing something fun and designing something that teaches. And I think that really all games teach you certain things, right? They teach you how to play the game. So we tried to design *Battle Lines* in a way where you could play the game and learn the skills of rhetoric—that those would be one and the same action. When you think of an educator designing a game, it's not ever very fun. So we didn't want to be educators designing games; we wanted to first become game designers. I think that when people get to go out in the real world and, it's not just locations, but even the people that you find there are now part of the game. That is just—it's so exciting. It's very pleasurable. And so it's a good way to have students feel like this trip was worth it, this class was worth it. And you want to do a good job and be a good player because it's so much fun.

ERIC: So we wanted to make a game that would—obviously— be educational, that would help students in rhetoric courses develop rhetorical skills, digital literacies, but we wanted also to make a game that would be enjoyable. One of the reasons we called ourselves the Immersive Environments group is because we wanted to create something that students would be able to immerse themselves in, and enjoyability seemed like an important prerequisite for that. So, for instance, in the audio level, we used clips from a commencement speech William James Battle, UT president, delivered in 1917. And we wanted students to engage with the rhetorical content of this speech, to note some of the things that William James Battle—

WILLIAM JAMES BATTLE: [crackling audio recording] Shall Texas have a university?

ERIC: —there he is now—had to say about the purpose of a university in a democracy. But we also wanted the level to be enjoyable. We wanted the audio file to have a certain aura to it; we wanted it to feel like part of a game and not just a dry exercise in listening to a 42-minute speech by a former UT president. In order to make this happen, we embedded the clips of the Battle speech in an audio file that also had some ambient clips of music from Austin legend Janis Joplin,

JANIS JOPLIN: [singing in clip from her song Me and Bobby McGee] Freedom's just another word for nothin' left to lose. Nothin', that's all the Bobby left me [fades out]

ERIC: that had various background noises to create a sort of ominous ambience [low rumbling tone fades in and out under narration]. What we found after the fact was that students did figure out the puzzle relatively quickly. They found the clues, the key words, buried under pieces of static in the original recording [static fizzles momentarily]. But they did not really engage at all with the actual content of the speech. They learned the digital lesson of how to manipulate files in GarageBand, but they didn't necessarily take anything away from the message that the clips from the Battle speech were attempting to convey. This gets at another issue that falls on the educational side of the tension between creating an enjoyable game and creating an educational game.

[5:19]

MENACING MALE ANNOUNCER: Round two.

ERIC: And that was attempting to construct a game that taught rhetorical goals as well as digital goals. So this is a place where students began to pick up on very quickly the technological skills and digital literacies they needed to beat the audio level, but they did not generally engage with the rhetorical content or context of the game in order to do that.

On the enjoyability side, another issue we faced was figuring out how to balance the narrative structure of the game, the overall story that was holding it together, with forming individual puzzles.

MENACING MALE ANNOUNCER: Round three.

[5:57]

ERIC: There are a lot of satisfying games out there that depend largely on narrative structure. Take a tabletop role-playing game where there's a lot of energy devoted to world creation, character development, and things of that nature. Then there are games that work really well by basically being structured around individual levels or individual puzzles. Take a successful gaming franchise like Mario [sound effect: Mario getting a coin]. Certainly there's a barebones narrative structure there: defeating enemies [sound effect: Mario killing an enemy], saving princesses, things like that. But it's pretty easy to play through the game without really interrogating the details of the story, like why in the world Mario's a plumber. And if you don't pay close attention it's pretty easy to ignore the name of the princess you're trying to save the whole time [sound effect: Mario shrinking]. In any case, we wanted both narrative and satisfactory puzzles in our game, and it wasn't strictly an either/or choice. But following up on narrative elements we set out in earlier stages of the game required a lot of organization and forethought. In the opening of the game, we'd established not only Amanda, but a potential love interest and one of her family members, and the Friends of Texas, all these potential loose ends and red herrings and characters you could come to care about as the story progressed. But with a constrained schedule, we couldn't put off coming up with the individual levels and puzzles that students would have to solve for the sake of developing a rich, thorough, and holistic narrative. For instance, for the audio level, students found the audio file they had to deconstruct in GarageBand on a wiki that Amanda had created. But there was no reference back to other characters from earlier levels—just a sense of growing conflict between Amanda and the Friends of Texas. We could have gone a more narrative route, integrating more of the earlier characters into the story, having additional email exchanges or conversations go on. Or we could have spent more time on puzzle formation: kept the narrative minimal and put more time into increasing the complexity of the audio clue students had to work with.

In any case, the three tensions we've discussed so far—balancing the game's pedagogy with its enjoyability [sound effect: Mario getting a coin], its rhetorical qualities with its digital aspects [sound effect: Mario getting a coin], and its narrative with the independence of its individual puzzles [sound effect: Mario getting a coin]—were all linked with a final issue.

MENACING MALE ANNOUNCER: Round—

ERIC: [interrupting] Nope! My turn this time. [pauses] We good? Okay then! Round four! [sound effect: Mario getting an extra life] Linearity versus freeplay. Here's Cate, another one of our *Battle Lines* team members:

[8:26]

CATE: The thing that's most fascinating to me are all of the false clues. It's a mine of ideas for future ARG puzzles and solutions.

ERIC: [interjecting] Yeah!

CATE: And I think it builds their analysis skills. I mean, they were literally analyzing the Twitter icon—

ERIC: [concurring] Yeah.

CATE: —of one of their own classmates, not realizing that it was one of their own classmates.

ERIC: [responding] Exactly, right?

ERIC: [narrating] And here's Kendall again:

KENDALL: I am so excited that they looked at all the stuff that we predicted they might not look at. In fact, I remember sitting in the office talking about whether students would be bothered by this little floating tag on Gmail that just says the word "cookies." And students latched on to that and it's—I just love it. And we were all like, Well, we don't have time to fix it. But that kind of stuff is fascinating and if we could have been, you know, more reflexive and involved about it, I would love to give them more to play with that doesn't necessarily go anywhere, right, rather than less.

It is hilarious because it shows us how—how little we can predict what our students are going to do and be able to find. We can Google stuff, but we'll always—they'll Google something different and they'll Google it a different way, or they'll put the pieces together differently than we did, which is the cool thing about this kind of game.

ERIC: Board games have, well, borders. You can only move your queen in certain directions in a game of chess. You can only move so many spaces in *Monopoly* after you roll the die, and if you're playing *Clue*, you shouldn't actually murder anyone [dramatic orchestral hit]. It was a lot harder to define these boundaries in *Battle Lines* just because the game interacted with the real world: Both the physical real world, where anyone potential place or person on campus could become a part of the gaming environment if students read it that way, and any piece of HTML code could become a clue or a hint, a direction or a misdirection, once again depending on how players chose to read the game's limits. Because we had certain time limits on gameplay, we had to make decisions about how much room to give students in wandering off the track and following red herrings, even if they weren't red herrings that we had intentionally planted. The freeplay that resulted from going off the rails often seemed responsible for some of the most memorable and enjoyable moments in the game for the student-players. At a certain point, though, because of time constraints or not wanting students to accidentally violate university policies, we had to reel them back in. So we did things like construct a Twitter feed to allow Amanda to drop hints to student-players as needed, and when we got to the end of the game and students weren't necessarily satisfied with the ending, well, we improvised. We added a bit more narrative, we made peace with the fact that the digital goals seemed to have outstripped the rhetorical goals of the game, and we followed William Battle's advice to—

WILLIAM JAMES BATTLE: [crackling audio recording] Note the following facts.

ERIC: —marking them down for ARG creators slash rhetoricians who might come after us, hoping that they—maybe you—will go into the game-creation process a little less clueless than they might otherwise.

*[retro video-game music over electronic beat fades in till end]*

### Solving Pedagogical Problems through Game Design

*Problem:*

One of our goals was to design clues that required digital media skills in order to solve. One of our earliest problems was ensuring students had no other way to advance in the game without learning the intended skill.

*How We Found It:*

One of the first clues we brought from planning to playing became Level 3: Images. We made up a fake concert poster for a Janis Joplin show and used it to embed QR codes that would enable players to download the poster's original Photoshop file. We intended for students to learn to use layers in Photoshop to reveal hidden library call numbers. Players who tested this level before the game went live to students found they could study the printed poster and visually make out some of the call numbers—thus circumventing the need to learn about layers in Photoshop.

*Our Response:*

We first of all obscured the call numbers visually so that players would have to turn off certain layers in the Photoshop file to see them. We also added a piece to this level that required students to use layers in Photoshop to create a digital collage with a rhetorical purpose (a successful collage earned players the trust of their in-game guide, the mysterious Amanda).

The innovation of adding a productive mode of gameplay (in which students created persuasive digital media) to the more investigative mode (in which students discover, assemble, and interpret clues) gave us a useful model for designing the other levels. It not only made it more intuitive for students to rely on the digital media skill they had just practiced when they encounter the next clue that required the skill, but adding a productive mode of gameplay also furthered our rhetorical goals for the game: asking students to respond to rhetorical exigencies with digital arguments.

*Problem:*

In the game's initial level, we wanted to introduce a compelling story about our main character (Amanda) along with a basic rhetorical skill: identifying better and worse paraphrases of an argument. The level stages an email exchange between Amanda and her brother and between Amanda and her boyfriend. The problem was getting students to focus on the arguments without overinterpreting all the other points of data in the level.

*How We Found It:*

We had hoped students would discover the heuristic of identifying the best paraphrases by reading each of the emails carefully and recognizing a dispute between interlocutors over whether their arguments were being represented fairly. We did not want to issue overt instructions about identifying paraphrases because we worried about direct instruction making the game feel like more work and less fun.

But, in the absence of focused instruction about what to look for, students began to overinterpret clues we hadn't meant to leave them! For example, some students printed out an archival telegram and tried to tie it to a physical location. Some found the garbled text embedded in email subject lines, but couldn't figure out how to assemble it into the URL we meant them to find. Others examined the source code of the web pages for further clues. They even tried to contact a real person through Facebook who had attended UT Austin and by coincidence shared the name of our main character! These red herrings were distracting students from what we had intended to be the relevant—and rhetorically salient—clues.

We thought of this problem in terms of students' ability to distinguish rhetorical meaning in context from a kind of paranoiac overreading that finds meaning everywhere (such that no relevant meaning can be discerned).

*Our Response:*

We knew we had to alert students that they were on the wrong track, but we didn't want to break the alternate reality we were creating. In order to help students focus when they were struggling with a clue, we created a Twitter account for our main character, Amanda: @amananadaTX. We tried to use the Twitter account to lead students in the right direction without simply giving things away. Although it took a while for us to learn to use it well, the Twitter account was useful throughout the game, and it helped preserve the sense of the story by making Amanda into a kind of in-game guide, challenging students with clues and puzzles but also helping them with cryptic hints.

*Problem:*

As *Battle Lines* was drawing to a close, we planned what we thought would be a dramatic conclusion to the gameplay: Students who completed a final declamation assignment received a code word they had to mention to a helpful librarian inside a campus building, Battle Hall. Each student received a custom-etched wooden coin as a unique memento of their participation in the game.

*How We Found It:*

What we didn't think about was bringing the game to an equally rewarding sense of narrative closure. The mysterious disappearance of the in-game guide, Amanda, had left some students wondering how her friends and family felt since her secretive activities with the players had resolved the digital and rhetorical teaching of the game, but not her story! Students made it clear they felt the game was somehow unresolved.

*Our Response:*

Because students wanted to know what happened to Amanda, we scripted and filmed a semi-campy narrative resolution in which Amanda breaks up with the boyfriend she had argued with in the first level and disappears into thin air. We released this film as a kind of bonus reward to the game's most outstanding players, who circulated it among their classmates. We hoped that our film, entitled The Good, the Bad, and the Friendly, would give students a laugh and our thanks for their perseverance throughout the game.

"The Good, the Bad, and the Friendly" video. https://www.youtube.com/
watch?v=EWY_rOtQNm4

Caption: This video opens on a woman—presumably Amanda—staring at a plaque
honoring William Battle. A man, James, enters and tries to approach her, but she
runs off before he can make contact. Amanda has dropped a letter on the ground.
There is a voiceover of the letter, which compliments the Friends of Texas and
indicates that Amanda will be leaving forever. It ends with a vehement "paraphrase
this!" When James looks up, there is a man in a Texas orange shirt and a cowboy
hat standing in the doorway. The man flips a coin, nods, and walks out the door.
Text on screen thanks players for participating.

## Conclusion

Designing *Battle Lines* and observing students play the game taught
us to let go of our presuppositions about what our game taught. We
would like to note how much the student-players privileged digital literacy skills over rhetorical and research skills, the latter two of which
were sometimes relegated to the background. While we had planned
for there to be a balance between digital literacy, rhetoric, and research, it was frequently the students' attention to digital minutiae that
got them to the next level. In the end, they gamed the game and the
game designers in order to win without completing all of our desired
objectives. They didn't entirely neglect the game's rhetorical dimensions, but they did tend to privilege the more concrete digital literacy
skills as an approach to solving clues. Below we detail the students'

successes in a variety of categories and make recommendations for future researchers.

## Rhetorical Goals

Throughout *Battle Lines'* narrative, students became aware of current and past debates regarding the involvement of government in education—the debate exemplified by the historical narrative between Battle and Ferguson, but also an ongoing debate between the president of their university, Bill Powers, and Governor of Texas Rick Perry. Their ability to analyze this debate and to join in—a result of playing the game—was of limited success. Students made visual arguments about funding university education in one level of the game and their final declamations also responded to this and related topics.

We were more pleased by the students' static images than by their final videos, actually. With more time to complete their Photoshop-based arguments, we believe that the students reached a greater level of sophistication than they did in their videos. We also suggest that the difficult and time-intensive process of video editing made this final level difficult to complete in such a short time frame.

Student Collage (Democracy and Education)

Caption: This collage includes cartoons and photographs to make an argument entitled "Democracy and Equality." Various images suggest that there is "right way" and "wrong way" to educate and point to arguments about the cost and purposes of education, the benefits of education to society, and methods for achieving social equality through education.

## Research Goals

Some of our design intentions were to create a game structure that could be easily revised for use in classes besides the experimental one. Many of our research goals fit this category—players, throughout the game, learned basic skills that would be helpful to any college-level researcher, including web-based and library research.

Some of these skills were simple: getting the students to engage in research with their physical environments and with human beings in real life, for instance. Other skills involved navigating the Library of Congress classification system, searching the web for a variety of resources, evaluating websites for veracity, distinguishing between informative and evaluative statements, and paraphrasing with accuracy.

While successes in terms of research skills were mixed—students never did figure out that we were trying to teach them paraphrasing skills, instead solving this clue by trial and error—we were successful at getting students to navigate the world around them, even if that navigation took place as part of a delegation model of collaboration—with some to go to outside venues while others stayed behind. Our approach—making clues solvable only by visiting oft-overlooked resources on campus—certainly pushed our student-players to understand the number of textual and interpersonal resources available to them.

### Digital Literacy Goals

Our digital literacy goals went beyond web-based research, pushing students to engage with a variety of software available on classroom computers in the Digital Writing & Research Lab, including GarageBand, Photoshop, and iMovie, as well as video cameras used to record their final declamation projects. In order to solve the clues, students had to learn how to navigate these three programs and be comfortable with their basic functionality. Through collaborating with others, student-players learned to manipulate image layers and music tracks as well as perform basic video-editing tasks.

While not all students completed final projects, we had moderate success among those who did—they increased their mastery of these three programs to include manipulating the images themselves, editing sound files, as well as recording and editing their own videos.

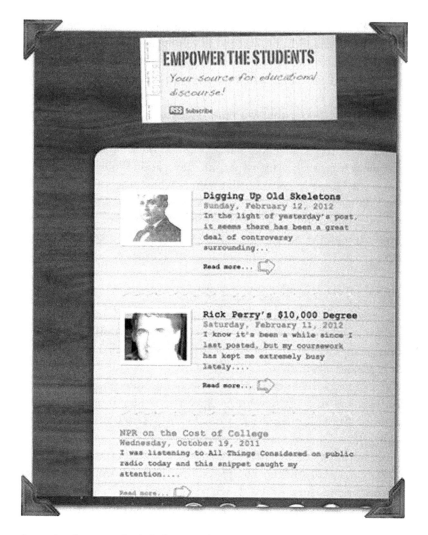

Screenshot from a student's declamation blog

Caption: This screenshot of a student's blog shows three posts that the student has made: one about the Battle/Ferguson controversy, one about Rick Perry's argument for $10,000 college degrees, and one about an NPR broadcast on the cost of college. The blog's title is "Empower the Students," and the blog theme makes it appear that the posts are written on notebook paper.

## Collaboration Goals

Student-players were particularly successful at collaborating online. From the start, the class wiki became a site of pure collaboration, but collaboration of a strikingly competitive kind: Students literally raced to share their work in this online document.

In the physical space of the classroom, however, the students tended to collaborate in small teams of 2–8 players formed through the convenience of proximity in the classroom. Despite the instructor's repeated "permission" to talk openly, open discussion was extremely rare. As a result, progress on clue-solving tended to progress in groups rather than en masse, despite the fact that, online, collaboration was practically absolute and almost all "solutions" were posted as soon as they were discovered.

Students additionally collaborated by delegating tasks, especially those that involved going outside the classroom. We also observed some students were operating on clues while their peers were researching solutions outside the classroom, and that they were not publishing their progress on the wiki or sharing with their classmates. The emergence of a more competitive approach to gameplay coincided with other students' willingness to allow clues to be solved for them.

## Final Words

For future developers, the designers of *Battle Lines* would recommend the following in order to increase attention to rhetorical goals:

1.  crafting a high-quality narrative that includes a satisfactory ending for the students, however difficult this might be even for professional game designers;

2.  designing each level based around a rhetorical or research goal in the hopes that students would give more attention to those goals than they did in our experiment;

3.  allowing more time for game completion so that students would have more time to revise their work, create high-quality arguments in each level, and improve their already excellent collaboration and digital literacy skills.

We hope our experience will be as highly instructive for you as it was for us. *Battle Lines* was our way of exploring the possibilities of educational games for rhetoric and digital writing, as well as experimenting with our own thinking about instruction, design, and play.

# REFERENCES

## Scholarly References

Alternate reality games. (n.d.) Wikipedia. Retrieved May 13, 2013, from http://en.wikipedia.org/wiki/Alternate_reality_game

Aoki, Keith; Boyle, James; & Jenkins, Jennifer. (2006). Bound by law? Duke University Law School, Duke Center for the Study of the Public Domain. Retrieved January 30, 2012, from http://www.thepublicdomain.org/wp-content/uploads/2009/04/bound-by-law-duke-edition.pdf

Barthes, Roland. (1977). Rhetoric of the image. Image–music–text (Stephen Heath, Trans.). New York: Hill & Wang.

Battle, William James. (1917). William James Battle commencement speech - 1917. UT History Central. Retrieved from http://www.texasexes.org/uthistory/audio.aspx?audio=battle

Berlin, James. (1988). Rhetoric and ideology in the writing class. College English, 50(5), 477-494.

Bernhardt, Stephen A. (2004). Seeing the text. In Carolyn Handa (Ed.), Visual rhetoric in a digital world: A critical sourcebook (pp. 94–106). Boston: Bedford/St. Martin's.

Bogost, Ian. (2008). The rhetoric of video games. In Katie Salen (Ed.), The ecology of games: Connecting youth, games, and learning (pp. 117–40). Cambridge, MA: MIT Press.

Boluk, Stephanie; Jagoda, Patrick; & Lemieux, Patrick. (n.d.) Speculation: An alternate reality game. Retrieved May 13, 2013 from HASTAC website: http://hastac2013.org/schedule-2/stephanie-boluk/

Burka, Paul. (2011, April). Old college try. Texas Monthly. Retrieved from http://www.texasmonthly.com/story/old-college-try

Burke, Kenneth. (1969). A rhetoric of motives. Berkeley, CA: University of California. (Original work published 1950)

Carr, Nicholas. (2008, July/August). Is Google making us stupid? [Electronic version]. The Atlantic. Retrieved January 16, 2012, from http://www.theatlantic.com/magazine/archive/2008/07/is-google-making-us-stupid/306868/

The Computer History Museum. (2008, December 16). Remix: Lawrence Lessig on IP in the digital economy. Youtube. Retrieved January 12, 2012, from http://www.youtube.com/watch?v=nS6IC5AWh5c

Csikszentmihalyi, Mihaly. (2008). Flow: The psychology of optimal experience. New York: Harper.

Department of Rhetoric & Writing. The University of Texas at Austin. (2012–14). RHE 312: Writing in digital environments. Retrieved November 14, 2012, from http://catalog.utexas.edu/undergraduate/liberal-arts/courses/rhetoric-writing/

Ehses, Hanno H.J. (2004). Representing Macbeth: A case study in visual rhetoric. In Carolyn Handa (Ed.), Visual rhetoric in a digital world: A critical sourcebook (pp. 164–176). Boston: Bedford/St. Martin's.

Fogg, B.J. (2003). The functional triad: Computers in persuasive roles. Persuasive technology: Using computers to change what we think & do (pp. 23–29). Amsterdam: Morgan Kaufmann.

Gee, James Paul. (2007). Good video games & good learning. New York: Peter Lang.

Gee, James Paul. (2008). Learning and games. In Katie Salen (Ed.), The ecology of games: Connecting youth, games, and learning (pp. 21–40). Cambridge, MA: MIT Press.

Gould, L. (1982). The university becomes politicized: The war with Jim Ferguson, 1915-1918. The Southwestern Historical Quarterly, 6(2), 255-76.

Gunderson, Erik. (2003). Declamation, paternity, and Roman identity: Authority and the rhetorical self. Cambridge: Cambridge University Press.

Hea, Amy C. Kimme; Zimmerman, Josh; & Howe, Sara. (2010, May 21). Press 'start': Critical reflections on the development and deployment of a large-scale alternate reality game (ARG). Paper presented at Computers and Writing: Virtual Worlds. West Lafayette, IN.

Hogg, W. C. (1917). His own words to discover his motives. Ann Arbor: University of Michigan Press.

Jenkins, Henry. (2006). Convergence culture: Where old & new media collide. New York: New York University Press.

Kress, Gunther, & van Leeuwen, Theo. (2001). Multimodal discourse: The modes and media of contemporary communication. London: Arnold.

Kress, Gunther, & van Leeuwen, Theo. (2002). Colour as a semiotic mode: Notes for a grammar of colour. Visual Communication, 1, 343–368. doi: 10.1177/147035720200100306

Kristofferson, Kris, & Foster, Fred. (1969). Me and Bobby McGee. [Recorded by Janis Joplin]. On Pearl [mp3]. New York: Columbia Records.

Lanham, Richard A. (1994). The implications of electronic information for the sociology of knowledge. Leonardo, 27, 155–163. Retrieved from http://www.jstor.org/stable/1575985

Lauer, Claire. (2009). Contending with terms: "Multimodal" and "multimedia" in the academic and public spheres. Computers and Composition, 26, 225–239.

Lauer, Claire. (2012). What's in a name? The anatomy of defining new/multi/modal/digital/media texts. Kairos: A Journal of Rhetoric, Technology, Pedagogy, 17(1). Retrieved September 4, 2012, fromhttp://kairos.technorhetoric.net/17.1/inventio/lauer/index.html

Lévy, Pierre. (1997). Collective intelligence: Mankind's emerging world in cyberspace. New York: Basic Books.

Manovich, Lev. (2001). The language of cultural interfaces. The language of new media (pp. 80–98). Cambridge, MA: MIT Press.

McCloud, Scott. (1993). The vocabulary of comics & Blood in the gutter. Understanding comics: The invisible art (pp. 24–93). New York: Harper Perennial.

McGonigal, Jane. (2008). Why I love bees: A case study in collective intelligence gaming. In Katie Salen (Ed.), The ecology of games: Connecting youth, games, and learning (pp. 199–227). Cambridge, MA: MIT Press.

McGonigal, Jane. (2011). Reality is broken: Why games make us better and how they can change the world. New York: Penguin.

McLuhan, Marshal. (2003). The medium is the massage. In Stephanie McLuhan & David Staines (Eds.), Understanding me: Lectures & interviews (pp. 76–97). Toronto: Stephanie McLuhan.

Plato. (1999). Phaedrus. (Benjamin Jowett, Trans.). Internet Classics Archive, Massachusetts Institute of Technology. Retrieved from http://classics.mit.edu/Plato/phaedrus.html

Selber, Stuart A. (2004). Multiliteracies for a digital age. Carbondale, IL: Southern Illinois University Press.

Selfe, Cynthia L. (Ed.). (2007). Multimodal composition: Resources for teachers. Cresskill, NJ: Hampton Press.

Solomon, Martin. (2004). The power of punctuation. In Carolyn Handa (Ed.), Visual rhetoric in a digital world: A critical sourcebook (pp. 282–289). Boston: Bedford/St. Martin's.

Warren, Scott; Dondlinger, Mary Jo; & McLeod, Julie. (2008, March 28). Power, play, and PBL in postsecondary learning: Leveraging design models, emerging technologies, and game elements to transform large group instruction. Paper presented at American Educational Research Association Annual Meeting. New York. Retrieved May 13, 2013 fromhttp://juliemcleod.org/portfolio/pdfs/power_play_pbl.pdf

Winterbottom, Michael. (1982). Schoolroom and courtroom. In Brian Vickers (Ed.), Rhetoric revalued: Papers from the International Society for the History of Rhetoric (pp. 59–70). Binghamton, NY: Center for Medieval & Early Renaissance Studies.

## Design Resources

Arjan. (2006). Stone dice 17 [Photograph]. Wikimedia Foundation. Retrieved January 5, 2013, from http://wikimediafoundation.org/wiki/File:Stone_Dice_17.JPG

Baum, Trevor. (2011). Haymaker [True Type font]. Lost Type Co-op. Retrieved January 10, 2010, from http://www.losttype.com/font/?name=haymaker

Clarke, Joseph Clayton. (1931). Pickwick playing cards [Illustration]. The World of Playing Cards. Retrieved January 5, 2013, from http://www.wopc.co.uk/uk/pickwick.html

Christopher, Kevin. (n.d.). Hooverville [True Type font]. Retrieved January 10, 2013, from http://www.kcfonts.com/

Coretuts. (2010). Photo corners [Photograph]. Coretuts. Retrieved January 10, 2013 from http://www.coretuts.com/vintage_photo_corner.php

Gone to Texas. (2007). GTT Map 2007 [Illustration]. Gone to Texas. Retrieved February 12, 2012, from http://www.utexas.edu/events/gtt/map.html

Guðsþegn. (2012). UT Tower - Main Building [Photograph]. Wikipedia. Retrieved December 20, 2012, from http://en.wikipedia.org/wiki/File:UT_Tower_-_Main_Building.JPG

johnny_automatic. (2006) Open mouth [Vector graphic]. Open Clip Art Library. Retrieved January 5, 2013, from http://openclipart.org/detail/1040/open-mouth-by-johnny_automatic

johnny_automatic. (2006). Pointing hand [Vector graphic]. Open Clip Art Library. Retrieved January 5, 2013, from http://openclipart.org/detail/1006/pointing-hand-by-johnny_automatic

johnny_automatic. (2012/1905). Ear [Vector graphic]. Open Clip Art Library. Retrieved January 5, 2013, from http://openclipart.org/detail/167173/ear-by-johnny_automatic

Macleod, Frances. (2011). Abraham Lincoln [True Type font]. Lost Type Co-op. Retrieved January 10, 2013, from http://www.losttype.com/font/?name=Abraham%20Lincoln

OCAL. (2009). Bull clip art [Vector graphic]. Clker. Retrieved January 10, 2013, from http://www.clker.com/clipart-26980.html

Outer surface of the human brain [Vector image]. (1894–95). Wikipedia. Retrieved January 5, 2013, from http://en.wikipedia.org/wiki/File:PSM_V46_D167_Outer_surface_of_the_human_brain.jpg

Seeger, Stuart. (2010). Texas State Capitol - Austin, Texas [Photograph]. Wikipedia. Retrieved December 20, 2012, from http://en.wikipedia.org/wiki/File:Texas_State_Capitol_-_Austin,_Texas.jpg

Steffman, Dieter. (2006). Verve [True Type font]. DaFont. Retrieved January 10, 2013, from http://www.dafont.com/verve.font

Vectorian. (2012). 85 Vintage Vector Ornaments [Vector graphics]. Vectorian. Retrieved January 10, 2013, from http://www.vectorian.net/download-free-vector-ornaments.html

Vintage Vectors. (2009–13). Antique optometry eyeglasses graphic [Vector image]. Vintage Vectors. Retrieved January 5, 2013, from http://www.vintagevectors.com/decorative/antique-optometry-eye-glasses-graphic/

Vintage Vectors. (2009–13). Old phonograph (gramophone) vector [Vector grahpic]. Vintage Vectors. Retrieved January 5, 2013, from http://www.vintagevectors.com/objects/old-phonograph-gramophone-vector/

All student media was used with permission per The University of Texas at Austin Institutional Review Board-approved study number 2011-10-0066.

# LITERACY IN COMPOSITION STUDIES

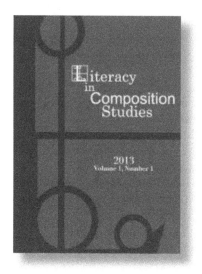

*Literacy in Composition Studies* is on the Web at http://lics-journal.org

*Literacy in Composition Studies* is a refereed open access online journal sponsoring scholarly activity at the nexus of Literacy and Composition Studies. With literacy and composition as our keywords we denote practices that are deeply context-bound and always ideological and recognize the institutional, disciplinary, and historical contexts surrounding the range of writing courses offered at the college level. Literacy is often a metaphor for the ability to navigate systems, cultures, and situations. At its heart, literacy is linked to interpretation—to reading the social environment and engaging and remaking that environment through communication. Orienting a Composition Studies journal around literacy prompts us to analyze the connections and disconnections among writing, reading and interpretation, inviting us to examine the ways in which literacy constitutes writer, context, and act.

## On the Social Consequences of Literacy

Vieira's essay was published in the inaugural issue of *LiCS*, part of the symposium that invited participants to explore the intersections between Literacy and Composition Studies. In this essay Vieira demonstrates how a Composition Studies perspective—with its focus on writing—enables new ways of exploring an "unpopular" question about the consequences of literacy. Vieira explores the social consequences of transnational movements on literacy, attending to the roles of technology, materiality, school, and family. The editors nominated Vieira's piece because we were impressed by how she draws on her ethnographic fieldwork to reanimate a seemingly settled theoretical debate.

# 10 On the Social Consequences of Literacy

*Kate Vieira*

I have sympathy for the bold, and currently unpopular, question that anthropologist Jack Goody and literary critic Ian Watt posed in 1963: What are the consequences of literacy? Goody and Watt argued that literacy's technical affordances allowed the objective recording of historical facts. Without the confusing subjectivity of face-to-face communication, culture could be passed on more or less accurately, distinguishing literate civilizations from oral ones. Writing within the contested field of anthropology from the 60s to the 80s, Goody feared cultural relativism had confused the bread and butter of anthropology, the study of "talking man," with the object of sociology, "reading and writing man" (Goody and Watt 304). Goody and Watt were trying to make some distinctions, based not on the newly politically embarrassing terms "primitive" and "civilized," but instead on concepts that were, in their view, less culturally biased but still worthy of attention: literate and nonliterate. They wanted to transcend the ethnocentrism that characterized nineteenth-century anthropology but were suspicious of what they called the "sentimental egalitarianism" that caused anthropologists to ignore crucial differences between civilizations (344).

The counterarguments to their claims are too numerous to rehearse here. Briefly, though, along with others, Brian Street (also an anthropologist) called attention to the variety of uses of literacy and orality in particular cultural contexts (namely Iran in the late 1970's, where he conducted fieldwork). To extrapolate about a society's capabilities from literacy's technical potential was, in Street's view, reductive, "technicist" (*Literacy in Theory and Practice*). For Goody and Watt, it was the central question of anthropology. In the ensuing decades, Goody qualified some of the terms of his argument and defended others. And scholars of New Literacy Studies, within and outside of anthropology, have produced careful studies of literacy's varied relationships to social contexts and to power. Literacy can index race, culture, age, gender, class, capitalism, identity; it leeches the meanings that organize our lives. In short, Goody and Watt's "autonomous" theory of literacy has been rebutted. And a scholarly field of inquiry has developed in its place.

Yet Goody and Watt's ambitious research question remains compelling: What are the consequences of literacy? I would like to know the answer. And I believe Composition Studies is an ideal disciplinary space from which to approach it. Some of us may make use of ethnographic methodologies, but we are not shackled to anthropological debates. Our unit of analysis is not culture, at least not centrally, but *writing*—how it happens, what it means, where it circulates, how it accomplishes its goals, whom it advances, whom it leaves behind, what it is worth and why. These processes entail the social, but do not require us to pin it down and watch it wriggle. Our attention can be more centrally trained on literacy.

There are consequences to literacy—large ones and, my own fieldwork suggests, often troubling ones. Can we explore them without dividing the world into oral and literate, without having to take. on debates that are not of our moment, and without sacrificing the crucial insights of New Literacy Studies? Are there new answers to old questions?

Brandt and Clinton, in an influential 2002 article, posed similar questions and answered affirmatively. They argued that literacy is not only a social product, but that it is also an object that actively constitutes the social. Seen in this Latourian vein, literacy's materiality is brought into bright relief. Viewed materially, literacy is a tool (though not a neutral one) that has particular potentials to be put to certain uses. This context-sensitive appeal to literacy's materiality avoids what Street condemns as "technicism" and also transcends what Brandt and Clinton term "the limits of the local." A focus on literacy's materiality is also timely: It resonates with contemporary scholarship on the affordances of new media (e.g. Haas; Kress) and of "old" media, such as paper (e.g. Hull; Kafka; Mortensen; Prendergast and Ličko). Brandt and Clinton encourage us to look *at* literacy instead of *through* it—precisely the work that compositionists' disciplinary training encourages, and perhaps a method of analysis that can yield new answers to questions that remain urgent.

What follows is a brief, and I hope suggestive, crack at such an analysis. My interests lie in the transnational, in the ways that literacy and people travel across borders, and in the ways that these trajectories are intertwined. Based on my recent ethnographic research with immigrant communities and their families, I am beginning to see literacy as a navigational technology that opens up some paths and closes off others, that orients and disorients, that routes and often reroutes.

## NAVIGATION

Here, then, are three attempts.

1. In my ongoing ethnography of a U.S. immigrant community, a young undocumented Brazilian man, Rafael, told me the following:

> *I'm in a public place, looking for something, or on the road, and I see a written sign in English, and I read it and manage to understand. . . this helps me when this happens. . .*

And a similar excerpt: A middle aged Portuguese immigrant, Cristina, told me the following about her efforts to get to Boston to take the literacy test to get her citizenship papers:

> *I'm very smart, because if you give me an address to go to Boston or to go anywhere, I'll go. You gotta give me the address. You write it down. You say I want you to go to the city of Boston, take your citizen papers. I told the city hall, I told the lady, I've never been there, but if you write it to me, I'll believe it. . . . See, I know how to read, but not like you . . . That's why I lost [failed] three times on the citizen papers.*

Here there is a curious connection between movement and literacy. Individual literacy allows Rafael and Cristina to orient themselves in unfamiliar surroundings, to read the world in a more literal sense than Freire had envisioned with his phrase. To chart a route to Boston on a map. To decipher a street sign in English through the windshield of a moving car. To go in a particular direction.

But Cristina's and Rafael's experiences suggest that literacy is not simply an individual navigational skill. It is also an infrastructure that regulates movement. Cristina, having lived in the U.S. for 34 years, wanted to naturalize. Literacy, for her, is an *obstacle* to overcome as she seeks to write herself into the nation. Even worse, Rafael has no papers. He cannot legally drive or work: "I'd like a paper, to live here legally," he told me. "Pretty soon they'll prohibit us from walking." The bureaucracy of immigration services has written him out. For Cristina and Rafael, literate infrastructures do not simply facilitate their movement. They also stall it.

The textual regulation of Cristina and Rafael is, to echo much work on literacy's social history, a sign of history in the present. European nation-states came into being, in part, by wresting the authority to control people's movement from religious institutions (Torpey). They consolidated their power in part through the passport—a textual apparatus that attempts to regulate the unwieldy movement of bodies. In our particular historical moment, many of these moving bodies are seen as problematically brown. Can migrants revise the narratives that write them in oppressive ways, as, for example, Morris Young's or Juan Guerra's or Tomás Mario Kalmar's work suggests? Sometimes, yes. Literacy can sometimes empower, but often it oppresses, disenfranchises, regulates. These are some of its consequences.

2.  If literacy regulates us, it also moves us. I am fascinated by pages 65 to 69 in Harvey Graff's *Literacy Myth*. These pages offer evidence that in the late 19th century, migrants to Ontario were highly literate compared to others in their birthplaces. One scholar has suggested that migrants were recruited through personal letters sent from family members abroad (Foner). Through these letters, moreover, people were taught how to use the postal system (Gerber), a transnational literacy institution. This brings me briefly away from papers to our current moment of mass migration and digital writing technology. Is there a cross-border literacy pedagogy at work in these

environments? I have recently been trying to answer this question by interviewing immigrants' family members in Brazil, the ones who didn't migrate, the ones who stayed home. They receive what I call "writing remittances"—the letters, emails, and computers that facilitate communication with their family members abroad. Writing remittances travel into their lives; and they participate in changing them.

Consider the experiences of two women I interviewed in a mid-sized town in Brazil: One woman, Maria, whose son migrated to Japan, was only able to complete the second grade and has difficulty writing and reading. She works as a domestic in other people's houses. The other woman, Eliana, whose brother migrated to the U.S., completed a college degree in accounting. She worked as an accountant before her children were born and then worked at home raising them. While Maria is not impoverished, and Eliana is not extraordinarily wealthy, they represent opposite ends of Brazil's entrenched class system.

But one social fact unites them: both women received computers from their family members abroad. Maria, with less formal education, can sign in, send photos, can Skype. Eliana, with more education, said that she only touches the computer to dust it. "I'm becoming illiterate," she told me twice in the space of our 90-minute interview. Eliana, once an accountant, cleans the computer sent from her brother in the U.S. In contrast, Maria, who cleans for a living, logs on. Writing technologies from abroad have facilitated a change in each woman's sense of her own literacy and of her social value. Their very places in the world seem to have shifted. They have been rerouted.

3.    For many migrants, the goal is to get ahead, *ir para frente*, as Simone puts it to me, as we sip bottled water in her family's tidy kitchen. She is a college student, a Brazilian immigrant to the U.S., whose undocumented status has dogged her efforts to leverage education for upward mobility.

In the required course for her major, she encountered her toughest professor, who demanded essays that, in her words, one could not "B.S.":

If he doesn't see what he wants, or if he sees what he doesn't want, he'll take off points. . . . You write *na na na*, he will "minus 2." It has to be exactly what he wants.

Because of Simone's subordinate position as an undergraduate in an academic hierarchy, her words need to be corrected, deleted, revised or face the consequences ("minus 2"). This is a view of college writing as a checkpoint: "*Passei na marra*," Simone said of the required writing course, a phrase that roughly translates as "I passed by the sweat of my brow." She added, "But I passed. Everything turned out alright."

While writing to "pass" may be a common orientation to literacy among undergraduates, Simone's anxiety is accentuated by other moments in which she needed writing to pass, namely at points in her college education when her documents were demanded. Here she describes her anxiety about being able to complete a required internship for her major:

When classes finish, there is a day in your junior year. You make a line there, and everyone shows their ID. I showed my [Brazilian] passport to her. She said, "You have a passport. That's okay." And I was worried, not for the fact that I had a criminal record. I don't have anything, you know, but um, I don't know, you know. The check turned out okay, I don't know what. And then, there was another: the paper that was to apply, you had to put your social security number. So there was something else that I didn't have. So it was like that.

Simone's pressing textual anxieties seeped into her orientation to academic literacy. The punishing realities of her lived experiences with textuality could not be extricated from the literate site of the classroom, could not be extricated from her writing itself. To pass a college class, to pass a checkpoint, to pass for a white American—passing speaks to an assimilationist logic that continues to haunt U.S. literacy history.

New Literacy Studies scholars have demonstrated literacy's profound connection to social identities (e.g. Dyson; Gee; Heath; Royster; Sarroub), insights that we often put directly to use in the composition classroom. But understanding literacy materially, in the lives of undocumented migrants, shifts the focus from *identity* to *identification*. For many, writing becomes associated not centrally with expression or culture, but with a national tracking system that can lead to deportation, the separation of families, and sometimes death. Texts, in this context, are strong.

## Strong Texts?

In *The Logic of Writing and the Organization of Society*, Goody argues that bureaucracies in the ancient near east depended on "the capacity for writing to communicate at a distance, to store information in files . . ." (89-90). The material affordances of particular kinds of literacies, in other words, buttressed ancient social institutions, including the post and the state. Such conclusions are specific to Goody's field site, but they also resonate across contexts. It is remarkable, isn't it, that writing's roles in the ancient near east and in the contemporary migrant communities I have sketched here are so similar? Developing such comparisons may point another way forward for literacy studies. Researchers at the University of British Columbia, for example, are building a database that houses qualitative studies of literacy practices, so that scholars can work across grounded case studies to advance more robust theories (Purcell-Gates, Perry, and Briseño). To return to Goody, where he fails to persuade is in his distinctions between oral and literate societies. What is compelling about his work, and what helps me as I progress with my own, is not what orality supposedly cannot do, but what writing *can*.

To be clear: To track the consequences of literacies' material affordances is not to uncritically rehabilitate strong text views of literacy, in which texts autonomously accomplish magnificent feats independent of the social. Instead, it is a radically social view of literacy—literacy understood from the perspective, in these cases, of migrants and their families—that brings me up against literacy's consequences. When viewed from my field sites, the theoretical distinctions between strong text and context-sensitive theories of literacy begin to collapse. From this emic perspective, if nation states, with armies and laws, agree that papers have the power to regulate movement, then they do. Texts are as strong as the strongest make them. Sure, there are subversions and forgeries and creative misuses of literacy. But there is also mass compliance exacted through fear and through habit. For many participants in my research—and perhaps for others in highly bureaucratic societies—literacy is a potent object that enters their lives, that makes things happen.

No field site, of course, is representative. As I understand it, the value of ethnography as a methodology is in its specificity. Ethnographers attend to lived experiences and practices, and we proceed with the belief that such practices have something to teach our theories. What my research reveals is the entanglement of literacy with the movement of people—with their upward or downward social mobility and with their physical mobility across transnational borders or through hostile city streets. Literacy, experienced in these communities materially, is a navigational technology. It places and displaces. It orients and disorients. It includes and it alienates. These are not metaphors for literacy. They are active verbs that correspond with the development of the nation state, the transnational post, and systems of social inequality. Literacy's material affordances have social origins, yes. And they are taken up as part of other social practices, yes. That literacy is shaped by its social context has been irrefutably established. These claims lead us back, or perhaps forward, to its far-reaching consequences.

## Notes

1 Parts of this article were first presented at the Conference on College Composition and Communication in St. Louis, MO, 2012.

2 Here is the relevant quote: "It has seemed worthwhile to enquire whether there may not be, even from the most empirical and relativist standpoint, genuine illumination to be derived from a further consideration of some of the historical and analytic problems connected with the traditional dichotomy between non-literate and literate societies" (305).

3 See the introduction to *The Power of the Written Tradition*.

4 In his 2003 response, Street argued that Brandt and Clinton risked making the global forces that acted on literacy seem "autonomous." New Literacy Studies, he suggested, already had the conceptual heft to deal with

the connection between the global and local through "literacy practices," a category of analysis in which both local and global forces are visible.

5 Historian Ben Kafka describes how a clerk rescued people from the Terror during the French Revolution by soaking lists of future victims in pails of water and dumping the pulp in nearby baths: "While everyone else was looking *through* the files for orders or for information, he looked *at* them, and recognized them for what they really were: ink and paper" (14).

6 Young's term for this is "minor revisions"; Guerra's is "transcultural repositioning"; Kalmar's research participants develop a subversive "wetback dictionary" to learn English on their own terms.

7 In the early days of New Literacy Studies, Deborah Brandt popularized the term "strong text," to represent what was wrong with previous theories: They were decontextualized and product-centered (*Literacy as Involvement*).

## WORKS CITED

Brandt, Deborah. Literacy in American Lives. New York: Cambridge UP, 2001. Print.

—. *Literacy as Involvement: The Acts of Writers, Readers, and Texts.* Carbondale: Southern Illinois UP, 1990. Print.

Brandt, Deborah, and Katie Clinton. "Limits of the Local: Expanding Perspectives on Literacy as a Social Practice." *Journal of Literacy Research* 34.3 (2002): 337-56. Print.

Dyson, Anne Haas. *Writing Superheroes: Contemporary Childhood, Popular Culture, and Classroom Literacy.* New York: Teachers College Press, 1997. Print.

Foner, Nancy. *From Ellis Island to JFK: New York's Two Great Waves of Immigration.* New Haven: Yale UP/ New York: Russell Sage Foundation, 2000. Print.

Freire, Paulo. *Pedagogy of the Oppressed.* New York: Seabury Press, 1970. Print.

Gee, James Paul. *Social Linguistics and Literacies: Ideology in Discourses.* New York: Routledge Falmer, 1996. Print.

Gerber, David. *Authors of Their Lives: The Personal Correspondence of British Immigrants to North America in the Nineteenth Century.* New York: New York UP, 2006. Print.

Goody, Jack. *The Logic of Writing and the Organization of Society.* New York: Cambridge UP, 1986. Print. Studies in Literacy, Family, Culture and the State.

—. *The Power of the Written Tradition.* Washington, D.C.: Smithsonian Institution Press, 2000. Print.

Goody, Jack, and Ian Watt. "The Consequences of Literacy." *Comparative Studies in Society and History* 5.3 (1963): 304-45. Print.

Graff, Harvey. *The Literacy Myth: Cultural Integration and Social Structure in the Nineteenth Century.* New Brunswick, N.J: Transaction Publishers, 1991. Print.

Guerra, Juan. *Close to Home: Oral and Literate Practices in a Transnational Mexicano Community.* New York: Teachers College Press, 1998. Print.

Haas, Christina. *Writing Technology: Studies on the Materiality of Literacy.* Mahwah: Erlbaum Associates, 1996. Print.

Heath, Shirley Brice. *Ways with Words: Language, Life, and Work in Communities and Classrooms.* New York: Cambridge UP, 1983. Print.

Hull, Matthew. *Government of Paper: The Materiality of Bureaucracy in Urban Pakistan.* Berkeley: U of California P, 2012. Print.

Kafka, Ben. "The Demon of Writing: Paperwork, Public Safety, and the Reign of Terror." *Representations* 98.1 (2007): 1-24. Print.

Kalmar, Tomás Mario. *Illegal Alphabets and Adult Biliteracy: Latino Migrants Crossing the Linguistic Border.* Mahwah: Erlbaum, 2001. Print.

Kress, Gunther. *Literacy in the New Media Age.* New York: Routledge, 2003. Print.

Mortensen, Peter. "Reading Material." *Written Communication* 18.4 (2001): 395–439. Print.

Prendergast, Catherine, and Roman Ličko. "The Ethos of Paper: Here and There." *JAC* 29.1–2 (2009): 199-228. Print.

Purcell-Gates, Victoria, Kristen H. Perry, and Adriana Briseño. "Analyzing Literacy Practice: Grounded Theory to Model." *Research in the Teaching of English* 45.4 (2011): 439-58. Print.

Royster, Jacqueline Jones. *Traces of a Stream: Literacy and Social Change Among African-American Women.* Pittsburgh: U of Pittsburgh P, 2000. Print. Pittsburgh Series in Composition, Literacy and Culture.

Sarroub, Loukia. *All American Yemeni Girls: Being Muslim in a Public School.* Philadelphia: U of Pennsylvania P, 2005. Print.

Street, Brian V. *Literacy in Theory and Practice.* Cambridge: Cambridge UP, 1984. Print.

—. "What's 'New' in New Literacy Studies? Critical Approaches to Literacy in Theory and Practice." *Current Issues in Comparative Education* 5.2 (2003): 77-91. Print.

Torpey, John. *The Invention of the Passport: Surveillance, Citizenship, and the State.* New York: Cambridge UP, 2000. Print.

Young, Morris. *Minor Re/visions: Asian American Literacy Narratives as a Rhetoric of Citizenship.* Carbondale: Southern Illinois UP, 2004. Print. Studies in Writing and Rhetoric.

# PEDAGOGY

*Pedagogy* is on the Web at http://pedagogy.dukejournals.org/

*Pedagogy* seeks to create a new discourse surrounding teaching in English studies by fusing theoretical approaches and practical realities. As a journal devoted exclusively to pedagogical issues, it is intended as a forum for critical reflection as well as a site for spirited and informed debate from a multiplicity of positions and perspectives. The journal strives to reverse the long-standing marginalization of teaching and the scholarship produced around it and instead to assert the centrality of teaching to our work as scholars and professionals.

## What New Writing Teachers Talk about When They Talk about Teaching

Heidi Estrem and E. Shelley Reid's "What New Writing Teachers Talk about When They Talk about Teaching" explores findings from a multi-year, multi-site study of new college writing instructors. First, the authors describe the principles that guide new instructors' teaching and reveal the number of resources that new instructors draw on beyond the pedagogy seminar. Secondly, they delineate how the kinds of classroom narratives these instructors chose to tell points to a range of understandings about what it means to teach writing. Ultimately, they argue that learning to teach writing is a complex process requiring sustained mentoring and support throughout the early years of teaching. Drawing on the research on TA mentoring, this multi-year, multimodal research project allows us to hear from graduate students in detailed and rich ways.

# 11 What New Writing Teachers Talk about When They Talk about Teaching

*Heidi Estrem and E. Shelley Reid*

As a discipline with academic roots in pedagogy (Harris 1996), composition studies has fostered increasingly visible and structured programs to mentor new writing instructors. Several recent essay collections compile examples of programs, thoughtfully theorized approaches, and careful explorations of how to best support and nurture new instructors of first-year writing (see, for example, Pytlik and Liggett 2002; Ward and Perry 2002). It is now common that new college writing teaching assistants (TAs) participate in at least one pedagogy seminar designed to guide them through their initial teaching experience and provide an introduction to composition studies (see Dobrin 2005). Additionally, individual accounts of new instructors like those by Wendy Bishop (1990), Elizabeth Rankin (1994), and Sally Barr Ebest (2005) help provide a rich context for further research on the pedagogical development of new writing instructors.

As two writing program administrators who have mentored new TAs and taught the pedagogy seminar for years now, we believed that our hours of work with these TAs — who are often simultaneously new to graduate study, new to teaching, and new to the concept of composition studies as a field — were affecting them positively. But how much, we wondered, did their encounters with new concepts about teaching and writing in our pedagogy course influence their approaches in the classroom? How did TAs make decisions about teaching, and why? To build on the important scholarship on TA mentoring, as well as to help us move from *belief* to *knowledge* about how TAs make decisions and articulate their beliefs about teaching writing, Shelley designed a multiyear, multimodal research project; Heidi then added her program as a second site. The three-year research project included extensive surveys of TAs and anonymous interviews at both sites (the full project is described in much more detail in Reid and Estrem forthcoming). The rich perspectives expressed within the set of interviews — what new instructors talk about when they talk about teaching — kept drawing our attention again and again: these new writing instructors shared their perspectives on teaching, their hopes and fears, their insights and questions, and their frustrations in ways that helped us revisit and rethink what we thought we knew about how instructors experienced teaching for the first time.

What we gradually came to understand as we reread the transcribed words is this: while research within composition studies has focused quite a bit on *teaching*, there's not been quite as much focus on *learning* — in this case, learning about teaching. From the interview transcripts, we gain different glimmers of insights into how people learn pedagogy — how they conceptualize it, narrate it, make meaning from it, and integrate new ideas into their practices. One key message these TAs' voices provide us seems obvious now both in a "We already knew that!" way and in a "Why weren't we thinking more about that?!" way: learning to teach (writing) is a protean and lengthy process, its uncertain and recursive progress often obscured by the myths of quick competence on which learners, teachers, and institutions rely.

In this article, we focus most closely on two particularly compelling areas of the interviews that help reveal the complexities of learning to teach writing: first, at the macro level, the *principles for teaching* that the interview participants named and what they identified as *the origins of those beliefs*, and second, at a very particularized level, the *stories of teaching challenges* they chose to tell. Together, these accounts help us, in turn, come to know more about how new instructors learn pedagogy: not just how they learn *about* it or learn to *practice* it, but how they begin to learn to become the reflective practitioners we hope for. Part of what these TAs are telling us — Heidi and Shelley individually and all of us as a field — is that we are one of many sources of information and values about teaching (writing) that aid new learners. And part of what they tell us, less directly, is that we need to more overtly acknowledge and teach toward a slower, more recursive, and more extended learning process for new writing teachers.

In the analysis that follows, we first briefly explain how the interview methodology itself opened up new possibilities for imagining alternate spaces for our mentorship of new TA instructors. Then, and most important, we turn to the words of the TAs themselves, exploring what they say about teaching and what that might reveal about their learning processes. Finally, these data lead us to reconsidering current institutional structures and the implicit expectations embedded within those structures. Through taking seriously what these TAs talk about when they talk about teaching, we can productively rethink how we might provide mentoring that is focused, directed, and appropriate to the developmental stages that TAs are in as learners themselves.

## METHODOLOGY AS PROCESS AND RESULT: CONTEXTS FOR DIALOGUE IN WRITING PROGRAMS

Although our interviews were initially structured as a data-gathering methodology, we have come to understand them as contributing to the thinking process, and especially the storytelling process, that the TAs participated in via our study. As Irving Seidman argues, "It is this process of selecting constitutive details of experience, reflecting on them, giving them order, and thereby making sense of them that makes telling stories a meaning-making experience" (2006: 1).

The methodological decisions made for this study helped illuminate TAs' stories in a different way than we had anticipated. While there are several excellent qualitative studies of TA development, and particularly of the graduate pedagogy seminar, we wanted to tease out possibilities beyond the local (for a fuller account of prior scholarship in this area, see Estrem and Reid 2012). Informed by our own instructional experiences, by the research of Rankin, Barr Ebest, and others, and especially by Mary M. Kennedy's *Learning to Teach Writing: Does Teacher Education Make a Difference?* (1998), we were confident we knew much of what the TAs we work with would tell us about teaching if we asked them directly. But we were curious about what they might say — particularly what they might say about their core beliefs and reasonings, not just their practices — if we weren't there.

So while we were mindful of Seidman's (2006: 7) concerns about all interviews conducted by those in positions of power — that it can be a "process that turns others into subjects so that their words can be appropriated for the benefit of the researcher" — Shelley ventured that a different approach to conducting the interviews might lessen (while of course not removing) the impact of our position as researchers of/ with/among our own instructors/students. We wanted to at least try to mediate that complicated world differently for these graduate student instructors. TAs who volunteered for the interviews, then, were informed that we would be reading the transcripts. However, the interviews took place in a neutral setting (a department conference room or empty office) with an undergraduate or graduate research assistant, and were transcribed without identifying data. Twenty-nine interviews were conducted at George Mason University over a three-year period; twelve were conducted at Boise State University over a two-year period. (Some students were interviewed in more than one year, but we were generally unable to track these repeated participants.) The interviews were designed to gain insight into how these new TAs negotiated situations in the classroom and what principles they identified for their teaching (and where they came from), and then to assess whether they applied those principles (or not) to various aspects of teaching, from planning a syllabus to responding to student writing. (See Appendix A for descriptions of the two sites and Appendix B for the full survey.)

This method had some surprising benefits; first, however, it seems appropriate to acknowledge its limitations. While one goal of conducting a two-site, longitudinal study was to gather data that would let us trace the impact of local pedagogical structures and TAs' development over time, we have no solid reports to make here on those counts. Although we gathered data about each participant's site, status (first- through third-year), prior experiences, and other demographic information, we saw few reliable patterns of difference along any of these lines. Whether that is a consequence of too limited a sample, too similar sets of participants (neither site grants PhDs or has many rhetoric and composition concentrators), or too short a time for observation of TA development is not clear. It's also conceivable that there really are few major differences across these lines of investigation, a possibility that could potentially affect TA preparation significantly; with limited data, though, we offer such suggestions guardedly in this article. In addition, the research assistants conducting the interviews did not always know the program as well as we did and therefore missed opportunities to follow up. Finally, the interviews still were clearly going to be reviewed by the TAs' supervisors and took place in the department's building and with questions designed by us, leaving TA participants still very much embedded in their institutional situations.

The design of the study does deliberately privilege a degree of anonymity for the participants over a concern for understanding their learning through what would be a more recognizably "contextualized" approach — for example, through a teacher-research approach or through a qualitative study of new TAs. However, as we read and analyzed these transcripts, it was clear that they were not *de*contextualized: they were differently contextualized, to be sure, but they were also grounded in our individual program values, our university contexts, even in the relationship between the interviewer and the TA. The interviews themselves came to function as "social interaction[s]," providing a way for participants to "generate new reactions" (Briggs 1986: 22). The social interactions in these interviews led to dynamic, grounded responses in a space different from those often used for research on new instructor development.

These social interactions occur as a kind of temporary context in what we might label a "thirdspace" (see Edward Soja's voluminous scholarship). While cultural communication theory operates at a dramatically different level than our own study does, Soja's metaphor gives us a lens for considering these conversations. As he explains, "Thirdspace is a metaphor for the necessity to keep the consciousness of and the theorizing on spatiality radically open. . . . It is a purposefully tentative and flexible term that attempts to capture what is actually a constantly shifting and changing milieu of ideas, events, appearances, and meanings" (1996: 50). But we found the interviews' thirdspaces (neither seminar nor office chat, neither department mailroom nor online discussion) allowed the TAs' stories of teaching identities to shift and deepen in meaning even as they were talking. The transcripts help us assess ways that we, as their mentors, might create other kinds of spaces for this development work. We aren't claiming that these interviews represent a deeper or more "honest" truth than, say, our own classroom-based research with these same TAs, or the largely qualitative, case-study-based research that's been done with this population of developing TAs up to this point. Instead, though, we do propose that these TAs' stories — as told through these interviews with a disinterested third party — convinced us that alternate spaces could change how teachers spoke, what they spoke about, and what knowledge was created through their talk about teaching, an idea we return to at several points in this article.

## WHAT TAS TALK ABOUT, PART 1: PRINCIPLES AND WHERE THEY COME FROM

Educational researchers remind us that new teachers are not new to the classroom, but just to the front of it. Jo Sprague and Jody D. Nyquist (1989: 44 – 45) identify beginning graduate students as "senior learners," on their way to becoming "colleagues in training" and then "junior colleagues." As a whole, the interviews elicit how these senior-learners- becoming-colleagues-in-training make decisions about preparing for class, writing a syllabus, and facing challenges in the classroom. In reading the transcripts, we have found that, indeed, "If given a chance to talk freely, people appear to know a lot about what's going on" (Bertraux, quoted in Seidman 2006: 39).

Table 1. TA principles about teaching

| Principles about teaching related to . . . | Number of times mentioned | Frequency |
| --- | --- | --- |
| Pedagogy of approach: | 45 | 37 percent |
|   Classroom practices (29) | | |
|   Engagement and community (16) | | |
| Pedagogy of content: | 46 | 37 percent |
|   Teaching writing as a process (22) | | |
|   Expanding students' understanding of writing (18) | | |
|   Teaching critical reading (6) | | |
| Focus on encouraging students | 16 | 13 percent |
| Focus on student learning | 14 | 11 percent |
| Other | 2 | 2 percent |

Embedded in the middle of the interview protocol are the two questions that produced the data we will first describe and then analyze in this section:

1.  What do you see as three to four key principles for your teaching or tutoring of writing?

2. Could you say where those principles come from or are related to?

### Categorizing TAs' Principles

Within the set of forty-one interviews, we identified and categorized more than one hundred identified principles or beliefs (123, to be exact). As we sifted and recategorized, these named principles gradually coalesced into four main areas (see table 1). TAs shared principles related to

- pedagogies of approach (what TAs might do in a particular class meeting);
- pedagogies of content (*what* to teach students about writing [and reading]);
- encouraging students; and
- student learning.

As so often happens, two TAs identified principles that we could not categorize neatly, and these make up the "other" category.

These principles are wide-ranging; they reveal TAs' beliefs about student learning, instructor behavior, what "good" classrooms look like, and what the day-to-day teaching of writing should be. Across both programs, TAs emphasize the importance of garnering student "engagement" and building a sense of classroom community; they value teaching writing as a complicated, messy, social process; they are committed to encouraging students and have begun to think about students as learners. And as they talk in this thirdspace, they articulate their principles in an amalgam of generalized and field-specific tropes, revealing even as they gain knowledge and experience that they remain in transition between "senior learner" and "colleague in training."

### Pedagogy of Approach

The responses coded as principles related to a pedagogy of approach document how TAs envision classroom practices and approaches to teaching. The twenty-nine labeled "classroom practices" comprise the most varied response category — and the most frequent. They include principles about general approaches ("whatever it takes to get the job done"), instructor preparation for a class session ("preparation about the subject at hand"), working with students ("ask questions," "listen before you talk"), and recommended classroom approaches ("it's okay to joke," "find a concrete metaphor to explain an idea"). Also captured within this category is a set of responses about the importance of creating a class that functions like a community and that emphasizes "engagement." These areas were mentioned frequently and consistently enough to warrant their own subcategory as an important aspect of approaches to teaching. The following are examples of the kinds of responses within this category:

> I would say one [principle] is student engagement, really finding ways to engage students not just in the classroom time, but also in the projects.

> [One principle is] developing a community feel in the classroom, so that they can go to other students and work with other students, and it's not just learning from me, who is kind of their peer. . . . And I think it's good to develop more of a community of writers rather than just like student/teacher.

## Pedagogy of Content

The next cluster of TAs' principles focuses on the content of the course. In these, TAs describe a commitment to teaching writing as a process, to expanding students' current understandings of writing, and to engaging them as critical readers. When articulating beliefs about writing process, they named twenty-two principles. For example:

> So, it's really important to make sure that students realize that writing is something that is important and valuable, but is mutable at the same time. That it's changeable. It's not set into stone.

> For me it was really teaching them that something comes before the draft so I really wanted to instill in them that whether you do an outline or a brainstorm map or just take notes you need to do something before you sit down at that computer screen 'cause you'll freeze.

These TAs identify also a number of principles (eighteen) related to challenging first-year students' initial conceptions of writing. They see their role as advocates for an enriched, expanded notion of what writing is and what it can do:

> Well, firstly, I want them to know that writing can be fun. It's not necessarily as one-answered single — there's no one answer. There's room when writing to play. Even when you're writing an academic research paper, there's room to make your own way.

> I really want to try to expose them even briefly to a real range, not just of writing styles or genres but also situations, presentations, conferences.

Additionally, a small but significant cluster of responses (six) addressed the importance of teaching critical reading.

## Encouraging Students

In both programs, TAs hold strong beliefs about the importance of encouragement: that writers learn by knowing what they're doing right, that encouragement leads to better learning, and that it should be a part of teaching. Sixteen beliefs were similar to the following examples:

> I think the second principle is to try and encourage students to be open to positive, constructive criticism.

> Number one is generosity; to care about the students' lives and not just their academic work.

> I try to think like a student who would struggle with the subject . . . I try to think, if I was a student who wasn't interested in writing, didn't feel I was good at it, all of these sorts of things, what would help me and what would help me at least appreciate it more or do better or at least see that I could get through it, even if it wasn't ever gonna light my pants on fire.

## Student Learning

The final category includes principles about how people learn and about cognitive development. Here, TAs name fourteen beliefs about the conditions for learning ("people learn by doing," "people don't learn by just hearing it once"); about what first-year students need to learn ("individual accountability in group work," "making them follow the prompt"); and how first-year learning fits in with the fuller college experience ("meta-knowledge," "connections to other classes").

## ANALYZING TAs' PRINCIPLES

Collectively, these named principles or beliefs about teaching have much to encourage those of us who work with new teachers. Within a short time frame — only a few years at most — many of these TAs have formed thoughtful, engaged principles (and some quirky ones as well). Even though we only read the transcripts, the earnest tones of their spoken voices come ringing through: these TAs care about teaching and teach based on deeply held principles. At the same time, TAs use a lot of generalized language here — even when prompted by the more "academic" word *principles*. TAs who, in the pedagogy seminar, routinely use phrases like *collaborative learning* and *recursive process* are talking in less specific language ("community feel" and "something comes before the draft"), causing us to wonder how much they are envisioning the rich traditions and scholarship of composition pedagogy and how much they are drawing on their own preferences as students and writers.

Moreover, some TAs' answers are so brief or underdeveloped that we are more keenly concerned. As one example, we can imagine some of the strategies that this TA might resort to in her earnestness to "get the job done":

> I don't really know if that's a principle, but I guess it's just sort of whatever it takes to get the job done. . . . You know, they definitely — I — I want them to have every chance to succeed, and to succeed means to meet those outcomes. So, like, if that means that I have to do things that I don't feel . . . is a proper (air quotes) use of time, then that's what I'll do. Right? 'Cause ultimately, I want them to be — when they leave this class to meet those outcomes, to have a decent grade, to be able to do what they're supposed to do in other classes.

The layers of responsibility this TA is beginning to articulate — to her students, to program-wide goals, to classes after first-year writing, to students' performance in the class — point to both an ethic of care and commitment as well as a kind of near-desperation that worries us, particularly when we peel back the next layer and look at where these principles come from. For this TA, this was nearly her full answer. She didn't identify where these beliefs come from, and if this is the extent of her beliefs about teaching, they seem, well, pretty thin.

Viewing the responses as a set also confirms for us the value in looking cross-institutionally. While there are, of course, site-specific references (to particular readings here and there; to tutoring, which was an experience all TAs had at George Mason University, and so was of course much more common in their replies), for the most part, the named beliefs were not readily identifiable by us — as their immediate mentors — as site specific. As we discuss in further detail in the next section, this similarity in their beliefs likely stems from the combination of beliefs they hold prior to teaching as well as the impact of composition teaching principles.

## IDENTIFYING WHERE BELIEFS COME FROM

We were particularly interested in understanding more about how TAs identified the *origins* of their beliefs through answering the follow-up question, "Could you say where those beliefs come from?" After all, nearly one-third of these interviewees were taking their pedagogy seminar during the semester that they participated in the survey. Within this set of questions — about naming their beliefs and the origins of those — it made sense that we might see the most impact of our work with TAs. We hoped to gain a stronger sense of how TAs integrated new and previous knowledge about teaching and learning writing.

For each named principle, we then listed and analyzed what the TAs identified as the origins for that particular principle. The TAs identified their principles or beliefs about teaching writing as being derived from

- formal study, including composition scholarship;
- personal experience, belief, family value, or intuition;
- experience teaching or tutoring; and
- the community of peers and mentors within which they work.

However, there is often not a one-to-one correspondence; many TAs identified multiple sources as the origin for any particular belief. For example, TA responses to the question "Could you say where those principles come from or are related to?" frequently looked like this:

> But I've done a lot of reading, obviously, about pedagogy and teaching and students. Then I've also been in the classroom and talked to students. So I think it's probably a mixture of all those things, not that I could specifically point to one instance or anything like that.

> I just think they come from my experience as both a creative writer and my experience in the two pedagogy courses that I've taken.

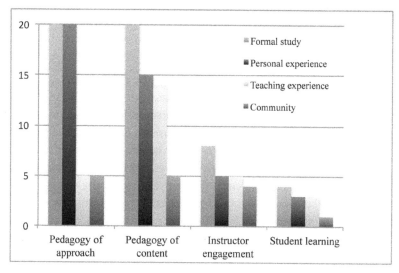

Figure 1. Origins of principles and beliefs

We separated each identified "origin statement" within each category (pedagogy of approach, pedagogy of content, engagement, and student learning) and then coded the identified "origin" for each statement as explained above. When all responses are analyzed, several patterns emerge.

For example, within the twenty-nine initial principles or beliefs identified as related to "pedagogy of approach," formal study and personal experience were both named twenty times, while teaching experience or the influence of peers/community were each mentioned five times. (A caveat: these charts are not intended to support any fine-grained quantitative analysis, but they are helpful in making general trends visible.) When asked to identify where their beliefs come from in all of these areas, for instance, TAs note the influence of *formal study* most frequently for all areas. Formal study principles are what we might expect (and hope) to see informing their beliefs: those new to teaching (and often new to the field of composition studies) are locating their principles for teaching in what they have learned through participating in pedagogy seminar(s), receiving training for Writing Center or teaching, or through reading articles. (In TAs' language, formal study was represented in a range of ways: "the pedagogy course," "Freire," or "that underlife idea [Robert Brooke].")

In the second set of teaching principles rooted in *personal experiences or beliefs*, sometimes TAs noted their own experiences as a student or writer; other times they noted the influence of family or personal values. For example, TAs noted that their principles came from "what I liked as a student," "[the fact that] my mom's a teacher and she approached it in that way," "[what] works for me as a writer." As fig. 1 shows, in each of the four categories of TAs' principles, personal experiences figure quite strongly. A third set, focusing on principles drawn from TAs' own prior *classroom teaching (or tutoring) experience*, figures most strongly in the category of "pedagogy of content." This makes sense: brand-new TAs likely know very little about the content of the courses, and so formal study and their own personal experiences still figure strongly in this area — and yet like the rest of us, TAs eventually base *what* they teach on prior teaching experiences. *How* they approach teaching first-year writing is influenced slightly less by prior teaching experiences. Finally, while in other areas of the interviews (beyond the scope of this article) our coding for *community of other instructors* is quite frequent, within their discussions of principles, fewer TAs name the influence of mentor TAs or peers. (In this category are responses like "watching my mentor TA teach" and "peer mentor.") They draw from their community of peers and mentors quite a bit when imagining a course, dealing with challenges in the classroom, or creating assignments (issues covered in other areas of the interviews) but do not link their beliefs or principles about teaching writing to their peers very often.

Overall, we find these patterns both encouraging and cautionary. Our work with new writing teachers in the pedagogy seminar and in one-on-one mentoring can directly affect their approaches to the classroom in ways they recognize and can name: they talk of concepts like encouraging engagement and inquiry or emphasizing peer review. Since many TAs never took first-year writing themselves, one potential high-impact area for us as mentors is in helping them rethink what the writing class looks like and feels like. It's also clear that their own experiences teaching or tutoring influence *what* they teach more heavily, and there is steady influence from a wide range of personal beliefs that we — and maybe they — may not know about unless we ask them directly. Moreover, when combined, these extracurricular sources (peers, teaching experience, and personal experience) outweigh our instructional voices in TAs' responses; again, this is not a new concept for educators to face, but we realize we have not always been so mindful of it in our pedagogy courses, where we are predisposed to see our effects on our students, and they are predisposed to remind us of our influence. And lastly, it seems that while TAs do turn to peer mentors for practical help, they have less frequent theorized or reflective conversations with peers — a pattern which reinforces our interest in creating new spaces where all TAs can engage in such conversations.

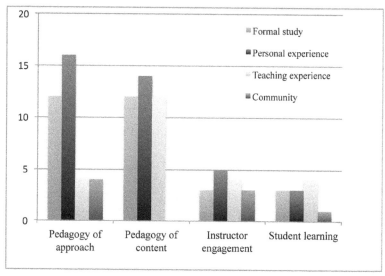

Figure 2. Origins of principles and beliefs: First mention only

Caught between pleasant surprise and mild doubts about seeing "formal study" informing TAs' core beliefs at higher levels than other sources, we also wondered how the data would look when only the *initial* responses given were coded. We had noticed that many respondents began by naming teaching experiences, or a personal experience, and then added phrases like "the readings too, but I can't say which one." So, when we look only at the *first* response given, the numbers distribute somewhat differently.

As a parallel example of the numerical groupings behind this chart, for all initial principles or beliefs coded as "pedagogy of approach," the number of *initial* identifications of the origins of that particular belief is now as follows: formal study, twelve; personal experience, sixteen; teaching experience and community, four each. This graph (see figure 2) makes visible how and when personal experience and classroom-based experience were *most readily* recalled as the source of each principle. In the category of "pedagogy of approach," personal experience comes quickly to mind for the TAs: though they also acknowledge sources like "the pedagogy course" or "readings I've done," they are more likely first to identify their principles as based in what they've experienced in the classroom as students, what they know and believe about human behavior, and what they value. (Their teaching/tutoring experiences are less influential within this area.) In other words, TAs draw on some principles about how to teach writing that they see as rooted in personal experience — values that are in place before an instructor sets foot in a classroom with which they have either no or very little personal experience.

In the area of "pedagogy of content," teaching experience and formal study are slightly secondary to personal experience, although all three areas are identified frequently by these TAs. In the area of principles related to the importance of encouraging students, the first named origin is most often personal experience, followed by teaching experience and formal study. In the area of student learning, teaching experiences become most important: new teachers' observations of their own students prevail over data and theories about writing and learning. Of course, the differences between these numbers are quite small. What interests us more are the trends we see here in where, how, and why these TAs name the origins of their beliefs.

Again, it's complicated. We're glad, in fact, to see new instructors of writing voluntarily identifying multiple sources that inform their teaching beliefs. These patterns are useful in two ways. As the mentors of these instructors, we can see more about the beliefs new TAs are developing or already have in place so we can build from those resources to expand their repertoires. Additionally, these responses remind us that if we choose to ignore the many areas of their lives and experiences that new (and continuing) instructors draw from as we teach, we're missing a large portion of the picture. Our TAs' talk reminds us that new learning does not replace earlier learning as much as it synthesizes with earlier understandings, sometimes wholly and sometimes partially, attaching readily when new and old principles match, and perhaps less strongly when there are conflicting principles. Some "resistance" might thus be productively reframed as a normal stage of TAs' learning processes, or lessened through inquiry about the origins of long-held values.

These conversations about principles reveal thoughtful, resourceful instructors who take teaching seriously and approach it with a wide range of perspectives — and whose voices sometimes surprise us with their certainty about their principles. Their beliefs help us understand more about what they think about teaching and where they locate their beliefs; as a next step, we can consider how we might encourage these TAs to continue revisiting and deepening these principles. Reading their words as they work with the interviewer to understand the question and to consider and name how and why they teach underscores for us the importance of ongoing reflection and reconsideration, of creating multiple spaces for reflection. It may matter to scholars and teachers in the field, for instance, that TAs encourage revision because scholarship demonstrates its value as a learning mode for writers rather than only because they just believe it's important. Moreover, their growth as reflective practitioners — as well as their ability to defend, change, or pass along their practices — may depend on how they perceive and articulate their reasons for taking pedagogical action.

We are mindful, as well, of an apparent lack of differences among responses from first-year TAs as opposed to second-and third-year TAs: our results strongly suggest that *all* of our TAs would benefit from more opportunities to name principles, connect them to multiple sources, and reflect on them. Without such prompting, new instructors might settle on a set of absolute principles quite early (e.g., "I *always* privilege classroom community"); the good news is that the transcripts also demonstrate how easily a space for guided teacher-talk can provide other opportunities for articulation and reflection. As mentors of these new instructors, we are reminded of how crucial it is to provide varying kinds of support for the kind of interactive intellectual work that new instructors need to do, and to time our support to match learners' developmental stages. For example, many pedagogy education programs ask new TAs to write a teaching philosophy as part of their course work in their first or second semester of teaching. However, our interview transcripts point to a different timeline: a structure for working with new TAs that might encourage them to name and *revise* principles for teaching throughout their experience in a program, drafting and redrafting these ideas in workshops, in colloquia, in online spaces, and through guided discussions that extend and amplify the pedagogy education process.

## WHAT TAs TALK ABOUT, PART 2: TRICKY, DIFFICULT, OR SURPRISING TEACHING SITUATIONS

While asking TAs to name *beliefs* necessarily leads to larger, philosophical perspectives, asking them to share *specific accounts of teaching* (and then to reflect on them) illuminates how new instructors identify and describe the particular. In this section, we focus on the responses to the following set of questions:

1. Please tell me a little about a tricky, difficult, or surprising situation you encountered recently in a writing class or while tutoring regarding a writing student.

2. How did you respond?

3. Why did you respond in that way?

Here, then, we take up what TAs talk about when they share anecdotes of teaching not directly related to their principles or beliefs for teaching. The ways in which TAs describe challenging situations they have faced stand out in the interview transcripts as some of their longest responses (see table 2). The forty respondents to this set of questions (one TA couldn't think of a situation) provided responses that we have coded globally as *stories of pedagogy* (understanding these teaching-related situations as teaching moments for themselves or as pedagogical issues) and *stories of students* (of resistance, of students learning how to be students, of appropriate student-instructor relationships). To approach these rich narratives in a systematic way, we first identified the two overarching patterns we saw in these accounts and then worked to code the narratives according to these main themes within the stories of pedagogy and stories of students.

Three accounts from the stories noted in table 2 have also been identified as "unsanctioned" accounts: detailed experiences identifying challenges or solutions that we — and often the TA — recognize as "out of bounds" of program norms and recommendations. We say more about those below.

## STORIES OF PEDAGOGY: REFLECTIVE PRACTICE

Fourteen participants use the prompt to describe and reflect on stories of pedagogy: stories about adjusting their teaching approaches, about lessons that went well and lessons that didn't. We have included longer excerpts from the transcripts here in part because they reveal how TAs are using the interview as a processing space, building an answer phrase by (sometimes hesitant) phrase. The narratives also demonstrate how single events — the kind that may occur in one's first, fourth, or even twentieth semester of teaching — provide opportunities for and sometimes even demand continuing learning about teaching.

Among the stories of pedagogy, three accounts demonstrate a particular stance that we've identified as "reflective practice" — that is, the TAs use the moment of the interview to discuss how they have rethought their own approach or their role in the classroom. For example, a third-year TA describes how she learns from students through thinking deeply about her own beliefs and approaches as well:

> I have a student who is Catholic and her papers tend to be — she tends to argue from a belief stance, and thesis statements of belief are very difficult in terms of how to lay out an argument, and I don't want to discourage her from exercising her faith and her passion, and so just trying to balance a respect for her faith and also help her to recognize some fallacies that can come into play with, you know, the world being the enemy and, you know, those kinds of things; so trying to help her explore the complexities of an argument that may be based on her belief system, but that she might not be able to argue from the Catholic standpoint, and have it be effective towards convincing someone who doesn't believe, who isn't Catholic.
>
> So, but she seems to be, you know, responsive to that. It's tricky for me, you know, in terms of — and I, you know, I'm

a Christian, so I want to make sure that I'm not biased too, so those are kinds of — that's probably one of the more unique tricky situations that I deal with is religion in the courses. You know, you have to be very careful about how I don't present a bias. . . . I have the students talk [laughs], you know, and if this is your religion, you know, I'd love to have you share it with the class and how it relates to this issue, and . . . I'll say "Okay, if you put this in a paper, what are some concerns that I would have about what you just said?" and they usually can tell me . . . I'm not as familiar with some of the diverse religions in this campus and I learn from them, and I think it's really important to not come across as the teacher is the know it all and they're the trash receptacles that I dump things in, and I think they bring a lot to the table in terms of discussion that I wouldn't have thought of so — and they respond very well to each other and very passionately, and if I don't get in the way of that sometimes they can create their own lesson, and to me that's a dynamic thing to watch.

While this narrative begins as a reflection on the challenge of working with one particular student, the TA quickly moves beyond this example so that it does not remain a story of student resistance. Instead, she reflects on her own awareness of her likely biases, and she reminds herself what she has to learn from her students. We were glad to see these kinds of accounts — where TAs turned voluntarily to deep reflection — but there were only three such stories. As mentors of these TAs, then, we are mindful of needing to create more opportunities for all TAs to solve (or at least untangle) their teaching "challenges" through reconsidering them, through exploring multiple angles and approaches, and through drawing on resources that they have readily available to them.

Table 2: Types of difficult teaching situations

| Theme | # interviews (total n=40) | Characteristics |
|---|---|---|
| Pedagogy: Reflective practitioner | 3 | These accounts identify the challenge as located (at least partially) in the instructor's choices, and demonstrate the willingness of instructors to learn from their students and adjust their approach. |
| Pedagogy: Classroom or program | 11 | These accounts position *teaching* events (organization, working with readings, adjusting after a substitute) as the key challenge. |
| Students: Resistance | 14 | These accounts identify the challenge as stemming specifically from what participants identify as student *resistance.* |
| Students: Studenting | 7 | These accounts note student *behavior* as a challenge — behavior that's not necessarily resistant but is about individual students learning to handle school, such as a student who misses a lot of class or who needs personal help beyond the classroom. |
| Students: Relationships | 5 | These accounts focus on the challenge of how to address the more general interpersonal arenas of teaching. They're stories of authority, age, and "appropriate" behavior. |

## STORIES OF PEDAGOGY: CLASSROOM OR PROGRAM

In other narratives related to teaching issues, eleven participants describe the challenges of teaching particular aspects of writing and how and why they made adjustments, though they do not explicitly articulate how they reflected on and learned from the experience. Indeed, many of them seem to be fully articulating the story, seeing all its pedagogical implications, for the first time, even reliving it as they create it. In the following account, a third-year instructor explains the challenge she faced when she hadn't integrated readings into her course very well:

> You know it was just that, I mean I guess everyone hates their text, the first one they do. My readings were grouped by like topic. And so one of the topics worked great and I did a little like literature review. The other topics were sort of _____ and gentle, and as I saw like kind of the decrease in quality in the reading responses and class discussion never really took off, I decided to kind of just make sort of a organic class decision that we would just start focusing on the writing, so we were getting into the bigger writing projects. I mean something that made sense to me, but at the same time I was like don't even buy this reader. It just never really panned out.
>
> I think because there are so many _____ in 101, that to me the main one was always the writing. I knew that they would have to focus on close reading in 201, so it was kind of like if you can't do everything, which of course I tried to do. You know I think I just decided that 101 goals put more emphasis on focusing on the writing projects versus the barely applicable readings.

While this "organic class decision" is not necessarily one we'd make or encourage as a mentor, her rationale for how she addressed this challenge is intriguing, reasoned, and based on her newly acquired professional knowledge: she knew that the next course in the sequence, an introduction to literature, would focus on close reading, and so she felt comfortable making this kind of one-time adjustment.

Several other transcripts also demonstrate that TAs often make decisions about how to address challenging situations by drawing on their knowledge about the program, course goals, or university culture. For example, another second-year student shares an experience in his second-semester class: drafts came in that didn't follow the guidelines for that assignment at all. He "knew," he said, that "101 knowledge wouldn't necessarily transfer" into his course — so he knew that he needed to teach and give time for revision. Because he had planned for it, he was able to respond by holding a "revision boot camp" in class, and as he'd predicted, the second drafts were much better. His already developing sense of how people learn through the arc of the program ensured that he faced this challenge with forethought rather than frustration.

A first-year instructor articulates a challenge that he also approached with a larger context in mind. He details the challenge of teaching students how to do exploratory writing rather than the argument-based writing they were more comfortable with, and he relays his struggle to really teach students how to explore in their writing. While he didn't have a lot of resources to draw from — his strategies for responding to this challenge were to "be there for the students when they struggle" — he shows awareness of the larger teaching goals at stake: he notes that "the goal is to teach. I want them to struggle, to experience cognitive dissonance." Accounts like these show instructors addressing pedagogical challenges through a sense of their larger goals for teaching and their role within a program. Their attention turns inward to their own decisions about what and how to teach in a writing class. However, these fourteen pedagogy-based accounts make up only about one-third of the narratives.

## STORIES OF STUDENTS

The majority of TAs, when asked this question, did not choose to tell stories about a pedagogy challenge. Instead, the stories involved students in a variety of ways. Fully seventy-five percent of these narratives (30 out of 40) revolved around challenges with students: stories of resistance (16), student behavior (9), or student-teacher relationships (5). We're treading tentatively here, as we want to be true to the data — and we are also aware of how carefully these new instructors were working to unpack teaching challenges and think through why they occurred. These new instructors, then, *weren't* blaming students. There were moments of frustration, but the frustration was rooted in not feeling successful with a particular student — and usually not in it being the student's fault. That said, for the majority of respondents, a "teaching challenge" was a "student challenge."

### Students — Resistance

In accounts we've coded as being about student resistance, these new instructors are stymied by teaching challenges that seem to be related directly to students' attitudes about the course and most use the word "resistance" in their account. For example, this first-year instructor explains his challenge:

> I currently have a student who hates technology, to the point where he wants to type all of his stuff out on a typewriter. And that would be okay with me, except that we build Web sites for unit one. So, that was a real challenge . . . he didn't want to talk to me. He didn't want to seek my help. He didn't wanna, like, anything else. And I just sort of had to keep telling him to come talk to me, but he never did. So, he ended up turning in his stuff late. And so now the dilemma is, like, according to my late policy, he should get docked a certain amount of points. And do I dock him for his resistance to technology, or do I — you know, so, that's sort of a challenge.

And another first-year instructor relates a similar tale of resistance and frustration:

> But I did have a tricky situation with my . . . class. When I first came to class, I had a student who was particularly challenging. Everything I said he questioned, and he was the worst enemy as far as peer support went. He wasn't very well liked in the class. Luckily, he didn't kind of turn the tide as far as the class was concerned. But I had to really work on my own judgment of him, because I didn't particularly care for his personality. But I had to listen to what he said, and I had to respond each time in a patient manner. Because letting yourself become impatient in front of the classes, I think, is not a good trait of a teacher. So he really tested my patience. Every day he had a challenge that he had for whatever it was I had said. And, you know, one time it was I told them that on their blog they couldn't use text messaging language. And he brought up some linguistics theory saying, like, "Doesn't language always change and aren't we the ones who create our own language?" which would've been, you know, interesting arguments and valid if he wasn't presenting them simply to annoy. I mean, he's just that kind of person. So on the one hand, I wanted to listen to his arguments and maybe discuss that. But I also didn't want him to take up too much of the class time with something that was disingenuous. Yep, he would also say things like — when I had them get into a

circle, he said, like, "That's hippie shit. My parents taught me not to trust hippies," you know. So he was also very aggressive. But he disappeared about couple months into the class if that, maybe month and a half. He just disappeared. So he took care of himself.

Students who don't respond to instructors' good intentions, to repeated attempts to provide support, or to the course in general are described as "resistant" in a variety of ways. For new instructors, clearly individual student reactions loom large.

## Students — Studenting

Other accounts stem from student behaviors, or what we call studenting: what to do with students who don't come to class, who come unprepared, or who are dealing with challenges in other parts of their lives. For example, this second-year TA tells a narrative that shares features with other stories in this category:

I had a student who e-mailed a couple of months ago and said that he was having some emotional issues and then he asked if I could work with him. He had only missed a couple of days of class at that point. I said, "Sure, I can work with you." But then I didn't hear from him for four weeks I think, so I had just kind of assumed at that point that he had dropped the class or that he wasn't planning on coming back to the class, because my attendance policy was pretty clear. But then he showed up in class and so this addressing this, having to talk to him about how I couldn't pass him in the class after he had missed that much class time. That was tricky.

A second-year TA explains the challenge of a certain kind of writing center consultation:

Well, I had something happen to me that happens not extremely frequently but sort of often where someone comes in, and it's not they don't want to be there, but they just sort of want to answer the questions themselves before really reflecting on it I think. And so at that point you do sort of have to try to ask more pointed questions and sort of try to slow things down I think; even directly saying, "Hey, let's just sort of — we don't have to rush; let's just kind of take things slower." Make sure you communicate it.

These accounts show how new TAs work to understand how learners behave, and why, and what their roles as instructors are. These situations require decisions about how — and how intensively — to intervene when a student is off track. Since even experienced teachers often make such decisions situationally rather than based on a consistent rule, these instances reveal a category of teaching challenges that involve reflective problem solving.

## Student-Teacher Relationships

Five of the accounts reveal these new TAs' struggles with appropriate student-teacher relationships. Since new TAs inhabit the roles of graduate students and of instructors, it's not surprising that some challenges arise here. The following account, from a first-year TA who is describing an experience while working in the writing center, exemplifies the kind of challenges within this category:

> My biggest problem as a tutor was a student who had actually violated the [restriction on the] number of sessions. . . . And he was a really nice guy, but he wanted me to do everything for him, and he just sort of lost sight of what the relationship was like as the tutor and as a student coming in for help with a paper. And he would come, like knock on one of the session room doors while I was tutoring someone else and ask for help, or he would have an appointment with another tutor and beg them to switch with me, or if I went outside to eat some lunch or have a conversation, he would follow me out with his laptop and just kind of follow me around the office. . . . And while they [writing center directors] were sympathetic, I was sort of expecting the system to be in place to kind of help me out, because I didn't want to hurt this guy's feelings or make him feel like tutoring wasn't okay or that I couldn't help him. I just needed the rules to be enforced. And since there was no one doing it, I kind of got stuck and he hasn't come back for a tutoring session since I had to say something about it.

> At first I just kind of let him take advantage of the situation, because I just felt uncomfortable establishing rules. And it wasn't like he ever came to me to talk about anything that wasn't directly related to his papers. It is just that he thought, for some reason, that I was magically the only person who knew how to do MLA or who would read his memos quickly if he showed up late and you know offer advice. So I felt really uncomfortable and I didn't do much, and then eventually I was just like, I am sorry. I can't help you unless you make an appointment, and when you make an appointment you need to show up on time. If you miss your appointment, you need to call and cancel beforehand and you can't make appointments in other people's names or just show up and yeah, so eventually I suppose I handled it in the way that I was supposed to have.

New TAs struggle as they learn how to be authority figures, how to establish boundaries and rules with others in ways they have never had to before. As this participant explains — but hasn't had much opportunity to reflect on, yet — part of her challenge here was realizing that while she had mentors, there wasn't a "system" to save her from dealing with complicated human relationships. For perhaps the first time, she had to be the enforcer of policy, and moving into that role was deeply uncomfortable.

## UNSANCTIONED TEACHING NARRATIVES

Three of the stories told in answer to this set of prompts elicited responses that we're pretty confident these instructors wouldn't have shared if we had been the ones doing the interviews — or at least not in the exact ways that they were reported here. One involved a behavior (a TA drinking a lot the night before a class so that she'd be sick and have a reason to cancel it) that is not a "sanctioned" response to a teaching challenge; in another account, a participant directly says "I don't know if I'm allowed to say this." While there are not many of these accounts, they hint at the kinds of complicated teaching experiences TAs face and point out the short supply of spaces for reflective conversation about such experiences: none of these stories made it to the mentor at the institution where the interview took place.

Two of these accounts, both by female instructors, involve intimidating male students. In one of these, the first-year instructor describes a student with whom she struggled all semester. An interviewer interpolates questions. The instructor says:

> Okay. [This student] talks a lot. And he has some buddies in there, too. And they're a little bit more controllable, but this particular student is just completely, like — I guess not uncontrollable, but he just talks all the time, and just will make comments, and while I'm in the middle of doing something or talking to another student, and he'll just be completely — I don't know — out of — I don't know — I can't even . . . I just be like, "Please don't talk."
>
> And the other day, he was way aggressive to me about a grade that I gave him. And I didn't think it was unfair, but he kind of was a little aggressive. And that was odd to me, because — I mean, he's a big guy, and he's a little scary. And he's been so obnoxious, really, in class, that I was just kind of — I think I handled it okay, but had to just remind myself not to get mad back at him, or react to his previous behavior. But it was scary.

*How did you respond?*

> Oh, yeah, I had to — I was like — I had to be calm, you know, "Hey, this is why I gave you the grade. I don't think it was unfair. These are the things you could have done better." But he was saying — he was just really, "I still don't understand . . ." And I just had to remain calm, and that's hard. And especially with a student who I've been kind of mad at for the whole semester. So, that was tricky.

*Why did you respond in this way?*

> Well, he, like — he was like, "Can you come talk to me?" And so I had to walk over there. It was after class; everyone else had gone, which was probably a little —

Unfortunately, she doesn't finish this thought, although the implication seems to be that it was not a wise choice to talk with this guy (who's "a little scary") alone in the classroom after class. This new instructor knew to "remain calm" even though she'd been "kind of mad" at him for the semester. Her story — about a student who made her mad all semester, a student she was scared of but met in private anyway, a student she did not tell the composition director about — reveals a new instructor trying to process what this experience meant for her and how she reacted. More generally, she tries to figure out whether this student is being appropriate in class or whether he might be "uncontrollable"; like other TAs, she might benefit from reflection and additional input into her analysis.

Another instructor, a second-year TA, relates a very different kind of ambiguous, challenging, ongoing experience that we have with students every once in a while — experiences for which senior faculty eventually develop a repertoire of responses. For her "tricky" situation, she describes a long and complicated account of working with a student who keeps insisting that she turned work in, and yet the instructor cannot find it. After this happens repeatedly throughout the semester, another mix-up occurs at the final portfolio time. The student hands in her portfolio to the instructor's mailbox — without a required second essay. However, because of the ongoing complications, and because it's the end of the semester and the instructor is confused herself, she gives the portfolio a passing grade even though it's incomplete. She explains:

> But that moment, I was just like — I was like — just wanted to be done with it. I read her portfolio; it didn't have the essay in it, but I just — I gave her like — I gave her a passing grade, trying to keep in mind that it was my fault that her paper was gone.

> It's probably like one of those moments that I'm not very proud of as a teacher, but I was really not — did not have a great semester, so I was just trying to get it done. But that was a really sticky situation, where I couldn't confront the student and say, "You're basically lying to me and I know it."

These unresolvable, uncomfortable scenarios are particularly tricky for new teachers, who haven't yet figured out what should be followed up on and what doesn't need to be. They're also the kind of scenario that is particularly useful for us as instructors: as mentors, we weren't aware of these situations, and so they give us glimpses into the decisions and reactions that new instructors make all the time whether we're available for feedback or not.

## TAs' Resources for Teaching Challenges

These lively, honest, human accounts from new instructors reveal engaged, thoughtful people working to grow: to learn from their students, to be tentative, to think through teaching challenges and why they've approached them in the ways that they have. They are neither the stories of rank neophytes nor the stories of experienced faculty. These stories of pedagogy and of students again point to areas of inquiry for those of us who work to support new instructors; we might work, for example, to provide space for discussing "student" challenges — and then for reframing those challenges and revising responses to them.

Collectively, the participants utilized a range of strategies for *how* they responded to these challenging or tricky situations. Within their accounts, they note that they tried the following:

- Clarifying the issue, approach, or class with students directly (8)
- Taking another teaching approach (11)
- Taking another communication approach (e-mail, conferences, printed written instructions) (5)
- Sticking to a course policy (3)
- Reflecting on teaching practices/context (2)
- Remaining calm and using humor (2)
- Talking to a peer or mentor (1)
- Acknowledging students' frustration and reframing it as an opportunity for revision (1)
- Following up with resources beyond the classroom (counseling center) (1)
- Redoing final grades to give students benefit of the doubt (1)
- Being there for students when they struggle (1)

Most of these strike us as healthy, productive reactions; it's wonderful that sixteen TAs identified ways in which they tried another approach after the initial teaching or communication approach wasn't successful, for example.

At the same time, we worry that simply "clarifying" an assignment, or "being there" for students, points toward a lack of resources: new instructors simply have not yet developed a large composition pedagogy repertoire. For example, a first-year TA first discusses his challenge of really getting students to write in an inquiry-based (rather than argumentative) way. His response, he says, is to "give the assignment and be there when they struggle." While he goes on to discuss this in a way that does echo program-wide goals, noting that he wants students to "experience cognitive dissonance," we wonder about the sparseness of approaches that he is able to recollect and apply.

Four TAs' accounts were unresolved or unsuccessful, but they acknowledged what they had learned for the next time they addressed a similar situation (developing models that they didn't yet have, for example, or intervening with a struggling student much earlier, or giving more guidance). For the majority of these TAs, the challenges were presented as resolved and they believed that they had learned from the incident. At the same time, the "unsanctioned" accounts and the accounts where TAs had few real resources for approaching these teaching challenges help us think about how to provide more effective and appropriate TA mentoring, across several semesters or even years, which we discuss below.

## LEARNING FROM TAs: IMPLICATIONS, POSSIBILITIES, CHALLENGES

As mentors of these TAs, we find that the implications of the two portions of interview data that we've focused on in this article loom large for us: what will we do now, knowing what we now know? Like so many of our colleagues, we teach in programs where the graduate curricular landscape is highly contested; we're experienced enough to know that institutional and cultural changes unfold slowly. Still, these data point us to reconsiderations for our own programs and for the teaching and mentoring of TAs in English departments, writing departments, and first-year writing programs across the country.

Just as scholars have worked hard within composition studies to make clear that first-year writing is *not* successful as a one-shot writing inoculation, so too do we need to make clear — in what we say, in our institutional structures, in our work with new TA instructors themselves — that one graduate pedagogy seminar is not and cannot be a one-shot teaching inoculation. Instead, we'll all benefit if we stop selling (or institutionally identifying) "the" TA pedagogy course as the one course to "get" it. Such a structure cre ates several unintended re-percussions. First, it tells our colleagues in other English subdisciplines that learning to teach is a relatively quick process to be moved through in a semester, and that graduate TAs are "done" after they've learned to teach first-year writing. This is the tale many of us were told, of course, and our own experiences years ago as TAs inevitably color discussions we initiate about supporting and mentoring TAs. However, the "we were given a textbook and did just fine" argument should not supplant data-based decisions, based on new knowledge about what it means to learn to teach.

Second, a one-semester approach — even a one-semester-plus approach, including lots of mentoring, meetings, informal workshops, and in-service/ in-services training — also tells these new graduate instructors that really they should be "done" after that initial experience (with perhaps some minor brushups here and there). As one TA in his third semester of teaching noted, he was "expecting to have ironed out some of these problems sooner." He continues, "I'm assuming that it's not just my inability to overcome problems [but] that it just seems that way . . . in a few ways, it's kind of frustrating just not being perfect." In contrast, we are reminded of Nancy Sommers and Laura Saltz's (2004) research on writing development over time: writing students are able to learn more, they note, when they are able to accept that they're novices and need to learn. When we communicate to new instructors early on that they can fully learn to teach in a short period of time, we short-circuit their opportunities for growth. If, instead, it's clear to them that learning writing pedagogy really is a long-term process, then they can approach it as a different kind of puzzle to work with — a longer-term, ongoing, thousand-piece puzzle, not a quick teaching game.

Instead of settling for an approach that leaves TAs frustrated about imperfection after three semesters of teaching, we can aim to do better in what we preach and how we practice it. To counter the institutional message that people can learn writing pedagogy in a one-semester seminar, we imagine a variety of approaches appropriate for different institutions. Just as some first-year writing programs recognize the need to "stretch" writing instruction over two semesters and to advocate for an overt structure for writing pedagogy across an institution's curriculum, we too see the clear need to stretch our institutional approach to learning pedagogy. Two seminars is one possibility; another is an ongoing, required internship or colloquium for graduate credit that establishes a structure for regular meetings, discussions and reflection. At the same time, departments and programs can articulate their commitment to nurturing teacher-scholars through mission statements and program outcomes — for *all* programs of graduate study — that include an expectation of involvement with learning about teaching throughout each graduate student's program of study.

Moreover, the very interviews we conducted, as a genre, indicate to us how vital added spaces for guided discussions of teaching are. Teachers use talk to process, interpret, and analyze teaching experiences; interactions with other peer instructors (Nelson et al. 2010) and mentors (Rust 1999) are crucial to teacher development and growth (Cohen 2008; Miller 2008). Our set of interviews makes visible a continuum of talk about teaching, from mediated to less mediated, with the more-mediated discussions of the pedagogy seminar classroom on one end of the continuum and the informal interactions of the communal TA office at the other end. To foster third (and fourth) spaces for pedagogy talk, we imagine networks of sites for talk: mentoring groups, teaching circles, colloquia, discussion boards. We can make the ongoing process of learning to teach more visible through guided discussions where we might ask instructors — before, during, and especially after their pedagogy seminar — to identify the origins of their beliefs and then to re-see those possibilities in conversations with peers. On the principle that we should help new teachers practice what we want them to be able to do as reflective practitioners, we can ask them, at various points over several semesters, to identify teaching challenges and tricky situations from their classrooms and then help them reflect on and work to understand those challenges in light of multiple scholarly and communal resources. Such approaches will help TAs broaden their repertoire of possible approaches as well as sharpen their skills at creating reasonable responses to challenging pedagogical situations.

Our interview data does not let us directly evaluate the pedagogy classes we teach, the in-service training we provide, or the mentoring we encourage, but because we take responsibility for helping new instructors begin articulating and shaping their beliefs about teaching and their approaches to the classroom, what we learn from these interviews does help us think about our work in these settings. Do we play a key role in these new instructors' lives? Of course. Many voluntarily brought up ideas they had encountered in our pedagogy seminars, teaching approaches they had learned there, meetings they'd had with us as individuals. And yet, our work with them is one (important, we still think!) influence among multiple streams of influences, cultural models and expectations, and experiences that new instructors are negotiating. Their voices speak back to us, reminding us all to approach learning writing pedagogy as being as much of a developmental process as learning to write.

## NOTE

Thanks to Jim Fredricksen for the phrase how people learn from pedagogy.

## WORKS CITED

Barr Ebest, Sally. 2005. *Changing the Way We Teach: Writing and Resistance in the Training of Teaching Assistants*. Carbondale: Southern Illinois University Press.

Bishop, Wendy. 1990. *Something Old, Something New: College Writing Teachers and Classroom Change*. Carbondale: Southern Illinois University Press.

Briggs, Charles. 1986. *Learning How to Ask: A Sociolinguistic Appraisal of the Role of the Interview in Social Science Research*. Cambridge: Cambridge University Press.

Brooke, Robert. 1987. "Underlife and Writing Instruction." *College Composition and Communication* 38.2: 141 – 53.

Cohen, Jennifer L. 2008. "'That's Not Treating You as a Professional': Teachers Constructing Complex Professional Identities through Talk." *Teachers and Teaching: Theory and Practice* 14.2: 79 – 93.

Dobrin, Sidney I., ed. 2005. *Don't Call It That: The Composition Practicum*. Urbana, IL: National Council of Teachers of English.

Estrem, Heidi, and E. Shelley Reid. 2012. "Writing Pedagogy Education: Instructor Development in Composition Studies." In *Exploring Composition Studies: Sites, Issues, and Perspectives*, ed. Kelly Ritter and Paul Matsuda, 223 – 40.Logan: Utah State University Press.

Freire, Paulo. 1970. *Pedagogy of the Oppressed*. New York: Continuum.

Harris, Joseph. 1996. *A Teaching Subject: Composition Since 1966*. Logan: Utah State University Press.

Kennedy, Mary M. 1998. *Learning to Teach Writing: Does Teacher Education Make a Difference?* New York: Teachers College Press.

Miller, Matthew. 2008. "Problem-Based Conversations: Using Preservice Teachers Problems as a Mechanism for Their Professional Development." *Teacher Education Quarterly* 35.4: 77 – 98.

Nelson, Tamara Holmlund, Angie Deuel, David Slavit, and Anne Kennedy. 2010. "Leading Deep Conversations in Collaborative Inquiry Groups." *Clearing House* 83: 175 – 79.

Pytlik, Betty P., and Sarah Liggett. 2002. *Preparing College Teachers of Writing: Histories, Theories, Programs, Practices.* New York: Oxford University Press.

Rankin, Elizabeth. 1994. *Seeing Yourself as a Teacher: Conversations with Five New Teachers in a University Writing Program.* Urbana, IL: National Council of Teachers of English.

Reid, E. Shelley, and Heidi Estrem. Forthcoming. "The Effects of Writing Pedagogy Education on Graduate Teaching Assistants' Approaches to Teaching Composition." *WPA: Writing Program Administration.*

Rust, Frances O'Connell. 1999. "Professional Conversations: New Teachers Explore Teaching through Conversation, Story, and Narrative." *Teaching and Teacher Education* 15: 367 – 80.

Seidman, Irving. 2006. *Interviewing as Qualitative Research: A Guide for Researchers in Education and the Social Sciences.* New York: Teachers College Press.

Soja, Edward. 1996. *Thirdspace: Journeys to Los Angeles and Other Real-and-Imagined Places.* Cambridge, MA: Blackwell.

Sommers, Nancy, and Laura Saltz. 2004. "The Novice as Expert: Writing the Freshman Year." *College Composition and Communication* 56.1: 124 – 49.

Sprague, Jo, and Jody D. Nyquist. 1989. "TA Supervision." *New Directions for Teaching and Learning* 39: 37 – 53.

Ward, Irene, and Merry Perry. 2002. "A Selection of Strategies for Training Teaching Assistants." In *The Allyn & Bacon Sourcebook for Writing Program Administrators,* ed. Irene Ward and William J. Carpenter, 117 – 38. New York: Longman.

## APPENDIX A: RESEARCH SITE CHARACTERISTICS

Table 3. TA education and mentoring at the time of the study

|  | George Mason University | Boise State University |
|---|---|---|
| Yearly cohort | Twelve to fourteen (mostly) MFAs per cohort; up to half of 3rd-year cohort moves from TAships to nonteaching fellowships | Roughly seventeen MA TAships (literature, rhetoric and composition) and seventeen MFA TAships (poetry or fiction) |
| Teaching responsibilities | 3-year TAship<br>*Year 1:* Writing Center tutoring (complies with Southern Area Colleges and Schools' 18-credit-hour rule for teachers of record)<br>*Year 2:* Teach two FYC in fall, two Intro to Literature classes in spring<br>*Year 3:* Repeat Year 2 (option for one Intro to Creative Writing section) | 3-year TAship<br>*Year 1:* Teach 1+2 1st-year composition (FYC) each year<br>*Year 2:* Teach 1+2 FYC each year; a few advanced opportunities for MA and MFA students (literature surveys, Writing Center, creative writing 200-level courses)<br>*Year 3:* MFA students continue to teach a combination of 200-level creative writing courses and 1st-year writing courses |
| FYC curricular structure | Learning-goals-based curriculum; TAs choose texts and create syllabi | Outcomes-based curriculum; course reader and syllabus initial outline provided to 3rd-year TAs; TAs choose texts and create syllabi for subsequent semesters |
| Preteaching support | Noncredit Writing Center education; observations of FYC sessions with mentor; composition pedagogy seminar | Online work during previous spring and during summer; 8-day presemester workshop in August |

|  | George Mason University | Boise State University |
|---|---|---|
| First-year peda-gogy education | Monthly small group mentoring and individual consultations; two class observations; literature pedagogy course in spring | Graduate composition pedagogy seminar in fall while teaching one section of English 101; two class observations of others; class observation |
| Continuing support | Informal mentoring in 3rd year | Informal professional de-velopment meetings twice monthly in 2nd and 3rd years; informal meetings and classroom visits with mentor TA |
| TAs as mentors | May serve as mentor TAs in 2nd or 3rd year | May serve as mentor TAs in their 2nd and 3rd years |

## APPENDIX B: INTERVIEW QUESTIONS

(*Italicized* questions are suggested for interviewer follow-up, if needed.)

1. What is your program status: first year, second year, third year?

2. Please state whether you are male or female.

3. How many complete semesters, including this one, have you tutored writing?

4. How many complete semesters, including this one, have you taught composition?

5. Did you teach or tutor somewhere else before you came to [uni-versity]? (*What, and for how long?*)

6. Which pedagogy classes have you taken so far — including any you are currently enrolled in?

7. Please tell me, what are some of your main steps or thought-processes as you prepare a writing-class syllabus? (*Are there any other issues or goals you consider?*)

8. Now can you tell me, what are some of your main steps or thought-processes as you prepare to teach/tutor a class meet-ing (or tutoring session)? (*Are there any other issues or goals you consider?*)

9. Please tell me a little about a tricky, difficult, or surprising situation you encountered recently related to teaching writing,

either in class [while tutoring] or regarding a writing student [client]. (*What was difficult or surprising about it?*)

10. How did you respond? (*How are you planning to respond?*)

11. Why did (*will*) you respond that way?

12. What do you see as three or four key principles for your teaching [tutoring] of writing? (*In other words, what do you think is important for you to do as a writing teacher [tutor]? What do you try always to do or not do?*)

13. Could you say where those principles come from, or are related to? (*Were they from something you read or learned, something you heard of or saw someone doing, some experience you had?*)

14. What one or two questions or issues remain most uncertain and/or challenging for you about teaching [tutoring] writing?

15. How do you cope with that uncertainty right now?

16. Do any (more) of your principles help you cope? [*Interviewer may remind interviewee of answers to Question 12.*]

17. Are there any other ways that the principles you mentioned earlier, or other principles, come into play as you plan classes or solve problems?

18. On a scale of 1 to 5 — with 1 being "not much at all" and 5 being "quite a lot" — how often do you find yourself thinking of your teaching-principles when you are involved in the following activities:

    • planning your syllabus (*even for those who are currently only tutoring*)
    • planning your class day or tutoring session
    • teaching/tutoring your session
    • responding to student writing
    • problem solving as a teacher/tutor

19. Do you have other comments about or reflections on your recent teaching or teacher preparation that you'd like to add to this interview?

# PRESENT TENSE

Present Tense is on the Web at http://www.presenttensejournal.org/

*Present Tense: A Journal of Rhetoric in Society* is a peer-reviewed, blind-refereed, online journal dedicated to exploring contemporary social, cultural, political and economic issues through a rhetorical lens. In addition to examining these subjects as found in written, oral and visual texts, we wish to provide a forum for calls to action in academia, education and national policy. Seeking to address current or presently unfolding issues, we publish short articles ranging from 2,000 to 2,500 words, the length of a conference paper.

### A Womb With a View: Identifying the Culturally Iconic Fetal Image in Prenatal Ultrasound Provisions

The editors of *Present Tense* believe that "A Womb with a View" represents the best in shorter-form academic publishing. Not only is Rochelle Gregory's work accessible, but it also tackles a politically important and powerful issue of current value and meaning. Further, this article is just as rigorous, critical, and, perhaps most importantly, timely, as any article published in more traditional academic essay lengths.

# 12 A Womb With a View: Identifying the Culturally Iconic Fetal Image in Prenatal Ultrasound Provisions

*Rochelle Gregory*

In the past fifty years, medical advances have allowed doctors to view human embryos (less than ten weeks' gestation) and fetuses (after ten weeks' gestation) via prenatal ultrasound technology ("Fetal Development"). These procedures allow doctors to identify potential birth defects and maternal dangers without imposing risks upon the mother or the viability of the embryo or fetus. Fetal images, though, are neither self-explanatory nor universally recognized and have become "sites of struggle for meaning" (Perlmutter 22), meaning that this article will attempt to explore by arguing that ultrasound visualization is a complex and transformative act.

For abortion opponents, prenatal ultrasound images offer a "definitive declaration that these pictures tell one story and unveil one truth—that life begins at the moment of conception" (Boucher 9). These images have been used, for example, to deter women from terminating their pregnancies in anti-abortion media such as the film The Silent Scream, at interactive mall kiosks like Truth Booth's A Window to the Womb, and on websites such as National Right to Life, Pro-Life Action League, Abortionfacts.com, and the Heritage House 76. And, since the mid-1990s, lawmakers in Texas and twenty other states have enacted legislation that "regulate[s] the provision of ultrasound" by requiring providers to perform or offer to perform an ultrasound on each patient seeking an abortion ("Requirements for Ultrasound").

Most recently in 2011, Texas Governor Rick Perry signed House Bill 15, more commonly known as the Texas Abortion-Sonogram Law; House Bill 15 is considered the most restrictive legislation of its kind in the United States since it requires doctors to display the images to the patient from live, real-time prenatal ultrasounds and to "make the heartbeat audible and describe the fetus' [or embryo's] dimensions, cardiac activity and internal and external organs" (Ackerman). Additionally, this legislation requires that "the provider must give [a patient] a detailed verbal description of the image unless she was raped, has a court order waiving parental consent or is ending the pregnancy because of a fetal abnormality" ("Abortion").

Proponents of ultrasound provisions have stated that such legislation's purpose is to dissuade women from terminating their pregnancies. During the House and Senate debates on the legislation, proponents including Governor Perry argued that the law would ensure that "Texans have access to all the information when making such an important decision" and that the legislation is a "critical step in our efforts to protect life" (qtd. in Tinsely), and Senator Jane Nelson of Flower Mound, Texas stated, "I believe that women will understand [with this bill] that if they choose to have an abortion, that is indeed a life" (qtd. in Tinsely). Critics of the bill, however, have argued that the law is an attempt to shame and humiliate a patient seeking an abortion in order to discourage her from terminating her pregnancy. Senator Wendy Davis of Fort Worth, Texas noted that the law is "cloaked under the guise of informing women ... but the intent is to torture women psychologically" (qtd. in Tinsely). As one online commentator noted, "Conservative legislators have fantasies of women seeing fully formed babies on monitors, bursting into tears, and running out of the clinics" (Marcotte).

Still, it is clear that for representatives like Nelson and Perry, prenatal ultrasounds offer self-evident images that require little explanation, interpretation, or mediation of the embryo or fetus as it exists within a woman's womb. Images of embryos and fetuses affect not only the "larger cultural climate of reproductive politics but also the experience and consciousness of pregnant women" (Petchesky 265) and often provoke strong reactions, including outrage. Ultrasound provisions, specifically, exploit the cultural significance of the iconic fetal image in order to dissuade a patient from terminating her pregnancy. In essence, these legislative measures encourage a patient to identify (inappropriately and incorrectly) her embryo or fetus as the culturally iconic fetus, one that is viable, fully developed, and autonomous.

## Transformation of the Culturally Iconic Fetal Image

At the onset, prenatal ultrasounds appear to offer photographic representations of embryonic and fetal development in utero. These images are perceived to be *indexical* signs that stand "unequivocally for this or that existing thing" (Peirce 4: 531) due to the perceived "genuine relationship" or "direct physical connection" between the embryo or fetus and the image (Peirce 2: 285). Other examples of indexical signs might include driver's license or passport photographs or an exit sign with an arrow pointing toward the door. The image of the embryo or fetus is a sign in which the "signifier is not arbitrary but is directly connected in some way (physically or causally) to the signified" (Chandler 37); in this case, an indexical sign of a fetus at six weeks' gestation might appear on screen as indistinguishable on a monitor (Figure 1). As an indexical sign, the prenatal ultrasound image conveys "a certain mystique in our culture that [might] be described by terms such as 'absolutely analogical' and 'message without a code'" (Mitchell 61).

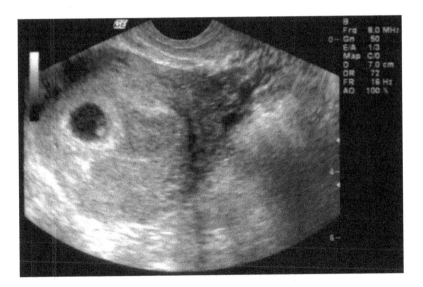

Figure 1 ("Sonogram Human Foetal Ultrasound Scan at 6 Weeks")

However, a closer examination of prenatal ultrasound images illustrates how they are considered to be persuasive tools that will dissuade women from terminating their pregnancies because prenatal ultrasound images of the embryo or fetus are attributed with the cultural status of being *iconic signs*. Iconic signs, by definition, resemble or possess a likeness of what they signify and "have the modality of direct perception" (Hodge and Kress 27). Additionally, while iconic signs are supposedly transparent, they reflect cultural conventions that often make these signs highly evocative (Chandler 40). In this case, the culturally iconic image is the autonomous, fully developed (regardless of gestational age), eight-pound, twenty-inch fetus (Figure 2).

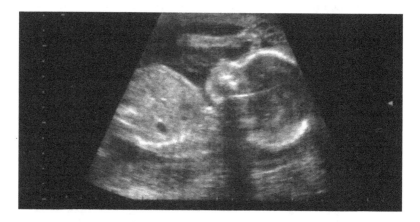

Figure 2 ("Sonogram Human Foetal Ultrasound Scan at 22 Weeks"

An examination of these fetal ultrasound images illustrates how they transform from indexical to iconic signs in the cultural contexts of reproductive legislation. Ultrasound legislation intends to dissuade patients from terminating their pregnancies because they are expected to visualize the culturally iconic image of a fully formed, healthy, miniature human floating in the space of its amniotic sac. In short, in the context of legislation like House Bill 15, the image of the embryo or fetus is perceived to be a persuasive tool for pro-life advocates and legislators because there is no recognition or awareness that a transformation of an indexical sign to the culturally iconic one has occurred during the visualization.

This shift—from the indexical sign to the culturally iconic image—is possible because, as iconic signs, prenatal ultrasound images vaguely represent the embryos' or fetus' physical features, are absent of color and definite form, and lack specificity. The culturally iconic image of embryo and fetus displaces the "mother" by representing "the fetus as primary and autonomous, the woman as absent or peripheral" (Petchesky 268). The prenatal ultrasound image reduces the "incidental elements" of the mother, the doctor, and the technology itself. As such, the fetus is completely independent from the womb and appears to be completely viable—irrespective of gestational development.

While research suggests that ultrasound provisions have no effect on abortion rates (Gold), legislators perceive these images to be effective rhetorical tools that would dissuade a patient from attaining an abortion because these images blur "the boundary between fetus and baby; they reinforce the idea that the fetus's identity as separate and autonomous from the mother (the 'living, separate child') exists from the start" (Petchesky 272). The significance of the culturally iconic image is evident considering that if a woman were viewing a prenatal ultrasound image prior to an abortion, the embryo or fetus on the monitor is (in most cases) less than twelve weeks' gestation.

Despite this significant distinction, ultrasound provisions seek to exploit the shift from an indexical sign to the culturally iconic image of the fetus in order to dissuade women from terminating their pregnancies. As Governor Perry issued in a statement, ultrasound provisions ensure that women, upon viewing the ultrasound image, understand "the devastating impact of such a life-ending decision" ("Statement"). Texas Right to Life Director Elizabeth Graham and Legislative Director John Seago concur that the legislation is intended to dissuade women from terminating their pregnancies by encouraging women to see themselves in the ultrasound images as mothers (to unborn, yet fully formed infants) rather than as naïve young girls: "A sonogram transforms a confused customer into a mother willing to rise off the table, walk out of the abortion mill, and choose Life. The last option [abortion providers such as] Planned Parenthood wants is for a frightened girl to take time, to even think, to have a chance to change her mind" (qtd. in Ertelt).

## IRREFUTABILITY AND TIMELESSNESS OF FETAL IMAGES AS ICONIC SIGNS

The persuasive appeal of the iconic fetal image is its supposed irrefutability and timelessness. As a culturally iconic sign, the fetal image reductively "epitomizes the distortion inherent in all photographic images: their tendency to slice up reality into tiny bits wrenched out of real space and time" (Petchesky 268). The fetal image as a sign relies on the outlines of objects and entails a "'reduction' of objects' outlines into a more elementary representational form, in which only the basic underlying structure is retained and many incidental elements are discarded" (Messaris 13). Iconic signs appear to be factual, positive, educational, and informative, but what we see when looking at a prenatal ultrasound image is a reflection of our experiences and desires. As David Blakesley writes, "What we see, even at the moment of perception, is a consequence of what we're looking for" (130). As such, legislation like House Bill 15 seeks to exploit this transformation of the fetal image from an indexical sign of a six-week fetus to the culturally iconic image of the thirty-two-week fetus. What viewers perceive to be the image of the fetus on the computer screen is really a collection of shaded pixels according to certain criteria programmed into the computer; the resulting image appears to be "human" although it must be interpreted and described by qualified technicians and physicians.

Additionally, the visualization and transformation of the fetal image relies on the technology to capture fetal images—technology that is neither invisible nor neutral. Technology is "impure" and can easily manipulate "humans and what it means to be human" (Burnett 141). Medical and scientific images that seem to "peer" into the body particularly challenge notions of "what it means to be flesh and blood" (141); visualization involves "the embodiment and the transformation of information into knowledge and understanding through human activity and the conversion of [that] information and knowledge by humans into material and aesthetic forms" (202). Despite the perceived transparency of the fetal image presumed by legislators, the prenatal ultrasound requires doctors and skilled technicians to interpret what appear to the patient as black and white dots. Nothing is inherently "life-like" in the image; rather, in this case, through the visualization of the image, it has transformed into a means of immersion, where parents become a part of the image and the experience, and a perceived connection and closeness with the image exists. As such, viewing has become a "haze of mediation, experience, and screen" (Burnett 7).

Burnett's point—that visualization and transformation are social acts—illustrates the complexities of prenatal ultrasound images. These images are, on the one hand, supposedly easily understood and representational images of gestational development that should be removed from biological contexts. In the scenario, then, of a woman seeking an abortion, the prenatal ultrasound image directly represents the embryo or fetus, which according to legislators should be a very powerful visual rhetoric against terminating a pregnancy. However, this scene illustrates the contradiction of such rhetoric considering that medical experts must interpret and describe the image in order to reinforce to the patient what she sees and hears during the procedure. In this scenario, then, only trained technicians who are able to "read" prenatal ultrasounds can administer them—a point that undercuts all claims to the indexical or self-evidentiary nature of these images. In other words, the abortion-sonogram legislation requires doctors to describe the images because, without such a description, patients would not make the appropriate transformation from an indexical sign to a culturally iconic one. Only an expert can interpret prenatal ultrasound images—a point that identifies any "doubts about the clarity of what is being seen" (Boucher 16). Prenatal ultrasound images are only considered "factual" by those who accept an ethos of medical technology as definitively and objectively "truthful."

Just as visual images' constructed meanings are not "transparent and universally understood, but culturally specific" (Kress and van Leeuwen 3), these images are hardly irrefutable and timeless because their rhetorical effectiveness relies on the cultural contexts in which the images appear. Prenatal ultrasound images are perceived to be factual, positive, educational, and informative in a cultural context that accepts them as such, and maternal bonding through the awareness of the human body is culturally specific and defined. While this awareness has been defined as unequivocally biologically linked, all "positive" awareness is culturally defined. As Petchesky notes, arguments that suggest the "timing of maternal-fetus or maternal-infant attachment is a biological given [...] contradict women's changing historical experience" (283).

An example of this transformation and mediation is clear in the popularity and appropriation by anti-abortion advocates of Lennart Nilsson's famous images of the fetus suspended in the womb in *Life* magazine on April 30, 1965 (later republished in "Drama of Life Before Birth: Landmark Work Five Decades Later") and in his book and on his website A Child is Born. While Nilsson's images have been widely used and distributed in anti-abortion literature, Nilsson's photographs were actually aborted fetuses, a point that illustrates how technology mediates and transforms an iconic sign:

> Although claiming to show the living fetus, Nilsson actually photographed abortus material obtained from women who terminated their pregnancies under the liberal Swedish law. Working with dead embryos allowed Nilsson to experiment with lighting, background and positions, such as placing the thumb into the fetus' mouth. ("The Lonesome Space Traveller")

These famous photographs have been manipulated in anti-abortion discourses as symbolic props that continue to shape reproductive rights campaigns some fifty years after they were first published.

The fetal image, like Nilsson's, presents what Roland Barthes referred to as a coded iconic message that requires little interpretation because "there is always the stupefying evidence of *this is how it was*, giving us, by a precious miracle, a reality from which we are sheltered" (44). In this case, the prenatal ultrasound offers a woman the opportunity to transform what is presented on the monitor into a baby floating within intrauterine shelter of the womb beyond culture and context. This iconic image of the fetus offers an "abstract individualism, effacing the pregnant woman and the fetus's dependence on her" (Petchesky 270). This iconic fetal image possesses a "symbolic transparency" that encourages us to "read in it ourselves, our lost babies, our mythic secure past" (270).

## CONCLUSIONS

As this article has shown, the iconicity of the fetal image is all the more relevant considering reproductive legislation has emotional, fiscal, and legislative repercussions on women's reproductive health and freedom. The significance of the cultural iconic fetal image is illustrated even as legislators currently debate, amongst other concerns, whether to require invasive trans-vaginal ultrasounds (internal ultrasounds that are often required in cases where the gestation age is less than six weeks gestation) and how 3D technology will change ultrasound provisions. Additionally, some advocates of abortion provisions have demanded legislative inclusions that require only doctors and sonographers who do not have a financial interest in the abortion decision to administer prenatal ultrasounds (provisions that would require a patient to seek out a doctor to perform the ultrasound procedure who had no financial interest the patient's decision to proceed with an abortion). These advocates of provisions have also demanded requirements that doctors must determine and explain to patients that they are terminating "viable pregnancies" (Glessner). These iconic images have continued to shape political agendas that have far-reaching implications on women's health, and considering that fetal images are afforded an iconic status that plays a significant role in women's reproductive rights, they require a contextuality that is often, but cannot be, ignored.

## WORKS CITED

"Abortion." *Guttmacher Institute*. Guttmacher Institute, 1 May 2012. Web. 15 May 2012.

Ackerman, Todd. "Judge Stays Sonogram Law." *Chron.com*. Houston Chronicle, 30 Aug. 2011. Web. 15 May 2012.

Barthes, Roland. *Image-Music-Text*. Trans. Stephen Heath. New York: Hill and Wang, 1977. Print.

Blakesley, David. "Defining Film Rhetoric: The Case of Hitchcock's *Vertigo.*" *Defining Visual Rhetorics*. Eds. Charles A. Hill and Marguerite Helmers. Mahwah, NJ: Erlbaum, 2004. 111-34. Print.

Boucher, Joanne. "Ultrasound: A Window to the Womb?: Obstetric Ultrasound and the Abortion Rights Debate." *Journal of Medical Humanities* 25.1 (2004): 7-19. *EBSCO Academic Search Premiere*. Web. 14 Oct. 2005.

Burnett, Ron. *How Images Think*. Cambridge, MA: MIT P, 2005. Print.

Chandler, Daniel. *The Basics: Semiotics*. New York: Routledge, 2002. Print.

"Drama of Life Before Birth: Landmark Work Five Decades Later." *Life*. Life, 2012. Web. 6 June 2012.

Ertelt, Steven. "Victory: Appeals Court Upholds Texas' Ultrasound-Abortion Law." *LifeNews*. LifeNews, 10 Jan. 2012. Web. 15 May 2012.

"Fetal Development." *Medline Plus*. U. S. National Library of Medicine and National Institutes of Health, 19 Apr. 2012. Web. 15 May 2012.

Glessner, Thomas. "Effective Lifesaving Ultrasound Legislation." *At the Center* 13.1 (Winter 2012): N. pag. Web. 15 May 2012.

Gold, Rachel Benson. "All That's Old Is New Again: The Long Campaign To Persuade Women to Forgo Abortion." *Guttmacher Policy Review* 12.2 (Spring 2009): N. pag. Web. 2 Jan. 2012.

Hodge, Robert, and Gunther Kress. *Social Semiotics*. Ithaca: Cornell UP, 1988. Print.

"House Bill 15." *Texas Legislature Online*. State of Texas, 19 May 2011. Web. 2 Jan. 2012.

Kress, Gunther, and Theo van Leeuwen. *Reading Images: The Grammar of Visual Design*. New York: Routledge, 2005. Print.

"The Lonesome Space Traveller." *Making Visible Embryos*. University of Cambridge, 2008. Web. 2 Jan. 2012.

Marcotte, Amanda. "Texas Passes Ultrasound Requirement." *XXFactor*. Slate, 11 May 2011. Web. 2 Jan. 2012.

Messaris, Paul. *Visual Literacy: Image, Mind, and Reality*. Boulder: Westview, 1994. Print.

Mitchell, W. J. T. *Iconology: Image, Text, Ideology*. Chicago: U of Chicago P, 1986. Print.

Nilsson, Lennart. *A Child is Born*. Lennart Nilsson, n.d. Web. 6 June 2012.

Peirce, Charles. *Collected Papers*. Eds. Charles Hartshorne and Paul Weiss. 6 vols. Cambridge, MA: Harvard UP, 1931-35. Print.

Petchesky, Rosalind Pollack. "Fetal Images: The Power of Visual Culture in the Politics of Reproduction." *Feminist Studies* 13.2 (1987): 269-92. JSTOR. Web. 14 Oct. 2005.

Perlmutter, David D. *Photojournalism and Foreign Policy: Icons of Outrage in International Crisis*. Westport, CT: Praeger, 1998. Print.

"Requirements for Ultrasound." *Guttmacher Institute*. Guttmacher Institute, 1 May 2012. Web. 15 May 2012.

"Sonogram Human Foetal Ultrasound Scan at 6 Weeks." *DHD Multimedia Gallery*. Damon Hart-Davis, n.d. Web. 3 Jan. 2012.

"Statement by Gov. Rick Perry on Federal Appeals Court Overturning Injunction of Sonogram Law." *The Office of Governor Rick Perry*. Rick Perry, 10 Jan. 2012. Web. 15 Jan. 2012.

# REFLECTIONS

*Reflections* is on the Web at http://reflec-tionsjournal.net/

*Reflections*, a peer reviewed journal, provides a forum for scholarship on civic writing, service-learning and public rhetoric. Originally founded as a venue for teachers, researchers, students and community partners to share research and discuss the theoretical, political and ethical implications of community-based writing and writing instruction, *Reflections* publishes a lively collection of essays, empirical studies, community writing, student work, interviews and reviews in a format that brings together emerging scholars and leaders in the fields of community-based writing and civic engagement.

### Prison Collaborative Writing: Building Strong Mutuality in Community-Based Learning

"Prison Collaborative Writing" was chosen not only for the research and writing, but for the way it empowers prison voices. Grace Wetzel believes that prison inmates, such as "Wes," must read, analyze, and write about the research on community-based learning as part of the empowerment process of critiquing his surroundings. By using reciprocal 'academic' and 'prison' scholarships, he eloquently critiques a prison system that robs inmates of their voices and thus humanization. It is this kind of reciprocity at many levels that makes this article the best.

# 13 Prison Collaborative Writing: Building Strong Mutuality in Community-Based Learning

*Grace Wetzel and "Wes"*

*Abstract: This essay explores the pedagogical lessons of student-inmate peer reviews conducted during a prison outreach project in a first-year composition class. Collaborative writing between inmates and students reveals the positive outcomes that can result from strong mutuality in community-based learning relationships. Through a qualitative analysis of student reflection papers and prisoner oral reflections, this essay shows how an emphasis on the personal during this project did not preclude systemic considerations, but rather produced productive, political outcomes. This essay concludes with a response from my community partner—a prisoner in a medium security facility and participant in the peer reviews. We hope to demonstrate how a reciprocal, relationship-based orientation can facilitate not only productive community-based learning outcomes for students and communities, but also a new type of scholarship—one more thoroughly enriched by community voices.*

Most service and community-based learning practitioners can recall Bruce Herzberg's seminal article, "Community Service and Critical Teaching," published in *College Composition and Communication* in 1994. Herzberg shared lessons from a course that investigated the power structures inherent in the educational system, while also engaging students in literacy tutoring at a homeless shelter. Yet this service learning component was not entirely successful. The problem, according to Aaron Schultz and Anne Ruggles Gere, was that while Herzberg's student tutors "cared for" others, they did not alter their beliefs in individualism and meritocracy. Herzberg himself concluded, "[i]f our students regard social problems as chiefly or only personal, then they will not search beyond the person for a systemic explanation" (309). Other scholars have echoed this warning. Margaret Himley worries that forms of service learning such as tutoring can uphold "power asymmetries," while Linda Flower contends that "[t]o rest in the mere personal puts one on the slippery slope of philanthropy and charity that preserves the status of giver and receiver, expert and client. It allows one to ignore or evade the larger social systems and logics that create a world of 'Others' in the first place" (Himley 417; Flower 2).

For many years, service and community-based learning practitioners were therefore cautioned to avoid the "mere personal" in favor of community work that illuminates systemic reasons for social problems such as imprisonment, poverty, and homelessness. More recently, however, scholars such as Tom Kerr, David Coogan, and Lori Pompa have helped turn attention back to "personal" or relationship-based orientations in service and community-based learning. Kerr, for instance, reports on his course "Writing for Social Justice, Writing for Change," a capstone senior seminar in rhetoric in which students corresponded with prisoners through "the intimate medium of personal letters." This medium enabled "embodied, personal dialogue" that transformed student attitudes towards prisoners through "connect[ions] with people" (67).[1] David Coogan also advocates personal dialogue in his article, "Moving Students into Social Movements: Prisoner Reentry and the Research Paper." Reflecting on students' work with a nonprofit prisoner reentry program, Coogan affirms the power of dialogue to inspire critical thinking capable of contextualizing processes of social change and promoting students' participation in these processes. For this reason, Coogan advocates outreach projects "that center on writing and the relationships that writing can form with community partners" (151). Finally, Lori Pompa's "Inside-Out Prison Exchange Program" joins students and prisoners in a semester-long course held in a local prison. This program positions students and prisoners in a reciprocal relationship as fellow learners: "[w]hen students attend class together as equals, borders disintegrate and barriers recede," Pompa explains. "What emerges is the possibility of considering the subject matter from a new context—that of those living within that context" (27).

Similar aims informed the prison outreach project discussed in this essay. This project occurred in conjunction with my course, "Containment and Liberation," a first-year theme section of rhetoric and composition. Exploring literal and figurative forms of entrapment and freedom in American Society, this course included a community engagement component that invited students to participate in a partnered, in-person peer review with a prisoner. Incarcerated participants were enrolled in a prison education program sponsored by a local Christian university with outreach ties to my former graduate institution (a large state research university). This education program offered prisoners associate degrees in exchange for five years of service within the state's Department of Corrections.[2] Prior to meeting in person, students and prisoners read and responded in writing to Herman Melville's "Bartleby the Scrivener," a short story which students interpreted in the context of Foucault's "The Carceral" and prisoners interpreted in the context of their own institutional experiences.[3] Student and prisoner pairs met for one hour during the exchange to read and discuss their papers together before reconvening for a group debriefing.[4]

My choice of peer review for this outreach project (a perhaps more manageable option for community-based learning practitioners lacking the resources to orchestrate a semester-long class) stemmed largely from the possibilities inherent in personal dialogue—those advocated by scholars such as Kerr, Coogan, and Pompa. By fostering student-prisoner dialogue around a common text, I hoped to "draw people normally separated by difference into new roles as partners in inquiry" (Flower 44). An exploration of this outreach project reveals the positive outcomes that can result from establishing strong mutuality in community-based learning relationships. Peer review levels the hierarchal structure of service models like tutoring, initiates dialogue about social and institutional containment, and thus carries potential for producing mutuality—defined here as "the sharing of ideas in a learner-to-learner environment by establishing a personal respect between parties as teachers/learners/scholars."[5] In view of this emphasis on mutuality, this essay therefore jettisons the term "service learning" (which implies a hierarchal outreach relationship) in favor of the term "community-based learning" (which better captures the reciprocity that informed this project). Even more importantly, this emphasis on mutuality extends to the reciprocal nature of this essay—a product of my collaboration with my community partner, a prisoner and peer review participant who has served as co-investigator and essay respondent for this article.

This scholarly reorientation builds upon Cushman's "Sustainable Service Learning Programs," which encourages professors to "view the site as one where research, teaching, and service can take place in collaboration with community members and students" (44). Yet there has been very little joint scholarly production between those in the field of Rhetoric and Composition and the community members with whom they work—at least in terms of the substantial, visible presence of community voices in published scholarship (by this I refer to co-authored articles, essay responses, etc.). Even Cushman—who advocates "creating knowledge *with* and for community members"— limits her claim by recommending that research "*harmonize*" with "community needs and perspectives" rather than more fully involve community members as co-investigators in, and fellow contributors to, scholarly production (Cushman 46, italics mine).

My community partner and I hope to demonstrate how a reciprocal orientation can foster not only productive outcomes for students and communities, but also a new type of scholarship—one more fully enriched by community voices. We take our cue from Lorelei Blackburn, who has recently argued for the importance of "organic relationships" in service and community-based learning. According to Blackburn, an organic (versus product-based) orientation privileges connections between scholars and community members that are rooted in respect and ongoing collaboration. This reorientation promises to "positively change the way we engage with communities, the way we teach students, and the way we conduct research" (6). This essay springs from one such organic relationship. It is a study that my community partner, a prisoner in a medium security facility, has helped define, develop, and write.[6] It is a study that has progressed in stages "within a sustainable and reciprocal relationship" that has outlasted the community-based learning project analyzed here (Blackburn 5).

Our reciprocal examination of this project reveals ways in which student-prisoner peer review fosters personal dialogue carrying political implications. Through a qualitative analysis of student reflection papers and prisoner oral reflections, we show how an emphasis on the personal during this project did not prelude systemic considerations, but rather produced productive, political outcomes (for the most part). Political in the context of prison outreach means several things: 1) carrying implications for impacting or changing public attitudes and policies; 2) raising student awareness of the systemic reasons for this social problem; and 3) mutually involving/ engaging those who are incarcerated in the process of working to ameliorate the American prison industrial complex. In conjunction with this definition, we understand "systemic" to mean of or relating to social structures—particularly as these structures perpetuate inequalities and "influences and biases, both realized and unrealized, that affect how a person thinks (and in this case, how a person writes and analyzes)."[7]

To challenge students to confront and critically reassess these influences and biases, peer review was chosen as a means by which to initiate mutual dialogue between students and prisoners by dividing tasks equally between parties. Each of the two authors was asked to initially assess his/her paper, to read his/her paper out loud while the partner followed along (making notes to use during review), and then to discuss the paper with his/her partner. Unlike certain other forms of prison outreach, this project did not involve a facility tour (which tends to promote voyeurism) or tutoring sessions (which tend to maintain hierarchal boundaries between students and prisoners). Rather, students entered the exchange familiar with peer review—a practice that had taught students to work collaboratively with others and consider new perspectives. As one student reflected prior to the trip, "this would be a great opportunity for me to open my horizons." Another noted that "[p]eer reviewing in general is very interesting and I think peer reviewing with someone different will be an interesting experience and I will be able to learn from someone different." This project's ability to build a learner-tolearner environment was further facilitated by both the prisoners' welcoming demeanor and the cozy library and classroom in which the peer reviews took place (an interior starkly distinct from more austere buildings throughout the facility). These inviting conditions, along with the peer-review model, helped cultivate an exchange that promoted personal dialogue and complicated cultural representations of prisoners.

Indeed, in this particular exchange, peer review fostered intimate conversations that challenged my students to look past "fragmented representations" of prisoners in *People* magazine, on CSI, and on CNN (Sloop 194). Students discovered that their partners were nothing like "what movies, television, and media portray as truth." As another put it, "I thought [this experience would be] eyeopening, but I didn't realize how much of a reality check it would be." These awakenings occurred alongside reciprocal dialogue. Students and prisoners conversed, questioned, and laughed with one another. "[The exchange] reminded me of any other class consisting of friends," a student wrote later. "[W]e were all students, we were all teachers," remembered an-other, "ready to learn and show the ideas that rest on the plains and corners of our minds." This last student comment is particularly no-table. Much like the literacy tutors Nancy Welsh discusses in a 2002 *CCC* article, this student foregoes common binaries[8] such as "subject-object, active-passive, knower-known" in favor of "a subject-subject logic in which all participants . . . are understood and composed as active, as knowing" (247).

Yet besides fostering reciprocal dialogue and complicating cultural representations of prisoners, this exchange was intended to illuminate systemic reasons for crime such as poverty, insufficient schooling, and unstable home environments—steering students away from solitary conceptions of personal responsibility. At several points during the exchange, however, prisoners volunteered such conceptions—embrac-ing personal responsibility for their crimes and admonishing students against following a similar path. One prisoner, for instance, told stu-dents out loud during the debriefing that they "could have been me had I made different choices while in high school, and can still be me if [students] don't keep [their] choices as being the right ones." An-other prisoner, according to one student's reflection paper, "drilled" into his partner's head "that he made a mistake and he knows he has to pay his dividends for his doing." A third student's reflection paper reported, "[w]hat surprised me was that [my partner] told me not to feel bad for him. He said that he made the decisions that put him in there." Finally, in a spontaneous essay entitled "Students Exploring Freedom: A Reaction to the Interaction" (written immediately after the peer review), my community partner and essay respondent, Wes, characterized his prison community as those "finding grace to bloom within any set of circumstances, even when those circumstances are self-created consequences."

While this emphasis on "self-created consequences" appears ini-tially problematic (the majority of these prisoners were primarily low-erclass African American males, many serving time for crimes related to drugs and gang violence), my students (unlike Herzberg's tutors) did *not* leave with reinforced notions of individualism that curbed their search for systemic explanations. Rather, students' reflection papers indicate how a reciprocal, relationship-based orientation—anchored in the personal—produced political implications.

It gave me the revelation that he and I are not two completely different species on different axes of the universe. We are both human and capable of doing the wrong, *the difference being that our society saw fit to punish his behavior.*

Darryl[9] really drilled in my head that he made a mistake and he knows he has to pay his dividends for his doing, but he seriously regrets what he did and would never do it again. He started to tell me about how life at a prison is a life that no one should end up with. They have no rights practically and they have no 'say' in what the United States does as a whole, inmates are just imprisoned in buildings and are a 'nobody' until they are released. Darryl will not get out until he is 63 years, and this made me feel for him because he was talking about all the dreams he has outside of prison. No one wants to die alone and no one wants to be told what to do every minute of every day. *Some crimes I believe are not worth the time they are given.*

It also gives you a reality check on…making good decisions because one screw up and any of us could end up in the system, just another number…[This experience] really *opened my eyes to the justice system now and how I perceive so many issues without really taking the time to see how the issues affect everyone. Also I feel that a lot of people argue against rights in prison but I wonder how many people have ever known someone in that position? Would they still support taking away their rights and all of the same legislation that they have up until this point?*

After the prison trip, *my mind was changed about education in the prison system.* Hearing about James's life story and his future plans it is obvious that this education system has helped him prioritize his life and realize what is really important.

These passages, to varying degrees, transform the personal into the political. Student one begins by aligning herself with her partner— both equally "capable of doing the wrong" but separated by *social custom* rather than interior moral agency. Her statement indicates an initial movement from individual to structure, with promise for further critical thought. Student two relates the story of Darryl's "mistake," but soon segues into a discussion of institutional dehuman-ization.[10] Rory notes that "[n]o one wants to die alone" or "to be told what to do every minute of every day. Some crimes," he concludes, "are not worth the time they are given." Here, Rory employs a train of logic that moves from personal to communal to political. Rory first reflects on Darryl's day-to-day injustices, then applies these injustices to col-lective human rights, and finally concludes with a political assessment. For student three, the personal promotes critical thinking about pris-oner rights and plants seeds for further public involvement. Rhetorical questions indicate her reassessment of the justice system—one attuned to structural considerations and carrying "implications for other, more extensive efforts" (Schutz and Gere 136).

Student four goes even further by acknowledging a change of po-litical opinion as a result of the outreach experience. Notably, this student posits a direct correlation between James's assumption of indi-vidual responsibility and her own support of prison education. A fifth student crystallizes the power of the "politicized" personal when she confessed during the car ride home, "This makes me change my mind about the death penalty. I could never stand to see any of those guys in there killed." Notable, this student had been paired with Jay—the prisoner who most fervently embraced individual choice. Like Kim, Kara left not contented by Jay's "just dues," but rather newly opposed to the death penalty. She extrapolated the personal to make it both political and collective.

Aaron Schutz and Anne Ruggles Gere worry that "personal" forms of service and community-based learning will remain unconnected to larger communities. As newly independent adults, however, my stu-dents will carry their critical thinking into the voting booth, onto their campus, and into their eventual careers—where it is my hope that they will "populate" public discourse both "productively" *and* responsibly (Coogan 150). More immediately, many students carried their critical thinking into future assignments for our course. Essay three, for in-stance, asked students to prepare a researched argument on a topic of their choice. Over half of those who participated in the prison writing exchange argued for increased educational opportunities for prisoners. One student, moreover, converted his essay into editorial form and submitted it for publication in the student paper.

Dan W. Butin recently lamented in his book *Service-Learning in Theory and Practice* that "while researchers have begun to articulate what positive outcomes may accrue from service-learning, there is almost no solid research on how such outcomes occur" (16). I maintain that outreach relationships built on strong mutuality can foster productive outcomes from community work. As one prisoner, Darryl, told me during a debriefing, the "struggles" he and Rory shared were the reason the peer review "went further than writing. It started a relationship—and produced good writing *because* it produced a relationship." Here, Darryl offers one answer to Butin's question about "*how*" positive outcomes occur, while also echoing Coogan's call for outreach projects that "center on writing and the relationships that writing can form with community partners." Positive outcomes stem from the personal relationships and sense of identification that peer review facilitates between students and community partners. Importantly, however, Darryl posits "good writing" as the *product*, not precursor, of outreach relationships built on strong mutuality.[11]

Other prisoner and student comments support the link between strong mutuality and productive outcomes. Ricky, for instance, remembered

> [w]hen they came in they were scared, but when we started talking you could almost see them struggling. There's things they'll ask me as a fellow man. Certain things they'll ask me that they won't ask you [the teacher] because we're worried about what everyone else thinks. He could ask me questions without feeling dumb.

Ricky recounts students' process of critical thinking ("when we started talking you could almost see them struggling") and inquiry ("[h]e could ask me questions...") rooted in a sense of mutuality. Ricky perceives himself as his partner's "fellow man"[12]—a position that affords the student a more genuine conduit for critical inquiry than that of the teacher. Importantly, students perceived incarcerated persons in similar ways: those who were "prisoners" and "criminals" before the peer review became "partners," "classmates," and "friends" during and after the exchange (a few students and prisoners even created nicknames for one another). This relationship-based orientation enabled students to (as one put it) "gain respect for the kind of person they are" and "learn from someone that has a unique understanding of this topic that I would never have."

For one prisoner, James, this process was anchored in humor—a means of deconstructing "Hollywood" representations of prisoners. "We crack jokes to let them know we're people too," James explained, "[t]hat's what I believe happened with your students. 'Oh man, I never would have expected that.'" A student's reflection paper recounts a similar process, remembering that during the debriefing, "we made jokes" and "talked like we had known each other for years." This lighted-hearted, relationship-building atmosphere helped students feel comfortable enough to ask "any questions that we had" and pursue the type of critical thinking that Coogan believes can invest students in social change. "It takes time," James qualifies, but "little by little it's broken down."

Ultimately, this outreach project demonstrates the value of a relationship-based orientation in community-based learning. In addition to producing a variety of political outcomes, the strong mutuality present during the exchange carried equally meaningful (and entirely unanticipated) personal effects for one community partner. "I had a selfish interest," Ramone confessed. "I have a son that age. [The peer review] was an opportunity to get some idea how he thinks . . . probin'. . . figuring out how to bridge the gap and relate to him." "It was challenging," Ramone concludes, "but also began to provide some ways of thinking to help me meet [my son] where he is . . . I hope one day I'll have a relationship with him." This passage posits the value of the "personal" in its own right— reminding us that community-based learning outcomes assessment must make room for the unexpected results that community partners find meaningful.

I want to close by acknowledging that this article would likely not exist if my community partner had not initiated critical analysis of this outreach project. Shortly after the peer reviews took place, he composed a voluntary essay entitled "Students Exploring Freedom: A Reaction to the Interaction." This essay made several important observations about the outreach project as a whole, including its relationship-based nature[13] and the "commonality" forged between students and prisoners, who "both want freedom in the most desperate terms. For the one," Wes explained, "freedom is defined as being released to make choices about the future; for the other, it is being released from the choices of the past." This essay crystallized two noteworthy aspects of the exchange: 1) a sense of mutuality between students and prisoners (albeit one underlined by crucial differences); and 2) prisoners' emphasis on personal choice. In doing so, his essay convinced me that this outreach project warranted further, scholarly investigation. I began the research process and continued my conversations with Wes, who offered further evidence (in the form of a counterpoint) that a reciprocal, relationship-based orientation yields productive community-based learning outcomes.[14]

The 2012 CCCC theme, "Writing Gateways," provided an occasion for Wes to enter scholarly discourse in a more formal, written capacity. "How does the discipline welcome in new teachers, scholars, and students?" the call for proposals asked; this question seemed ripe for building a gateway for community voices at our convention. I formed a roundtable entitled "Lessons from the Inside: Reconsidering Rhetorical Concepts through the Lens of the Prison Writing Classroom" that would feature three scholarly presentations followed by a series of prisoner responses. In January 2012, I completed a conference version of this article and sent it to Wes (now at a different prison having graduated from the associate degree program). He sent back a four-page written response that was read, along with my essay, at the 2012 CCCC Convention. From here, the next natural step seemed revision and development, followed by submission to a scholarly journal. *Reflections* was chosen because of its commitment to community-based writing, and we hope that our article will make an original contribution in this area.

To close my portion of this essay, I return to Blackburn, who asserts that when outreach relationships "gro[w] organically, around mutual interests and respect," they will not necessarily end when the service project does. What has made this outreach relationship so remarkable is our mutual interest in the outreach project itself—our shared desire to better understand its dynamics and contribute to a body of knowledge about prison literacy work. It is worth considering how more of these types of scholarly collaborations might enrich the fields of Community-Based Learning and Service Learning studies.

## Response To: Prison Collaborative Writing: The Outcomes of Community-Based Learning Relationships Built on Strong Mutuality

I believe it is wise that I preface all of my observations within the proper context of my own qualifications, or the lack thereof. I have been graciously invited into a conversation with wise scholars, and in that respect I see myself as the guest in this discussion. Yet I am a member of a marginalized community that so many educators reach out to affect, and in this respect my observations carry some weight. So I humbly offer my observations to the brilliant minds of the scholars while realizing that I speak as a sophomore in the truest sense of the word—a "wise fool."

I was deeply impressed by the approach of Dr. Grace Wetzel's peer review project *because* of its relationship-based nature. My original voluntary essay reflecting on the project emphasized two important observations relative to this collaborative article. The first regards the impact I experienced from being allowed to be viewed as a "peer" by university students who were not incarcerated. Specifically, I was intrigued by how the peer review morphed into conversations about life lessons in a manner that clearly indicated prisoners and university students related to one another as true peers. The second observation regarded the sense that I had that a project of this nature could actually impact the institution of American prisons if the university students were truly affected by the experience. I wrote, "University education should actually be combined with practical application lessons so students can actually *live out what they learn*" (emphasis added). I now understand this concept as the hope that the students would politicize their experience; that is, that they would critically analyze their views about crime and punishment and engage in a productive stance regarding criminal justice issues. I had no idea at the time that my simple set of honest observations would speak to the heart of a discussion about service learning models.

As Grace began to converse with me about a deeper analysis of the project, she shared with me copies of articles, encouraging me to consider the implications of my observations through the lenses of the scholars. Among others, I read Linda Flower's concern about the "social systems and logics that create a world of 'Others'" and how she feared the "mere personal" would continue to enable those systems. I considered the observations of Aaron Schultz, Anne Ruggles Gere, and Margaret Himley concerning the potential weaknesses of tutoring in breaking down individualism and meritocracy. And then David Coogan's idea that service learning projects could create "social movements" and Tom Kerr's discovery of the potential of "embodied personal dialogue" as a catalyst for critical thinking about the prison industrial system expanded my considerations of the learning project in which I had participated with Grace. I noted a similarity between these two scholars and her motives to use our peer-review project to level hierarchal structures and promote "positive service outcomes" and, in this case, possibly produce "productive, political outcomes." But it was while reading Lorelei Blackburn's description of an "organic relationship" model, which values "relationships" above service learning projects and products, that an original observation came into focus for me.

Evidence suggests there is a difference between the personal element in this community-based project and the "mere personal" about which the scholars warn. While the "mere personal" may "preserve the status of giver and receiver, expert and client" and continue to enable systemic influences, the personal in the instant project was a *mutual* element that did not flow only in one direction *from* the students to prisoners. This personal functioned in a reciprocal relationship, flowing from one learner to the other regardless of whether that learner was a member of the marginal or the majority community. My portion of this article will attempt to demonstrate how I see mutuality as the dynamic that allows for a personal interaction which enables positive community-based learning outcomes (in the instant case politically productive outcomes), while simultaneously contributing to the field of scholarship.

To recap my university partner's observations about the benefits the personal element created for her university students, notice how this personal is distinguished in its function in this project. Without the dialogue stemming from personal interaction there would have been no "reality check," no realization that the students and the inmates were not "two completely different species on different axes of the universe." There would have been no humanization of Darryl as a fellow man with rights and "dreams," and no insight that "any of us could end up in the system." Without the personal element, James would still be a faceless prison number without "future plans" and life priorities, and men on death row would not have been transformed into the affectionate handle of "those guys in there" who could be executed. The realizations sprouting from this person-to-person dialogue were apparently more than students simply relating to prisoners as their fellow-man. Grace demonstrated how the students moved from the individual to critical thinking about political and systemic issues such as "social custom," "institutional dehumanization," reassessment of the criminal justice system, and the death penalty. Even though the prisoners had emphasized self-created consequences within their individual stories, the students were still able to recognize where the lines of personal culpability were drawn and where the influences of social and political systemic factors began. One might argue that systemic factors were highlighted through the personal stories of the prisoners as preconceived hierarchies were deconstructed and the students were able to consider how they themselves could make similar choices and become entrapped by the social system. It seems mutual dialogue privileged a relational exchange, which in turn prevented the students from hiding within safe confines away from the world of "Others." Therefore systemic factors were obvious rather than obscured. I conclude that mutuality functioned as a catalyst which allowed objective consideration of larger social issues.

In fact, evidence of this project suggests when mutuality is absent, revelation of systemic influences may also be absent. Consider a counterpoint. When I first read my university partner's initial paper which highlighted the responses of the university students to the project, I naturally sought for comments from my own peer review partner. When I found no reference of his remarks, I inquired of Grace and found the student had confessed that his preconceptions of inmates had not changed at all. Although I felt a bit narcissistic, I remember the emotions I experienced as I considered the fact that, after spending over an hour with me, he was unmoved about whether my punishment was just, untouched by my unique set of circumstances, and generally unaffected with my plight as a prisoner. Needless to say I had been hoping for results such as these and I remember wondering whether I was *that* bad of a guy. I then began reflecting upon the time I had spent with my peer partner and I remembered how I had attempted to help him relate to me by being approachable and open to any personal questions he might have had about me. However, he chose not to ask any personal questions about my life, family, or crime.[15] He was a great guy with a good paper, but he never heard my story, preferring rather to let the conversation comfortably center around the writing project alone. It was then that I said to Grace, "Think about what didn't happen with [my peer review partner] that *did* happen with all the others - it never got personal." And without the presence of a reciprocal relationship perhaps "Other" structures were maintained and political affect never happened. It seems that the evidence of this project leans in favor of mutuality as a benefit for the students, not a barrier.

However, mutuality did not yield positive outcomes only for university students. As an objective investigator reading the reflections of my fellow prisoners, the relational element of the project stood out to me in its value to the incarcerated. It is without any bitterness against society that I suggest the personal element is noticeably absent within the prison community in general. I suspect most prisoners would lament that we are seldom spoken to as much as we are spoken about. Inmates are often grouped together and misrepresented by the social media and entertainment industry, and even by the security system of the department of corrections,[16] which robs the prisoner of his individuality while creating that world of "Others" at the same time. If followed to its extreme, in my experience, the non-personal works in my sub-society to promote dehumanization. But note how the prisoners grasped at rehumanizing themselves through reciprocal relationship. Darryl chose to speak of the good writing the project produced in terms of *shared* "struggles" with his peer partner. Ricky recognizes himself as his partner's fellow man and admits his partner had an avenue of inquiry with him that the instructors did not have, but he phrases his description in terms that shows how *he* relates to the same challenges. "Certain things they'll ask me that they won't ask you [the teacher] because we're worried about what everyone else thinks." Ricky's use of the inclusive term is insight into his desire to relate to his peer. He is not thinking in terms of inquiry benefitting the service learning project, he is rehumanizing through relationship. James also strove for a sense of humanization through humor. He admittedly worked through "crack[ing] jokes . . . to let them know we're people, too" until perceived misrepresentations "little by little" were "broken down." My own reflection paper sought to demonstrate the importance that I placed on being permitted to be viewed as a fellow student among peers. (Imagine what being invited to co-author a scholarly article is doing for my self-esteem!)

This evidence of how mutuality benefitted my community is not just the value of the personal in its own right, as Grace described it in Ramone's case. Prisoners often assume people in different social classes cannot relate to their plight—not *will not*, but *cannot* relate. While my fellow prisoners and I resisted the misconceptions we perceived in those who were outsiders to our community, our own assumptions were inevitably affected once we felt we were on common ground with peers. Rehumanization as a positive outcome brought with it the hope that we are not so different from those reaching out to educate us. This demonstrates how the personal was flowing *from* us *to* the university students in mutual benefit.

Prisoners also further benefitted from the community-based learning project's mutuality by being allowed to analyze the project along with Grace. While we are aware of the social challenges we face as prisoners, we are mostly ignorant of how educational scholars view our challenges. We can express how we would like them to be viewed, but are not always privileged to listen in on the discussion. Therefore, we remain ignorant of the social discourse of our plight and unable to objectively examine it without the bias that our own pain creates.

However, when reciprocal relationship produces joint collaboration and analysis, we become aware of the potential of our society toward improvement, aware of the challenges facing our educators, and even aware of which data is most valuable for analysis. Without scholars involving my community in relationship, we remain blinded to the discipline as a whole. Grace returned post-project and asked for our analysis, allowing us to glimpse the social discourse for ourselves. This knowledge seems directly proportional to the prisoner's hope for the future.

This particular aspect of mutuality within this project truly intrigued me. Consider that Grace's desire for producing positive outcomes was geared in part toward the political activism of her students. She desires them to "carry their critical thinking into the voting booth, onto their campuses, and into their eventual careers" where they might "'populate' public discourse both 'productively' and responsibly." *But what about the inmates? I wondered. Can we politicize through the personal, too? Are we limited to only participating in the activism process by allowing ourselves to be subjects of study?* Actually, it seems to me that a reciprocal relationship may have powerful political potential for a project's community members through mutuality that the "mere personal" can never obtain. Once I realized that the personal element in this project was not limited to merely being an ingredient in the one hour peer review but that it also extended to the analysis of the project, specifically *this* collaborative article evolving from an organic relationship, I realized that my and my fellow prisoners' participation in the political process was no longer indirect. Therefore by extension, perhaps marginalized groups that are allowed to analyze community-based learning projects side-byside with scholars have an avenue to *directly* participate in both the grander issues affecting their communities, and the scholarship of the discipline, ultimately creating a new type of scholarship. I want to make the case for this observation in two ways.

First, I submit that a community member's analysis is valuable to the scholars; that is, it is true analysis and not merely one's opinion about a project's strengths and weaknesses. Grace did not inquire of prisoners after the project merely to gather data. For my part, for example, she invited me to consider implications and affects of both systemic structures in service and community-based learning and the dangers of the "mere personal" in such projects. When I shared my thoughts in my response to her essay through the 2012 CCCC Convention, she validated my observations as true analysis. Allow me to briefly summarize those thoughts that I shared in that response.

I noticed that her initial impression of the service learning project lacked insight about certain systemic affects *upon* the personal simply because, as an outsider of my community, she was not aware of certain contributing factors. While I clearly argued in favor of keeping the personal in community-based learning projects involving prisoners, I felt it should probably be emphasized that systemic influences should never be completely removed from consideration. No learning project occurs in a systemic vacuum, and even the individual person involved in a relational exchange brings with him his own systemic influence. For example, much might be read into our actions of volunteering our own personal culpability for our crimes, but it should be noted that the particular program that sponsored our education is a religious based program that emphasizes personal culpability in light of a Biblical world view. Perhaps then this personal element was a systemic influence, at least in part. Furthermore, such a world view holds to a type of mutuality as a foundational conviction of education; specifically that Christ-like love and charity to one's fellow man is the most effective means to educate him. It should be asked, then, how much those systemic convictions influenced my own initial critical observations of the peer review project that I wrote about in my voluntary essay, where I celebrated the relational nature of an educational experience. After all, it is easy to observe what one already believes and is already expecting to see. And one more example may be found in the case of Jay, who so drastically affected his peer review partner's opinion on the death penalty. Prior to entering the educational program, Jay was actually trained to share his personal story in another program which brought troubled youths into the prisons in order to hear stories of convicted criminals for the purpose of helping to steer the youths away from making poor choices that may lead to a life of crime. Perhaps it was not the "personal" at all that affected his peer partner as much as it was Jay's former training in motivational speaking. Each of these observations highlight that the personal itself may have been an element of another system—a system motivated by a particular political point of view.

Although my analysis lacks the depth and insight that scholarly training might produce, Grace's validation of my analysis from a scholar's perspective highlighted the strength and potential that a relational side-by-side collaboration can produce. Without an organic relationship continuing beyond the boundaries of the initial peer review project, she would never have known the facts about Jay's prior training, and may never have considered the systemic effects upon the personal element that I noticed because of being *in* the community affected by those unique systems. At the least, my analysis uniquely contributed to the field of scholarship by providing a data source for this study while provoking critical thinking about the balance of personal and systemic considerations in service and community-based learning.

Therefore, and my second point in arguing the unique productive potential of mutuality in learning projects, because a community member's analysis *is* valuable to the public discourse of his community's larger issues, giving voice to that analysis privileges the member with influence toward an ever-widening audience with that discourse. The reciprocal relationship in the instant case, allowed me to politicize the personal through this collaborative article, thus being heard by those in the voting booths, on the university campuses, and those whose career choice is in the field of education. Mutuality is here demonstrated to be a productive element for community members in that it empowers their voices to break out of the confines of the project at hand, join in with the social discourse, and be heard by the field of scholarship. I do not believe the "mere personal" that allows service learning participants to be the "knower" and the community member to be the "known" (Welsh)—a personal element that flows in one direction—could allow such a productive effect.

In conclusion, I believe the evidence of the analysis of this peer review project supports my university partner's claims that the personal can be productive in community-based learning and can clearly contribute to scholarship in the field of pedagogy, but only if the personal aspect flows in mutual exchange. I am honored that my opinions and observations in this matter were not only asked for, but were allowed to be represented in my own words. I'm excited to see how other collaborative articles and discussions may contribute to and refine the analysis of future community-based learning projects. I am also excited at the potential of affecting my incarcerated community through such an approach.

## NOTES

1. Kerr explains, "[i]t is one thing to read an anthologized personal account of prison life or of experiences leading up to prison, yet quite another to be addressed by name and to have one's own questions taken up thoughtfully by currently incarcerated people. It is the difference between disembodied, relatively risk-free 'academic' discourse, and embodied, personal dialogue that carries with it possibilities and risks connected to any human involvement" (67).

2. Graduates serve as mentors and assistants to the education of other prisoners, in addition to AIDS Ward workers or hospice care assistants, for instance.

3. Should I conduct a similar project again, I will offer prisoners the opportunity to read Foucault as well. During this project, I taught a guest lesson in the prison on Foucault's "The Carceral," but I now recognize the importance of assigning the actual text.

4. Student-prisoner pairs were selected voluntarily as opposed to being assigned. During the group debriefing, each student-prisoner pair shared lessons learned and new perspectives gained (on both their essays and institutional containment) with the class.

5. This definition was developed with my community partner, a prisoner in a medium security facility who participated in the peer reviews and who has served as co-investigator and respondent to this essay. I use quotations because although my community partner and I have developed this definition together, this phrasing is his own.

6. A word about methodology. This research study emerged organically through a shared interest in (and subsequent investigation of) an outreach project *as it unfolded*. Consistent with Eli Goldblatt's advice that we develop relationships "before we…set up research projects," I did not enter the service site with a pre-defined research methodology (283). Rather, a voluntary

essay by my community partner entitled "Students Exploring Freedom: A Reaction to the Interaction" (written immediately after the peer reviews took place) sparked the research study. For this reason, I do not have tapes or transcripts of the peer reviews. I draw instead from student reflection papers and prisoner oral reflections gathered during a debriefing after the outreach project took place.

7. The phrasing in quotes is that of my community partner. The definition was collectively assembled.

8. As Patricia Webb, Kirsti Cole, and Thomas Skeen recount, much service learning in the 1980s-90s "posited the student as 'knower' and the members of the community as the 'other' who needed the 'knower's' expertise" (238-39).

9. All prisoner and student names have been changed to pseudonyms.

10. Note that Darryl himself politicizes the personal when arguing that despite his "mistake," "life at a prison is a life that no one should end up with."

11. While Coogan posits writing as a conduit for relationships, Darryl suggests that good writing stems from strong relationships.

12. Ricky articulated a reciprocal position at other points as well, remembering for instance that "[t]hey [students] young and wild and I remember the days I was young and wild."

13. Wes wrote that "what happened" during the project "is proof-positive that humans are social creatures rather than merely intellectual; Bartleby served as a platform of learning, but it was life lessons that dominated the conversations."

14. Wes said to me: "Think about what didn't happen with [my peer review partner] that did happen with all the others—it never got personal."

15. These observations about my peer review partner should not be taken as contrary to the initial impression given in my voluntary essay (that of feeling like a "peer"). My initial reflection paper had reviewed the project as a whole, based mainly on the statements and responses I had heard during the group debriefing following the one-hour peer review. Furthermore, the essay was written before I was aware of my peer review partner's lack of response.

16. *University partner's note on this point*: It is worth mentioning that when I sent Wes a manila envelope of scholarly articles for this project over the summer, the articles were confiscated as a potential threat to security and held and examined for over a month before they were deemed appropriate and finally delivered to Wes.

## WORKS CITED

Blackburn, Lorelei. "The Affordances of Organic Relationshipbuilding in Civic Engagement Projects." Conference on College Composition and

Communication. America's Convention Center. St. Louis, MO. 22 March 2012.

Butin, Dan W. *Service-Learning in Theory and Practice: The Future of Community Engagement in Higher Education*. New York: Palgrave Macmillan, 2010.

Coogan, David. "Moving Students into Social Movements." *Active Voices: Composing a Rhetoric for Social Movements*. Eds. Sharon McKenzie Stevens and Patricia M. Malesh. Albany: SUNY Press, 2009.

Cushman, Ellen. "Sustainable Service Learning Programs." *College Composition and Communication* 54.1 (September 2002): 40-65.

Flower, Linda. *Community Literacy and the Rhetoric of Public Engagement*. Carbondale: Southern Illinois UP, 2008.

Goldblatt, Eli. "Alinsky's Reveille: A Community-Organizing Model for Neighborhood-Based Literacy Projects." *College English* 67.3 (January 2005): 274-295.

Herzberg, Bruce. "Community Service and Critical Teaching." *College Composition and Communication* 45.3 (October 1994): 307-19.

Himley, Margaret. "Facing (Up To) 'The Stranger' in Community Service." *College Composition and Communication* 55.3 (February 2004): 416-438.

Kerr, Tom. "Between Ivy and Razor Wire: A Case of Correctional Correspondence." *Reflections* 4.1 (Winter 2004): 62-75.

Pompa, Lori. "Disturbing Where We Are Comfortable: Notes From Behind the Walls" *Reflections* 4.1 (Winter 2004): 24-34.

Schutz, Aaron and Anne Ruggles Gere. "Service Learning and English Studies: Rethinking 'Public Service'." *College English* 60.2 (February 1998): 129-149.

Sloop, John M. *The Cultural Prison: Discourse, Prisoners, and Punishment*. Tuscaloosa: University of Alabama Press, 1996.

Webb, Patricia, Kirsti Cole, and Thomas Skeen. "Feminist Social Projects: Building Bridges between Communities and Universities." *College English* 69.3 (January 2007): 238-259.

Welsh, Nancy. "'And Now That I Know Them': Composing Mutuality in a Service Learning Course." *College Composition and Communication* 54.2 (December 2002): 243-263.

# THE WRITING LAB NEWSLETTER

Volume 37, Number 1-2      Promoting the exchange of voices and ideas in one-to-one teaching of writing      Sept./Oct., 2012

*The Writing Lab Newsletter* is on the Web at https://writinglabnewsletter.org/

*The Writing Lab Newsletter* (beginning in Sept. 2015, the journal will change its name to *WLN: A Journal of Writing Center Scholarship*), a peer-reviewed publication with five issues per academic year, provides a forum for exchanging ideas and information about writing centers in high schools, colleges, and universities. Articles illustrate how writing centers work in an intersection of theory and practice, underpinned by theory and scholarship. *WLN* aims to inform newcomers to the field as well as extend the thinking of those who are more knowledgeable and experienced. Authors also report on research and describe programmatic models that can be adapted to other contexts.

### Lexicography: Self-Analysis and Defining the Keywords of our Missions

Writing center professionals repeatedly use words and phrases, such as "independent writer," in mission statements to define the tutor's goal for the student. But how are such terms understood and internalized by others? As Rendleman describes the method of textual analysis he used, drawn from contemporary lexicographic practice, the result invites colleagues to consider how terminology used by tutors, teachers, students, and writing center directors both converge and diverge in meaning. Drawing on lexicographers' methodology is representative of how writing center scholars turn to other fields to introduce and incorporate new approaches to familiar concerns. In this case, colleagues are challenged to take a fresh look at familiar terminology in mission statements.

# 14 Lexicography: Self-Analysis and Defining the Keywords of our Missions

*Eliot Rendleman*

After returning from a class visit last fall to advertise the mission and services of the writing center I direct, I sat at my desk with an emerging concern over a statement that I have dogmatically repeated to myself and to others since 1996: "One of the major goals of the writing center is to help you become independent writers." As usual, I quickly moved on to answer any questions from the students and the teacher without qualifying exactly what I meant by "independent writers." And why not move on without qualification? Wouldn't everyone know what I mean by the term, especially in the land of Independence Day, famous bootstrap narratives, and technological visionaries? But obviously, this was an ill-founded assumption. I should have known better. As most of us would agree, meaning is elusive and socially constructed. The meaning of our words is elusive partly because individuals can use the same term and mean different things in kind and degree, depending on the context, and it's socially constructed in that we develop meaning or the sense of terms through our dialogue and experience with others in broad and narrow contexts of the world. What I mean by "independent writer" might not be what you mean. What I meant by "independent writer" fifteen years ago might not mean the same thing for me now. How I define the "independent writer" might depend on my audience (students vs. teachers, educators vs. politicians) and my rhetorical purpose, further complicating the matter. I couldn't help myself as this process of self-reflection gained momentum. As Dave Healy writes, "Writing center folks tend to be a self-analytical lot" (1).

This essay has two purposes. First, I want to encourage colleagues to reflect formally on most, if not all, of the key terms found in their own mission statements, online descriptions, assessments, training material, marketing documents, and, even boilerplate speeches. Other terms besides the "independent writer" might include "writing process," "proofread," "edit," "feedback," and so on, words that we often take for granted and that we need to clearly explain to the students we visit and who visit us. Though the definitions of each of these terms appear obvious or self-evident, sustained research and formal analysis may prove otherwise, showing both the striking and subtle similarities and differences in each of our conceptions of the words.

Second, I want to share a method for such a reflection, and I offer a narrative that illustrates my study of the open compound word (Jackson 5) "independent writer." To guide my research and analysis, I appropriate contemporary lexicographic practice. Using lexicography's criteria for composing definitions, I examine the ways in which writing center stakeholders—scholars, writing center administrators, teachers, consultants, and students—define or use the term. From this analysis, I develop a comprehensive and flexible definition for my center and for other directors and consultants to work with and against as they define the term for themselves and their local constituents. The motivation for this essay is not to come up with the "definitive" definition. Rather, it is about a process of research and analysis that will reveal shared terminology as a means to construct a definition that might resonate with students and colleagues and that might contribute to the clarification of what we do at each of our institutions. After all, it appears we won't be able to "really get rid of" such a term (Healy 3), as a few have hoped, so we might as well take the lead on constructing the definition of a term with the words of particular stakeholders. In the end, I offer ways to use the working definition of an independent writer to market a writing center and to conduct a portion of consultant training.

## A LEXICOGRAPHIC METHODOLOGY

Since this essay attempts to develop a working definition of "independent writer," I borrowed partially from lexicography. Lexicography is the study and practice of defining words and compiling dictionaries, and I sought guidance from Howard Jackson's *Lexicography:*

*An Introduction.* The methodology for this study borrows from the lexicographer's planning, data (collection), and methods stages. For the planning stage, I designated my primary audience: students at our school, which would remind me, for example, to limit jargon. Based on Jackson's description of the data stage, I focused on computer corpora, that is, writing center scholarship found in searchable online archives, writing center websites, and anonymous electronic surveys of teachers and students. Using this data, I felt confident I could gather the language and senses of the word among the various stakeholders who might encounter the eventual definition. For the method stage I was only concerned with the definition, "the major function of dictionaries" (86), not the word's pronunciation, etymology, and so on. A lexicographer tries to write definitions that "capture" the meaning, or sense, of a word (18). Word meaning has four aspects: denotation, or reference to something in the "real world" (15); connotation, or "often emotive" positive and negative associations (16); sense or semantic relations, such as synonymy, antonymy, hyponymy, and meronymy (17); and collocation, or the "likelihood that two words will co-occur" (18). With these basic lexicographic concepts of planning, data, and method in mind, I discovered during my research and analysis common terms that I could employ to compose a definition that captures the meaning of the word and that would be persuasive or acceptable for most, if not all, of our constituents and those of other writing centers.

Using the four criteria of word meaning, I gathered data from writing center websites, writing center journal articles, and surveys. Websites and articles offered ready-made and easily searchable computer corpora for a representative community of writing center administrators and scholars, while the surveys presented data of the terminology used by my primary and secondary audiences, out of which I could create my own computer corpus. Using Google and various combinations of the keywords "writing center," "writing studio," "writing lab," "rhetoric and writing center," and "independent writer," I discovered twenty-four writing center websites of two- and four-year institutions that used the word. To discover what journal articles in writing center studies might implicitly or explicitly define the word, I searched the archived PDF files of the *Writing Lab Newsletter*, the PDF files of the *Writing Center Journal* at The Writing Centers Research Project, and the HTML files of *Praxis: A Writing Center Journal*. During this search, I found six articles that use the term. I distributed an online survey to the students who use our center's services, the consultants who staff our center, and English department faculty members of our institution, who recommend the majority of students who come to us. One-hundred-seventeen students, five consultants, and eleven faculty members responded to the following prompt: "The goal of the writing center is to help [you/students] become an independent writer. What do you think 'independent writer' means?" With a popular spreadsheet application, I collated the words in the immediate vicinity of "independent writer(s)" that offered as a referent a "person, object, feeling, action, idea, quality, etc.—in the real world" (Jackson 15); that suggested positive or negative feelings or associations; that demonstrated a similar, opposite, "kind of," or "part of" sense (17-18); and that appeared frequently with the word.

## THE SENSES AND A WORKING DEFINITION

As one might expect, the results of analysis show that each group's senses and aspects of the independent writer converge and diverge. The words that all the groups use to explicitly define or to implicitly describe the independent writer converge on positive mental states, inventory of knowledge, habits of the mind, awareness of the self, and emphasis on isolation. Regarding mental states that invite positive connotations, the groups say independent writers are confident, proud, fearless, and empowered. They possess knowledge about the strategies for invention, drafting, revision, proofreading, and editing. The minds of these writers are organized. According to the stakeholders, independent writers are people who can envision the "big picture" of writing assignments and can formulate, conceptualize, construct, or structure projects. Independent writers are self-aware, knowing their strengths and weaknesses. As they compose assignments, these kinds of writers find momentum from their strengths and know what to do to manage their weaknesses. And the final area of convergence includes the emphasis on isolation. Independent writers invent, draft, revise, proofread, and edit alone—rarely, if ever, seeking opportunities for collaboration.

The words each group uses to explicitly define or to implicitly describe the independent writer diverge from words to express concerns about the forms and goals of writing, the quality of written products, voice, audience, critical thinking and interpretation, research, and degree of collaboration. Students, writing center administrators, and scholars say the independent writer can write in many different forms or genres and for many goals, while consultants and faculty members are silent on the subject in my corpus. Students and consultants remark on the quality of the products independent writers produce, saying that their writing is good (sometimes perfect), purposeful, clear, concise, and error free, while faculty, administrators, and scholars are silent in the survey and literature. Voice and self-expression matter to students, faculty members, and scholars when the independent writer is mentioned, while I discovered that administrators exclude this concern on their writing center websites. Students and faculty mention that independent writers recognize their audience and compose work that engages and affects their readers, while consultants, administrators, and scholars exclude words that denote or connote this concern when presenting the term. When students, faculty, and administrators use or define the term, I often found the words "critical thinker" and "can interpret," while these words were absent in the corpus for consultants and scholars. All the groups, except my representative consultants, mentioned something about independent writers' abilities to suc cessfully research and find resources. And in the final area of divergence—degree of collaboration—students and faculty members say independent writers mostly work alone, yet they must seek some feedback to test ideas and the quality of writing during most, if all, recurring stages of the writing process.

Based on these results of converging and diverging senses of the independent writer, I would like to offer a working definition, incorporating the terms that all these groups should recognize and find reasonable. After some words or phrases of the definition, I include in parentheses the lexicographic criterion that helped guide data collation, analysis of the results, and composing of the definition:

> *Independent writer*: a person or a kind of writer (denotation, semantic relation) who is reasonably confident (connotation) about his or her ability to apply an array of strategies to the writing process stages of project planning, invention, drafting, revision, proofreading, and editing; who is aware of his or her strengths and weaknesses (connotation), finding momentum from strengths and strategies to accommodate weaknesses; and who takes sole responsibility for his or her writing and often works through the writing process alone (collocation),

yet seeks some feedback to test ideas and the quality of writing during most, if all, recurring stages of the process.

The definition offers a reference to things in the real world, emotive associations, sense relation, and words found in collocation among the corpora. Since I synthesized this definition from the words of writing center stakeholders, it should be comprehensive enough to address most, if not all, of the senses of the word "independent writer" that would resonate to one degree or another with my primary and secondary audiences. The practical application of this definition, the initial reason for starting this study, is in marketing our center. But after my analysis of the corpus—discovering that my representative consultants' senses of independent writer exclude concerns about the forms and goals of writing, audience, critical thinking and interpretation, and degree of collaboration—I can see that this process of defining a central tenet of the work we try to do at our writing center reveals potential gaps in my consultant training.

## APPLYING THE DEFINITION TO MARKETING AND CONSULTANT TRAINING

Writing center administrators can apply the method of defining words and the comprehensive definition of *independent writer* I presented above (or one that they compose for their particular locales) to marketing and consultant training. First, administrators and consultants can use the definition as a presentation checklist or outline at the beginning of consultations for new clients and during classroom visits, orientations, and other student-centered events. Instead of stating the word in passing, as I did in the opening narrative, speakers of the word should give a definition and describe what the writing center does to address each major component of the definition. For example, to explain how we help students build confidence as an aspect of independent writer, we can explain, with Albert Bandura's forces of developing self-efficacy in mind, how we model strategies of the writing process, allow students to master skills with consultant guidance, acknowledge successes and strengths, and offer a comfortable and inviting environment to help mitigate anxiety. To address the part of the definition that mentions strategies of the writing process, we would list one or two of them for each process stage, such as clustering and listing for invention, or reading aloud or reading "backwards" for proofreading.

And we would continue like this, in brief, for each element of the definition. The definition becomes much more than a mantra that we invoke as a formality each time we speak the term. Rather, it becomes a productive tool of delivery that ties a writing center's services into this mission or goal. The definition also becomes a clear, professional, and persuasive way to influence how "others see our missions, goals, and methods" (Simpson 4).

The second application of defining a word and the resultant definition is to consultant training. The specific applications include a curriculum checklist, a frame for critical reflection, and an assessment. As a checklist, similar to the marketing application, administrator-teachers can present the definition at the beginning of the semester in their peer writing consultation course, and for subsequent meetings they can show consultants how particular activities tie into the ultimate goal of developing independent writers. For example, most administrator-teachers conduct mock and real consultations during their class meetings. During the post-consultation reflection and critique, students can analyze what part of the consultation reinforces an element of the definition. They might begin, "How did the consultant's praise contribute to the development of the independent writer?" or "I noticed that the consultant showed the student how to use clustering with a topic outside of the student's essay. How does that help develop the independent writer?" Besides using the definition as a critical frame during class, I can use the definition as a checklist for planning my syllabus calendar. As I lay out the activities and after I've written the calendar, I can review what activities support the senses of the independent writer. More than mantras, comprehensive definitions of our key tenets can become central to curriculum planning and reflective practice.

In addition to creating a checklist for marketing, curriculum planning, and critical reflection, the process of defining the keywords of our missions can lead to a partial assessment of consultant training. The process might uncover what consultants have acquired from training and what they are conscious of. At the same time, of course, the process might reveal what they have failed to retain, what they've ignored, or what might only lie at the unconscious level. If one of my major goals for our writing center is to develop independent writers, then, according to the above definition and the results of my analysis, the consultants at the writing center I direct are conscious of and, I assume, engage in activities during a consultation that create positive mental states, that offer strategies for the writing process (i.e., inventory of knowledge), promote various productive habits of the mind, encourage an awareness of the self, and help plan for the next step to write away from the writing center (i.e., emphasis on isolation). While the results of my analysis highlight what consultants are conscious of based on their training and experience, they concurrently suggest potential gaps in the course curriculum. The representative consultants are not conscious of helping students understand the forms and goals of writing, audience awareness, skills for critical thinking and interpretation, strategies for research, and plans for when to collaborate or gain feedback. As the definition can be used as a checklist to confirm that class activities and assignments support the ultimate goal of the independent writer, the results can be used in the same way.

Defining the keywords of our mission statements is more than just an exercise in self-analysis. The process of defining these words and the definition can produce the type of influence Jeanne Simpson advocates in "Whose Idea of a Writing Center Is This, Anyway?" To help influence students during class visits and other occasions, an inclusive definition, such as the "independent writer," becomes a verbal checklist to present the services in an orderly fashion that supports a clearly stated goal. To help influence consultants, the definition can assist with making concrete connections between classroom practice and abstract goals. And by revealing the senses consultants possess about an administrator's writing center goals, the lexicographic method and resultant definitions can influence the investigators themselves, to maintain the activities and assignments that clearly support the elements of the tenets and revise those that don't.

## Works Cited

Bandura, Albert. "Self-efficacy." *Encyclopedia Of Human Behavior.* Ed. V. S. Ramachandran. Vol. 4. New York: Academic P, 1994. 71-81. Print.

Healy, Dave. "Countering the Myth of (In)dependence: Developing Life-Long Clients." *Writing Lab Newsletter* 18.9 (1994). 1-3. Web. 5 May 2012.

Jackson, Howard. *Lexicography: An Introduction.* London: Routledge, 2002. Print.

Simpson, Jeanne. "Whose Idea of a Writing Center Is This, Anyway?" *Writing Lab Newsletter* 35.1 (2010). 1-5. Print.

# WRITING ON THE EDGE

Not Just to Bear Witness: An Interview with Jeffrey Gettleman

Counter-Coulter, by Rebecca Jones and Heather Palmer

Sister, short fiction by Andrew Lam

Volume 23 Number 1 Fall 2012

*Writing on the Edge* is on the Web at http://woe.ucdavis.edu/

*Writing on the Edge*, now in its 25th year, is a University of California, Davis sponsored journal about writing and the teaching of writing. We publish articles, essays, creative nonfiction, cartoons, short stories, poems, collages, and whatever else works in the creative energies of writing teachers. In each issue we also publish interviews with writers (e.g. Toni Morrison, Calvin Trillin, John McPhee) and writing teachers (e.g. James Berlin, Linda Flower, Victor Villanueva). We believe that articles about composition need not lose themselves in the wilderness of academic abstraction, but can be lively and enlightening in equal measure. We are a journal to be read for pleasure rather than duty.

## Counter-Coulter: A Story of Craft and Ethos

"Counter-Coulter…" traces one of those rare moments that teachers desire and dread at the same time: to actually put into practice, in a very public way and before a hostile audience, the principles that drive their teaching and their scholarship. Jones and Palmer tell the story of preparing and delivering a live, public response to a speech by conservative commentator Ann Coulter. Not only do they offer a blistering critique of Coulter's confrontational brand of political rhetoric, they also manifest a central value of our mission at *Writing on the Edge*—to publish work that is both insightful and engaging.

# 15 Counter-Coulter: A Story of Craft and Ethos

*Rebecca Jones and Heather Palmer*

"If you talk the talk, you have to walk the walk."

While we discourage our writing students from using clichés, we start with a common one. Quite simply, it fits. After years of teaching students about the power of rhetoric and the importance of participating in public discourses, we realized we had been doing a lot of talking and very little walking. What follows is a story about this walk—one that led us into the public world outside our offices and, as we discovered, back to the very core of our discipline.

In the fall of 2009, after months of research, writing and revision, and many sleepless nights, we found ourselves briskly walking over to the Fine Arts auditorium where Rebecca would deliver the speech we worked so hard to write in response to a talk titled, "Evaluating the Change in American Government," given by the Burkett Miller Lecture Series invited guest at our university: Ann Coulter. Outside of the auditorium, we made our way through a meager crowd of anti-Coulter protesters and through the prodigious gathering of her Tea Party fans and community conservatives. For those readers who live outside of the current fray of partisan politics, Ann Coulter is a conservative pundit and self-described liberal hater often featured on FOX News. Since her presentation style of choice is highly vitriolic and invective, we steeled ourselves before walking backstage because we expected her demeanor to reflect such divisiveness.

Before heading onto the stage, we were surprised to find ourselves chatting amiably with Coulter in the wings about rather inane things like whether or not she studied Aristotle in college, how much Sarah

Palin makes per speech (not as much as Ann herself, as she regretfully pointed out) and how much she likes the *Grateful Dead* and *Phish*. When out of the spotlight, in the crafty way of artifice, she was personally charming.

However, chatting backstage with Ann Coulter is the end of our story, not the beginning. Before Rebecca walked onto the stage, we had to do all of the hard work. What follows is a story about this experience meant to inspire our colleagues and students to recognize emergent possibilities for ethical discourse even in the most adversarial of rhetorical situations.

We first learned about the event in the spring of 2009 through an email from the University of Tennessee at Chattanooga's Probasco Chair of Free Enterprise, Dr. J.R. Clark. He is charged with finding an annual speaker for the lecture series as well as a local respondent. Speakers in the past have included Nobel Prize winners in economics and dignitaries such as the Prime Minister of Estonia. Dr. Clark sent the following email to members of the Women's Studies program:

> Seek [ing] a faculty commentator from any discipline, preferably with views significantly differing from those of Ms Coulter, to offer 8 minutes of commentary/critique on her speech. …It would seem to be an excellent opportunity to express differing views, gain significant visibility for the women's studies program, and set a positive example of what successful women professionals can do in their careers.

Within an hour, in our roles as Rhetoric, Writing, and Women's Studies professors, we separately sent response emails claiming interest in the project along similar lines: we wanted to address how Coulter's divisive rhetoric is pernicious for a vibrant deliberative democracy and to offer a healthy alternative. We wanted to present a lesson on the highly refined 2500 year old art of rhetoric rather than reduce the encounter to a cat fight between professional women. In the past few semesters, Rebecca had taught Introduction to Rhetorical Analysis and Theories and Methods of Argument and Heather several sections of Persuasion and Propaganda. Often, the courses made us feel guilty about our arm-chair lifestyles as academics. In short, since our classes dealt with issues of civic importance, we missed the passion of activism—we felt the lassitude that sometimes comes from too much theorizing from the sidelines as lived history happens outside the walls of the academe.

We found it strange that Dr. Clark targeted the Women's Studies program rather than Political Science, Communication, or even English (with its strong rhetorical emphasis). In talking with Dr. Clark, we came to understand that he simply wanted a female academic representative with a very different ethos than Coulter to represent the university. He hoped we would counter Coulter's sarcastic vitriol with calm rationality. While this is laudable, we know from experience and recent work, such as Sharon Crowley's *Toward a Civil Discourse: Rhetoric and Fundamentalism*, that calm rationality may offer an alternative vision, but it does little to make change or even initiate dialogue with others holding strong beliefs about a particular topic. Additionally, though Dr. Clark did not say it, we imagine he thought there might be something to say about HOW Coulter presented herself, as a woman, in public. There are many inappropriate discussions on the internet about Coulter's masculinity and, ironically, about her weight. We made it clear that we were not interested in discussing these topics or the *ad hominem* attacks against her, and he happily engaged our services as rhetorical scholars with something to say about the state of public discourse in America.

Before we discuss the heart of this essay, the writing and performing of the speech, we have to explain two things: first, the reaction to our acceptance of this task and, second, why we felt so passionately about participating in this project. When news spread that we were going up against Coulter (as if this were a boxing match or a cat fight), we encountered a variety of reactions. Many people wondered what would make a mild-mannered professor pit her shriveled capacity for extemporaneous speech against a public figure known for eating people alive. Some people were actually afraid and quickly transferred their own fears of public speaking onto us. In addition to fearing for our reputations (which we assume they thought would be ruined after we humiliated ourselves), others were angry that we had lowered our standards and had accepted an invitation to be in the same room with someone like Coulter who many on the left and who care about language see as the very root of the problem with politics and partisan discourse in America. This second reaction, anger, we did not expect, especially an anger that seemed to stem from the very fact of participating. We both agree with *Power Politics*, Arundhati Roy's critique of academic abstentionism, which points to much of academic discourse as lacking the "passion, the grit, the audacity, and if necessary, the vulgarity to publicly take a political position" (2001, 23). Her critique is well-founded since it is through such disdain that the divide between the academic and the activist is falsely maintained. However, we could understand our colleagues' reticence, motivated as it was by both concern and respect for our work and academic character (decidedly not as vulgar as Coulter's in their minds).

The primary concern voiced by our colleagues was that, by engaging Coulter directly, we would somehow be condoning her communicative style. For many feminists and rhetorical scholars, it seems that public discourse in America has come to resemble the trash-talking and taunting that now pervade male sports. One sharp objection to this culture of invective and demonization comes from Deborah Tannen, who articulates the problems with such a culture in her 1998 book, *The Argument Culture: Moving from Debate to Dialogue*. Unfortunately, American public discourse did not make the move to "dialogue" and over a decade after publication we were set up to critique a situation worse than the one Tannen describes. Tannen criticizes the "pervasive warlike atmosphere that makes us approach public dialogue, and just about anything we need to accomplish, as if it were a fight" (3). Tannen questions the metaphors of war and combat that unconsciously and automatically shape our thinking. The argument culture, Tannen writes, urges us to approach our environment with an adversarial frame of mind (3-4). It assumes that opposition is the best way to accomplish anything: As she puts it:

> … the best way to discuss an idea is to set up a debate; the best way to cover news is to find spokespeople who express the most extreme, polarized views and present them as "both sides"; the best way to settle disputes is litigation that pits one party against the other; the best way to begin an essay is to attack someone; and the best way to show you're really thinking is to criticize. (3-4)

Where some colleagues wanted us to be conscientious objectors in this war of words, others encouraged the upcoming brawl. Those friends and students that admired our gutsy move wanted us to attack her, in fact, and hoped with all their hearts that we would crush her publicly and win one for the team. These reactions are complex and warrant their own article. Suffice it to say that all the reactions were personally and politically motivated, but they also depended largely on perceptions of our ethos (boring, theory-driven professors or radical lefties) and on the speakers' political views. Of course, our individual ethoi are much more complex than these stereotypes. In short, those who loved us as individuals, feared for our lives. Those who created us in their minds as leftist prevaricators either thought we could do better by rising above the situation, refusing to engage such vulgar display, or wanted us to kick butt.

Absorbing all of these reactions forced us to articulate to ourselves why we wanted to participate in this public discussion. So, despite this complex external pressure, we held tightly to our initial gut reaction. We think public discourse is important. We worry, along with many others in the academy and the media, that the partisan brutality has gotten worse and has a corrosive effect on our democracy. We know from our own experience as teachers that students feel disengaged from national politics because they do not see a place for themselves within the vicious back and forth. Ultimately, we both feel that this was an opportunity not only to put our words into action, but also to test the theories of rhetoric and writing that we promise our students daily are useful in the world.

## THE WORK

We were heady with the notion of making a public appearance, but the euphoria of getting the gig did not last long as we began a rather grueling writing process: a process that would lead to an eight-minute commentary on Coulter's presentation. We were diligent scholars and tried to follow our normal academic writing routines. We read and took notes on Coulter's primary works. We read secondary sources on Coulter, American Conservatism, politics, and contemporary media issues. Rebecca ordered ALL of Coulter's books and read them. Heather started watching Coulter on FOX news and thinking more carefully about her delivery. We logged onto her weekly column and tried to plot out a trajectory in her commentary that might lead to her October 5 presentation. We were entering the turbulent shallows of political punditry, looking for a way to effectively model a counter to Coulter's divisive rhetoric, in both style and content.

Before Rebecca stepped onto the stage, different audiences assigned us different ethoi (academic, liberal feminist, etc...), and we knew that part of the challenge involved crafting an ethos for Rebecca for that particular day. While this issue was unresolved at the start, we understood that we, personally, have very divergent writing and presentation styles. Heather writes/speaks like a scholar, a traditional philosophy scholar. Rebecca enjoys watching people listen to Heather talk about her work with puzzled expressions as they try to follow the quick-paced highly theoretical language. Rebecca worked for a small newspaper for a short time and has a more minimalist approach to language, preferring the practical to the theoretical. These differences posed an initial problem. We had a few arguments about using words like adumbrate or pernicious in the speech. Pernicious made it, adumbrate did not.

From these discussions, key questions arose: 1) how to weave together these style differences, 2) how to choose a credible ethos that answered to the demands of such a unique rhetorical situation, and 3) how to choose a style that adequately projected our chosen ethos. More specifically, we struggled to situate a credible, cohesive voice without fulfilling the largely conservative pro-Coulter audience's expectations that we would live up to the static stereotypes of the liberal humanist professors: on one hand, that we are godless radical activists shaping the impressionable young minds of future generations with our liberal anarchic agendas, or that we are so disengaged from the world as to be completely irrelevant to the concerns of today's world (in short, boring).

In the run-up to the event, these expectations were voiced on a number of platforms, most alarmingly on the Tennessee Gun Owner's website, which posted rather hostile comments about our academic research topics (from women's studies to protest rhetoric) that were listed on the department website, our likely militant liberal views, and even comments about our physical appearance. One comment sums it up rather nicely, "Tolerant liberals - haaa - Frickin fascists is more like it" (tngunowners.com). Clearly, several sectors of the public wanted to turn this into a fight, a spectacle which had clearly delineated losers and winners. And this included many self-declared liberals (on a different forum), who actually threatened to plant bombs that involved excrement in the lecture hall. We offer this rather lengthy description of the rhetorical backdrop to provide a point of entry into the concerns we had moving into the composing process, since as rhetors we were keenly aware of the kairotic dimension of the event. Our task was to provide an eight minute long response to Ann's speech, itself 45 minutes long, and to possibly participate in a lengthy question and answer session afterwards. But, as we were to find out, the task involved so much more than just the actual writing and delivery of an eight min-ute long response. In the end, these diverse and impassioned reactions helped us to evolve an ethos that we feel productively engaged many hostilities, fears, and hopes.

## A COLLABORATIVE COMPOSING PROCESS

While the prep work was daunting and intimidating, it was the writing that proved the most grueling. Feeling confident after our research, we decided to just start writing and see what happened. Our first draft was, well, "shitty"—as Anne Lamott would say (*Bird by Bird: Some Instructions on Reading and Life*). After more than ten years of telling students that even good writers MUST revise, we both continued to harbor the secret hope of every writer that *this* first draft would be per-fect. We imagined, "certainly, veteran writing teachers can crank out a decent speech in a week or so." Looking back, we were completely delusional.

Our first meeting to discuss Draft I was both casual and exciting. We started with a few pages of paragraphs. When we actually dug into the language, Rebecca remembers feeling her chest tighten with panic. The writing had felt cathartic after so much research and reading, yet we knew it was desperately off track in about ten minutes. While we felt most confident in the general topic we had chosen (the problems with and consequences of combative, partisan public discourse), we were unclear about the shape and scope of the argument and especially about the style in which we planned to deliver it. We had not answered other basic rhetorical questions concerning audience and ethos.

The first draft did many things wrong. The most egregious in-cluded a mild insult to the organizers of the event and a sarcastic tone that felt aggressive and peevish. We began like this:

> Before we begin, I do want to note that Ann Coulter is only the third woman invited to be a part of this lecture series that began in the early eighties. While this might not be signifi-cant to Ann, it is to us.

> I only have 8 minutes, so I'm going to jump right in: here's what I'm not going to do today. I am not going to "take on Ann." Anyone in the audience who wants to witness that

kind of spectacle can turn on the TV most nights and see the slaughter for themselves. This Southern daisy does not care to be trashed by the Yankee vixen. Stop. That last line does exactly what I don't want to do: stereotype, name call, and reaffirm the strong oppositions we see in the news every day. (Draft I)

We open by insulting the organizers in arguing that they are sexist and whine that we are only given eight minutes to speak. Next, we insult Coulter by assuming she doesn't care about feminist issues ("while this might not be significant to Ann"). Both insults serve to build brick walls between speaker and audience. While these are interesting issues, if we really only had eight minutes, we were wasting them. The southern/ yankee dichotomy offers a regional divide and the daisy/vixen a worn-out cliché about the only two choices women have as public characters: angel or devil, and a seductive one at that. Of course, we meant all of this to be sarcastic and serve as an example of bad rhetoric. However, by opening with insults and dichotomies, we severely limit any possibilities we have of connecting to a hostile audience. No matter how many times we say, "We don't want to reaffirm the strong oppositions" we have already done it.

It turns out that this was a strange form of rhetorical imitation. We now know that this gut reaction draft was due to an overexposure to Coulter's rhetoric. In a sense, we had become immersed in the war of words. After reading all of Coulter's books and watching countless hours of "news" talk shows, we were arming ourselves for the fight. When we read Coulter's writing or watched talk news, we felt as if we were being pummeled with words and backed into a corner. Views, beliefs, ideals, and public actions are pulverized and not in an effort to find solutions to an actual problem, but in an effort to humiliate and insult another into submission. Here are the first lines of some of Coulter's books: "Liberals have a preternatural gift for striking a position on the side of treason" (*Treason* 1); "Historically, the best way to convert liberals is to have them move out of their parents' home, get a job, and start paying taxes" (*How to Talk to a Liberal: If You Must* 1); "Liberals love to boast that they are not "religious," which is what one would expect to hear from a state-sanctioned religion" (*Godless: The Church of Liberalism* 1). Al Franken is not much better in his book *Lies and the Lying Liars Who Tell Them*. He opens with an insult to Christians: "God chose me to write this book. Just the fact that you are reading this is proof not just of God's existence, but also of His/Her/Its beneficence. That's right. I am not certain of God's precise gender. But I am certain that He/She/It chose me to write this book" (xv). Sure, we get that these openings are jokes. Both writers, whether Coulter admits it or not, are comedians. They are using comedy as a rhetorical strategy to wage war against their opponents instead of actually engaging in a political argument. In our first draft, we felt this drum beat. We felt it so deeply that we even tried out their war-like wit. While "argument is war" is a difficult metaphor to dislodge (see Lakoff and Johnson *Metaphors We Live By*), the one thing we knew for sure we wanted to do was to offer a different example of argumentation. The first draft fails miserably in achieving this aim.

Witnessing our own devolution on the page, we started to think more about audience and how many different audiences we needed to accommodate in this speech: Coulter, Coulter's "followers," Coulter's dissenters, students, and those who believed in us. We knew that in this draft we were mimicking a negative and aggressive style and limiting ourselves to addressing an oppositional audience. We needed to ask, instead, what ethos could we craft to suit multiple audiences and still be true to our notions of the task at hand? This question guided us in our revision of Draft II.

## DRAFT II

After toning down some of the harshest rhetoric and getting rid of the daisy/vixen sexist remark, in this draft we worked to add more academic components as well as some narrative as alternative ways to make our points.

The first opening was still intact as we, clearly, were not ready to give up our attempts at sarcasm. In this draft, we continue to acknowledge the divide between the speaker and the audience up front as well as the audience's expectation of a fight. We do, however, introduce new images:

> It has become apparent that the expectation for today is yet another polarized debate. Ann says liberals are liars and I say conservatives are crazy (do you like my alliterations). When one person gets 40 minutes and the other 8, the only thing that can happen is she said, she said. So…Ann argues college professors are undercover liberal conspirators brainwashing

the nation's youth, I argue they are not. That seems pointless and slightly redundant. And... I mean, come on—the conservative fireball versus the boring commy professor, at High Noon. Can't yall hear the sound track from a Clint Eastwood movie bursting through the speakers? And two women to boot!

Ironically, this cat fight was actually slated to begin at noon. We couldn't pass on the opportunity for humor after so many people had commented on our upcoming "fight." While the metaphor is rather grossly mixed (communists and cowboys), it attempts to acknowledge the divisiveness and obvious feminist issues with a lighter tone. If this were not bad enough, we even added some gun metaphors: "Right now, we have only two sides. Both are pointing guns and firing (even if one side says they don't like guns!). The noise is deafening. And I mean literally, we are all deaf to any argument that doesn't fit our pattern." The good news is that after the gun metaphors, we begin to dig into a serious and more appropriate discussion about the state of public discourse, our theories about the problems, and some possible solutions.

In one section, we fall into familiar academic discourse: "Our very lives are divided down partisan lines. Bill Bishop and Robert Cushing's *The Big Sort: Why the Clustering of Like-Minded America is Tearing Us Apart* argues that we are more segregated in the United States now than ever before." We continue by discussing social psychologist Jonathan Haidt's studies on the divergent moral codes of liberals and conservatives. These sections felt more comfortable to us with their basic logic and argument/proof dynamic. However, we worried that these kinds of sentences would not play well out loud (think about how conference papers sound).

At the end of this draft, we begin to show some promise. We write ourselves into a possible style. The final paragraph ends with this:

> Here's the problem as we see it. Polemics, demagoguery, attack politics are offered AS IF they are THE NEWS, as if they are researched, thoughtful arguments. It is the AS IF that is so troubling. Sure, it's fun to watch Ann and James Carville talk over each other on *The Today Show*. However, this format, a split screen holding ideologues of a different flavor shouting out platforms, does not help me sort out the issues or help think seriously about social problems. By the way, Ann, are

the networks so cheap now that they can't afford to fly their
speakers to the same town so that they can be in the same
room when they talk? (Draft II)

This paragraph starts off well. It is casual but not as biting as our opening. It is not strictly academic as we experiment with the confluence of
witty public speech and academic discourse, "As IF" and "demagogu-
ery" in the same sentence. Toward the end of the paragraph, we dive
back into sarcasm. The calling out of "Ann" makes the sentence aggressive when the question should be calling out media conglomerates
for creating the expectation of debate and delivering only a simulation.

For this draft, we decided to get outside opinions. We asked two
colleagues to listen to what we had and offer suggestions. We sat in a
circle at Heather's house, staring at each other in anticipation. When
Rebecca read the draft aloud, she could feel a bit of tension, both her
own and from our colleagues. This draft was not working either.

The first reaction was a short silence. They clearly thought we
could do better. Their major complaint was about the aggressive opening and, to be honest, once we read it aloud we knew that the tone was
still too angry. Another complaint, and one perhaps more difficult to
take, was that our message was unclear, buried in witticisms. However,
as we started chatting and brainstorming about the possibilities of our
little moment in the limelight, it was clear that they too were under the
thrall of partisan discourse. At this juncture, we had found a few online forums related to our upcoming speech. When we shared some of
the more worrisome ones (something about excrement and the stage),
one of our colleagues suggested we somehow incorporate the online
angst into our speech. So, while they both seemed to dislike our attempts at sarcasm, they also felt we could not ignore the elephant in
the room: when people talk politics in America, it gets nasty. Despite
this dilemma, incorporate the ugliness or not, this discussion yielded
the most useful advice. One of our friends commented, "you two are
teachers, so teach us something." She reminded us of our original goal:
show our students how good rhetoric can work, show them there is
another option. We still had a long way to go.

## DRAFT III

In some ways, we felt more confused after our second draft than we
had at the beginning. We were definitely developing a clearer idea

about what we wanted our text to accomplish, but could not quite pinpoint the arrangement and style issues. While we did not want to match Coulter's vitriol, many Americans find her funny and engaging, so we felt a great deal of pressure to deliver both intellectual content AND fabulous form. We think this is why we continued to hang on to many awful lines we thought might be funny. Additionally, we were becoming aware of the real restrictions of an eight minute speech. We were used to leading hour and fifteen minute discussions on particular points or offering three hour graduate classes on one article. Brevity was not our strength. We had about four double spaced pages to accomplish our task, a task we realized included critiquing Coulter's rhetoric without sounding dogmatic, teaching the audience about rhetoric, arguing for an alternative model of public discourse, making ourselves and our students proud, speaking in public in an engaging way, not getting booed (or worse) by the audience, and developing a ethos that could accommodate all of these goals.

Draft III was the draft of hard realities. This is the draft that made us cry and ultimately pushed us to write the version we are proud to have presented. The major change in this draft can be found at the end. We take our friend's advice to "teach us something" and begin to develop a list of the components of a "good argument." This step in the process represents a shift from the defensive rhetoric we had been clinging to toward a more proactive and positive position. Rather than merely "engage" Coulter, we offer an alternative vision of argumentation that certainly functions as a critique but with a very different rhetorical stance. We don't pull apart Coulter's rhetoric. Instead, we attempt to offer a clear discussion of what we believe is good public argument and let the audience do the critical work. Of course, our still "witty" opening hoped to push them toward a particular kind of critical work.

Our list of "advice" developed from a discussion of the rules for "critical discussion" created by Van Eemeren, Grootendorst, and Snoeck- Henkemans as an alternative way to discuss rhetorical fallacies in their book *Argumentation: Analysis, Evaluation, Presentation* and our own experience teaching and thinking about public argumentation (109). We decided to discuss several rules and to offer both a clear definition of how the rule functions as well as an example of how a party might break the rule. In this draft, we only had the barest of outlines though we had decided to address the following issues:

staying on topic, agreeing to the terms of the debate, listening to another's position, and being willing to concede the point. We knew that these would sound very utopian but we hoped that through examples we could demonstrate their necessity and benefits. As the end of our presentation, we knew it was vital to make these four pieces of advice concise, engaging, and, most importantly, clear. This was a very difficult task. We reworked these short passages countless times before the final version felt right.

While we felt good about the end of the presentation in terms of our message, the opening of our speech still had major style issues. We read this draft to Heather's husband because he is a local performance artist and has a background in public presentation and teaching. The draft we read to Dennis was a toned down version of earlier drafts, but it still started in a confrontational manner. We continued to address our differences with Coulter up front while claiming we were not equipped to meet her using her weapons of choice: "I realize (from friends, a few really scary forums, and excited students) that the expectation today is for me to stand here and "take on Ann." I can only assume we are supposed to engage in a brawl in which one opponent vanquishes the other." We then move to a description of what current political discourse looks like using words like "spectacle," "memorable soundbites," and "cable news mayhem." We end the opening with a much smoother version of the Clint Eastwood/high noon joke.

When we read this to Dennis: he balked. His basic complaint, "this isn't you." For Dennis, we had a major ethos problem. He did not have a problem with the language per se, but he had a problem with Rebecca delivering it. For one, he did not envision a professor being so sarcastic and secondly did not think that Rebecca, personally, could get on stage and pull it off. This was another difficult criticism to deal with. As scholars of rhetoric, we knew that getting our ethos wrong was the beginning of the end. Dennis's comments made us ask ourselves the big questions again: what is our aim, what ethos helps us achieve this aim? We also had to admit that this snarky beginning made it seem as if we did not respect our audience. In our efforts to match Coulter's thrilling delivery, we had lost sight of our own goals that simply could not be accomplished by mimicking her style, even in a milder form.

We stepped back and began to think about ethos, as a concept. In some ways, this project called for basic Aristotelian rhetoric: a speaker uses her personal credibility to talk to a particular audience about a particular topic. For our student audience, this conception might work. However, in terms of the pro-Coulter audience, we had no credibility in the classical sense (as professors and even as women) because of the negative ethos they conferred on us. These complications required newer notions of ethos. Bitzer's "rhetorical situation" where ethos and response arises "naturally" (5) or even Vatz's response that focused on the speaker were too discrete (as Biesecker complained) and did not offer a complete vision of what we needed. We needed a feminist approach that went beyond invitational rhetorical and allowed us to take a strong position without becoming incendiary (as Nancy Welch argues in "Taking Sides"). We were two women trying to combine our styles, we had a mixed audience in terms of age, race, gender, and political belief, and we had pressure from many different fronts to "be" a certain kind of public speaker.

As we look through the notes we made on this draft, we read our own strong admonitions: "Get to the point. One sentence that gets to the seriousness of the work. Be more factual. Be straightforward. So, don't be flippant (Draft III)." We realized that a more serious paragraph that clearly demonstrated the problem we hoped to address should go first and that the cowboy-shoot-out-high-noon joke was the end of our speech and not the beginning. Additionally, we started to see important arguments we had left out. We wanted the audience to know that this was not about advocating the opposite of agonism. We had been so concerned about not living up to the audience expectations about a cat fight, we forgot that they might also expect us to make a "let's all hug instead of fight argument." We did not want that ethos either.

Even though we were disheartened when we realized we still needed major revisions, the shape of the speech seemed clearer and within reach.

## FINAL DRAFT

In the end, we crafted an ethos that fit a teacher. However, this teacherly ethos was not a stereotype (either radical or boring) but felt, at least to us, rhetorically savvy and even a little funny. We wrote brand new paragraphs for the opening that were unlike anything we had written so far. It was a radical revision in the strictest sense in that we reimagined our ethos. We had been "crafting" too much in the beginning and needed to find a more comfortable style, for us and for the audience.

Here is what Rebecca read as the opening on October 5, 2009[1]:

> I'm here today in my role as a professor of rhetoric and argumentation. I'm concerned about the divisive tone and timbre of political discourse because it negatively affects students' willingness to participate in the political process.
>
> The university setting offers a unique space for people from different points of view to engage with one another in the open exploration of arguments. I see productive thoughtful argumentation in my classes every day. Unfortunately, this type of interaction is not reflected in the current model of political discourse we see on network and cable news and hear on talk radio. (Final Copy)

While this opening lacked the punch of early drafts, it was an opening that met audience expectations for a professor while also challenging the speech we had all just heard. We continued with a critique of war rhetoric from both sides of the aisle and spoke from the heart by including more subjective observations and sentiments. We found ways to "confront Ann" by challenging her style rather than copying it:

> Few people hear someone like Ann Coulter, Rush Limbaugh, James Carville or Al Franken and think, "Hey, I'd love to hash it out over coffee with them. This sounds like fun!" I mean, who is crazy enough to try and argue with Ann? This is precisely because this kind of discourse doesn't leave space for argument. It's not meant to. (Final Copy)

Finally, we emphasized our passion for the deliberative process that served as the primary reason for participating in this event:

> We've come to a place where a "good" argument doesn't seem to matter, where we are more interested in politics as a zero sum game, in who can embarrass the other more thoroughly with vicious language, in politics as spectacle, than political engagement as a way to solve problems critical to our future. We are here to say that it *does matter* that public figures offer ethical, thoughtful discourse because whether they want to or

> not, they serve as models for young people about how to par-
> ticipate as citizens in America. (Final Copy)

The lines above were particularly poignant after Coulter's speech because it was especially divisive on this occasion as she used the Roman
Polanski rape case in an ethically questionable argument about politics.

We even gave ourselves some space for our beloved joke, but it did
not come until page four of a five page speech. After we offered our
three examples of "good" argument, we added

> [1]The full text of the speech can be found in NCTE's Gal-
> lery of Writing: http://galleryofwriting.org/writing/1578503.
> I know that many people here today were hoping to see a
> good fight—the kind of spectacle offered up each night on
> the "news" shows, where Ann chants "liberal lies" and I say
> "conservative crackpot." This stuff is really funny. Ann is the
> master of one-liners. Our fight might have made for an en-
> tertaining spectacle—the conservative fireball versus the bor-
> ing commie professor and at High Noon. Can't ya'll hear the
> sound track from *The Good, The Bad, and the Ugly* bursting
> through the speakers? And two women to boot. (Final Copy)

This is all that remained of the sassy opening we had obsessed over
for so many weeks. By prefacing with a more professional ethos, we
were able to offer this critical sentiment in the end without seeming
too flippant.

While we were tempted to end with the joke, we did not. We ended
with an ethos that conjured teacher/activists challenging the audience
to be critical of themselves:

> Whatever your emotion, don't let it stop here. Passion is inven-
> tion. If getting mad or fired up is the beginning, then we've
> got a good start today. So, don't sit and stew or forget. Do
> some research, talk to your friends, your parents, your profes-
> sors. If you are confused about healthcare, ask those working
> in the trenches, like a nurse practitioner; if you want the pulse
> of the economy, talk to small business owners.

Decide what you believe based on your own research and not hearsay or one late night talk show. (Final Copy)

As we look back at this process, we cringe at those early drafts. In some ways, this article is embarrassing as we admit our struggles with the very things we teach our students each semester. However, this process has become our best lesson. We both use the early drafts in class to demonstrate how revision works, and we feel so much more prepared to help struggling students move past their own bad joke.

## The Performance

While the focus of this paper is the writing, we wanted to comment on the actual performance of the speech: terrifying. True to her normal form, Coulter delivered a scathing discussion of liberal politics, Obama, and anyone else within target range. Rebecca had to sit on the stage while she spoke and noticed that her speech was actually written as one-liners with spaces between each jab. After a rousing applause, Rebecca stepped up to the podium to a restless silence. It turns out that there was some kind of problem with the distribution of free tickets that resulted in an audience primarily made up of local conservatives while most of the students were in an overflow room watching a screen. The animosity was palpable as Rebecca stepped up to the podium. At one point, early in the speech, Rebecca was describing the shape of current political rhetoric and delivered the following lines: "Negative and polarizing rhetorics guarantee division, entrenchment, argument for argument's sake, yelling or, in the worst cases, silence and, sometimes, even violence (consider the finger biting incident at a recent tea party) (Final Copy)." This line was meant to illicit at least a little chuckle from the audience. There was nothing. Rebecca stopped and commented, "This really isn't my audience, is it?" The remark was spontaneous and more a response to bad energy than anything else. However, it worked to break up the wave of animosity.

After our response, Coulter stepped up to the podium to answer questions. She actually said, "While I would like to comment on Rebecca's response, I really want to focus on the questions from the audience." So, in response to a direct critique of her rhetorical style, she took questions from the audience rather than address the issue. Unfortunately, she continued her vitriol. A young woman in the audience, obviously a Coulter fan, asked Coulter why she often commented that women should not be allowed to vote. Coulter's response was patronizing and did not veer from her regular routine. She received a standing ovation for arguing that the demise of the country started when women got the right to vote in 1920. After her recitation of her argument, the young woman was pointedly ignored as Coulter moved to the next question. Her overall performance can be summed up as a set of biting one-liners that serve to reinforce a particular set of beliefs. She was a powerful speaker, but did not offer anything new.

Ultimately, the whole process of engaging directly with Coulter seemed a way to move our lessons about rhetoric and civic discourse out of the classroom and onto center stage. As the discussion of the final draft explains, we eventually agreed that the event needed to be for our students and serve as an exemplar of our work as rhetors—to engage social action critically and publically.

While we learned many small lessons along the way, it was our understanding of ethos through revision that was the most powerful lesson. The question of character takes up one of the fundamental ethical principles of communication, our need to assign communicative expression in some foundational way to a singular character. In thinking about crafting an ethos to meet the exigencies of such a unique rhetorical situation, we had to carefully tend to the tensions, contradictions, presuppositions, and adversarial ground such a forum presented to us. Instead of crafting a solid, stable, foundational ethos that would simply reflect Rebecca's views on Ann Coulter's politics and appeal to shared audience values, we used an invented ethos which provided us a greater flexibility by recasting the reductive personal agent of language as an exterior force, inseparable from relations with others. In dealing with the specific exigencies of the rhetorical situation such as a potentially hostile crowd, expectations and pressure from our colleagues and students, the heightened adversarial atmosphere due to the heated political climate, crafting an effective ethos had to move beyond the standard conception of ethos as representing the character of the speaker. For this situation, *ethos* became a calling of an invented self into being through language.

In order to understand how our sense of ethos evolved, we had to factor in the pathos inherent in such a heated ideological conflict. The intensity of pathos meant that there were many factors that preceded this rhetorical situation and prevented us from following Bitzer's advice to "speaking naturally in the situation": in fact, the question for everybody became how to speak at all, how to find a voice against such odds. Crowley's *Toward a Civil Discourse* was on target for our project in admonishing "liberal" rhetors that pure logic cannot adequately confront fundamental emotionally driven beliefs.

## On Courage and Community

We found that putting our rhetorical commitments to work in useful and public ways by engaging with Coulter inspires students to take part in public debate even with voices that are intimidating (and even scary). Re-engaging rhetoric as a practical art in the face of powerful and often antagonistic institutional structures provides the courage necessary for such action. We also realized that engaging in productive rhetorical combat raises some interesting questions such as those Nancy Welch asks in *Living Room: Teaching Public Writing in a Privatized World*: how do we work in relationship with others and build a rhetoric that values agitation as much as affinity? (70-72). Upon reflection, such a challenging and uncomfortable speech act, speaking in an unfamiliar and adversarial setting outside the classroom or conference hall, pulled us out of our discrete separate identities into a field of intersections with others—we realized in a very real, affective way that ethos occurs in a socially created space, at the intersection between the rhetorical and the personal, reaching outward to a third space, toward community. Since our concern is providing productive examples of rhetoric as a practical and public art for our students, we were pleased to be students of our own lesson about ethos and community—most rhetoric that makes a lasting and useful impact works in relationship with others. This is a particularly valuable lesson for students since, as Nancy Welch also points out, "most of our students' futures will depend on what they learn now about collective, not individual rhetorical strategies" (71). Our relative success at crafting a collective ethos is borne out by the surprising number of favorable responses to our speech, particularly from those who were at first in favor of Coulter and ideologically predisposed to resist what we had to offer. We conclude with the audience's reactions and written comments sent to us after the event. We received many emails from friends with the general message: "Bravo!" However, by the next day we started getting some unusual emails from strangers with the same general message: "I am a Coulter fan, would probably disagree with you politically, but, despite this, really appreciated your speech." Here are a few excerpts from the surprise emails that landed in our inboxes. This first one is the most articulate:

> My expectations were such that I had pictured you delivering a vigorous and scathing critique of Miss Coulter's rhetoric. Instead, I feel that I learned something from your calm and sensible message about the value of good argument. Admittedly, a word fight would have been very entertaining, however, you rightly pointed out that polarizing criticism is divisive and discourages rational debate. I feel your response was very powerful and effective because you criticized the current climate of political discourse rather than criticizing Miss Coulter's message point by point.

Here's another response that appreciated our educative approach: "Although I won't take you up on your invitation to take a rhetoric class, I will do some research and learn something about the art of good argument." Others offered kind and heartfelt compliments: "I wish her overall presentation had been as professional as yours. I'm thankful the students at UTC are given the opportunity in your class to get beyond entertainment-driven politics. Keep up the good work." However, the following was Rebecca's favorite. The writer explained that he "hated" politics because of the constant bickering and then added, "Both sides of the isle are more interested in discrediting each other than proving their own worth. I did not know how much positive feedback you have received so I just wanted to say your alright for a commie lib (LOL)."

We discovered that meaning was created by us in conjunction with our audience, as adversarial as they may have been, and that it was critical for us to move beyond an understanding of ethos as arising "naturally" from the rhetorical situation. Far from robbing us of our ability to make meaning, and speak this meaning directly, we found that understanding ethos as craft gave us possibilities for multiple types of authorship, and emphasizes our creative potential *as rhetors* to collaborate with the exigencies of the rhetorical situation. The value of such an approach to ethos is what we hoped to communicate to our students, specifically those in our writing classrooms who often struggle with voice. It is this struggle that we want to share with our students—to remind them that the creative process can be a richer ground for invention under such constraints.

## WORKS CITED

Bishop, Bill and Robert Cushing. *The Big Sort: Why the Clustering of Like-Minded America is Tearing Us Apart.* New York: Houghton Mifflin, 2008.

Biesecker, Barbara. "Coming to terms with Recent Attempts to Write Women into the History of Rhetoric," *Philosophy and Rhetoric* 25.2 (1992): 140–161.

Bitzer, Lloyd. "The Rhetorical Situation." *Philosophy and Rhetoric* 1.1 (1968): 1–14.

Coulter, Ann. *Godless: Church of Liberalism.* New York: Three Rivers Press, 2007.

Coulter, Ann. *How to Talk to a Liberal (If You Must): The World According to Ann Coulter.* New York: Three Rivers Press, 2004.

Coulter, Ann. *Treason: Liberal Treachery from the Cold War to the War on Terrorism.* New York: Three Rivers Press, 2003.

Crowley, Sharon. *Toward a Civil Discourse: Rhetoric and Fundamentalism.* Pittsburgh: University of Pittsburg Press, 2006.

Franken, Al. *Lies and the Lying Liars Who Tell Them.* Penguin Press: New York, 2003.

Haidt, Jonathan and Jesse Graham. "When Morality Opposes Justice: Conservatives Have Moral Intuitions that Liberals may not Recognize." *Social Justice Research* 20.1 (2007): 98–116.

Lakoff, George and Mark Johnson. *Metaphors We Live By.* Chicago: University of Chicago Press, 2003.

Lamott, Anne. *Bird by Bird: Instructions on Writing and Life.* New York: Anchor Books, 1994.

Roy, Arudhati. *Power Politics.* Massachusetts: South End Press, 2001.

Tannen, Deborah. *Argument Culture.* New York: Random House, 1998.

Van Eemeren, Franz H., Rob Grootendorst, and A. Francisca Snoeck-Henkemans. *Argumentation: Analysis, Evaluation, Presentation.* New Jersey: Lawrence Erlbaum and Associates, 2002.

Vatz, Richard. "The Myth of the Rhetorical Situation." *Philosophy and Rhetoric* 6.3 (1973): 154–161.

Welch, Nancy. *Living Room: Teaching Public Writing in a Privatized World.* Portsmouth, NH: Boynton/Cook, 2008.

Welch, Nancy. "Taking Sides." *Teaching Rhetorica: Theory, Pedagogy, Practice.* Ed. Joy Ritchie and Kate Ronald. Portsmouth, NH: Boynton/Cook, 2006.

# About the Editors

**Steve Parks** is associate professor of writing and rhetoric at Syracuse University where he teaches entry-level and advanced courses in composition theory and practice. He also leads seminars on community publishing and community organizing. He has published two books: *Gravyland: Writing Beyond the Curriculum in the City of Brotherly Love* (Syracuse University Press 2010) and *Class Politics: The Students' Right to Their Own Language* (Parlor Press 2013). He has also published articles in *Journal of College Composition and Communication*, *College English*, *Community Literacy Journal*, and *Reflections*. He established New City Community Press (newcitycommunitypress.com) in Philadelphia as well as Gifford Street Community Press (giffordstreetcommunitypress.com) in Syracuse. Over the past two years, he has been working with democratic activists in the Middle East and North Africa.

**Brian Bailie** is a PhD candidate in the Composition and Cultural Rhetoric program at Syracuse University. His work focuses on the intersections of protest and media, technology and transnationalism, identity and material rhetoric, and the ways activists exploit, expand, resist, and utilize these intersections to their advantage. Bailie has served as contributor, associate editor, and special issue editor for *Reflections: A Journal of Writing, Service-Learning, and Community Literacy*. His most recent publications have appeared in the *KB Journal* and *Composition Forum*.

**Heather Christiansen** is a PhD student in the Rhetoric, Communication and Information Design program at Clemson University. Her research interests include visual rhetoric, the rhetoric of brand communities, identity, and user experience design. She currently serves as the managing editor of *The WAC Journal*.

**Elisabeth Miller** is a PhD candidate in Composition and Rhetoric at the University of Wisconsin—Madison. She is currently completing a dissertation, *Literacy beyond Language*, on the literate practices of persons with aphasia, or language-related disability caused by stroke or other brain injury. She has taught introductory and intermediate writing, served as Assistant Director of Writing Across the Curriculum at UW-Madison, and acted as coordinator for the Madison Writing Assistance community writing program. Her work has appeared in *Community Literacy Journal* and *Writing Lab Newsletter*.

**Morris Young** is professor of English at the University of Wisconsin–Madison. His book, *Minor Re/Visions: Asian American Literacy Narratives as a Rhetoric of Citizenship* (Southern Illinois UP, 2004) received the 2004 W. Ross Winterowd Award and the 2006 CCCC Outstanding Book Award. With LuMing Mao, he coedited *Representations: Doing Asian American Rhetoric* (Utah State UP, 2008), which received an honorable mention for the 2009 Mina P. Shaughnessy Prize from MLA. He is currently working on a project that examines the conceptual and material spaces of Asian American rhetoric.

www.ingramcontent.com/pod-product-compliance
Lightning Source LLC
Chambersburg PA
CBHW031235050326
40690CB00007B/811